Refashioning India

Refashioning India

Gender, Media, and a Transformed Public Discourse

Maitrayee Chaudhuri

Orient BlackSwan

REFASHIONING INDIA: GENDER, MEDIA, AND A TRANSFORMED PUBLIC DISCOURSE

ORIENT BLACKSWAN PRIVATE LIMITED

Registered Office
3-6-752 Himayatnagar, Hyderabad 500 029 (Telangana), INDIA
e-mail: centraloffice@orientblackswan.com

Other Offices
Bengaluru, Chennai, Guwahati, Hyderabad,
Kolkata, Mumbai, New Delhi, Noida, Patna

First published in hardback 2017
This paperback edition 2026

ISBN 978-93-6973-539-6

Typeset in
Adobe Jenson Pro 10.5/12,5
by Manmohan Kumar, Delhi

042649

Printed in India at
Kensington Printing & Packaging, Noida 201 301

Published by
Orient Blackswan Private Limited
3-6-752, Himayatnagar Hyderabad 500 029
e-mail: info@orientblackswan.com

For my sons, Abhik and Sarthak

Contents

Publisher's Acknowledgements

Chapter 2, 'Citizens, Workers and Emblems of Culture: An Analysis of the First Plan Document on Women', was originally published in *Contributions to Indian Sociology*, Vol. 29, Nos. 1–2. Copyright © 1995 Institute of Economic Growth, New Delhi. All rights reserved. Reproduced with the permission of the copyright holder and the publisher, SAGE Publications India Pvt. Ltd, New Delhi.

Chapter 3, 'Gender in the Making of the Indian Nation-state', was originally published in *Sociological Bulletin*, Vol. 48, Nos. 1–2, 2000. Reproduced with the permission of *Sociological Bulletin*.

Chapter 4, 'Gender and Advertisements: The Rhetoric of Globalisation', is reprinted from *Women's Studies International Forum*, Vol. 24, Nos. 3–4, pp. 373–85, May–August 2001, with permission from Elsevier.

Chapter 5, '"Feminism" in Print Media' was originally published in *Indian Journal of Gender Studies*, Vol. 7, No. 2. Copyright 2000 @ Centre for Women's Development Studies, New Delhi. All rights reserved. Reproduced with the permission of the copyright holder and the publisher, SAGE Publications India Pvt. Ltd, New Delhi.

Chapter 6, 'A Question of Choice: Advertisements, Media and Democracy', was originally published in *Media and Mediation Volume 1, Bernard Bel (ed.)*, Copyright 2006 @ Sage Publications, New Delhi. All rights reserved. Reproduced with the permission of the copyright holders and the publisher, SAGE Publications India Pvt. Ltd., New Delhi.

Chapter 7, 'Nationalism is not What it Used to be: Can Feminism be Any Different', was originally published in *Nivedini: Journal of Gender Studies*, November–December 2010, pp. 120–145. Reproduced by permission of the Women's Education and Research Centre.

Chapter 8, 'Indian Media and its Transformed Public', was originally published in *Contributions to Indian Sociology*, Vol. 44, No. 1–2. Copyright@2010, Institute of Economic Growth, New Delhi. All rights reserved. Reproduced with the permission of the copyright holder and publisher, SAGE Publications India Pvt. Ltd., New Delhi.

Chapter 9, 'Gender, Media and Popular Culture in a Global India', was originally published in *Routledge Handbook of Gender in South Asia*, Leela Fernandes (ed.), Chapter 10, Part III, pp. 145–159, 2014. Reproduced with permission from Taylor and Francis.

Chapter 10, 'National and Global Media Discourse after the savage death of 'Nirbhaya': Instant Access and Unequal Knowledge', was originally published as 'National and Global Media Discourse after the savage death of Nirbhaya: Instant Access and Unequal Knowledge' in *Studying Youth, Media and Gender in Post-Liberalisation India*, edited by Nadja-Christina Schneider and Fritzi-Marie Titzmann, 2015, pp. 19–44. Reproduced with the permission of Andre Horn—Frank & Timme GmbH.

Abbreviations

AAP	Aam Aadmi Party
AIDWA	All India Democratic Women's Association
AIWC	All India Women's Conference
ANP	Applied Nutrition Programme
BJP	Bharatiya Janata Party
BSP	Bahujan Samaj Party
CDP	Community Development Programme
CII	Confederation of Indian Industries
DDA	Delhi Development Authority
FMCG	Fast-Moving Consumer Goods
IIs	International Institutions
INC	Indian National Congress
INGO	International Non-governmental Organisation
INS	Indian Newspaper Society
IPL	Indian Premier League
IRS	Indian Readership Survey
JNU	Jawaharlal Nehru University
MRUC	Media Research Users Council
NDA	National Democratic Alliance
NPC	National Planning Committee
NRI	Non-resident Indian
OBC	Other Backward Classes
PBD	Pravasi Bharatiya Divas
RSCI	Readership Studies Council of India
RSS	Rashtriya Swayamsevak Sangh
SCW	Sub-Committee on Women
TCC	Transnational Capitalist Class
TOI	*The Times of India*
TRAI	Telecom Regulatory Authority of India
VHP	Vishva Hindu Parishad
WCAR	World Conference against Racism
WIA	Women's India Association
WRPE	*Woman's Role in Planned Economy*
WTO	World Trade Organization

Images

Acknowledgements

I have acquired many debts over the twenty-five years it has taken me to write this book. I refrain from naming them, both because there are too many and also because I fear that I may err in missing out some of them. My sincere thanks to colleagues, friends, and students who have all contributed in different ways to my thinking on the issues that I explore in this book. I owe a special debt to Patricia Uberoi, T. K. Oommen, Joanna Liddle, Rajeswari Sunder Rajan, Biswajit Das, Yogendra Singh, U. Kalpagam, Satish Deshpande, Nandini Sundar, Leela Fernandes, and Nadia Schneidar, for without their invitation and support, I would not have written the ten chapters that form the mainstay of this book. My sincere thanks to Mimi Choudhury, Moutushi Mukherjee, and Proteeti Banerjee for the support they extended from Orient BlackSwan. Needless to say, the shortcomings are entirely mine.

CHAPTER 1

INTRODUCTION

The Indian state formally initiated India's new economic policy towards greater integration into global capitalism in 1991. This marked a radical break from a long period of state-initiated development based on import substitution and a focus on equity rather than growth. It was a new beginning in the history of contemporary India. It marked the advent of not just new economic policies, but of new political visions and cultural imaginings. I seek to map this process of new visualisations with a focus on public discourse from the vantage point of gender as it played out in the quarter century after India initiated economic liberalisation. This I do through the chapters here, written at different points in time from the early 1990s, through the next two decades up to mid-2016. The chapters therefore rest upon an analysis of media texts at different points in time and have been organised chronologically. An unintended, but fortunate consequence of this is that it helps to convey two things. One, an ongoing sense of the substantive changes in public discourse that recast India; and two, the feel of how, as they say in corporate parlance, the 'rapidity of change has changed', perhaps most evident in the transient nature of contemporary media headlines. For things have sped up: 'markets shift faster, products evolve quicker, customers are more fleeting ....'[1] I cite this quote from a consultancy firm of intelligence professionals knowingly, for evident through this volume is also the story of how a corporate managerial discourse is increasingly pervading media discussion, political campaigns, policy formulations, and even everyday middle-class conversation. This is the language of the new social imaginary of a refashioning India.

If print media advertisements and new look newspapers with colourful commercial add-ons were the big thing in the 1990s (Chapters 4, 5, 6), it was the communicative abundance of television among India's transformed public that was grabbing headlines in the 2000s (Chapter 8), while the 2010s saw the rise of new media and social media politics (Chapters 10, 11). In that sense, the book can be read as a chronicle of contemporary India, written by one who is as much a participant member as observer of everyday life in a changing India.

The chapters are primarily based on textual sources. Chapter 2 begins with the analysis of a state document, the First Plan Document on Women in India, one of the twenty-nine sub-committees of the National Plan

Committee (NPC, 1947), which was foundational to the way the Indian state was discursively constituted. This chapter serves as a baseline against which one can gauge the shift in India's dominant public discourse. The other chapters range from analyses of advertisements to media debates and representations in contemporary India since the 1990s.

Analyses of the texts are, however, informed as much by a historical perspective[2] as by the ethnographic sensibility[3] of a middle-class woman participant observer: seeing one's familiar newspaper undergo a complete makeover; spotting for the first time an advertisement for men's beauty care and one of a Mercedes car; thumbing through weekly magazines, with a new gloss, borrowed from neighbourhood 'lending libraries' (erstwhile video libraries) run from scooter garages[4] of Delhi Development Authority (DDA) apartments;[5] daily conversations among homemakers regarding advertisements of new detergents and ready-to-use garlic and ginger paste; new juices and snacks in unfamiliar tetra packs, which then become a must-have at children's birthday parties; watching the evening news change from news reading by a single person to two (a major change in the late 1980s), to the cacophonic nightly debates on television every night; the excitement in the neighbourhood at watching and voting through text messages for the first Indian Idol; shared discussions about a new generation who earn more than their parents did at retirement, and think nothing of changing jobs and taking unheard-of amounts as loans; the transformation before one's eyes of the mobile phone as an aspirational, up-market object to an indispensable necessity, cutting across social class; and the rise of social media politics and the ubiquitous troll.[6] It will be evident below how this approach, buttressed by a comprehensive use of notes, informs both the order of the chapters and their treatment.

The newspaper that I have virtually grown up with through the 1970s and 1980s, *The Times of India* (TOI), underwent a dramatic transformation. For a start, the price was reduced, and in exchange, one got glossier and bulkier newspapers. This was a new and exciting experience. I was born a decade after independence and was brought up in an India that had no television and where one switched on Radio Ceylon to listen to Hindi film songs, and where the earliest advertisement that I recall was a postage-sized, black and white shot of a gentleman with an Aspirin tablet in hand. This was the world of urban, middle-class India when 1991 happened, and created a new, 'shared'—albeit differentially—everyday world of the nation.[7] It is a story of what changed, and how it changed, in India's public discourse.

THE ARGUMENT

Central to this book is the following line of reasoning: *one*, that modern public discourse can be fruitfully understood as the 'presentation of the nation's self', its identity, and image; *two*, that the mutually imbricated economic, political, and cultural articulations are embedded within specific configurations of capitalism and class formations; *three*, that the central site of ideological production varies in different contexts, for instance, the state directly in the first decades of independent India (Chapters 2, 3) and a media constitutive of a changed relationship between the state and the market in the twenty-first century (Chapter 4 onwards); and *four*, that not only is national identity deeply gendered (a recurring theme through the book), but 'gender' also acquires new meanings in new contexts. I provide below a synoptic account of how these four points anchor this book.

Modern nation-states are self-conscious entities. They are most often wilfully imagined and built. However, they are not built entirely as they wish, for contexts impinge and constrain, even as they offer possibilities. It is in this sense that I argue that public discourse, articulated variously in the rhetoric of nationalism or of globalisation, evinced in state policy documents or a market-fuelled refashioned media, tells us as much about the nature of capitalism as about the identity of the nation. These texts offer us crucial insights into the contexts within which the nation's identity gets shaped and recast. Contexts are important. The challenges of a fledgling and diverse nation such as India, pursuant on a path of self-reliant growth with equity in a Cold War world, are dramatically different from the challenges of globalisation, the growing dominance of a corporate capitalism that was increasingly transnational, and the ascendency of a neoliberal ideology as the new common sense.

The context was different in 1947. After independence, the state became the centre of India's political and economic life. It was the central site of ideological production, crucial in making some of the key policy visions and state shibboleths as part of everyday and public discourse (Chapter 2). The state also continued to be the most important mediating apparatus in negotiating between conflicting class interests for four decades.[8] What appeared to change thereafter was a shift in both these functions. The media after 1991 increasingly became the dominant apparatus for ideological recasting, with a reworked relationship to the state.[9] Further, the autonomy of the state in relation to the dominant classes altered. The earlier role of what can be described as the generally urban middle classes in leading and operating, both socially and ideologically, the autonomous interventionist activities of the developmental state weakened significantly. An ideological trend among the urban middle classes to view the state apparatus as ridden with corruption, inefficiency, and populist political venality grew, as did much greater social acceptance of the professionalism and commitment to growth and efficiency of the corporate capitalist class (Chapter 8). Significantly, the state itself underwent a makeover and re-presentation of self.[10]

This was, however, not the only change. The 1990s was a turning point not only in terms of India's new economic policies, but it was also the time that marked, politically at one end, the rise of the Bharatiya Janata Party (BJP) and its majoritarian Hindutva agenda. If the shrillness of Hindutva rhetoric dimmed between 2004 and 2014, sans state support,[11] it acquired unprecedented scale, intensity, and brazenness after 2014 (Chapter 11). At the other end arose a comprehensive assertion of Dalits and Other Backward Classes (OBC) with issues of social exclusion, discrimination, and an agenda to seize both political and cultural space from the hegemony of 'upper castes' in a post-Mandal epoch. This appeared for a while as an important plank of opposition to the majoritarian actions of the Indian government, particularly since the tragic death of Rohith Vemula.[12] However, the storyline appeared to change rapidly as the ruling party sought to aggressively woo both Backward Classes and Castes, and Scheduled Castes. This seemed to have worked in the 2017 Uttar Pradesh Assembly elections and the party is at work on similar lines in Bihar (http://www.sundayguardianlive.com/news/8941-bjp-woos-backwards-bihar; accessed 12 May 2017).

Further, this was also a time when the gains of the second phase of the women's movement in the 1970s became increasingly mainstreamed. Gender did not just get 'refashioned'. It became a pervasive presence and the book seeks to show how it became crucially intertwined in complex and contradictory ways with the recasting of India. Historically, the gender question in India has been inextricably linked to the histories of nationalism, the politics of religion, caste assertion, and communitarian politics (Chaudhuri 1993). The script is being played out once again, but anew. The ongoing debate on triple talaq is but one instance of this.[13] Gender, I therefore argue, offers a very productive vantage point from which to map and analyse the transformation of Indian public discourse.[14]

The Indian media played a key role in this process of recasting. This book is therefore as much a study of India's changing public discourse as it is a study of the dramatic growth and transformation of the media, from dependence on state patronage to a dependence on the market,[15] to increasing evidence of its control by political parties, which are active players both in matters of the state and the market.[16] In the early years after liberalisation, the media itself carried debates on what its role ought to be in India: between a section who chose the 'sunny side of journalism' and those who batted as 'watchdog over the system of governance' (Chapter 6). The media emerged as a central site and ideological apparatus for the transformation of public rhetoric and in the making of a new social imaginary of India (Chapters 4, 5, 6).[17] It did not stop there, but grew to become an actor that mediated the manner in which politics gets to be played out (Chapters 8, 9, 10, 11).

I began with the contention that a study of the changing public discourse offers an understanding of the nation-state's changing identity. It is in order, therefore, that I return to the image of 'India' and 'Indians' that was built assiduously, but not without its share of contestations, during the long years of colonial rule, initially during the middle-class, nineteenth-century social reform movement and then during the early twentieth-century anti-colonial nationalist movement. This historical perspective alone would make it possible to understand the nature and scale of the recasting that took place. Both the structure and the content of this book reflect this attentiveness to the past. It is in this spirit that I begin here with a schematic historical account of the making of modern India's identity and its defining elements.

Public Discourse and the Identity of India

A nation and its state are founded on a very self-conscious articulated notion of identity. India first encountered the question of national self-definition in the course of its anti-colonial struggle. It was engaged in the historical task of creating a new India, and it was inevitable that the question of what they meant by India would be extensively debated through the nineteenth-century social reform movement and the twentieth-century national movement. A dominant, if not general agreement evolved that Indian civilisation was plural, and in spite of periods of intolerance, these bodies of ideas enjoyed considerable freedom of expression, engaged in a critical dialogue, challenged or borrowed each other's ideas, and created over time a distinct and internally differentiated composite culture (Parekh 2008). As a historical space, India has been no more or less virtuous than any other part of the world. And views in sharp disagreement persisted at the ground level. For instance, the ideology of fanatic Hindu nationalism, the kind that inspired the assassination of Gandhi, has been a recurrent theme within the many contending ideas of India. The idea of religion as the defining marker for nationhood, evident in the making of Pakistan, likewise challenged the idea of a composite culture. Such visions have haunted the story of contemporary India. They have been occasionally strident, but for the most part, have remained muted and, surprisingly, appeared to retreat almost wholly from the dominant national public discourse, only to reappear with renewed vitriol.[18] This has been most evident since the formation of a new BJP-led government in 2014. The language of transnational capitalism, and the new India's feted consuming middle class, so evident in many of the chapters written in the first decade of liberalisation, seem curiously out of sync in a 2016 India marred by state-driven strident cries of bigoted nationalism.

I do not see the two as completely unrelated. *One*, the BJP, perceptive to this new India's aspirational class, strategised on a rhetoric of development and growth in the 2014 election campaign. But this is neither unexpected nor unexplainable. Contained in the BJP's rhetoric is a systematic use of two registers: one of brute passions, the other of reason and statesmanship. This second register is a deeper story. It is the story of a party wedded to an ideological core of majoritarian impulses, coupled with grandiose ideas of a nation feted for its economic power and international clout. If a rhetoric of democracy and diversity is part of a strategy of doing global business, so be it (see Chapter 11). This in no way stands in the way of a free play of majoritarian politics. For the 'government speaks consistently with (at least) two voices' (http://www.bbc.com/news/world-asia-india-34943206; accessed 20 April 2017). *Two*, I argue that a general culture of vacuous consumerism over the decades has led to the cultivation of a middle-class sensibility towards instant and ready to consume ideas of cultural pride and nationalism.

Apart from the idea of pluralism, a more general agreement had developed over decades, that since the vast majority of Indian people were poor and the nation, as it were, was lived in its villages, democracy and freedom would mean little unless the needs of the poorest were addressed.[19] This found expression in very diverse ideological strands that constituted both social reform and national movements, from Vivekananda's invocation of *daridra narayan*, to Gandhi's choosing to wear what India's poorest of the poor wore,[20] to the socialist focus on the peasant and worker, to Ambedkar's forewarning of the challenges of political equality in an unequal society (Chapter 2). The spirit of austerity was seen as a virtue that drew moral sanction from Gandhi's lasting impact on Indian nationalism. It was not only Gandhians, but also the early Communist leaders in India who led frugal and austere lives. It is not that austerity as a virtue went unquestioned, as evident in the Dalit critique.[21] This public deference to austerity was to change quickly and dramatically from 1991.[22] The transformation of the media with the exceptional growth in advertisement[23] not only ushered in new images, but also heralded new ideas of a good life and the good Indian as a 'consumer citizen' (Rao 2012). The stress was on success, and an exclusive and glamorous lifestyle[24] that effectively displaced the larger section of Indian men and women from public discourse. This was the time when new words such as 'celebrity', 'glam quotient', and 'Page 3' came into circulation. Within this context, the Indian woman learnt that 'thrift' was no longer a virtue and 'shopping' is a legitimate pleasure, while Indian men learnt that looking good is not a woman's prerogative (Chapter 4). In this entire process of refashioning the 'nation', the constituent elements of Indian nationalism were reconfigured, as choice rather than constraint and extravagance rather than thrift became the new rhetoric of globalisation.

The point that I wish to make is that India's identity as a nation therefore rested not on an idea of culture, which was about markers alone—such as language, custom, festivals, dance, music, dress—but was also centrally about values.[25] Two important values that defined India's identity were thus the constitutional recognition of India's plural and diverse people and their ways of life, and an economic resolve to address the rights of the poor and alleviate inequality[26] (Chapter 3). Democracy in India therefore became integrally linked to development and redistribution, as well as the recognition of cultural diversities and identities (Fraser 1998). The first principle of redistribution entailed a clear economic programme of development. Development was considered a goal that was good in itself by most policymakers of the early twentieth century. But there were strong differences regarding competing models of development. The achievements of the capitalist path of growth associated with Western powers and their modernity were admired, but not entirely uncritically in India. This was also invariably associated with the devastating impact of colonialism and imperialism. As I mention in Chapter 3, 'economic critiques of colonialism were a key component of Indian nationalism'. Gandhi was critical not just of capitalism, but of mechanised modernity at large. This was a time when a serious challenge to capitalism was being offered not merely ideologically, but in a real attempt to build a socialist economy. The Indian national movement was influenced by socialist ideas and many in the Indian National Congress (INC), most noticeably Nehru, were inspired by the Soviet experience. This in part explains the formation of the National Planning Committee (NPC) in 1938, which drew a road map of development for independent India (Chapter 2).

The idea of a mixed economy where private business and public enterprise would work together thus formed a critical element in the identity of India. We shall see later in this book that after liberalisation, the media hailed business leaders; however, political parties, even as they emphasised the importance of capital investment and growth, had to repeatedly affirm their first commitment to the poor.[27] A marked feature related to this model of development was a curious hesitancy in public discourse till very recently to even use the word 'capitalism'.[28] The reservations about capitalism stemmed from the strong legacy of anti-imperialism within the national movement, a legacy that not incorrectly identified colonialism with the rapacious greed of capitalism. Just as being 'socialist' remained unacceptable[29] for mainstream twenty first-century United States of America, professing free market economics and 'capitalism' with no caveats about equity was unacceptable in mainstream Indian political discourse. This had to change if the new economic policies from 1991 were to work. It is a central contention of this book that the media played a vital role in refashioning India's public discourse, which included making 'capitalism' legitimate, consumerism desirable, and profligacy acceptable (Chapter 6). From another context, recent years have also seen capitalism being debated afresh within the Dalit movement[30]

(Chapter 8), even as the national question of Dalits has been increasingly revisited (https://dalitnation.com/about-3/).

In the early decades of independent India, the discourse thus ran that India was neither 'socialist' nor 'capitalist', but 'mixed', borrowing the best from each (Chapter 2). The chapters will show how the years from 1991 saw an increasing and often strident criticism of Nehruvian socialism and the forced deprivation that the Indian middle class had had to undergo. This grew sharper over the years, but no fundamental attempt was made to redefine basic principles of secularism or socialism or a broad commitment to the poor. What changed was the spectacular victory of the BJP[31] in May 2014, which saw more direct views expressed in public discourse that the expiry date of 'socialism' was long gone by and that its mention in the Preamble to the Constitution could be dropped.[32] The media, which had been arguing the same for long, was in full agreement. But significantly, the idea that 'secularism' too could be done away with was met with considerable opposition. This debate is another story and we return to it in Chapter 11.

The equidistance that we saw regarding a midway between capitalism and socialism also found place in India's foreign policy, its commitment to non-alignment, and staying away from partisan support to either socialist Soviet Union or the capitalist United States of America, the two superpowers of a global era marked by the Cold War. If one were to proceed with the idea that state domestic policies are integral to the identity of a nation, we also need to take into consideration the foreign policy of the state, which also bears down upon the identity and self-presentation of a nation-state. This equidistance was seen as founded not from strategic reasons of hard realism, but an independent foreign policy based on an idea of a Third World morally grounded on a shared past of colonial exploitation and a universal striving for a just world order. [33]

However, as the years rolled on, discontent spread and aspirations changed. Poverty and inequalities remained. Globally, the feeling grew that India counted for little in the world except as a huge market. It was in this context that a new view of India's identity gained ground. This view, tentatively mooted in the late 1980s and gathering momentum since, subscribes to the idea of Indian identity not as civilisational or even as a culturally embedded nation-state, but as a state like any other. The way forward was the practice of realpolitik to at once gain the world's respect and promote national interest through economic and military strength. This idea of India had the active support of the globalised techno-managerial elite, large Indian business houses with global markets in sight, an ambitious middle class eager to benefit from working abroad, from outsourcing, and elated at India's international status. This was the new easy, 'feel good nationalism' that could be consumed. It was a vision of India that also enjoyed great popularity amongst large sections of the media, drawn from the same middle class and from among major groups of non-resident Indians (NRIs).

There is, however, another twist to this story with the active engagement of the BJP in building their influence among the NRIs.[34] The extravagant programmes showcased to welcome Prime Minister Modi abroad are indicative of this, as is his eagerness to be with them. Indicative also is the fact that as the diasporic 'Indian loses physical ties to the colonized nation ... identity is suspended in time and space ... frozen, nurtured and protected' (Fruzzetti and Perez 2002: 55–56). The BJP is not alone in wooing NRIs, although the political agenda differs amongst different groups. An influential global Dalit network has been active in its engagement with various international institutions to press forward its own political agenda, such as the recognition of caste as racial discrimination in the United Nations or the special recognition of discrimination in specific nation-states such as Britain (Chapter 7). More recently, Punjab, which went to elections in 2017, has seen active campaigns with the Indian diaspora.[35]

If big business and NRIs are part of what constitutes the 'global', one also needs to look at the role of the bureaucracy. The fact that several influential individuals in the government have worked in international institutions, or were closely associated with them and have managerial backgrounds, ensures that this vision has a receptive audience (Parekh 2008). Both the 'global' and the 'managerial' parts are important. The 'managerial background' is important for, across sectors—health, education, media, and entertainment—we see increasing evidence of corporate and managerial discourse. The global presence redefines the idea of a national public sphere, understood as one wherein citizens raise and debate issues of their concern and often address these to the state. The shared everyday life of citizens within the nation is crucial here. In the global context, this is redefined for various reasons, such as the role of international institutions, the global corporate presence, and the increasing visibility of the non-resident Indian. In such situations, nationalism cannot but get altered, a point I develop in

Chapter 7. Here, special mention has to be made of the increasing role of international institutions (IIs) in a range of issues, among which women's empowerment and gender rights are central. This, I argue, has (among other reasons) played a role in the hypervisibility of gender, and why both nationalism and feminism have changed (Chapters 9, 10, 11).

The NRI is not the only actor here. The resident transnational capitalist Indian is as much an actor here. The interests of the two may coalesce at some and differ at other points. The visibility of the NRI in the 'national' public sphere does alter it in significant ways.[36] The diaspora was specially invoked in the President's address after the new BJP government took office in May 2014.[37] I discuss the implications of the return of the 'diaspora' and India's media and transformed public in Chapter 8. While the incremental building of the idea of India as a great power is evident in the chapters of this book, a full-blown expression, or perhaps aspiration to being a world power was most evident in Prime Minister Modi's proactive foreign policy and its role in recasting India (Chapter 11). But before I move on to the next section, a quick summing up of the key markers of India's identity as a modern nation-state in its first decades after independence is in order: diversity and plurality; equity and social justice; austerity; a state-led mixed economy; and non-alignment in its foreign policy. It is the refashioning of these values that the book seeks to map.

THE CONCEPTUAL FRAMEWORK

There are a couple of key ideas that provide the conceptual wherewithal to make sense of the processes involved in refashioning the image of contemporary India—its 'makeover', to use a more context-appropriate description. Some of these are *capitalism, nationalism, state, ideology, gender, democracy, individualism, freedom, choice*, the *media*, and the *public sphere*. Even if each of these terms is not overtly present in the title of this book, they are implicit therein. They provide the analytical framework through which I can make sense of what otherwise would have been an interesting, but discrete study of gender images in nationalist rhetoric in general and in the media in particular. I did begin with a study of women's representation in print media advertisements (Chaudhuri 1998b), but soon realised that the story of the recasting of women cannot be seen as an isolate. It could be more fruitfully understood as an integral part of refashioning

India in the context of neoliberal capitalism: a reworking of state–market relations; a reconfiguring of the global and the national; the emergence of a transnational capitalist class; growth of new aspirations and achievements; ascendancy of consumption and pleasure as reigning ideologies; and the unprecedented role of communication, publicity, brand-building, and self-presentation. The emphasis is on grappling with the interconnected play of trends in a specific historical context. Thus, for instance, when discussing nationalism, I do not restrict myself to identifying markers and tropes, but seek instead to understand the changing rhetoric of nationalism and its changing relationship with capitalism.

This is not to suggest that capitalism itself was not changing. What remain constant are its unchanging imperatives of profit-making, incessant expansion, and innovation. What transform are its mode of operation, spirit, and language, as the nation no longer remains the central playing field for capital. Our study of the media over the years shows how it has recast its earlier role as harbinger of a self-reliant nationalism towards an unabashed batting for global capitalism at one end and hyper-nationalism at the other. Gender, likewise, is not addressed as a fixed and extraneous category that has its script determined and set for nationalism, but as an organising principle of society that works in tandem in expected and unexpected ways with capitalism and nationalism. It is critical therefore to accord importance to both the immanent logic of capitalism and to the reflective, thought-out strategies of decision-makers in the state, international institutions, and the many think-tanks associated with the global assemblage of organisations, so as to rein in or give specific direction to that logic. Professional firms specialising in marketing research, media training, publicity relations, management, and advertising provide not only tangible practical expertise, but also create new normative visions of self, the nation, and even transformative politics. Along with NGOs, they function as a new apparatus for ideological production (Chapter 9).

My contention, therefore, is that it is necessary to recognise the free-market project's adaptive (and co-optive) capacities, rather than 'relying on cartoon-like versions of its supposedly invariant essence, or resorting to a left-critical version of hobgoblin-spotting'. Neo-liberalism is in here and this calls for 'a careful parsing of the costs and consequences of (various forms of) market rule, in the context of a wide array of cohabitative arrangements' (Peck 2010: 276). It therefore calls for grounded assessments, not blanket pronouncements. Labelling something, or someone, as 'neoliberal'—which has become a political swearword—cannot be the end of the conversation. The task at hand is a process-based understanding of neo-liberalism, as an evolving pattern of regulatory restructuring (Rajagopal 2016; see section on 'Regulatory Anarchy'). It is within the broad processes at work that one can make sense of the hyper-visibility of gender, of the media's constantly changing contours, and the transformation of public discourse. This is the understanding that informs the book's attempt to map the minutiae of the everyday ideological restructuring and refashioning of India. It is important to recognise that 'all ideologies mix together factual description and the analysis of situations with moral prescriptions about what is right and good and technical considerations of prudence and efficiency. It is this peculiar mixture of factual content and moral commitment that gives ideology its appeal and enables it to guide political action' (Thompson 1984: 78).

This book rests on the understanding that the changing rhetoric and practice of nationalism and culture cannot be understood away from the changing nature of capitalism. The new spirit and practices of capitalism constructs new 'global' cultures, whether of consumption or of managerial discourse, or ready-to-consume platitudes of feel-good nationalism.[38] At the same time, drawing upon one of the central insights of sociological theory, I proceed with the assumption that economic practices and institutions are themselves embedded in wider social, cultural, and institutional relations (Smart 2003: 7). This helps us to understand why the family continues to matter and Indian women remain cultural emblems of the nation; but culture had to change, as the 'thrifty' Indian housewife turned 'profligate' in keeping with the 'new spirit of capitalism'.

Central to my conceptual framework, therefore, is the integral way in which capitalism and nationalism are interlinked, a point that was eclipsed by the cultural turn that dominated the study of nationalism and the nation alike. There are many very disparate quarters from which the view of the nation as primarily 'cultural' has arisen. In Indian politics, there is the cultural nationalism of the BJP. Within academics, there has been an increasing trend to analyse the nation as essentially a cultural construct, critiqued rightly for its hegemony and exclusion. This critique, however, falls short of a comprehensive analysis in its failure to address two central points: *one*, the political-economic contexts of nationalism and the way it can impinge upon the very different trajectories that nationalism can take; and *two*, the 'potential' political-democratic or authoritarian possibilities of a nation-state, depending on the ideologies that it rests upon. Within the diaspora, again, we have imaginings of the nation as an essentially cultural entity—'an imagined community' that is global in its spread, but essentially contained within 'bounded' cultural groups[39] (Chaudhuri 1998a). Globalisation is a strange beast. This cultural focus renders invisible the political-economic contexts until they acquire a stridency that is difficult to ignore. What we have to draw attention to is that globalisation did lead to the emergence of a transnational capitalist class that does not appear to see territorial residence, political belonging, and accountability to the state as integral to nationalism. In India, it played out in a specific fashion with a concerted attempt to delegitimise the state and celebrate the market (Chapter 7). In the West, it has played out at one time with the rhetoric of a flat world and blurred boundaries, and in more recent years with an increasing assertion by right-wing powers for economic protectionism and cultural profiling of the 'other'.

In India, we will see the emergence of a kind of 'trans-nationalism' mapped in the following chapters. This 'trans-nationalism' draws its strength from its access to global services, business, and objects of consumption. It is '... vacuous at times in terms of validation of its intellectual premises', for it draws its strength from 'the materiality of objects of consumption globally available if you can pay for them', and service under 'multinational corporations and new international civil services connected with global non-governmental and inter-governmental organisations, etc.' (Bhattacharya 2005; see Chapters 4, 8). The empty nature of this new nationalist imaginary as an ascending trans-national economic power, I argue, had no mean role to play in laying the grounds for the acceptance of a vacuous cultural nationalism, dressed up in the technologically savvy format of media advertisements with the necessary 'feel-good nationalism' factor (Chapter 11). It is important to note that the new middle class, since the 1990s, has been largely socialised in an educational system[40] and media discourse[41] that privileged managerial knowledge, in the very limited sense of fixing and strategising, to the exclusion of any familiarity with the humanities and social sciences that would have perforce acquainted them with the rich legacy of India's national movement and its role in the making of modern India.

Structurally, one has to recognise that the political economy of this 'proud to be Indian' nationalism of the new transnational capitalist class is not located within the everyday of the nation. What is of particular interest here is not only the tension between the universal imperatives of capital and particular passions of nationalism, but also how the same tension can play out differently in different contexts.[42] Media reports of the business investments of Indian capital in distant shores were initially flagged off as measures of the success of Indian capitalism, and therefore of Indian nationalism.

What is also discernible in the shift of the dominant ideological paradigm in India is that an earlier relative privileging of workers as nation-builders (Chapter 2) has been replaced by an almost entirely capitalist or 'captains of industry' nation-builders (Chapter 8). Later reluctance of the same class to invest in India was seen as a failure of their patriotic duty.[43] The reader will recall the way capitalism was invoked—or, more accurately, *not* invoked—in dominant public discourse. Significantly, 'socialism' was added on explicitly in the Preamble of the Constitution only in the 1970s.[44] The idea of economic self-reliance had been a central element in the story of Indian nationalism. With globalisation, this idea appeared to become dated. Even universities had to be 'global'. Recent events such as Brexit and Donald Trump's presidential victory, which have rested on the idea of national economic protectionism, have led commentators to wonder whether they mark an end to globalisation (https://www.theguardian.com/business/2016/nov/17/does-trumps-election-spell-end-for-globalisation).

I argue, therefore, that to understand nationalism in global times, one has to bring into the discussion the constitutive role of classes in the contemporary global stage of capitalism in the making of state, nation, and nationalism. I have already alluded to the growing presence of the NRI in Indian public discourse. An observation by Bhikhu Parekh on the Pravasi Bharatiya Divas (PBD) held in January 2015 (on the day that Gandhi had returned to India from South Africa) may help to elucidate the changing relationship of capitalism and nationalism. Since the celebrations to mark PBD drew so much from Gandhi and his return to India in particular, it would be interesting to imagine what Gandhi himself would have said, had he been asked to address the meet. Gandhi is '... a little surprised that the PBD falls' on the day of his return from South Africa, wondering that he 'had returned for good' and that surely 'the government of India does not want all Pravasi Indians to follow' his 'example'! (Parekh 2015).

What we see unfold in this book is the story as much of cultural constructions as of the changing configuration of social forces that have redefined at once capitalism, nationalism, and democracy. Robinson, for instance, emphasised that 'the nation-state is not transhistoric', but has to be understood in the context of 'the historically specific correspondence between production, social classes, and territoriality—a correspondence that led to a given political form that became the nation-state' (Robinson 1998: 565). This book rests on the broad argument that 'the material basis for the nation-state tends to be superseded by globalization' and a 'truly transnational studies requires the return to a theoretical conceptualization of the state, not as a "thing" but as a specific social relation inserted into larger social structures that may take different, and historically determined, institutional forms, only one of which is the nation-state' (ibid.).

Most critics of nationalism would concur with Robinson's argument that 'viewing the interstate system as an immutable structure in which social change and development occur has resulted in a nation-state reification' (Robinson 1998: 565). What they would usually not do is either historicise or seek to understand the specific configuration of production relations within which the structural and cultural form of nation-states takes place. With the focus on culture, the state as an entity is often critiqued for its cultural dominance and hegemonic exclusions, but is rarely seen as embedded within dominant social relations of production, a point I elaborate in Chapter 2 as I seek to make sense of the contestations within the First Plan Document on Women.

What is of interest to the broader argument I make in this book is that the state, which commanded the nation in the early decades, came under sharp critique by the media after 1991. The grounds here were not about exclusion or hegemony, but its incompetence vis-à-vis the efficiency of the corporates. In the immediate aftermath of the Mumbai terrorist attack of November 2008, the Indian media witnessed unprecedented bashing of the state and political parties. The state was no longer the flag bearer of the new nationalism on display. The market was. In Chapter 8, I draw from a newspaper article written in the context of the Indian Premier League (IPL) cricket matches being asked to reschedule in light of the 2009 General Elections in India. The IPL owners decided to shift the venue to South Africa, arguing that a globalising India '... has to become a little more accountable to the rest of the world .... The public is learning its lessons. It's a cocking a snook [*sic*] now, with the corporate sector taking the lead. *Our politicians couldn't provide leadership, so these business leaders are taking the helm ...*' (Varma 2009; emphasis mine).

I do not enter here into the scandal around IPL 2010 that hit both the state and the corporate world.[45] But what I would draw attention to is that a corporate global was redefining older ideas of the state, nationalism, corporate sector, and importantly, the public. It is simply not enough to be theoretically lazy and sweep complex processes under blanket terms such as 'globalisation' or the 'post-national'. There are two points that I make here, therefore: *one*, that it is important to delineate the political, economic, and legal structures that 'globalisation' has put in place, within which the media industry operates; and *two*, that one must take into account the radical changes that the media has brought about in redefining the social and the political. I shall return to the latter, but first, an attempt to delineate what constitutes the new global assemblage and how that impinges upon the national.

For long, states were the central players in much of modernity, scripting a homogenous national discourse, flattening out differences. Globalisation has ushered in a host of new transnational players, such as corporate funded think-tanks, international institutions (IIs), international non-governmental organisations (INGOs), who script a global discourse, within which the national can tell its story. The state remains a key actor, but is now in a transformed relationship with other significant global players. The pervasive presence of the global discourse draws its legitimacy from the hegemonic position that IIs occupy in the world order. This is what I had in mind when I argued a little earlier that it is critical to accord equal importance to both the immanent logic of capitalism and to the strategies of individuals and institutions to regulate or deregulate capitalism. However, the presence of this global discourse within the national space would be impossible without the technology that makes media convergence possible. It is within this convergence that I have sought to capture the themes that emerge in the multiple discourses in the aftermath of Nirbhaya's tragic death (Chapter 10). The resultant public discourse has therefore to be analysed in terms of both its content and its form.

This book argues that the media in India has played a salient role in making legitimate a new public discourse or a new 'dominant ideology' (see Althusser 1971), a new spirit of capitalism which 'theoretically has the ability to permeate the whole set of mental representations specific to a given era', infiltrating political and social movement discourse and 'furnishing legitimate representations and conceptual schemas to journalists and researchers, to the point where its presence is simultaneously diffuse and general' (Boltanski and Chapello 2007: 57). I argue through this book that advertisements, advertorials, research reports, corporate features in the media, and management literature work in consonance to recast public discourse. I concur with Boltanski's point that management literature can be read on two different levels—'one turned towards capital accumulation, the other towards legitimating principles'. Readers will notice through the chapters how images of India's new women and men are built. They are not composed only of practical recipes for improving appearances and efficiencies.

> It simultaneously has a high moral tone; if only because it is a normative literature stating what should be the case, not what is the case ... their orientation is not constative, but prescriptive .... In the style of manuals of moral instruction, they select the cases according to their demonstrative power ... what is to be done as opposed to what is not to be done—and take from reality only such of its aspects as confirm the orientation to which they wish to give some impetus (ibid.: 58).

But it is precisely insofar as they constitute one of the main vehicles for the diffusion and popularisation of normative models in the world of enterprise that they are of interest to us here.

My analysis of the media, intensively studied for a month in 2007, shows the manner in which corporates shape public discourse (Chapter 8). On the other hand, my analysis of media reports after Nirbhaya (Chapter 10) suggests that along with corporates, international institutions, whether financial IIs or human rights IIs, began to increasingly define the content and tone of public discourse. I argue therefore that IIs and INGOs, as they actively engaged with states, academia, and the media, emerged as central sites of both knowledge production and opinion-making. Examples are the increasing use of a language of governance, development, gender, and human rights broadly crafted by IIs such as the World Bank, World Trade Organization (WTO), The United Nations (UN), and a host of human rights agencies.[46]

It is in this context that we need to understand the visible and audible presence of global human rights discourse in the content of the responses in the aftermath of Nirbhaya's rape-murder in December 2012. This admonishment at a human rights violation is evident in the travel advisories issued by foreign states; statements by international institutions; commentaries in the international media, transnational feminist academia, and sundry blogs; and corporate commentaries. I argue that while 'global' discourses impinge upon the 'national' public sphere, the latter is not yet entirely subsumed within the global.

I now turn to the question about the *form of discourse*, and what one can term the magical possibilities of the media (Chapter 10). The purported boundaries between old and new media seem to collapse as we witness, in the multiple discourses, a seamless continuity in both content and form. One of the profound ways in which the Internet and new media change the public sphere is through a change in temporality—our relationship and experience with time. Information and images travel the world instantly. The Internet is a highly mediated and highly capitalised form of circulation organised in the 24x7 instant access. The consumer has instant access, but the processes and structures within which messages are constituted and multiply mediated remain invisible to the consumer (Warner 2002). This makes it difficult to fully understand how people read a text or image in specific locales. Further, we know little about how this 24x7 instant access, coupled with abbreviated and context innocent message, shapes opinions and propels political agency.

This matter of localised readings gets further skewed because, *one*, there are unequal levels of global knowledge and ignorance within which both the making of media content and instant access takes place; and *two*, that while the Internet is global, its use is still defined by communities and cultures that could well be spread across the globe (such as diasporic communities), but are essentially bounded in specific cultural groups. WhatsApp messages, whether of virulent or banal content, in circulation is evidence of this. There is, in other words, a dissonance between content and transmission, reflecting a deep-seated hierarchy and a form that expedites instant uploading and access.

The other dimension relates to the altered form of new media and its role in transforming the 'social and political' to mediatised entities. This is of great consequence to how people, or the 'public', in a democracy experience both its everyday and the nation's critical events. For experience today is mediatised. Television debates do not allow the 'time-consuming process of marshalling evidence' that social science demands. The contemporary mediatised world is guided by the 'idea of instantaneous persuasion', which works 'through an appeal to the senses and thus to the embodied person'. They speak more 'eloquently' for they address the 'now' (Chakravarti 1992). The focus on the 'here and now', the sensational, is facilitated by both the new technological, economic structure, and cultural and aesthetic sensibilities of the Indian media industry.

An extraordinary instance of this happened in January 2016. A television channel aired a doctored video of students at Jawaharlal Nehru University (JNU) shouting slogans against India. This was played repeatedly while television anchors spewed venom on the 'purported' 'anti-national' students, and very soon on the 'anti-national' university. A few days later other videos in circulation appeared, as did evidence of deliberate doctoring and connivance on the part of the television channel, political groups, and the government. Arrests of students were carried out. The Home Minister stated that there were terrorist links. The Human Resource Minister spoke of how she would not tolerate any comment on Mother India (http://www.ndtv.com/india-news/2-videos-of-jnu-event-manipulated-finds-forensic-probe-sources-1283105; accessed 14 May 2016). The astonishing part of this story is that while the fact that the video was doctored was proven, the initial message of the doctored video travelled far and wide, and that message appeared impervious to correction. I am tempted here to invoke the matter of rumour and gossip, long thought of as unreliable sources (unlike newspaper reports) by historians. The critical point is not that 'rumour was news that one later learned was false', but that 'what characterized rumors was the intensity with which they were spread'. It is not the 'importance of the truth of stories' but 'the importance of how or why they were told' (http://publishing.cdlib.org/ucpressebooks/view?docId=ft8r29p2ss&chunk.id=ch2&toc.depth=1&brand=ucpress; accessed 16 June 2016). Perhaps the new term 'post-truth' fits in here, where objective facts are less influential in shaping public opinion than appeals to emotion and personal belief.

The BJP understood this. Not surprisingly, BJP spokespersons repeated the slogans on a daily basis on 24x7 television, strengthening the initial message that the university was a den of 'anti-nationals'. As Chapter 11 will show, the BJP was a party that had sensed the power of the media (old and new) early and used it to great advantage. In a world of unequal ignorance and instant access, the truth of a story rests on the effectiveness of communication. In such times of instant persuasion and impoverished absolutes, the need for liberal education and history cannot be overemphasised. Knowledge of history may make the *aam aadmi* more self-critical and less xenophobic—the best antidote to hubris (http://www.hindustantimes.com/columns/a-knowledge-of-history-is-an-antidote-to-hubris/story-y6Cuh9xhC8Zk0EdGj9pRxK.html).

I would like to pursue this point of instant persuasion, instant access, unequal ignorance, and greater 'visibility' of public personages further. It is widely believed that these help to safeguard accountability to the public. This, I argue, calls for careful scrutiny for what we witness in public discourse are: a retreat of a substantive and democratic collective political vision; the 'narrowcasting' or creation of specialised or fragmented audiences, which is probably the media system that has had the most dramatic consequence for mass politics;[47] and an all-out ideological attack on the political sphere, sometimes with a shrill celebration of the corporate world (Chapter 8), and sometimes with shrill cries of hyper-nationalism (Chapter 11). Neera Chandhoke (2016) observes that there has been a 'failure to value the normative component of statecraft', which has led to a 'dumbing down of political discourse'. I would argue further that it is not the failure to value the normative component of statecraft, but a recasting of statecraft to strategic management. Buzzwords and advertisements are more conducive to the state politics of today. Instant persuasion, not the marshalling of evidence and normative visions, is the order of the day. Both nationalism and democracy are about strategies and communication. And questions of historical wounds and mediatised experience have been central to recent political uses of the past. In such instances, 'mindless nationalism' empties out 'the coffers of political discourse', where people are forced to mouth a vacant 'Bharat Mata ki Jai' (ibid.). The story of refashioning India that this book seeks to convey is a story of nationalism severed from its place, 'as a property of a political community which nurtures a sense of belonging', which 'comes through experiences of justice' and not through the 'mouthing of pointless slogans' (ibid.).

THE STRUCTURE OF THE BOOK

The chapters of this book, as stated earlier, have been arranged in the order in which they were written. The issues that they raise reflect the spirit and concerns of the day. The book as a whole, thereby, tells the story of the unfolding changes in India's public discourse after 1991. This order also reflects my own shift from the study of the past[48] to the study of contemporary India. What binds them, however, is the focus on the dominant ideas produced and circulated in a modern society, its gendered nature, and its necessary yet conflicting relationship to both capitalism and nationalism.

Chapter 2 is an analysis of India's first plan document on gender, one of the twenty-nine sub-committees set up by the National Planning Committee in 1938, and finally published in 1947. The intermittent years of war led to the delay in publishing this set of documents, which are statements of the vision and identity of the new nation-state. I place this at the very start of the book not only because I wrote it earlier than the others, but also because inhering in it is the story of the ideological contestations that went into the making of the dominant blueprint of how the Indian state was imagined at the time of independence. It is the recasting of this vision that the subsequent chapters seek to map.

Chapter 3 provides an overview of the way women have been addressed in both the making and the running of the nation-state. Unlike Chapter 2, which is a text-based analysis, here the focus is not confined to the text or stated vision of the state alone, but on the actual ways that these ideological tensions evident in the earlier chapter play out in society. It identifies the three major ways in which the national movement, and later the Indian state, imagined the role of women. These are women as: (*i*) agents and recipients of development; (*ii*) women's participation as equal citizens of a democratic state; and (*iii*) women as emblems of national culture. If the first two dominated public discourse for the first four decades after independence, the mid-1980s saw a shrill ascendency of the rhetoric of women as cultural emblems of the nation and as members of communities. The two incidents in this period which brought the conflict between the rights of women as citizens and the rights of religious communities and 'culture' to the fore were the case of sati in Deorala, Rajasthan and that of Shah Bano, who was granted maintenance rights by the Supreme Court. It is from this point that we witness a greater and overt communalisation of Indian polity and society. If Chapter 2 provides a historical sense of the dominant nationalist vision, Chapter 3 conveys a more sociological sense of public discourse in the period just prior to 1991.

Chapter 4 is about advertisements and gender images in the English print media in India in the 1990s, and rests on the assumption that the shift in the Indian state's economic policy was accompanied by a shift in the media discourse. Some images of Indian women remained traditional (the homemaker and mother), but many were new (the globe-trotting corporate leader). Male models became more conspicuous with newer notions of power and success. There appeared a definite effort to incorporate very strong notions of individual achievement, pleasure, and identity for both men and women. The emphasis on austerity as a defining attribute of Indian identity retreated with a new emphasis on consumption, while the focus on success and a glamorous lifestyle effectively displaced the larger section of Indian men and women from public discourse.

Chapter 5 is a study of how the term 'feminism' was used in print media in the period between 1993 and 2000. Locating the issue of feminism in the institutional context of the print media, we discover two popular versions of feminism that the media promoted, a feminism of 'choice' and a more 'traditional feminism'. I use the term 'traditional feminism' with due caution. At the same time, media discourse seemed to express hostility, both covert and not so covert, to organised women's movements. This simultaneous co-option and backlash reflects at one level a sign of a consensus over some of feminism's demands, such as equality, while at another level it alters the agenda of feminism itself—in the interests of both a newly liberalised economy and a resurgent majoritarian political movement. This is one of the many kinds of cohabitative arrangements of neoliberal capitalism that one has averred to earlier.

Chapter 6 interrogates the idea of 'choice' and 'freedom', which entered and acquired salience in the Indian media with the wave of advertisements in the first decade of liberalisation. A principal tenet of liberal democracy is that a free media is the fourth estate of democracy. Exponents of modern market economies argue that advertisements create the necessary conditions for 'free choice', a prerequisite for the successful functioning of democracy. Critics of that position argue that the media's financial dependence on corporate advertisements logically erodes its autonomy, and thereby its role as the fourth estate of democracy. This is an old debate, but it acquired significance in India with the onset of liberalisation. Issues of paid news, corporate lobbying and espionage, convergence and cross-ownership, addressed in later chapters, had yet to acquire the salience that they did a decade later.

Chapter 7 analyses the transformed structures of power in contemporary India. I contend that the key to understanding India's transformed structure is a set of two disparate developments that together and at once impinge on the structural and ideological formations of contemporary India. One pertains to the assertions of subaltern groups, and the other to the changing nature of capital. While the first interrogates the exclusive and hegemonic character of the 'nation-state', the other seeks to redefine a national order that is more in sync with the imperatives of global capital and a now transnational Indian capitalist class. This, I argue, helps us to appreciate why nationalism, feminism, or the state is not quite what it used to be.

Chapter 8, based on an intensive study of the media for a month in 2007, argues that the unprecedented growth of India does not necessarily lead to a greater democratic participation, for the very idea of the 'public' has undergone transformation. This is evident in the ideological content of the media, the extra-national membership of the public sphere, and the interactive form of publicness. The chapter argues that the media plays a critical role in transforming public discourse, which is rendered more effective because of the synergy between style and substance. An often-strident appropriation of the 'nation' by the Indian middle class, aligned with the project of liberalisation, is manifest in the media. This is deemed 'the public'. The appropriation takes place in two ways: by an overt ideological defence of the market and an attack on the idea of a welfare state; and by the everyday quotidian features and news that inscribe corporate and managerial speech, to create a new imaginary of a global Indian middle class.

Chapter 9 argues that any discussion of gender, media, and culture in contemporary India needs to recognise three contexts: the constitutive influence of three decades of institutionalised feminism; the imperatives of neoliberal economic policies; and the scale of the media and communication industry in the making of popular and public culture. Further, that this constitutive influence has been largely made possible through knowledge produced by a new set of firms specialised in market research and communication, which are interested in understanding the Indian market. These firms function across the media industry, developmental sector, and advertisement and management firms. They reflect the changed nature of the media industry—a proliferating site of media and communication studies. Thus, the firms are linked not only with each other, but also with the academia. The fast and thick flow of images and ideas on gender, which I focus upon in this chapter, has therefore to be understood not as free-floating and self-propelled, an unintended consequence of new technologies in a globalised world, but as products of these agencies. For instance, as we shall see, marketing agencies take cognisance of the impact of feminist ideas of 'freedom' and 'autonomy' on the new Indian woman consumer, and further reconstructs these ideas in alignment with neoliberal ideas of self-realisation through achievement and pleasure. In a sense, this pushes the point articulated in Chapter 7.

I also focus here on the significant influence of the West—undeniably in the corporate world of media and advertisement, but also in academia. While there is a new focus on India in Western academia, including a new attempt to provincialise the West, the influence of theoretical paradigms generated in the West is paradoxically more insidious in sectors of Indian media discourses. I develop this argument through a discussion of post-feminism and the growing market for chick-lit fiction in India. While Western audiences today are more familiar than ever before with the Indian culture industry (for example, with Bollywood, Indian fashion, music, and cuisine), I still hold that in the broader institutional and ideological apparatus through which this familiarity is produced and transmitted, 'gender', 'sexuality', 'cultural diversity', and 'race' are usually configured as elements in the business of consumption in a global market. The questions that I pose, therefore, are the following: How has the idea of feminism been redefined in neoliberal times? How does gender travel? How do we look at the hyper-visibility of gender from a critical feminist perspective?

Chapter 10 is based on a thematic analysis of public discourse in the aftermath of the 'Nirbhaya' rape. I argue that although there is a growing convergence between 'national' and 'global' media discourse, important differences still persist in the content and tenor of the two sets of discourses. Important structural transformations define the relationship between Indian and international media. It is through a comparative study of the two on Nirbhaya that this chapter seeks to examine how and why they differ. A central point argued here is that the 'inequality of ignorance' holds true today in most key sites of knowledge production other than the academia, such as international institutions, global think-tanks, corporate research institutions, and NGOs. These institutions hold great influence in the contemporary global order and we shall see how they also form key sources of information for contemporary media and for the emerging global public sphere (Chaudhuri 2010b). While this asymmetry of knowledge has perhaps been long true, what is new is a potent convergence of 'ignorance' and 'instant access' that new technologies have made possible. It is within this configuration that I analyse both the *content* and the *form* of the mediated discourse in the aftermath of the gang-rape.

Chapter 11 describes the unprecedented role of media and communication in the 2014 General Elections on the one hand, and the centrality that gender acquired in the campaign. While the earlier chapters focused on the manner in which ideas about consumption and austerity were redefined, we notice that in the first year after the elections it was the challenges to the ideas of diversity and plurality that acquired prominence in public discourse. Into the third year we increasingly witness a government that understands that media news is instant, and that the best way to dislodge 'bad press' is to launch a 'new' product that the media could play upon. India thus witnessed 'surgical strikes' against Pakistan, to be quickly followed in the media by 'demonetisation'. There was a quick image makeover of a government supposedly in support of the rich, to one that was the custodian of the poor.

Early in the introduction, I had made the point that alternative ideas of the nation and state were always present, but it is only in specific contexts that they either grew sharper or muted. When the brute power of the state is coupled with dexterous use of the media for instant persuasion, along with a splurge of catchy phrases and acronyms to define social justice, we have a potent combination to fundamentally recast India. Chapter 11, I had felt,can therefore also be read as an Epilogue. However, events since 2016 have been so rapid and so far-reaching that one felt the need for a separate Epilogue.

The Epilogue is titled 'From Certitude to Uncertainty' for the spirit of optimism and certainty in the heady days of globalisation and consumption appear to have retreated from public discourse. Today, some declare that globalisation has met its end. Others argue that it needs a reset. Some contend that neoliberalism is in decline, others that it is even stronger. My own focus, however, is the relationship between neoliberalism and authoritarianism, and its gendered nature. Two examples may help show this. One is the rise of the strong man, the Bahubali, which is reflective not just of hegemonic masculinity but of a weaponised state that legitimises brute force as a sign of a strong state. Democratic norms and procedures are seen as entirely dispensable and a sign of a weak state. This is in sync with the rise of global leaders for whom might is right, as evident in the war between USA, Israel and Iran. The other is the rise of what is often termed as 'femo-nationalism' as evident in naming a military conflict 'Operation Sindoor', invoking a dominant marker of married Hindu women. Such trends exploit 'feminist' ideals to advance nationalist and militaristic agendas. Indeed, governments worldwide are 'weaponising gender' to transform their violent actions into moral and progressive acts.

NOTES

1. There are fifty million Twitter messages posted everyday. See https://www.jimcarroll.com/2005/04/the-rapidity-of-change-has-changed/#.VyhnOmOKe8U (accessed 3 May 2016).

2. 'Any attempt to construct an autonomous and homogenous object of linguistic analysis ... conjures away the social-historical condition under which a particular language or competence is constituted as legitimate, is acquired by some speakers, imposed on others, and reproduced as the dominant form of language use' (Thompson 1984: 7).

3. The stress in anthropology has been on 'experience, of being in spatial proximity with the "other" with its concomitant emphasis on sensory perception'. Another 'practice' employed by anthropologists, but which has been 'downplayed' in discussions, is the 'analysis of the widely distributed "cultural text"' (Gupta 1995: 377; also see Herzfeld 1992). The newspaper, television, and now social media increasingly mediate modern experience. They are critical not only in the discursive constitution of the state, nation, and market, but also of selves and of the world at large. WhatsApp visuals reach a non-literate section in ways that the old media could not.

4. In the late 1980s, the popular Bajaj scooter was sold at a premium and had a waiting period of many years.

5. In two decades, these colonies, which had been planned for middle-class Indians who used two wheelers to commute, faced a severe parking problem, with families now owning two to three cars each.

6. 'Celebrity television journalist Rajdeep Sardesai today deleted his Twitter account after alleging that his account was "hacked" by some miscreants. Rajdeep is often trolled on Twitter and most of the time he is abused as soon as he comments on the microblogging website. Earlier Rajdeep had claimed that he and his wife Sagarika Ghosh are constantly harassed by Twitter trolls, whenever they post their opinions against the Bharatiya Janata Party and the NDA government (http://www.india.com/news/india/rajdeep-sardesai-quits-twitter-after-allegedly-hurling-abuses-in-direct-messages-to-haters-1149466/ [accessed 21 June 2016]).

Ravish Kumar, celebrated Hindi journalist, said, 'I have stopped tweeting because social media space is no longer a citizen's space. It has been usurped by political parties to peddle their ideology and propaganda. It's an online lynch mob where anyone with organisational support of 500 can send out 10 lakh tweets and declare me a thief. But this sort of opposition hasn't ever bothered me. My silence on social media is directed at the coward liberals who are silently watching from the sidelines and are not willing to speak out against this online mob' (http://scroll.in/article/762857/the-ravish-kumar-interview-our-lazy-liberal-class-was-always-opportunistic [accessed 23 June 2016]).

7. The point I am making is not that exclusion ceases to be a defining feature of Indian society (see Badri Narayan 2016). The point is that the media is increasingly defining new social and political spheres. Influential sections within marginalised groups also use social media in new, imaginative ways, even as they find access to the old media difficult. Also see http://www.ndtv.com/india-news/mayawatis-elephant-gives-social-media-a-chance-online-blitz-coming-soon-1648362 (accessed 3 February 2017).

8. See Rao 2005; Rao analyses how, through successive historical periods, 'becoming a citizen' has involved a gradual extension of equal membership to more and more persons and groups. However, the promise of equality masks the exclusionary framework of caste hierarchies, gender differences, and religious divides, which determine the actual experiences of citizenship.

9. Large regional and national newspapers ceased to be dependent on political financing. The brisk growth of the advertising industry—which reached the giddy heights of over 30 per cent growth per year—has supplied a highly attractive source of income (Jeffrey 2000: 58; Rajagopal 1999: 57–100). The consequences of commercialisation are greater freedom in political writing, at the cost of a high pressure to conform to corporate interests (Sahay 2006).

10. An early example is the new slogan of *equity with efficiency*, coined by the then Finance Minister of India from the National Democratic Alliance (NDA) led by the BJP during the presentation of the annual budget (*The Hindu* 2002). The President's address after the BJP came to power in May 2014 invoked the same, albeit with a technological spin. '*E-governance brings empowerment, equity and efficiency*' (https://in.finance.yahoo.com/news/full-text-of-the-president-s-speech-to-parliament-074449489.html [accessed 10 June 2014]; emphasis mine) Events since 2014 have seen persistent and often violent efforts by the state to flex its muscles, with bigoted macho nationalism on the one hand and mantras of globalisation on the other.

11. States such as Madhya Pradesh, Chhattisgarh, and Gujarat have been under prolonged BJP rule, but power at the Centre and power in the states are two quite different things.

12. Rohit was a PhD student at the University of Hyderabad who committed suicide on 17 January 2016. … In July 2015 the University reportedly stopped paying him a fellowship of 25,000 rupees per month after he was found 'raising issues under the banner of Ambedkar Students Association (ASA).' as part of institute's disciplinary inquiry. He left behind a letter where he wrote, 'The value of a man was reduced to his immediate identity and nearest possibility. *To a vote. To a number. To a thing… Forgive me if I fail to make sense. My birth is my fatal accident.*' http://indianexpress.com/article/india/india-news-india/dalit-student-suicide-full-text-of-suicide-letter-hyderabad/#sthash.rgCeUHY5.dpuf emphasis mine (accessed 3 May 2016).

13. The Modi government has, through an affidavit in the Supreme Court, supported a ban on triple talaq. It emerged as a central issue in public discourse in April 2017, with PM Modi stating that women's rights is a development issue (see http://www.hindustantimes.com/india-news/women-rights-is-a-development-issue-don-t-politicise-triple-talaq-pm-modi/story-VDaGsDF4isPDsOuOdM94YM.html; accessed 18 April 2017).

14. Thus, even as the BJP battles for the rights of Muslim women, the country is witness to the most regressive statements and practices on gender. The Chief Minister of UP, Yogi Adityanath, wrote: '*Shastras* have talked about giving protection to women. Just like *urja* (energy) left free and unchecked causes destruction, women also don't need independence, they need protection and proper channelization' (http://www.ndtv.com/india-news/yogi-adityanath-belittled-women-in-article-should-apologise-congress-1682656; accessed 18 April 2017).

Also see https://thewire.in/74667/triple-talaq-statement-muslims/; accessed 18 April 2017. I would like to draw upon another instance which shows the intricate ways that *gender*, caste, and class conjoins in a protest against the state, globalised consumerism, and caste discrimination. The *BBC* reported that 26-year-old Jaya PS, who has a Masters degree in art, paints her body with a type of dark eye shadow when she walks out in public. 'Caste is closely related to color, and whatever is black is not welcome in the Indian society … I decided to paint my body black while appearing in public after Rohith Vemula died,' she told the *BBC* …. skin lightening creams are a very lucrative business in India …. In 2010 the industry was worth $432 million … Indians consume more lightening creams than Coca-Cola (http://atlantablackstar.com/2016/05/02/blackness-around-the-globe-dark-skinned-dalits-fight-an-oppressive-caste-system-whatever-is-black-is-not-welcomed/; accessed 3 May 2016).

15. As Paranjoy Guha Thakurta observes, corporate ownership of the media has a long history and, as had been pointed out in the reports of the first two Press Commissions, the pattern of ownership of the press had a huge influence on how

government policies were critiqued. However, what has inexorably changed is the nature and extent of cross-media ownership: horizontal, vertical, and diagonal consolidation; and digitalisation (see Rajagopal 2016). These changes have an extraordinary bearing on Indian democracy.

16. Links as recent as mid-2016 between electoral politics and the media industry were revealed in the report, 'Star in race to acquire DEN as Talks with SITI stutter'. DEN has a market cap of Rs 685.68 crore. 'The valuations will include the premium that it enjoys for its near monopoly position in UP, which is a key market for media companies, given the *forthcoming elections in the state next year*,' said people connected to the negotiations. DEN had thirteen million cable subscribers and 95,000 broadband subscribers as of 31 March 2016. '"*Entry to DEN will open access to an estimated ` 1,200 crore worth local ad spend in election marketing in UP*,' said Ashish Kaul, a media and entertainment expert' (http://www.pressreader.com [accessed 12 June 2016]; emphases mine).

17. For the making of this new social imaginary, see Mazzarella (2005). In his seminal work *Shoveling Smoke: Advertising and Globalization in Contemporary India*, he perceptively argues that the advertising business in India positioned itself as 'an alternative social ontology' (p. 145). He discusses how 'Indianness' has been used by advertising professionals in India as a differentiator in brand positioning, and also explains how the globalisation of consumer markets has influenced the commercial application of 'Indianness' in India.

18. Groundwork by communal organisations is an ongoing effort. It is only in specific historical moments, particularly with state power, that they gain ascendancy in the national public discourse.

19. Prime Minister Modi, on the occasion of the 'big bash' celebration of two years in power, reiterated his commitment to the poor (http://www.thehindu.com/news/national/government-is-accountable-propoor-says-narendra-modi/article8651361.ece [accessed 15 June 2016]).

20. Prime Minister Modi's decision to wear a suit with his name emblazoned all over during President Obama's visit to India as a guest on Republic Day 2015 drew considerable flak from the media for its narcissistic insensitivity and 'socio-economic audacity'. The allusion to Gandhi was unmistakable in one of the commentaries, titled 'From loin cloth to lion cloth' (see Chapter 11).

21. Teltumbde reads in Ambedkar's own self-presentation 'a counter to Gandhi's belaboured austerity' and 'a representation of modernity as against Gandhi's anti-modern views' (http://www.ambedkar.org/Babasaheb/postambedkar.htm [accessed 27 April 2016]). Others have remarked that 'Mayawati's "ostentatiousness" and her sartorial preferences can in fact be read as her symbolic countermove that mocks Gandhi's attempt at representing poverty and mourning through the semiotic transformation of his body' (Gordon, et al. 2010: 254).

22. See Chapter 9, where the media expressed its strong disapproval of Prime Minister Manmohan Singh's speech to the Confederation of Indian Industries (CII), wherein he proposed an unusual model of austerity to his corporate audience, suggesting that 'industry needs to be moderate in emolument levels' as higher salaries, unless matched by rising incomes 'across the nation', would stoke disaffection among those outside of the growth parabola.

23. Independent India has had a history of a print media which believed that freedom from the commercial imperatives of sponsors alone would enable it to function as the fourth estate of an economically poor democracy. No newspaper or magazine can be commercially viable without advertisements. Industry sources show a dramatic rise in the total advert revenue. From Rs 3,000 crore in 1994–95, it shot up to Rs 82,000 crore in 1999–2000. Of this, 56 per cent is from the print media and 36 per cent from television. It is in this context that I had argued then that ads refashion the new normative Indian.

24. This was interestingly also the time when 'exclusion' became a buzzword in academia and policymaking.

25. Pawan Varma's warning that if '*India's liberal and secular image is tarnished, there will be a global spillover*' is followed by an explication of the question:

> What constitutes the image of a country? This is a particularly complex question for a country like India which is not only a young Republic but also an ancient civilisation. To my mind, India's image, for the outside gaze, rests on several factors: the fact that it is the world's largest functioning democracy; it is an ancient land, with a culture that is marked by antiquity, diversity, assimilation, continuity and peaks of unparalleled refinement; it is a country which has consciously chosen the path of respect for plurality; it is a nation which believes in religious tolerance, ... it is a country ... with a great deal of economic promise ... the fact that it still has too many of the abjectly poor... and, finally, that it is a country that is essentially liberal in its outlook, with space for dissent and debate, and, therefore, unrelentingly opposed to the monolithic fundamentalisms that are sweeping across large parts of the world.. (Varma 2015)

26. Political parties in India since the 1990s have found that ignoring the question of inequality is fraught with risks of electoral defeat. The National Democratic Alliance (NDA) led by the BJP lost the General Elections in 2004 despite the Shining India campaign. Also see Chapter 12, where I look at debates about the urban poor and the dispossessed in analysing the huge victory of the Aam Aadmi Party (AAP) in the Delhi Assembly elections in February 2015. The fourth budget of the Modi government has been described as a budget for the poor (see http://economictimes.indiatimes.com/news/economy/policy/india-unveils-

budget-for-recovery-and-the-poor-after-cash-crackdown/articleshow/56927634.cms; accessed 2 February 2017).

27. In the run up to the 2014 General Elections, for instance, the Congress reiterated that it has always seen the business community and the poor as crucial partners for India's economic progress. Mr Gandhi [Rahul Gandhi] said that the economic programme of the Congress was different from the BJP's, and dismissed the suggestion that he was obsessed with redistribution and cared little for growth. 'I believe poverty cannot be fought without growth' (http://www.thehindu.com/news/national/its-a-contest-of-two-of-two-competing-ideals-of-india/article5941163.ece?ref=relatedNews; accessed 27 April 2014). Likewise, the BJP, faced with a united opposition to the Land Ordinance Act 2014, sought to dispel any misgiving that it was against the interests of the poor, while signalling that it was also for the corporates (*The Hindu*, 25 February 2015). One of the grounds on which the former finance minister Chidambaram criticised the Union Budget of the BJP government was that it went against the grain or ethos of India by being anti-poor (NDTV press conference, 28 February 2015). Two years into the government, Modi reiterated his government's accountability to the poor (see http://www.thehindu.com/news/national/government-is-accountable-propoor-says-narendra-modi/article8651361.ece; accessed 15 June 2016).

28. A more recent usage has been 'crony capitalism', to criticise undesirable practices such as corruption. But this also suggests a wider acceptance perhaps of 'real capitalism' (Chapter 12).

29. Bernie Sanders had to repeatedly 'explain' his 'socialism' in the early months of his Presidential Primaries.

30. More recently, debates within the Dalit movement has brought in the question of whether Ambedkar was a free market proponent (http://blog.mises.org/16519/ambedkar-the-forgotten-free-market-economist/).

> A new radical reading of it visible in the experiences of the Ambedkar-Periyar Study Circle at IIT Madras or Ambedkar Students Association at HCU or at the other end of the *spectrum people who venerate globalisation as the panacea of Dalit's ills or tell us that with advance of capitalism castes will vanish away* are also there to proclaim that they are the true legatee of this vision (Gatade 2016, wa-research.ch; emphasis mine).

31. Historically, the Jana Sangh, the earlier avatar of the BJP, was ideologically committed against 'socialism'.

32. 'On a day when the entire country is expected to honour and celebrate the enactment of India's 66-year strong Constitution, the Modi government, in a print advertisement issued by the Ministry of Information and Broadcasting,

made a glaring error in the Preamble of the Constitution removing the words socialist and secular' (http://www.firstpost.com/india/republic-day-blunder-modi-govt-ad-omits-socialist-secular-from-constitution-preamble-2066447.html; accessed 15 June 2016).

33. A leading strategic analyst remarked in the context of President Obama's visit that 'non-alignment meant standing on the sideline'. And would the shift to multi-alignment allow India to keep its independent foreign policy? (The Big Fight, NDTV, 31 January 2015). In June 2016, Nirupama Rao wrote: '*What sets the current India-U.S. relationship apart is its political and economic heft and the growing geopolitical and security dimensions of the friendship*' (http://www.thehindu.com/opinion/lead/lead-article-by-nirupama-rao-on-indiaus-bilateral-relations-contours-of-a-natural-alliance/article8710549.ece; accessed 15 June 2016). See also the repeated reference to India's 'heft' .

34. For at least two decades now, the BJP and its sister organisations have worked actively among Indians in North America. NRIs have helped to fund the Vishva Hindu Parishad (VHP) and the Rashtriya Swayamsevak Sangh (RSS); according to one study, between 1994 and 2001, some $2.5 million were repatriated to groups associated with the RSS and the VHP. Within the United States, NRIs have campaigned to elect legislators sympathetic to Indian interests, and to have school curricula amended to remove references seen to be slighting Hindus or their faith (Guha 2015).

35. A curious situation emerged, highlighting the challenges to the public discourse of nation-states when 'Punjab Congress chief Capt. Amarinder Singh's public meetings in Canada' were cancelled. 'He was to hold political rallies in Toronto and Vancouver.... This, after he was informed by Indian Foreign Secretary, Dr S Jaishanker, on phone that Canadian law, under the Global Affairs Policy, prevents foreign governments and individuals from conducting election campaigns in Canada'. He finally opted to Skype (http://www.thehindu.com/news/national/capt-amarinder-reaches-out-to-nris-via-skype/article8524733.ece; accessed 28 April 2016).

> The Bahujan Samaj Party (BSP) is focussing on wooing NRIs this election season, particularly those from Doaba region—Jalandhar, Hoshiarpur, Kapurthala and Nawanshahr districts. Dalits and NRIs are a sizeable populace in Punjab, one that every political party wants to tap. The Doaba region has a large chunk of Dalits. In the 2014 Lok Sabha elections, NRIs are said to have played a major role for AAP, which got around 24 per cent vote share in Punjab on debut (http://indianexpress.com/article/cities/chandigarh/bsp-reaches-out-to-dalit-nris/#sthash.I1iGBTZl.dpuf; accessed 4 May 2016).

Commentators report: 'The unforeseen looping of the Punjabi NRI with local politics opening up a political space for a totally new, "nonstate" entrant into the state is a fascinating phenomenon' (http://economictimes.indiatimes.com/articleshow/56975837.cms?utm_source=contentofinterest&utm_medium=text&utm_campaign=cppst). Also see http://economictimes.indiatimes.com/news/politics-and-nation/how-the-great-upstart-aap-and-the-foreign-hands-of-diaspora-are-changing-politics-in-punjab/articleshow/56975837.cms (accessed 5 February 2017).

36. 'The opposition cornered the government in the Rajya Sabha over its urgency to grant voting rights to NRIs at a time the Election Commission has already declared itself logistically incapable of ensuring voting rights of migrant workers who are displaced within the country, rather than abroad .... K. T. S. Tulsi asked if the preference for NRIs is based on their financial clout. 'If there are ten million non-resident Indians according to statistics, that will mean that there will be 18,000 votes per constituency on average and if all of them were to be given a franchise, it could significantly alter the voting pattern, and also the result of elections. I want to ask the government how is it that you are giving greater preference to non-resident Indians and lesser preference to resident Indians and migratory labour? Is it only because they have more money? Is that the reason for discrimination?' (Ghosh 2015)

37. 'Across the world, we have a vibrant, talented and industrious Indian Diaspora that is a source of great pride for us. They have done pioneering work in diverse fields, held the highest public offices and have worked hard to support their localities and families in India. While they have contributed immensely to their adopted country, they also carry a little flame of India in their hearts that can light up the promise of change in our country. A hundred years ago, in 1915, India's greatest Pravasi Bharatiya, Mahatma Gandhi, returned home and transformed the nation's destiny. The next Pravasi Bharatiya Diwas in January 2015 will thus be a special occasion' (https://in.finance.yahoo.com/news/full-text-of-the-president-s-speech-to-parliament-074449489.html; accessed 10 June 2014).

38. This holds true even as we witness the rise of hyper-nationalism, expressed in acronyms and buzzwords.

39. See n 34–36.

40. This is not the space to develop this point. But I would like to flag the necessary link between the decline of liberal education and the rise of a chest-thumping nationalism. It was precisely the period after the 1990s that saw the closure of humanities as a stream in many privileged schools, and the rush of the 'brightest' students to the commerce stream.

41. Every year, the top salary offers to students from the prestigious Indian Institutes of Management (IIMs) would be carried on the front pages of newspapers.

42. See the debates in the Indian and French media over Lakshmi Mittal's bid to merge with Accelor.

> Ever since he took over Europe's Arcelor in 2006, Mittal hasn't been able to shed his image as the big-bad mega-rich Indian who came to France to lay off workers and drive French steel industry to ruin. His company, Arcelor Mittal, though, is more of a European entity than it is Indian. It was born out of a merger between Europe's biggest steel producer, Arcelor, and Mittal Steel (headquartered at that time in Rotterdam). (http://www.business-standard.com/article/companies/lakshmi-mittal-household-name-in-france-for-all-the-wrong-reasons-112112900034_1.html; accessed 14 May 2016).

Also see Fraser (2005) for a discussion on the transnational public sphere.

43. See https://greatbong.net/2011/08/13/patriotism-and-the-nri/ (accessed 14 May 2016).

44. The forty-second Amendment of the Constitution (Forty-second amendment) Act, 1976, was enacted during the Emergency (25 June 1975–21 March 1977) by the INC government. The forty-second Amendment is regarded as the most controversial constitutional amendment in Indian history. It attempted to reduce the power of the Supreme Court and High Courts to pronounce upon the constitutional validity of laws.

45. See http://www.thatscricket.com/news/2010/12/16/ipl-scandals-and-controversies-of-2010.html (accessed 13 May 2016).

46. I have argued elsewhere how issues initially articulated by social movements, whether the women's rights movement or labour movements are taken up by IIs and often appropriated within their broad framework (see Introduction, Chaudhuri 2010).

47. See 'Frédéric Martel, The Different Identities of the Internet'. The argument here is that seen from afar, the globalisation of information and communication technologies might appear to be leading to uniformity. However, in reality, countries, governments, and populations are shaping the way the Internet is used to suit themselves (https://www.youtube.com/watch?v=x_wv6U_2UWo).

48. My early work was on the dominant ideological trends within the women's movement and their complex links with the national movement (Chaudhuri 1993). Chapter 2 represents this.

CHAPTER 2

Citizens, Workers, Emblems of Culture
An Analysis of the First Plan Document on Women

The historical context of the 1938 Sub-Committee on Women

The National Planning Committee (NPC) was established in October 1938 under the Chairpersonship of Jawaharlal Nehru to draw an outline for independent India's planned development. One of the twenty-nine subcommittees established by the NPC was on 'Woman's Role in Planned Economy'. The formation of the NPC clearly expressed the intention of the Congress to adopt planning as the most effective means for the comprehensive economic development of the new nation. Nehru was probably the most vocal advocate of planning, and was primarily responsible for putting it on the national agenda as the only viable instrument for alleviating the poverty of the Indian people. He was aided by Subhash Chandra Bose, during whose first tenure as Congress President the NPC was constituted. Gandhi, however, was firmly against the planning exercise, and even asked his followers not to cooperate with the Planning Commission, believing as he did that 'the whole of planning is a waste of effort'.[1]

This is only one, and the most obvious, of the conflicts within the national movement about the path of development that the new nation should adopt. Gandhi's view, however, finds no place within the Woman's Role in Planned Economy. Even amongst those who were agreed upon the significance of centralised planning, there was considerable ideological disagreement on questions of gender, nation, religion, class, development, and the state, to mention the more salient issues being disputed at that time. Many of these contradictions have left their mark on the proceedings of the Sub-Committee on Women (SCW) and its eventual report entitled *Woman's Role in Planned Economy* (*WRPE* 1947).

This chapter will seek to explore the various tensions which have gone into the making of the NPC and which surface from a reading of the *WRPE*. The chapter rests on the assumption that the NPC has to be understood as a concerted effort of the Congress and the Indian business section towards formulating a policy document for the impending Indian state.

The Congress in 1938 had come to represent the promise of some meaningful changes. It had done extremely well in the 1937 elections, winning 711 out of 1,585 provincial assembly seats, with absolute majority in five out of eleven provinces. For millions of Indians, the 'vote for Gandhiji and the yellow box' signified appreciation of patriotic self sacrifice, plus some hope of socio-economic change (Sarkar 1983: 349). At the same time, elections on a wider (but by no means universal) franchise demanded more money and the cultivation of links with locally dominant groups, businessmen in towns, and landlords and dominant peasant groups in the countryside.[2] Through the period the Congress was under the contradictory pressure of both Left and Right political forces, and the NPC in a very important sense embodied these conflicting pressures. To quote Nehru, the NPC was 'a strange assortment of different types'. There were 'hard-headed big businessmen' as well as people who are called 'idealists and doctrinaires, and socialists and near communists' (Nehru 1966: 419). Indian capitalists, while retaining close ties with elements in the Gandhian 'Right', like Patel and Rajaji, had also started cultivating sections of the Congress 'Left'. Nehru's vision of a modern industrialised India fitted much better with bourgeois aspirations than did the Gandhian evocation of rural simplicity and handicrafts. And there were enough indications that Nehru's socialist flourishes were manageable (Sarkar 1983: 343). In a letter to the Editor of the NPC on 13 May 1938, Nehru conceded the need to accept 'to a large extent the present structure, at any rate as a jumping off ground' (Krishna 1945: 49). These developments are significant for understanding the process by which the Congress, while fighting the Raj, was slowly becoming the Raj. The realignment between the Congress and the Indian business section also helps to make sense of the curious manner in which the *WRPE*, while presenting a radical class analysis of the women's question, also forecloses the possibility of its realisation.

THE SCOPE OF THE SUB-COMMITTEE REPORT: WOMAN'S ROLE IN PLANNED ECONOMY

On 16 June 1939, the NPC appointed the Sub-Committee on Woman's Role in Planned Economy (*WRPE* 1947: 27). The *WRPE* is a comprehensive account of the status of women in India of that period. It is also an outline of a plan for changing the status of women in independent India.

The terms of reference of the Sub-Committee, which sought to 'deal with every aspect of women's life and work', were as follows:

> This Sub-Committee will deal with the place of women in the planned economy of India, including consideration of her social, economic and legal status, her right to hold property, carry on any trade, profession or occupation and remove all obstacles or handicaps in the way of realising an equal status and opportunity for women. In particular it will confine itself to:
>
> (a) the family life and organisation, and women's employment in the house and the changes therein in recent years;
> (b) marriage and succession and the laws governing these;
> (c) the conditions of industrial employment of women and the protection of working women in mines, factories, plantations, workshops and cottage industries as well as domestic employment and retail trade;
> (d) social customs and institutions which preclude women from taking her full share in India's planned economy;
> (e) the types and methods of appropriate education to play her due role in household work, in the profession and social and national services; and
> (f) any other questions connected therewith (*WRPE* 1947: 27).[3]

The terms of reference, though extensive, laid special emphasis on providing women with equal opportunities as a matter of right to enable her to take 'full share in India's planned economy'. Entry into the production sphere was seen as the key to resolving the unequal status of women. This is a radical departure from the concern of nineteenth-century reformers and early nationalists with middle-class women's issues stemming wholly from their lives within the family. However, this departure is in turn marked by its own bias, namely the very cursory mention of women in the agricultural sector. Such an omission would have been possible only in a context where this silence could go uncontested. Women in agriculture are not completely invisible in the document, but the kind of detail that characterises the section on women in industry and even in cottage industries is missing.[4] Incidentally, the *Report of the sub-committee on labour* in its terms of reference also clarifies that its scope extends only to 'labour *other than agricultural labour*, including the problem of employment' (*The sub committee on labour* 1947: 11; emphasis in original).

Entitled *Woman's Role in Planned Economy*, the 265-page SCW report contains a Preface and Introduction by K. T. Shah, who was also the Editor of the other reports produced by the various sub-committees. The main text is divided into three principal sections: Section 1, on the individual status of women, has four chapters, namely 'Civic rights', 'Economic rights', 'Property rights', and 'Education'. (Why the chapter on 'Education' does not have 'rights' appended to its title, we do not know.) Section 2 on the social status of women has two chapters, entitled 'Marriage and its problems' and 'Family life'. Section 3 on miscellaneous issues begins with a chapter titled 'Miscellaneous', dealing with caste, widows, widow remarriage, widows' home, unmarried mothers, abortion, illegitimate child [*sic*], prostitution and traffic, women and children [*sic*] prostitutes, commercial prostitutes, courtesan and temple prostitutes. Then follow the 'Summary statement of policy' (Chapter 8), and the 'Summary of recommendations'. The final chapter contains the resolutions of the NPC on the report of the SCW.

The separation of 'Individual status' from 'Social status' in the report hinges on the basic understanding of the SCW that the individual is the legitimate unit of society, while the social—understood as 'marriage, family problems, caste and religion'—refers to the encumbrances that impinge upon the individuality of the woman.

The *WRPE* opens with a long Introduction by K. T. Shah, one of the three economists in the NPC (along with Radha Kamal Mukherjee and M. Visvesvarya). It plays an important role in placing the document, standing between the reader and authors and clarifying its meaning and significance in a way that may even be at variance with the intentions of the report. In this light, the clarificatory remarks made by K. T. Shah about the personnel of the Sub-Committee are telling:

> While the personnel of almost every other Sub-Committee was made of people claiming special knowledge of the subject or personal experience, this Sub-Committee was formed largely of women who might, without injustice, be described as lay persons. They were, no doubt, highly educated and distinguished in the public life of the country by their service or sacrifice; but not all of them could claim personal expertise on all the variety of topics falling within the scope of this Sub-Committee.

> The results are nevertheless such as would do credit to any body of experts; and that is the only justification for the writer to make such a special mention, which, he hopes, will be found to be neither invidious nor impertinent (*WRPE* 1947: 24–25).

Notwithstanding their lay status, the members of the SCW, consisting 'largely of women', were 'highly educated' and 'distinguished in the public life of the country' (*WRPE* 1947: 25), and therefore party to the central ideas of their time. The *WRPE,* in this sense, embodies the dominant ideological debates, tensions, and ambiguities of the period.

The Introduction begins with the following statement:

> This report considers the entire structure of Planned Economy with Woman as the focus. On the ground of examining socio-economic position of woman [*sic*], the Sub-committee has reviewed every field in which woman operates or should operate, to contribute her share of the nation's wealth and the people's well-being. While considering principally the material aspect of Woman's Role in Planned Economy , the cultural or spiritual position of women under a National Plan, and its reaction on the nation's life and work is by no means ignored (*WRPE* 1947: 17).

The deference to women's 'cultural' and 'spiritual' role, the significance accorded to the 'material' aspects of 'woman's role', and the privileging of the 'nation's wealth' are important cues for entering the text.

PERSPECTIVE AND METHODOLOGICAL OBSERVATIONS

In this chapter, I seek to read the *WRPE* as simultaneously the voice of its authors, a product of a historical period, and as an ideological text which nonetheless contains within it voices that are not intended. That is, the text is a plan document authored within the dominant trend of the national movement (itself containing multiple tendencies) and disclosing the various discourses of the period at work, processed dialogically (Bakhtin 1988: 131). The *WRPE* is a kind of hybrid sum of institutional and discursive practices bearing on the nation, family, class, gender, religion, and community. We have here divergent languages, often encapsulating antithetical worldviews. We have images of a liberal nationalist worldview jostling with visions of cultural revivalism and socialist utopias. The hegemony of the liberal nationalist view is finally established, although not without a concerted struggle with the other views. The *WRPE* reflects the basic ideological thrust of its time. It contains the ideas of the grand narratives of the West, which had such a powerful impact on the English-educated middle class, but which were interpreted in the specific context of colonialism, a context peculiarly gifted with the potential of endowing new meanings. This potential for transformation is, of course, located in the very process of the skewed development of colonialism.[5]

This chapter can in no way do justice to the report. Reading it today, almost eighty years after the SCW was constituted, reading it in the light of the issues which the women's movement has raised over the past few decades, it is remarkably contemporary. To mention but a few of the issues that were widely debated in the *WRPE* then, and which have continued to be debated since, the report considered: the nature of household labour and the need to recognise its value (p. 104); the rights of the unmarried woman; the irrelevance of legitimacy for determining the rights of children so far as the state is concerned (p. 204); and even issues like 'identical moral standards' (p. 38).

The *WRPE* is also remarkable as a well-documented status report, the first of its kind, based entirely on primary investigation in an era when such exercises were not the order of the day; and on women, an area where paucity of data continues to be a major problem. This data itself is based on an understanding of the complex ways in which the lives of women are structured by the economic, social, political, cultural, and religious spheres, thereby grappling with the perplexities of the woman's question in Indian society. In this respect, the report puts many studies on women in India of the late 1960s and 1970s in a poor light.

The central focus of the ensuing discussion will be to unravel the key concepts which directly and indirectly shaped the analysis and recommendations of the SCW. This focus unfortunately also forecloses any detailed discussion on the rich body of information contained within the *WRPE*, and also an analysis of the reasons why the document in a very real sense receded from the public eye,[6] even while planning itself acquired a certain urgency in independent India.

In our attempt to analyse the text, we will identify certain themes which run through it, and which derive from earlier discourses. A reading of the text clearly shows the imprint of the ideas of liberalism and socialism. However, these ideas, whether about the 'nation' or about 'democracy', whether about 'citizenship' or 'family and property', are not derived unchanged from the earlier discourses but, either in the form of worked-out critiques or class resistances, are incorporated in the discourse itself. To give an example, a critique against unbounded individualism in a liberal worldview and a plea for state intervention are incorporated into the discourse of the *WRPE*, a discourse which nevertheless is arguing for a liberal social order. This shift in emphasis is never complete, however, and what we observe is a constant but subtle contestation of the concept of 'individualism' within the *WRPE*. This is but one example of the several ways in which the 'text' gets inflected by the 'context' and whereby the 'context' is already textualised.

This dialogic relationship works in a particular fashion in a colonial society where the 'texts' offering emancipatory models were alien and Western. We thus also have a tension between nationalistic pride in tradition and the modern commitment to change which the liberal and socialist paths were offering.

Conflicts between these models exist at the ideological level and also at the level of realpolitik (if such distinctions are viable), for instance, in the ongoing ambivalence of the Indian business classes to the Congress and the subsequent rapprochement by 1938. Historically, we should remember that the communist movement in India was gaining strength, and that the Soviet Union was a great inspiring model for all nationalist movements.[7] Amidst these various sets of conflicts, the woman's question itself was being defined and redefined. The most explicitly stated (although not hegemonic) model evident in the *WRPE* for changing the status of women is the socialist model. The argument is that the emancipation of women becomes possible only when women are enabled to take part in production on a large scale, and when domestic duties require their attention only to a minor degree. This had become possible as a result of modern large-scale industry, which not only permitted the participation of women in production in large numbers but also actually called for it; and, moreover, which also strove to convert private domestic work into a public industry (Engels 1948). The marginalisation of agricultural labourers in the text has already been mentioned. Gandhi would not have approved. Other Congress leaders would not have approved either, but more on account of their conservatism with regard to women than for any concern about the logic of 'modern large-scale industry'.[8]

While the socialist model is the one that is most frankly advocated, emphasis on key liberal concepts like 'citizenship' (*WRPE* 1947: 36–38), the 'individual as the primary unit' (ibid.: 153), and 'private property' (ibid.: 118) run through the *WRPE*. This is but one of the lines of conflict regarding political options. The other discernible tension is that between the avowed aim of the *WRPE* to reorganise society by doing away with the past, with the family and existing forms of marriage, and stray comments within the *WRPE* which reaffirm the past, the gendered nature of the family, and the role of traditional religion.

The SCW, like the other sub-committees of the NPC, was trying to outline a society based on secular principles. That this was not an issue likely to pass uncontested is clear in the report not only from a manifest mention of differences (*WRPE* 1947: 232, Appendix I), but also from the manner in which issues such as the Uniform Civil Code (ibid.: 229–31) are presented, and in evidently ambiguous views regarding religion.

The following analysis of the *WRPE* will be more or less confined to the set of conflicting lines of thought just identified: (*a*) the ideas of liberal democracy, centred around the sanctity of the family and private property, and the ideas of socialism, premised on the understanding that the two institutions have to be done away with for the emancipation of women; (*b*) a vision of the inevitability of historical progress paving the way for a new social order, and the historical evocation of a golden past with an enviable record on the status of women; (*c*) the proclamation of a secular order, that is, a break with religion, and a simultaneous celebration of a past when the true spirit of religion had not yet been tainted; and (*d*) the prioritisation of the individual on the one hand and the nation-state on the other.

While we will try to focus on these issues separately, compartmentalisation is difficult: these ideas are so densely woven into the text and are so often interworked within the same phrase, sentence, or paragraph (as the case may be), that exposition of any one will invariably draw in several others.

Apart from this complex set of ideas is the disconcerting fact that the text is now being read by a particular person with particular orientations almost eighty years after the Committee set down to work. The weight of hindsight is immense and there is no way of suspending the armoury of concepts through which the text is being read; hence this preliminary disclaimer.

PRIVILEGING THE NATION, THE INDIVIDUAL, THE CITIZEN, OR THE WORKER

The *WRPE* had separated 'individual status' from 'social status' (see the previous section) with what seemed a clear preference for the 'individual'. This preference is, however, marked by a tension between the unfettered individual free to develop his/her potentialities unhindered by social problems and the call of the nation-state for useful citizens and productive workers. The note of dissent by Miss K. Khandwala argues that the perspective which had informed the SCW to start with had been eventually waylaid by the *WRPE* (*WRPE* 1947: 232). That perspective had clearly foregrounded the individual.

> The only social status to be recognized in planned society will be that of the *individual worker*, or the child who has to be the *citizen or worker* of tomorrow, or of the aged, disabled, defective person, who will have to be dealt with separately. The social status, therefore which presents the most serious question of social reform, will not, I take it, matter at all in planned society. Neither motherhood, nor wifehood, nor, *a fortiori*, widowhood matter at all (ibid.: 238; emphasis in original).

The SCW accords the individual woman an unequivocal centrality, but what is significant is that the aspects of the individual accorded the highest premium are those of the 'useful citizen' and 'the productive worker' (*WRPE* 1947: 36). The underlying assumption is that this usefulness and productivity of the individual are to be evaluated in terms of her contribution to the making of the nation. While societal barriers in the way of women's progress are sought to be pushed back, the retreat of society and the celebration of the individual are not absolute. For now the *nation-state* emerges as the central actor and the question of women's individual progress becomes a question of the nation's progress. For instance, on education the *WRPE* writes: 'All restrictions which prove a handicap to the *free and full development of woman's personality* shall be abolished' (ibid.: 219; emphasis mine).

On trade unions, the view is similar: 'Trade unions should accept the principle of equality between men and women and recognize the *individual as a unit*' (ibid.: 114; emphasis mine).

On the question of leisure we have: 'Every human being is entitled to a certain amount of leisure for self development. The effect of routine tasks performed monotonously each day has a deadening effect on the *individual* reducing his or her *capacity to contribute to national progress*' (ibid.: 41; emphasis mine).

And again on the matter of recreation: 'It is the *civic right of every individual to expect from the State* suitable parks and open spaces in the city where they may spend their leisure and *preserve the health necessary for carrying on their work efficiently*' (*WRPE* 1947: 43; emphasis mine).

On health, we have: 'Any steps taken to protect the health of the women workers should *not be considered as for their exclusive benefit only*, but as taken *in the interests of the whole nation*' (ibid.: 209; emphasis mine).

On widowhood:

> We are strongly opposed to widowhood being considered as a perpetual condition and every effort should be made by education, social reform and even legal reform, to put an end to the evils that result from such condition. We desire that the widow, instead of being the *nation's liability* be turned into a [*sic*] *useful member of society* . . . (ibid.: 182; emphasis mine).

On birth control, the document notes that 'from the national point of view, birth control is very important' (ibid.: 175), and 'From the eugenic point of view the Indian stock is definitely deteriorating for want of proper selection as well as due to poverty, malnutrition, etc., factors which are detrimental to the nation's health (ibid.).

Although this tone is not dominant in the *WRPE*, the *Report of the subcommittee on population* does read like this for the most part.

Elaborating on the condition of women in industrial employment, the *WRPE* uses the phrases 'in the interests of social economy' and 'the interests of the community' to argue for 'protective measures' for women working in 'occupations involving disproportionate physical strain', and for 'expectant mothers' in 'industrial or other exacting employment' (*WRPE* 1947: 45–117). A constant process is underway to ensure the free development of the individual, while also making sure that this individuality at no point transgresses the interests of the nation. For the point is not to grant rights for the 'exclusive benefit' of the individual, but 'in the interests of the whole nation' (ibid.: 209).

The interest of the whole nation is itself understood in the particular sense of 'growth', the basic value underpinning modern social thought. This is reflected in the chapter on 'Civic rights', which argues that: 'In order to help woman to become a useful citizen and *productive worker* she must be assured of her fundamental rights' (*WRPE* 1947: 209; emphasis mine). Apart from the obviously utilitarian vision that informs the *WRPE*, we have a certain prioritisation of the nation as a collective unit. Social organisations other than the nation are seen as hindrances to the growth of the individual. 'The rigidity of the caste system has affected the *individual rights of man and woman*, by preventing them from marrying outside the caste and thereby limiting their choice (ibid.: 177; emphasis mine).

And, 'Marriage from a rational view point can no longer be a divine dispensation but a voluntary association of two *individuals* with rights and obligations attached to it (ibid.: 153; emphasis mine).

What we have is a hierarchical placement of the community (caste, religion) at the base (understood as a legacy of the past, and therefore transitional until a point when the nation becomes the community), the individual (understood as citizen and worker), and finally the overarching state.

'Individual families will and should continue, but as far as the State is concerned, the *individual* must be the basic unit to which consideration should specifically be given' (*WRPE* 1947: 221; emphasis mine).

For in a planned society, the basic unit would be the *individual*. All groups (for example, the family, the caste), however tied together, must be 'voluntary associations' regulated by their own codes (ibid.: 153; emphasis mine). This emphasis on choice, on 'voluntary associations', is a necessary part of the package of liberal individualism. So we have the 'right to adopt a child' (ibid.: 174), an '*individual right*' which cannot be interfered with, but with the qualification 'that adoption of a son for purposes of inheritance is undesirable' (ibid.). Married women must have 'the *right to choose* their own nationality in the event of their being married to a non-national, or residing in Indian States or foreign countries' (ibid.: 43). Similarly, the report opposed those who sought to give 'the woman a vote not in her own right as an individual but as a wife' (ibid.: 37).

The *WRPE* reflects this emphasis in content, balance, and form. It is significant that Section 1, dealing with 'individual status', is spread over 115 pages (pp. 35–150), including seventy-two pages (pp. 45–117) devoted to 'Economic rights', while Section 2 concerning 'social status' was limited to forty-eight pages (pp. 151–97). Despite the neglect of women in agriculture, the report's detailed investigation on women's economic life and role is of special significance in relation to planning in independent India, for the very idea of the woman as a productive worker was subsequently eclipsed in state and academic discourse, except with reference to the new middle-class working woman.[9] It was only in 1974 that the Committee on the Status of Women in India raised the matter of the invisibility of women workers, and only as late as the 1993 Census that a concerted attempt was made to both redefine women's work and communicate to the people a more comprehensive understanding of 'work'.

In contrast, the chapter on 'Economic rights' in the *WRPE* expresses a very clear understanding about the process of marginalisation of women's work and the significance of the notion of a 'right to work'. "The right to work is a claim to something more fundamental than a mere chance of earning an independent income. Out of the total female population of about 180 million, nearly 50 million are wage earners (*WRPE* 1947: 199).

And:

> In both rural and urban areas women of the working classes are recognized as instruments of labour. A fairly large proportion of them are found engaged in all types of manual labour, agricultural, domestic and industrial occupations. This labour must be recognized as a separate unit of production and not as it is today, a corporate part of the family work (ibid.).

Special mention is made of the invisibility of work done in the precincts of the 'home' and the need to recognise household work.

> A great many women will confine their activities to the home, in any event, a great part of their work will be done in the home. This home work, though not recognized in terms of money value, is an essential contribution to the social wealth of the State and should be recognized as such. The aggregate of social wealth under planned economy will include all kinds of work, whether rewarded in money value or not (ibid.: 200).

As mentioned, we have a substantive thrust on 'Economic rights', and an empirical focus on working-class women, but an ideological tilt in favour of bourgeois rights—the right of women to hold private property (ibid.: 118), the right of citizenship, and the individual woman's right to choose (ibid.: 37). On the one hand, the liberal view contains the socialist position; on the other, the nation-state contains the individual.

THE HISTORICAL PROJECT: THE DENIAL AND RETRIEVAL OF THE NATION'S PAST

Much of the *WRPE* is about the significance of the period, and about the historical task at hand of defining the nature of the unborn nation-state and the status and place of women in it: 'In the world today great changes are taking place, and we are told that this is a period of transitions, so also in India where a new order is being born, not only political but also social and economic' (*WRPE* 1947: 32).

And again: 'Circumstances have altered so radically in recent years that the old frame no longer fits the new picture, and hence it has become necessary to make some changes' (ibid.: 32).

The present seems to be a time like no other, an epoch irrevocably burdened or blessed with the gift of choice. The phrase 'new social order' occurs repeatedly. The social unit for change is the 'nation', the legitimate form of self-representation in a world order marked by the simultaneous birth of the sovereign nation-state and a global world. It is within the new global order that the status of each nation was to be judged. This is the broad vision which informs the SCW.

The new order was to be brought in but, as the *WRPE* states, time was needed in order 'to bridge the gulf between existing conditions and what might seem at first glance to be drastic recommendations' (*WRPE* 1947: 32). These 'drastic recommendations' would be based on the 'rational explanation of scientific thought', for 'An essential characteristic of our time is the rational application of scientific thought and experience to all vital problems and it is in this spirit, desirous of finding practical solutions, that we have tried to approach each subject' (ibid.: 32).

The *WRPE* today strikes us as remarkable in its spirit of optimism, its faith in unending progress, and its belief in the state as an agent of change.

The *WRPE* shares this utopianism with both the French Enlightenment and the more hard-headed new science of political economy offered by the socialist model, but we also hear in the *WRPE* echoes of cultural revivalism, a harking back to the past. In this revanchism, however, the hope of society still resides in the future, when the essence of the nation's past would be realised. Commenting upon the altered circumstances of the modern period and the need for changes, the *WRPE* clarifies that it in no way belittles past traditions:

> This does not imply condemnation. It merely seeks to make the system more fitted for the task before it by an effort of conscious planning. It is not our desire to belittle in any way these traditions, which have in the past, contributed to the happiness and progress of the individual and have been the means of raising the dignity and beauty of Indian woman hood and conserving the *spiritual attributes of the Indian Nation*. We do not wish to turn woman into a cheap imitation of man or render her useless for the great tasks of motherhood and nation-building (ibid.: 32–33; emphasis in original).

Yet, notwithstanding this conscious deference to the past and to tradition, the *WRPE* is marked by a broad view that 'deleterious social customs' act as 'hindrances to women' (*WRPE* 1947: 255), and that every custom or usage likely to militate against the freedom and equality of women as citizens and workers must be progressively put an end to. Thus, regarding 'the idea of the sanctity of marriage' (ibid.: 153), the *WRPE* observes that such ideas arose in 'times when most of the human institutions flourished with the sanction of religion. The domination of religion—doctrinal religion—has done much harm to the individual in the past and continues to harm him today wherever such domination exists. With the growth of a rational outlook on life such a domination is bound to go' (ibid.). The past must go, but the past must be retrieved; traditions have been a bane for women in the past, but they also 'have been the means of raising the dignity and beauty of Indian womanhood and conserving the spiritual attributes of the Indian Nation' (ibid.: 33).

WOMEN AS EMBLEMS OF NATIONAL CULTURE AND INVENTED TRADITION

The constant weaving of the language of cultural revivalism and the language of rationalism, which we witness above, is common to much of nationalist discourse. The *WRPE* marks a departure from this trend, insofar as the middle-class woman's experience (as perceived by the middle-class man) has not been generalised to encompass the entire gamut of women's experience. Attention to working-class women has necessarily shifted the tenor of the report away from questions of sati and widow marriage, from purdah and cultural identity to the productive sphere, to questions of wages and working hours, to factory legislation and creches. However, as already noted, this retreat from an understanding of women as representatives of culture and tradition, and as the pillars of family and society, to a recognition of women's role in the productive sphere is never absolute. As the report puts it: 'we do not wish to turn woman into a cheap imitation of man or render her useless for the great tasks of motherhood and nation building' (*WRPE* 1947: 33).

The *WRPE* contains a number of allusions to a utopian past:

> Polygamy was first permitted to man by the Hindu Law in case when there was no male issue by the first marriage. In course of time this permission was exploited by man and the Kshatriyas began to marry more than one wife for political reasons and later it became a general privilege for every man who wished to marry again (ibid.: 155).

On the issue of inter-caste marriage, similar views are expressed: 'Hindu marriage lays down certain restrictions about inter-marriage within the castes. *These restrictions were not always there.* In Vedic times inter-caste marriages were not unknown (ibid.: 150; emphasis mine).

The underlying assumption is that these customs are not part of the 'real' Hinduism, that: 'Age long customs have grown around the institution of marriage resulting in greater rigidity or greater relaxation for marriage bonds for different sections of the Hindu society' (ibid.: 154).

On divorce, the *WRPE* observes:

> We find, however in the earlier religious texts authorities like Parashar and even Manu allowing a woman to marry again in certain circumstances. Kautiliya has definitely laid down detailed rules of divorce intended for the couples who found it impossible to live together. They were, however, applicable only to Asura, Gandharva, Kshatra and Paishacha marriages. The institution of marriage underwent a radical change during the years immediately preceding the Christian era when Hindu society came under the grip of ascetic influence. We refer to these instances merely to emphasise the point that *even in very early times* divorce and remarriage were recognized but *this practice was discontinued.* This tightening of the bond of marriage created obstacles in the way of the social advancement of women (ibid.: 163; emphasis mine).

The sentiment expressed here, namely that the sorry state of affairs in colonial India is an aberration, is typical of nineteenth-century reform movements. So is the view that the West may have taught us a great deal, but that this knowledge is not intrinsically alien to our culture; we have always been privy to modern enlightenment, 'even in very early times'.

Since these 'early times' of modern enlightenment tend to refer to the period prior to Muslim rule, we have a simplified but powerful image of two contrasting historical periods—the golden age of ancient India, and the dark age of medieval India (De 1963–64). This version of history was essentially a Hindu[10] reconstruction of the past. While there was also a Muslim rendering of the past,[11] the hegemony of the Hindu view in the national movement and subsequently in the Indian nation has led to a transformation of the Hindu view into the Indian view, the patriotic and natural view.

We have in the *WRPE* a curious juxtaposition of two utopias, belonging to two worldviews and to two language games. The woman as 'productive worker' and equal 'citizen' is never replaced, but the woman as 'culture' and 'tradition' has an unerring tendency to intrude into the text. This point is worthy of attention for ideas of cultural revivalism run counter to the manifest tone of the document. Although the past is never actually eulogised in the *WRPE*, at different stages the point is made that 'due to social degeneration certain common malpractices have crept into almost all communities' (*WRPE* 1947: 100). Nonetheless, the past has to be redeemed and retrieved, for a nation without history is no nation at all.[12]

If the project of nation-building is crucial to the whole exercise of planning, the reconstruction of the past, what Gellner calls 'memory and forgetfulness', is essential to the enterprise of nation-building. In this, we witness the contestation of the various community identities before an apparent collapsing of these identities within the supreme identity of the sovereign nation-state.

Another curious turn takes place vis-a-vis the perception of history, where essentially modern understandings of concepts like 'state' and the 'individual' are inserted into the past. The particular becomes the general to the extent of becoming 'natural', as the very first lines of the chapter entitled 'Civic rights' suggest:

> The individual in India has little or no conception of his duties to the State and the State on the other hand has not discharged its duty to the individual. This lack of harmonious cooperation between the two has led to the lowering of civic ideals and has been harmful alike to the individual, the community and the State (*WRPE* 1947: 36).

In this closed world of modern discourse, 'the individual in India' is abstracted and appears as a constant throughout history, awaiting only a more correct definition of his relationship with the 'state', the other necessary constant. Similarly, both 'India' itself and an image of 'Indian woman hood' become entities located outside history, 'givens', meriting the status of the natural. Indeed, as we move through the text, this collapsing of the social into the natural recurs time and again.

A class view of the national project: In defence of the family and private property

The question of the nation is central in the *WRPE*. The interests of individual women, citizens and workers, classes and castes, voluntary associations and families are subordinate to the nation-state, which both encompasses and overrides them.

The nation-building scheme, of which the NPC and the *WRPE* are integral components, has to be seen as a class project. I argue so not only because of the historical context, the attitude of the Indian capitalist section to the Congress and the NPC (see Section I above), but also because of the manner in which the right of property is written into the *WRPE*, thus foreclosing the fulfilment of the promise of equal rights for all women. For this promise that the *WRPE* initially holds up is eventually granted only to the woman likely to have property, for: '. . . so long as the system of private property remains the foundation of the social structure, woman shall have the same rights as man to hold, acquire, inherit and dispose of property' (*WRPE* 1947: 201).

Nehru, if we remember, had clarified that the Congress had 'not in any way accepted socialism'.[13] If that was so, phrases such as '. . . *so long* as the system of private property remains the foundation . . .', seem a deliberate ploy to give the impression that if the pace of change is slow, the onus rests on the conservativeness of the people, not in the class character of the Congress. Such contradictions within the text are explainable only when placed against the overall social and political context.

An examination of some of the contrary views that emerge in the text may elucidate the point. What we have is a play of categorical statements about doing away with 'private property' and the 'family' on the one hand, and a kind of hedging and setting of actual limits on the other. For instance, the dissent note, which states what the role of the family should be in a planned society—a view which we can assume informed the Sub-Committee at a wider level—is unequivocal on the need for doing away with the responsibilities of the family as they exist in today's society: 'Once these two responsibilities are taken over frankly by the State as a collective concern and not as individual liability, the foundation stone of the twin institutions of *family and property* will have been removed, and the institutions rendered as unnecessary as they are objectionable today' (*WRPE* 1947: 240; emphasis in original).

The *WRPE* draws a well-defined line between the long-term objective and the actually possible; yet, at no point is the impression given that the original goal has been given up. We thus have express intentions of doing away with private property (ibid.), but when discussing proposals for industrial housing, we find: 'We realise that this would mean extra financial strain on the industry and to meet this we recommend that the State and the *employer* would co-operate to meet the cost' (ibid.: 75; emphasis in original).

It appears that, when drawing out the macro model, the SCW has a utopian vision, but when it comes to the micro clauses spelling out actual proposals, it is Nehru's position that the Congress 'approval' of socialism does not imply an 'acceptance', and that the 'present structure' has to be 'accepted' to a 'large extent as jumping off ground' that gains ascendancy. The introductory passages of the section dealing specifically with property are skilfully worded, capturing the apparent ambiguity of the SCW on this question:

> Private property is the root cause of many inequalities. In a planned society the object of which will be to regularise and control the acquisitive impulses of men, efforts will, we hope, be taken to levelise [*sic*] inequality, by placing property in its true perspective, so that it is no longer mistaken for privilege and power, and so that every man, woman and child within the country has an equal opportunity in life. This does not mean the negation of the right to private property. It simply implies the recognition of an identity of response to primary needs and the claim of each citizen on the social dividend (*WRPE* 1947: 118).

It is clearly the intent of the NPC to reassure the captains of industry that the Indian state, once it comes into being, will continue with a system based on private property. Yet, the very next paragraph of the document begins with the now familiar phrase of the SCW, 'so long' as the system 'of private property' continues: 'So long, however, as the very foundation of society is based on a system of private property, women cannot claim equality with man unless she has the same rights as men to hold, acquire, inherit and dispose of property' (ibid.).

As part of the NPC, the SCW is an essential component of the story of the Congress drawing an agenda for the nation as the state-to-be. Significantly, the determination of the SCW on its basic stance on 'property' was much firmer than on issues like 'marriage', 'divorce', and 'religion'.

A DEFENCE OF MARRIAGE, FAMILY, AND 'RELIGION'

Returning to the issue of marriage, the SCW disapproves of the idea of the 'sanctity of marriage', and writes that in 'the new social order that we are planning, it will therefore be the State which will lay down and enforce the law of marriage and for the State, therefore marriage will only be a civil contract' (*WRPE* 1947: 153). But this is followed by:

> This however, does not mean that religion will be a taboo or that the State will not recognize any marriage which is not performed under the civil law of the State. It only means that, for the purposes of protecting the rights and enforcing the obligations of the parties concerned who enter into marriage, the State will not recognize any marriage which is not performed under the civil law of the State (ibid.).

This clarification about the relationship envisaged for the still unborn Indian nation-state and religion suggests that the SCW was responding to reservations that were probably being raised at that time, and an attempt was made to introduce a caveat that all religions are not to be dismissed, but only those which are 'doctrinal': 'The domination of religion—the doctrinal religion—has done much harm to the individual in the past and continues to harm him today wherever such domination still exists. With the growth of a rational outlook on life such a domination is bound to go' (*WRPE* 1947: 153).

The remedy for the 'diversity of laws which exists today is a common civil code including inheritance, marriage and divorce laws, which should be optional to begin with but universally enforced' within a 'reasonable period of its passing into Act' (*WRPE* 1947: 217).

The addition of the word 'optional', even if it is only to begin with, reflects the kind of opposition that such moves were generating. The SCW itself bears witness to the dissenting voices. A Note[14] on this subject states that 'considerable discussion took place on this resolution' (*WRPE* 1947: 229), and that a great deal of disagreement was expressed (ibid.). The other issues on which differences were expressed were on resolutions on divorce,[15] on property rights for women,[16] and on the recognition of the rights of the illegitimate child.[17]

A sharp schism divides what the SCW overtly set out to do—the 'drastic recommendations' (*WRPE* 1947: 32) to bring in the new social order—and what it eventually does. The shift does not appear in the text as a retreat, but only as an adjustment for a transitional period:

> The change from what is old and established to something new and untried always contains an element of danger. This fact is very evident in the realm of women and requires special care on the part of the planning authority so that the new measures adopted are effective and do not become obstacles in the way of advance. We have, therefore, referred in our report to such a period to bridge the gulf between existing conditions and what might seem at first glance to be drastic recommendations for the future (ibid.: 312; emphasis mine).

Changes in the status of women are seen as a threat to the social order. It is but natural therefore that the proposals of the SCW for altering the terms of marriage and property rights, and the role of religion are hedged in by so many caveats.

An interesting comparison can be made between the language used in the carefully worded caution regarding the 'drastic recommendations' and the arresting melee of images that capture the vision of the new woman and man. The spirit of optimism, progress, enlightenment, and equality, images of the brave new order, 'of man and woman, comrades of the road, going forward together, the child joyously shared by both', 'a reality' which cannot 'but raise the manhood and womanhood of any nation', are tangibly present in the *WRPE* (p. 33). The new times are special times, where all 'superstitious beliefs' will be abandoned in the 'new social order' in which the 'searchlight of reason' (ibid.: 153) would be shining.

On the other hand, the language used when deliberating on the constraints on implementing the recommendations is matter-of-fact, pragmatic, and cautious. The actual recommendations are straightforward, but their substance is diluted both by the subsequent elaboration of specific recommendations, and by the repetition of the phrase 'transitional period' (or words to that effect) in reference to the phase 'before the new measures actually come into effect'.

For instance, we have a long explanation about the actual intention of the proposed marriage reforms:

> In advocating divorce, our desire is not to break up the home but to make marriage more happy, and, therefore, more stable. If we turn to the evidence of writers like Pammine Halle, Beatrice and Sidney Webb and others, we find that even in Russia where the experiment of divorce under easy conditions was tried, it has resulted actually in strengthening the bond of marriage. It does not follow therefore, that by conceding the right of divorce to women the State will be undermining the foundations of marriage, and, therefore, of society. It will rather, we think, help to make the foundation more secure (*WRPE* 1947: 164).

This is a far cry from the view that, with the state taking over certain responsibilities, the twin institutions of the 'family' and 'private property' would be rendered 'as unnecessary as they are objectionable today' (ibid.: 240); or that 'private property is the root cause of many inequalities' (ibid.: 118); or that 'in planned society the basic unit would be the individual'.

It is relevant to mention the dissent note of Miss K. Khandwala to support our point on the eventual centrality which the *WRPE* accords to the institution of the 'family' and 'private property' for, as she herself states, the only reason that prompted her to write the note is 'that the Authors of the Report have departed materially from the general basis agreed upon in the Sub-Committee meetings when that body decided on the fundamental issues or principles which were to guide us in preparing our Report' (*WRPE* 1947: 232).

CONCLUSION

The *WRPE* is self-evidently about the role that women would play in a planned economy. Contestation within the *WRPE*, however, arises not only on the question of 'the role of women', but also regarding the very concept of a 'planned economy'. The major turnabout within the *WRPE* on the issue of private property (see the previous section) discloses that, notwithstanding the stated emphasis on 'planned economy', the nation-state is set to pursue a market economy. Likewise, the substantive emphasis is on working-class women, as 'instruments of labour' (ibid.: 199), but the ideological stress is on the rights of the bourgeois woman 'to hold, acquire, inherit and dispose of property' (ibid.: 201), apart, that is, from the general thrust on the unfettered development of the individual. This is a fundamental contradiction so far as the socialist perspective is concerned, for political economy understands '*private property*' as 'the product, the result, the necessary consequence of *alienated labour*' (Marx and Engels 1984b: 89; emphasis in original).

The retreat of the socialist perspective and the hegemonic establishment of the national liberal model has to be understood at both a theoretical level and in the immediate context of the political struggle within the NPC between the 'socialists and near communists' and the 'hard-headed big businessmen' (Nehru 1966: 419) over the path of development which the Indian nation-state was to adopt.

This class project is incorporated within the national project and the state is deemed instrumental in its realisation. The state supposedly represents the will of the entire nation. Glossing over both historical specificities as well as class and community inequalities, the state comes to be thought of as the nation itself, 'absorbing the entire society' (Gramsci 1971: 260) . In this state-centric vision of the *WRPE*, it can be argued that women were subsumed within the more privileged categories of the citizen and of class. I would stop short of such an assertion, for to my mind the *WRPE* does break out of the gender-blindness that characterises liberal theory. It questions the persistent tendency of much of modern theory to dehistoricise the private sphere, celebrating male entry into the public sphere and condemning women to remain in the 'timeless universe' of domesticity and doomed to 'repeat the cycles of life' (Benhabib 1987: 86). By acknowledging the 'home work' done within the house (*WRPE* 1947: 200) as well as by arguing for the recognition of women's labour as a 'separate unit of production' and not as 'a corporate part of the family work' (ibid.: 199), the entire set of public-private dualisms—the dualisms of universal/particular, political/apolitical, economic/familial, instrumental/expressive, formal/informal—are challenged. To this extent, the socialist perspective informs the liberal discourse.

While the liberal and socialist perspectives inform the *WRPE* theoretically, they do not contain all other ideological tendencies. The colonial subject's ambivalent relationship to the West is not easily dismissed. This is apparent in the rhetoric on women 'conserving the spiritual attributes of the Indian Nation' (ibid.: 32–33) and the fears that 'cheap imitation' may 'render her useless for the great tasks of motherhood and nation-building' (ibid.: 33).

It is in this strand of the *WRPE* that the most explicit patriarchal resistances surface. The *WRPE* clearly retreats from its initial views on the issues of marriage reforms, of divorce (*WRPE* 1947: 164), of the adoption and maintenance of children (ibid.: 230), and of the role of religion in the making of laws (ibid.: 227–31). Not surprisingly, these issues all pertain to the private, domestic sphere. In the section on the analysis of labour, the *WRPE* breaks the public/private dichotomy. In the discourse on family reform, this dichotomy is reaffirmed.

I have two possible explanations for this. The first is that the identity of 'Indian womanhood', resting on the attributes of motherhood and other qualities connected with domesticity, is class-based. The working-class woman is seen entirely in terms of production (as in the seventy-two pages on 'Economic rights'). Not so the middle-class woman. While the need for her economic independence is recognised (*WRPE* 1947: 105), her responsibility to 'create a cultural environment in the home for the proper nurture of the children' and not 'merely to cook, wash and attend to the needs and comforts of the family' (ibid.: 104) is emphasised to improve the low standards of life in the country (ibid.). These differential role expectations draw attention to the ways by which class itself is gendered.

The second explanation for the selective gendered analysis of the public/private split can be traced to certain limits to the production paradigm, even if production is taken to be both 'production of things' and 'production of life'. Recent feminist philosophy has asked whether 'the concept of production, which is based on the model of an active subject transforming, making and shaping an object given to it' can adequately comprehend traditionally female activities such as child-rearing and care-giving, 'which are so thoroughly intersubjective' (Benhabib 1987: 2). The *WRPE* attaches great 'national' significance to these activities (*WRPE* 1947: 104) but thereby also reifies them, alienating them from the subject.

This raises the question whether the woman as subject has any presence in the *WRPE*. The word 'subject' has a dual meaning—as the signifier of the individual who has subjectivity, and as the signifier of one who is under the authority of another. Poststructuralist theories have stressed the coincidence of these meanings. I would, contrarily, emphasise the subject as the site of agency—potentially resistive, but also implicated in domination. Both facets are visible in the *WRPE*. Significantly, all twenty-seven members of the SCW, including Chairperson Rani Lakshmi Rajwade, were women. The disparate views, the patriarchal resistances, the 'drastic recommendations', the eugenic view, the contestation and the eventual hegemony of the liberal model in the analysis have to be attributed to them. Since I do not see the theorisation of hegemony as contradictory to the theorisation of resistance (they are in fact part of the same project), I would not hesitate both to acknowledge the hegemonic project of the *WRPE* and yet to argue that the other resistive strands within the *WRPE* open up a new space for the woman's question, even if the possibilities thus opened up are foreclosed in the text.

NOTES

1. Gandhi to Amrit Kaur, 29 June 1939, quoted in Gopal (1975: 247). Gandhi had also written to Nehru: 'I have never been able to understand or appreciate the labours of the Committee . . . . I have not understood the purpose of the numerous sub-committees. It has appeared to me that much money and labour are being wasted on an effort which will bring forth little or no fruits' (Gandhi to Nehru, 11 August 1939 in Nehru 1958: 378–79).

2. Birla contributed Rs 5 lakh for the Congress Central Parliamentary Board headed by Patel, while R. K. Dalmia provided Rs 27,000 out of Rs 37,000 raised by the Bihar Pradesh Congress Committee (PCC). Since such amounts were evidently inadequate (election costs came to at least Rs 2,000 per seat), most candidates were expected to provide their own finances—which meant in practice a clear preference for propertied men. In Bihar, for instance, numerous Kisan Sabha militants were deprived of nomination under local landlord pressure, and the Congress leader A. N. Sinha admitted that most of his party candidates came from the zamindari class (Sarkar 1983: 350–51).

3. All quotes are in the original language used in the *WRPE*, despite the occasional awkwardness of expression.

4. A possible explanation for this neglect could be the *WRPE* view that: 'Already more than 60 per cent of our population depend on agriculture . . . a percentage which the land can hardly support', and that therefore 'fresh avenues of employment to women' should be opened up (*WRPE* 1947: 94).

5. For a discussion on the limits set by colonialism on the articulation of the women's question in India, see Chaudhuri (1993).

6. Significantly, however, *Samya shakti*, the journal of the Centre for Women's Development Studies (CWDS), carried a summary of the *WRPE* in the early 1990s (see Kasturi 1991–92).

7. In a letter to his daughter Indira, Nehru had written: 'The argument about the success or failure of the Five Year Plans is rather pointless. The answer to it is really the present state of the Soviet Union. And a further answer is the fact that this plan has impressed itself on the imagination of the world. Everybody talks of ... Planning ... now . . . the Soviets have put magic into the word' (Nehru to Indira, 917/1937, in Nehru 1962: 887).

8. The dithering and stalling on the Hindu Code Bill and the subsequent resistance by the Congress members are good indicators of this conservatism (see Chaudhuri 1993).

9. For an analysis of the theoretical traditions responsible for the significance attached to the entry of middle-class women in the workforce, see Chaudhuri (1982).

10. By 'Hindu', we are of course confining ourselves to the upper-caste, middle-class Hindu rendering of the past.

11. For a discussion of the manner in which the two communities reconstructed their 'past' in an attempt to legitimise the effort to improve the status of women in their respective communities, see Chaudhuri (1993).

12. Decrying the lamentable state of the Bengali nation, Bankim Chandra had commented that it could not be otherwise since this nation does not even have a history of itself. The two projects were linked. This significance of 'imagining history' is discussed in Kaviraj (1988: esp. 7–8).

13. Nehru contended in his speech of 21 December 1938 that the Congress had in no way accepted socialism (Krishna 1945: 49).

14. 'Mr. Shuaib Qureshi expressed his disagreement with it. Mr. G.M. Sayed was of opinion [*sic*] that the Civil Code would be made compulsorily applicable to all, and that there should be no option about it. Some other members were in sympathy with this view, but they felt that, under the existing system, it was preferable to make the applicability of the Code optional. The representatives of the Sub-Committee stated that their members, including Begum Hamid Ali and Begum Shah Nawaz, were in favour of an optional Civil Code. Mrs. Zarina Currimboy and Mrs. Ismail also expressed their agreement with this view' (*WRPE* 1947: 229).

15. The resolution stated that 'divorce shall be available at the option of either party, subject to such conditions as may be laid down by the law in that behalf'. One of the notes attached states that: 'In this connection the question of *mehr* in Muslim Law must be considered, without prejudice to the principle laid down.' In another note, Messrs. Shuaib Qureshi, Syed Mahmud, and Nazir Ahmed add: 'This shall not affect the Muslim personal law, according to which

the two parties to a marriage contract could, as the law stands even now, have, as part of the contract, equal rights to divorce. As to the right of maintenance of children, that too is fully safeguarded under the Islamic Law' (*WRPE* 1947: 230).

16. The 'State should follow a policy to assure women the same rights as men.' And again we have a note by the same gentleman that this should be without prejudice to Muslim personal law (*WRPE* 1947: 231).

17. The resolution reads: 'There should be no restrictions made either by law or custom between children born in or out of wedlock.' Mr A. D. Shroff did not agree. Mr Shuaib Qureshi recorded his dissent as follows:

> Such claim should be confined to
> (i) the parent of the child;
> (ii) in case of a child born out of lawful wedlock, to maintenance, parental care, and education, but would not affect the law of inheritance.

CHAPTER 3

Gender in the Making of the Indian Nation-State

Introduction

I attempt here a very broad mapping of the manner in which women have been addressed in both the making of the Indian nation and in the running of the Indian state. As I understand it, there are three major ways in which the national movement first and the Indian state later imagined the role of women. These are: (*a*) women as agents and recipients of development; (*b*) women's political participation in the nation as equal citizens of a state that does not discriminate on grounds of gender; (*c*) women as emblems of 'national culture'. These three facets of women's location within 'nationalism' and 'nation-building' reflect three aspects of the 'national movement' which were 'germane to the making of the Indian nation'. *One*, it was based on 'a well-developed critique of colonialism in its economic aspects and on an economic programme leading to independent economic development' (Chandra 1999: 17). Economic self-reliance, sovereignty, and growth with equity were part of the very identity of Indian nationalism. *Two*, the movement was committed to political democracy and civil liberties, which were seen as the building blocks of nation-making (ibid.). The political participation of women, both in the national movement and then in the running of the independent state, was therefore important. *Three*, Indian nationalism was also a cultural critique of colonialism and an assertion of 'national culture'. In this assertion, the image of 'Indian womanhood' was significant.

This chapter rests on the idea that history plays a defining role both in the ways that we imagine the nation and its past, and in the ways we practise our everyday contemporary lives. I therefore return to the past many times in the course of this chapter, including the section on conceptual clarifications. The past is, however, very generally invoked, both within academic and popular writings, when narrating the story of the status of Indian women. Indeed, the need for a historical past is an inextricable part of modern nationalist consciousness. The nation, itself a modernist enterprise, nonetheless has to summon a legacy stretching to an ancient, time-immemorial past. The story of the Indian woman can therefore only begin with a customary reference to her high status in the Vedic period. The contentiousness of such a project has been increasingly questioned (Chakravarti 1989), and I for my part am happier to locate myself in the colonial past as the starting point of India's journey to modernity, to state, nation, and the woman citizen.

My reasons for doing so are not very complex. India entered modernity and capitalism through colonialism. Nationalism and the modern states, which are posited as nation-states, are essentially modern. Likewise, the women's question has to be understood as part of the modern democratic project. But liberal democracy's relationship with the question of the rights of women was never simple. Thus, while equal rights necessarily meant the rights of all, men and women, it was not unusual to define citizenship as exclusive of both women and the dispossessed. On the other hand, modernity, with its corollary processes of capitalism and the refashioning of households and families, meant that women were recast as creatures of domesticity, and to be a housewife came to represent once more both a full-time and a natural vocation. It was also part of the nineteenth-century package of ideas that claimed that the status of a nation ought to be gauged by the status of women. Indians were thus berated for their inability to attain heights as a nation because of the pitiable condition of their womenkind. Indian social reformers responded to this challenge and we had a major recasting of women in modern India. In this recasting, we had a construction of middle-class domesticity, much along the lines of Victorian England, which defined the normative Indian woman as gentle, refined, and skilled in running a 'home'. We also had a simultaneous assertion of the virtues of an ancient Hindu past and culture.

With the intensification of the national movement, however, new ideas of socialism, of equality, and development also gained ground. The actual entry of women in political action altered the parameters of imagining women's role in the nation. And at the same time, the issue of cultural pride for a colonised society continued to be of great importance. It is only correct, therefore, to locate the making of both the nation and the women's question in this complex crucible of the colonial encounter. For therein lay the seed of much of the discord that marked contending ideas of women as democratic citizens and women as markers of culture, or women as dependent housewives and women as independent workers.

STATE, NATION, AND WOMEN

Perhaps a few conceptual remarks about the modern *state*, about nationalism and women may not be out of order here. I attempt below to etch (with a very broad brush): (*i*) the ambiguous relationship between the liberal state and women; (*ii*) the specificity of women's role in the nation; and (*iii*) the historical legacy of colonialism.

WOMEN AND THE LIBERAL STATE

The state is not a unified entity. It is a multidimensional phenomenon, the nature of which varies across time and space. Here, our concern is with the *modern liberal state*, with its legally circumscribed structure of power with supreme jurisdiction over a territory. Such a view may find echoes in ancient texts, but clearly could not prevail while political rights, obligations, and duties were closely tied to property rights and religious tradition. Similarly, the idea that human beings, as 'individuals' or as 'a people', could be active citizens of this order—citizens of their state—and not merely dutiful subjects of a monarch or emperor could only develop in modern conditions.

I proceed with Held's definition of liberalism as an effort to delineate 'a private sphere independent of the state and thus to redefine the state itself, i.e., the freeing of civil society—personal, family and business life—from political interference and the simultaneous delimitation of the state's authority' (Held 1984: 3). Liberalism was about a world of 'free and equal' individuals with natural rights. Politics came to be understood as the defence of the rights of these individuals. And the mechanisms for regulating these individuals' pursuit of their interests were to be the constitutional state, private property, the competitive market economy—and for us here, the most important—the distinctively patriarchal family.

While liberalism celebrated the rights of individuals to 'life, liberty and property', it was the male property-owning individual who was the focus of attention. The liberal state by definition had an uneasy relationship with women 'individuals'. While the West granted universal franchise only after bitter battles, in India, where a more critical understanding of liberalism was part of a nationalist discourse, the tension persisted. I have shown elsewhere that eventually even in the 1938 Plan Document where 'near communists' were members, the rights 'to hold, acquire, inherit and dispose of property' won over the view voicing the rights of working-class women as 'instruments of labour' (Chaudhuri 1996: 227–29). More significantly, however, the rights of bourgeois women as independent individuals were themselves challenged on the basis of customary practices. We witness this in the incredible opposition to the Hindu Code Bill after independence, where it was opposed tooth and nail on the grounds that the very fabric of Hindu society would collapse (Chaudhuri 1993: 182–92). We also witness this in the debates over the first Plan Document, expressed in the view that the 'State should follow a policy to assure women the same rights as men' but without 'prejudice to Muslim personal law' (Chaudhuri 1996). And we see this in the conflicts between the Church and women's rights (Roy 1991).

The problem is not just attitudinal but one bolstered both by structures[1] and theoretical legacy. Theoretically, within liberalism women were not easily accepted as citizens. Rousseau excluded all women from 'the people', that is, the citizenry, as well as the poor. For citizenship is made conditional upon a small property qualification and/or upon the absence of dependency on others (Held 1984: 23). Wollstonecraft (1975) thus wrote:

> But to render her really virtuous and useful, (women) must not, if she discharge her civil duties, want individually the protection of civil laws; she must not depend upon her husband's bounty for her subsistence during his life, or support after his death; for how can a being be generous who has nothing of its own/or virtuous who is not free ...? (https://www.marxists.org/reference/archive/wollstonecraft-mary/1792/vindication-rights-woman/ch09.htm)

Structurally, the family and the community mediate between the 'individual woman' and the state. An inevitable gap therefore exists between the liberal state's commitment to gender equality on the one hand, and to a patriarchal family, male property rights, and free market on the other.

NATION, NATIONALISM, AND WOMEN

Scholars have repeatedly warned us of the dangers of conflating state and nation (Oommen 1997: 13). Modern states, however, continue to posit themselves as 'nation-states', irrespective of the fact that there could be more than one 'nation' encompassed in them, or that there would be members of the same 'nation' under the rubric of another state. The desire for cultural recognition and identity—hallmarks of modern nationalism—has a tendency to get mixed up with the right to have a state to practise one's cultural distinctiveness and also be equal in a world of 'nation-states'. This conflation of terms is precisely the manner in which that curious entity, the 'nation-state', operates. Anderson (1983) had emphasised the misplaced nature of studying nationalism in political theory when we ought to really address it as a package with family, kinship, and marriage. But herein lies the tension between the coupling of the modern, bureaucratic, rationalised state and the passion of a nationalism that can both kill and get killed in the glory of the nation.[2] One can rightly speak, as Anderson does, of 'political love', a love that retains the fraternal dimensions of medieval caritas but also incorporates a maternalised loyalty symbolised domestically; *the nation is home and home is mother* (ibid.; emphasis mine).

Hence, it is not surprising that Rousseau, who, as we saw a little earlier, had no place for women as citizens, eulogised the Spartan mothers. Rousseau repeated Plutarch's 'Sayings of Spartan Mothers', reproducing tales, anecdotes, and epigrams of the Spartan woman as a mother who reared her sons to be sacrificed at the altar of civic necessity (Elshtain 1991: 546–47). The Spartans, models for later civic republicans and early modern state builders, honoured but two identities with inscriptions on tombstones—men who had died in war and women who had succumbed in childbirth, both embodying the sacrificial moment of civic identity (ibid.: 549–50).

This theme of *women and sacrifice for* the nation is woven into the body of Indian nationalist thought. For the militant nationalists, India herself became the mother, at whose altar men and women were sacrificed. More often, they were called upon to play a very special role as mothers and daughters of the nation. Gandhi's views resonate with this idea. Gandhi stated that 'woman ... (is) ... mother to the Nation ...' (1917).

> The economic and the moral salvation of India thus rests mainly with you. The future of India lies on your knees, for *you will nurture the future generation* .... The destiny of India is far safer in your hands of a government [*sic*] that has so exploited India's resources that she has lost faith in herself (Gandhi 1921; emphasis mine).

Drawing from different historical experiences, Yuval-Davis and Anthias (1989) sum up the ways in which women have tended to participate in ethnic and national processes and in relation to state practices. These are: (*a*) as biological reproducers of members of ethnic collectivities; (*b*) as reproducers of the boundaries of ethnic/national groups; (*c*) as participating centrally in the ideological reproduction of the collectivity and as transmitters of its culture; (*d*) as signifiers of ethnic/national differences—as a focus and symbol in ideological discourses used in the construction, reproduction, and transformation of ethnic/national categories; and (*e*) as participants in national, economic, political, and military struggles.

In practice, these would tend to blur into each other. The above propositions do hold true for India. But I would like to contend that the specificity of an anti-imperialist nationalism also brought questions of political participation and development centre-stage to the women's question. At the same time, I would argue that the inherent contradictions of a liberal state—wedded to equality on the one hand and patriarchal private property on the other, to individual rights of women on the one hand and to the rights of 'cultural and 'religious' practices on the other—inevitably led to a bind that this chapter looks into. To repeat, I seek to analyse these within the three axes on which I see the women's question defined in the Indian context: (*i*) women as agents and recipients of development; (*ii*) women as politically equal citizens; and (*iii*) women as cultural emblems of the nation.

LEGACIES OF THE COLONIAL ENCOUNTER

Generations have studied the nineteenth-century reform movement as simple, straightforward measures to do away with sundry social evils like sati and child marriage. Since the mid-1970s, we have witnessed a plethora of literature in this field, belying any such notion and foregrounding both the complexity and ambiguity of these processes. Central to this problematising of social reform was the exploration of the far-reaching implications of the fact that the early initiatives on the women's question had been taken largely by men; that the reformers belonged mostly to the upper castes; and that the specific problems addressed and the mode of addressing were very often restricted by region and caste location. A more dramatic instance of how these researches have made us rethink issues is the case of the Widow Remarriage Act, which legally allowed upper-caste widows to remarry, but simultaneously through codification of laws obliterated the rights that lower-caste widows had traditionally availed of under their customary laws (Chaudhuri 1993: 31–38). This move towards an increased homogenisation and *construction of a monolithic image and practice of Indian womanhood* persists to this day.

The other process initiated was the reinterpretation of 'Indian culture' and the special role within it for 'Indian women'. In this cultural regeneration are embedded complex ideas of what constitutes culture. Cultural practices often chosen as emblematic of community identity pertain to women's mobility and control of sexuality, for example, child marriage, purdah, sati, and the social death of widows. But if *women are icons of Indian culture,* the contentious question in a plural society like India is which of its women and which of its cultures ought to become the 'national' icon. And one of the most vexing issues of modern India has been fought over the *rights of community identity versus the rights of women and the rights of the state.*

While the concerns of the nineteenth-century reform movement left their mark on the women's question, it is important to emphasise that with the intensification of the national movement and the spread of *internationalist ideas of socialism and democracy,* the women's question could not be contained within the restrictive parameters of one or the other reformer. Women within women's organisations like the All-India Women's Conference and women within the national movement insisted on greater political and economic participation. The legacy of women revolutionaries, trade union activists, and underground nationalists is as much a part of the historical legacy that the independent Indian state inherited. Unfortunately, however, the persistent tendency of much of modern theory to dehistoricise the private sphere, celebrating male entry into the public sphere and condemning women to remain in the 'timeless universe' of domesticity and 'doomed to repeat the cycles of life' (Benhabib 1987) seems to have had the final say after India's independence.

WOMEN AS AGENTS AND RECIPIENTS OF DEVELOPMENT

Economic critiques of colonialism were a key component of Indian nationalism. With independence, the state's commitment to the nation was expressed in the pledge to development. Much before India actually attained independence, serious thought was given to the question of development. The Indian National Congress constituted the National Planning Committee (NPC) in 1938 to chalk out blueprints for independent India's development. One of the twenty-nine sub-committees formed was on 'Women's Role in Planned Economy' (*WRPE*, as discussed in Chapter 2). The formation of the NPC clearly expressed the intention of the Congress to adopt planning as the most effective means for the comprehensive economic development of the new nation.

What has baffled scholars is the complete turnabout in the manner in which women were understood in the development paradigm once India attained independence, and once planning really began. Indeed, women virtually disappeared from the idiom of development, even work, and entered wholly the world of welfare. The Central Social Welfare Board was established by the government in 1953 with a nation-wide programme of grants-in-aid for promoting welfare and development services for women and children. The Planning Commission's Plans and Prospects for Social Welfare in India, 1951–61, spells out social welfare services as intending to cater to the special needs of persons and groups who, by reason of some handicap—social, economic, physical, or mental—are unable to avail of, or are traditionally denied, the amenities and services provided by the community. Thus, women were considered handicapped by social customs and values, and social welfare services were thought of to rehabilitate them. This is a far cry from the systematic analysis of marriage and family, rights to property and rights at work which marked India's first plan document, the *WRPE*.

The break with the past seems absolute. A new, fresh beginning has taken place with distinct ideological moorings. The analysis shifted from addressing questions of systemic powerlessness to behavioural issues to be addressed by training. The origin of the women's programme has to be now studied within the context of the overall rural development programme, known as the Community Development Programme (CDP). The CDP was formulated soon after independence, in 1952, with American aid. The objectives of the CDP were essentially two-fold: material and psychological betterment of villages. Material improvement was to be brought about through government aid (financial and technical) for agricultural development. The government also planned to provide the villagers with welfare services, such as educational, recreational, and health facilities, wherever possible. The psychological aspect concerned the creation of community consciousness among villagers so that they became aware of their own needs and responsibilities. However, this programme, with its main focus on agriculture, had nothing to offer those who were not large agriculturists.

Women were integrated into this programme almost as an afterthought, when it was realised that the lack of participation of women was responsible to a considerable extent for the programme not having the desired impact. Later, when they introduced the women component in the rural development programme, it was designed after the Home Science Extension programme. In this programme, women were taught some practical skills aimed at making them better housewives and using their time more fruitfully. Mahila Mandals in the rural areas were visualised as the catalysts for such development. Accordingly, in the belief that better home-making skills would improve standards of living, the government devised the Mahila Mandal scheme in 1954 to integrate women into the CDP. Needless to say, this programme did not merit any success because of its sheer irrelevance to the needs of the rural masses.

After the CDPs receded into the background, the focus of policy regarding women throughout the period of the Second to the Fifth Plans (1955–86) was welfare (Government of India 1995: 24–30). Health and family planning concerns about women found explicit expression. In the Third Plan period, we had the Applied Nutrition Programme (ANP), with the objective of imparting nutrition education to mothers through demonstration feeding, production programme, and the training of women functionaries. Similar measures persisted until the Sixth Five-Year Plan (1980–85) was being drafted, when a group of national women's organisations asserted that the strategies recommended by these working groups needed incorporation in the Five-Year Plan. The Planning Commission responded by including for the first time a chapter on Women and Development in the plan document. Simultaneously, the commission initiated a discussion on science and technology in development and the Ministry of Social Welfare appointed a Working Group for this purpose. Reviewing the outcome of these policy debates in its Report to the United Nations in 1985, the Government of India noted that the major result was:

> A shift in recognition—from viewing women as targets of welfare policies in the social sector to their emergence as critical groups for development

> .... This shift represents reassertion of the principle of women's equality of rights—to participate effectively in the process of development, ensuring thereby movement in the direction of the Constitutional goals. It is also a reassertion of an ideology enunciated by the Father of the nation that the future of India cannot be built without the willing and conscious participation of one half of its population—women ... (GOI 1985: 6).

What is of significance here is that the tone is not of a new beginning, but a return to the constitutional goals and commitments of the 'Father of the Nation'. But even here, the first plan document goes unmentioned. In 1995 the government brought out yet another document, 'Towards Empowering Women', in response to the felt need of many 'in the context of the Fourth World Conference on Women at Beijing'. The document has little except a listing of women-specific and women-related initiatives towards 'empowering women'. It has little to say on poverty and exploitation, but has pages of tables indicating projects sanctioned and the number of women benefited.

At one level, the concept of empowerment could be read as being in continuity with earlier discourses of economic rights and political participation. On closer scrutiny we find that this is the buzz word of international aid agencies who have, over the past decade, appropriated 'the past years of research, activism and government action in India' (John 1996: 3074). As John has sought to show,

> [A]s the 'agency discourses' have been saying for some time now, the informal sector is at the heart of the market economy and represents its prime mode. In their view, although 'restrictive' third world state regulations are responsible for the growth of the informal sector in the first place, it is nonetheless here that high productivity is possible with low capital costs (ibid.).

This was of defining importance at a time when the Indian state was in the process of liberalising the economy, initiating and implementing structural adjustments and speaking of empowering the poor. What is also to be noted is that production is no longer definitive for national identity. I have argued elsewhere that consumption perhaps is (Chaudhuri 1999).

It is not as though the Indian state is oblivious to the implications of liberalisation. The Country Report 1995 has an entire section on macro-economic policies and their impact on women (GOI 1995: 54–57).

While fearing that the new economic policies may lead to an increase in employment with 'women bearing a disproportionate share of the brunt', it ends with the remark that the 'feminisation of "work" that may be a consequence of the policies may, therefore, throw up both challenges and opportunities' (ibid.: 54–55). The aid agency discourses and increasingly the state discourse, however, shift away from macro-economic policies to micro-interventions for the 'empowering' of women.

There are two points that I wish to underscore. *One*, the gap between the state's intent to address women as workers and contributors to national production and the unfailing lapse into a more powerful discourse of women as passive recipients of welfare and of women as dependent members in male-headed households. *Two* is the fact that with liberalisation and the exit of the socialist bloc, we have entered a new world where aid donors like the World Bank, committed to the entry of global capital, also appropriate the findings of the women's movement and women's studies to argue that poor women are 'more efficient economic actors' with 'greater managerial and entrepreneurial skills than men'. Therefore, what they need is credit and social services, not 'the conditions of employment that obtain in the formal sector, which would stifle productivity' (John 1996: 3074). Although recent government reports seek to connect the new discourse of empowerment—political or economic—to the legacy of nationalism, it is important to demonstrate that the two are not linked.

WOMEN AS POLITICALLY EQUAL CITIZENS

That nationalist leaders desired women's political participation[3] and that women participated in the national movement are accepted facts.[4] Less accepted is any consensus on what exactly political participation meant for the women and for nationalist leaders. One view would argue that 'even the most cursory examination of women's organized activism from the beginning of the twentieth century explodes the myth still being pursued by many, that women's role in the national movement(s) against imperialism was male-dictated and male-manipulated' (Kasturi and Mazumdar 1994: 16). The other, as Mies points out, is:

> To draw women into the political struggle is a tactical necessity of any anti-colonial or national liberation struggle. But it depends on the strategic

> goals of such a movement whether the patriarchal family is protected as the basic social unit or not. The fact that the women themselves accepted their limited tactical function within the independence movement made them excellent instruments in the struggle. But they did not work out a strategy for their own liberation struggle for their own interests. By subordinating these goals to the national cause they conformed to the traditional *pativrata* or *sati* ideal of the self-sacrificing woman (1980: 121).

Other scholars like Gail Minault and Geraldine Forbes (1999) argue that the concept of the extended family in Indian culture[5] could extend virtually indefinitely and be used to justify women's concerns beyond the kin group. The metaphor of the extended family certainly assisted middle-class women's performance of some public roles through their associations (Minault 1982).

While at one time an uncritical lauding of women's political participation in the national movement was common, more recent views have veered around to the belief that women's political participation 'gave the illusion of change while women were kept within the structural confines of family and society' (Jayawardena 1986: 107). Partha Chatterjee has further blurred the boundaries between the nineteenth-century Bengal reform movement and the political activism of women at an all-India level in the twentieth century to pronounce what he calls the nationalist resolution of the women's question (Chatterjee 1989). The argument is that by separating the colonial, material, public world from the indigenous, spiritual, private world, the nationalists defined what the parameters of women's change ought to be.

I would contend that active political participation often challenges the boundaries of intended models. And I would not see the question of political participation of women only from the confines of a set of reform ideas. Indian women also had a history of militant participation in political struggles—in working-class strikes, in peasant rebellions, in anti-imperialist and democratic movements—for a long time. It was not simply ideas (important as they were) which led to the Congress adopting the Fundamental Rights Resolution in 1931.[6]

As in the case of development, women's political rights were not seriously addressed in independent India's state discourse, where women were primarily understood as recipients of welfare as wives, mothers, and daughters. The state documents themselves accept that 'while women have often been in the forefront in mass movements, their presence has not been felt strongly in structured decision-making and institution' (GOI 1995: 67). The reason, they argue, is that 'working in a predominantly patriarchal structure with no gender sensitivity has made it difficult to bring about real and sustained changes for women' (ibid.). No further explanation is given about what gender sensitisation may mean, but we are left with the feeling that state policy debates have left the kind of interrogation of structures evident in the first plan document in favour of a discourse on attitudinal changes.

Not surprisingly, the failure of the state led to a resurgence of the women's movement in the 1970s, along with wide-ranging left and democratic movements. The state was confronted with the questions that the women's movements were raising, among which were: land rights; the gender-blind nature of development; political representation; laws pertaining to divorce, custody, guardianship, or sexual harassment at work; about alcohol, dowry, and rape. The women's movement in turn interrogated their own relationship to the state. While on the one hand women, particularly poor women, faced the violent edge of the state, it is the state from which the women's movement sought ameliorative intervention.

It is important to recall that a decade after the upsurge of democratic and radical movements, the state opted for economic liberalisation in the late 1980s, with the concomitant presence and pressures of international aid agencies in the country. Today, we are in a time when two parallel processes are underway. On the one hand international financial organisations, the Indian state, and Western states herald India's entry into the global market and encourage the withdrawal of the state from 'welfare' activities. On the other hand, the same set of actors promote economic and political empowerment of grassroots women. Economically, this implies, as we saw in the previous section, a valorisation of poor women's efficiency and a championing of the informal sector as the heart of the market economy. Politically, I would go along with the view that transnational capital supports the idea of 'low intensity democracy' or 'polyarchy' with the aim of legitimising internal orders that favour foreign investment and provide stable social and political conditions for its operation (Chimni 1999: 342).

The Indian government projected the new economic policies as representing a consensus above 'politics'. Along with the stress on production, a commitment to what is called 'empowerment' of the people is reiterated. We can look at the 73rd and 74th constitution amendment acts of 1993 reserving one-third of the total seats for women in all elected offices of local bodies in rural and urban areas in this light. The 1995 Country Report thus states, 'Women have thus been brought to the centre-stage in the nation's efforts to strengthen democratic institutions' (GOI 1995). State documents suggest that at last we are returning to the constitutional pledges of political rights, irrespective of caste, creed, and gender. I am sceptical of the intent and would go along with Mohanty's argument that 'empowerment, civil society and democratization form the new package of liberalization discourse which on their face value respond to the long-standing demands of struggling groups' (Mohanty 1995: 1435). At the same time, it would be spurious to dismiss the significance of these measures. That these are not empty gestures is evident in the fact that the promise to legislate 33 per cent reservation for women in Parliament has been repeatedly scuttled.

Recent years have seen abortive efforts to introduce what has come to be known as the Reservation Bill for women. That women are not adequately represented in the Parliament is widely accepted. In the twelfth Lok Sabha, out of 547 members, only thirty-two were women. It has been observed that as long as the promise of 33 per cent reservation 'remained in the realm of pious hope and pontification', there was 'uniform goodwill towards women and their cause' (Natarajan 1996). In parliamentary circles, the main opposition to the bill came from those who demanded sub-reservation for OBC women within the 33 per cent quota. Critics[7] have wondered what 'these champions of the OBC had been doing these 50 years long ...?' (ibid.). The other views opposing it were *one*, that 'women were not yet ready for political office' and have to be 'sensitised and educated', and *two*, that 'reservation for women will lead to the perpetuation of dynastic politics'. In a political clime where a large number of male members in both the Parliament and legislatures are 'charged in cases ranging from murder and dacoity to rape and economic offences' (ibid.) and where nepotism is widespread, both criticisms sound hollow. That the bill was unsuccessfully sought to be introduced after 1996 only shows a very concerted attempt to oppose it.

There is a strong tendency to project a view that in the past, political space for women in India was granted to women without resistance. Debates on women's suffrage in colonial Bengal, which I draw upon as only one illustrative evidence, suggest otherwise. Opposition to a woman's right to vote was made on various grounds. *One*, that since 'she is quite unfit for defence and administration of a country, franchise cannot be her birthright'

(Southard 1995: 100). *Two*, that it would lead to 'discontent with domestic duties and neglect of husband and children, "even during illness", that "politics and other brainworks"' [*sic*] would make women 'unable to breastfeed her children' (ibid.: 101). It was the active intervention and struggle of women's organisations that got women their right to vote. Today, too, political participation of women is a contested terrain, between a hesitant state, double-faced political parties, international aid agencies, and growing womens' movements.

WOMEN AS CULTURAL EMBLEMS

This chapter is premised on the assumption that notwithstanding the liberal 'nation-state's' pledge for women's political and economic participation in the nation, women continue to be seen primarily as biological reproducers of members of nations and as cultural reproducers of national/ethnic boundaries. If '*the nation is home and home is mother*', women cannot but be signifiers of ethnic/national differences. They participate centrally in the ideological reproduction of the collectivity and as transmitters of its culture. It is in a discourse on 'national culture' that women are therefore most often and most 'naturally' referred to. Most 'naturally' for the middle class who dominated the 'national' debate, women's economic participation was cognitively invisible and political participation was alien. Women's role in the 'home' was natural. And we know that the etiology of common sense is central to hegemony.

It is well-documented that both the 'home' and the 'Indian woman', which were being eulogised as eternal, were specific to a particular historical moment and marked a definite break from the past. Indeed, the nineteenth-century reformers and nationalists alike wanted to liberate the upper-caste woman from her world of superstition and ignorance. An audience of educated men was thus asked whether they did not feel in their daily lives that their mothers and wives were 'great impediments' in the way of their own intellectual and moral improvement (Chaudhuri 1993: 470). Reformers thus wanted to devise a system of education for females that would 'enable the wife to serve as a solace to her husband in his bright and dark moments ... to superintend the early instruction of her child, and the lady of the house to provide those sweet social comfort, idealized in the English word—Home' (ibid.). This 'home' is therefore new, but 'homes', like 'nations', appear as natural entities with a history that extends to a past that is 'time immemorial'. This process also happily coincides with what I have referred to earlier as the persistent tendency of much of modern theory to dehistoricise the private sphere, condemning women to remain in the 'timeless universe' of domesticity (Benhabib 1987).

Thus, while the economic and political spheres are 'alien' spaces that women have to enter, the 'home' is the 'natural' realm where women already exist. Western feminists have claimed that in the Western world, women have been seen as nature and men as culture. In India, we know that women are represented as cultural emblems. But what I want to argue further is that this 'culture' is at once 'nature', in the sense that like the 'family', the 'home', and 'women', 'culture' here evokes a past beyond history. It is primordial and thus inspires a passion that 'development' and 'political participation' can only be envious of.

Culture and nation are thus seen as natural. On the other hand, culture in the modern nation-state can really be understood as a 'garden' culture, not wild and therefore not natural. While wild culture, like wild nature, can grow unattended and still look beautiful, artificial gardens can be left unattended only to be destroyed. Likewise, modern 'national culture(s)' are thought-out entities which are administered under the specialised services of the state. Debates on cultural policies within Indian nationalism and nation-building were important. Defining what constitutes 'national culture', however, was a contentious project from the very start. Both the trends towards a hegemonic, homogenous, Hindu, upper-caste notion of culture and a well-articulated idea of a 'composite culture' with the far-sighted slogan of 'unity and diversity' fought themselves through the trajectory of Indian nationalism and the doings of the Indian state. For women, it implied once too often a conflict between women's rights as equal citizens and a community's rights to cultural practices that hinged upon gender discriminatory practices, be it sati, purdah, child marriage, the denial of inheritance rights, or polygamy.

Even in the national and women's movements in the colonial period, fissures had clearly cropped up between the promise of political and economic equality for women and equality for cultural practices that more often than not were discriminatory to women. Members of the Constituent Assembly, Amrit Kaur and Hansa Mehta, had objected to the guarantee of religious propaganda and practice. They felt that the terms 'propagation' and 'practice' might invalidate future legislation prohibiting child marriage, polygamy, unequal inheritance laws, and untouchability, as these customs could be construed as being part of religious worship. Kaur suggested that freedom of religion be limited to religious worship (Chaudhuri 1993: 185).

I have been arguing that while culture is perceived as 'natural', it is a very artificial construct in the modern state. Groups which have the power seek to shape the content of 'national' culture. In a culturally diverse society like India, in a clime where women came to represent 'culture', community leaders actively defined what constituted the authentic cultural practices of a community. It has been argued that the women's question itself became a site for defining what tradition is. Women's political activism sought to question this, as we saw in Amrit Kaur's attempts. But that the opposition to this was strong is evident from the fact that her views did not have the final say. Today, we thus have a Constitution with Article 15 which deals with the right to equality. But the constitution also contains articles dealing with other categories of rights, like the right to Freedom of Religion, as embodied in Articles 25–28. The question that A. R. Desai raised and one that continues to haunt India today is whether a State that proclaims opposition to gender-based discrimination can allow the persistence of religious personal laws (Desai 1994).

Almost sixty years later, the fears of India's early feminists have come true. Worse still, today the state's secular credentials are so weak that there is almost all-round consensus that the Uniform Code bill is best kept away. The demand for a uniform civil code has been appropriated by the Bharatiya Janata Party (BJP). It is important to recall today, therefore, that the stiffest opposition to the Hindu Code bill had come from the then Hindu Mahasabha. One of its leading members, Chatterjee, had argued that the act would encourage the conversion of Hindus to Islam. And Amrit Kaur lamented that '"religion" in danger is a very potent caveat which scares even seemingly intelligent persons ...' (Chaudhuri 1993: 190).

Questions of culture, community identity, and scriptural sanctions have been very much part of the manner in which the women's question emerged in India. One of the first issues where this came up is the sati dispute. While the Brahmo Samaj marshalled enormous Shastric evidence to show that sati was not mandatory, the Dharma Sabha pleaded with the British to disallow those who know nothing of their customs and religion so as to deter them from speaking. Raja Rammohun Roy argued that Manu enjoined a widow to live a life of denial and austerity, while the Dharma Sabha petitioned 'that in a question so delicate as the interpretation of our sacred books, and the authority of our religious usages none but Pundits and Brahmins and teachers of holy lives, and known learning ought to be consulted—not men who have neither faith nor care for the memory of their ancestors or their religion' (Chaudhuri 1993: 17–21). The Age of Consent Bill that raged through India at the end of the nineteenth century asserted the natural and nationalist right of a community to decide when and how to reform, rejecting the right of an alien and unresponsive state to legislate on the private matters of Indians (ibid.: 68–74).

While the establishment of an independent state in a way alters the terms of discourse, the problem of differing identification of communities to the state persists. The majority community 'naturally' identifies with the 'nation-state', while degrees of discomfort persist with the other communities. The fact that India attained independence with the partitioning of the country and unprecedented killings on 'communal' grounds has marked the discourse of state and communities till date. So far as women are concerned, the questions persist: Who decides who speaks legitimately for a 'community'? Who decides what constitutes the 'culture' of a community?

The Shah Bano case dramatically brought all these questions to the fore. On 23 April 1985, the Supreme Court of India passed a judgement granting maintenance to a divorced Muslim woman, Shahbano. The court awarded Shahbano maintenance of Rs 179.20 per month from her husband and dismissed the husband's appeal against the award of maintenance. The judgement of the Supreme Court sparked off a nation-wide controversy. The principal argument put forward by conservative Muslim opinion was that the Muslim Personal Law was based on the Shariat, which is divine and immutable. Although sections from the Muslim community defended the judgement, the state was more willing to listen to the voices of conservative spokespersons of the community. Shahbano herself was pressurised to such an extent that in an open letter, she denounced the Supreme Court judgement:

> ... which is apparently in my favour; but since this judgment which is contrary to the Quran and the hadith and is an open interference in Muslim personal law, I, Shahbano, being a Muslim, reject it and dissociate myself from every judgment which is contrary to the Islamic shariat. I

am aware of the agony and distress which this judgement has subjected the Muslims of India today (*Radiance* 1985).

The state passed the Muslim Women's Bill and the Hindu communal forces saw this move as an appeasement on the part of the state to the minorities. Significantly, the fact that it was Muslim women who were at the losing end passed them by. The question that arose is: Who exactly was the bill seeking to protect—community leaders, divorced husbands, or women? (Pathak and Rajan 1989).

It is important to emphasise that the tendency of the conservative leadership of a community to affirm gender-discriminatory practices as authentic culture is not confined to the minority community. Soon after the Indian state passed the Muslim Women's Bill, an 18-year-old widow, Roop Kanwar, was burnt alive on her husband's pyre in full view of about 3,000 spectators, 'accompanied by the full panoply of Rajput valour' (Bhasin and Menon 1988: 12). Despite the Rajasthan High Court's directives to the state government to prevent the celebration of 'Chunari festival' in honour of Roop Kanwar, it was celebrated. About two lakh people assembled at the Chunari Mahotsava and paid obeisance to the *sati-sthal* (site of the self-immolation). Many leading politicians participated. The women of the Rani Sewa Sangha, a voluntary social movement to preserve India's *'ancient traditions'*, dressed as brides and marched through the streets of Chandni Chowk, Delhi, to commemorate 'the historic act of self-immolation'. Sati was projected as the highest ideal of female spirituality and renunciation, the highest achievement of *naridharma* and *pativrata*. And it was imbued with the aura of sacrifice associated with Rajput history (Sangari 1988: 26). The sentiments expressed at the sati case were perceived to be in keeping with the 'natural cultural' and 'national' sentiments of the people. The state perceived no threat, unlike in the Shahbano case, which was widely projected as an instance of a community's disloyalty to the state and nation. Quite clearly, to be the cultural emblems of the nation, women have to conform to a particular culture.

CONCLUSION

The kind of synoptic view that this chapter has sought to present necessarily falls short of a nuanced understanding. The basic argument that it has put forward is that the Indian state has perceived women primarily at three levels: women as agents and recipients of development, as citizens, and finally, as cultural emblems. While India's specific colonial history and national movement have shaped these issues in a particular manner, this chapter also believes that some of the basic anomalies which we perceive between what the state says and what it does flow from the very logic of a liberal state. In other words, the liberal state is formally committed to the economic, political, and cultural rights of individuals. But so far as women 'individuals' are concerned, the state tends to relate to them through the 'family' and 'community', as evidenced in all three cases of development, political participation, and culture. This process gets further aggravated in India, with its complex legacy of colonial history and embittered community relationships.

This chapter has also sought to identify the major shifts in the policies of the Indian state and has attempted to understand the implications of the state's liberalisation policies on the women's question, be it development or political participation. The question that may arise is: Where does 'culture' come in? But, as has been argued all along, culture is not something that is added on. It is intrinsic to the imaginings of nations and the doings of states. Empirically, we know that along with liberalisation, we have had heightened ethnic and communal tensions where the issue of women as emblems of culture has meant the negation of women's political and economic rights. Theoretically, this chapter rests on the assumption that the 'nation-state' couples in itself a commitment to a rule-bound order premised on the equality of all individuals (where women are equal citizens and economic actors), a 'natural' and supreme love for the nation and its culture, where nation is the home (and mother), and on the freedom of the market, which is increasingly disinclined to allow a state to protect the weak and the marginal.

Notes

1. For details on how inheritance, marriage rules, and command over property determine the status of women in South Asia, see Agarwal (1994).

2. The war at Kargil repeatedly brought images of bereaved women who had lost their sons or husbands in the battlefield.

3. '... unless women of India work side by side with men, there is no salvation for India, salvation in more senses than one. I mean political salvation in the greater sense, and I mean the economic salvation and spiritual salvation also' (Gandhi 1925).

4. 'It was a stirring spectacle, that of tens of thousands of women, who for centuries were chained to the narrow domestic life and whom an authoritarian social system had assigned the position of helots at home, stepping out into the streets and marching with their fellow-patriots in illegal political demonstrations' (Desai 1994: 46).

5. As I write and the 1999 elections to the Lok Sabha heat up, we have the BJP pitting Sushma Swaraj as the '*desi beti*' against Sonia Gandhi, the '*videshi bahu*' who asserts her claim to the nation through her marriage, children, and widowhood.

6. Significantly, the Lahore Congress of Asian Women for Equality, the Geneva International Conference on Women's Equality, and the Congress of the Chinese Communist Party adopted a resolution on gender equality in the same year.

7. That the Lok Sabha in 1996 had some 169 OBC men (in the unreserved category) and no women finds no mention in the whole debate (*Sunday*, 1–7 June 1997).

CHAPTER 4

Gender and Advertisements
The Rhetoric of Globalisation

Introduction

This chapter is about advertisements and gender images, and hinges on the argument that they can be fruitfully understood as the rhetoric of India's project of globalisation. It rests on the assumption that the shift in the Indian state's economic policy in favour of globalisation has accompanied a shift in public discourse as evidenced in the media. My focus is on advertisements in the English print media—a media whose hegemonic significance cannot be wished away by its apparently inconsequential numerical strength. Since the focus is on 'shift', I make frequent forays into the past for purposes of comparison. By 'the past', I refer to the decades preceding the Indian state's far-reaching economic reforms in the latter part of the 1980s—a process commonly termed 'liberalisation', referring to the opening up of the Indian market and its integration into the global economy. This process, I argue, marks a break with the Indian state's stated sympathy with socialist ideas, with the notion of growth with equity, and a public discourse where there was near unanimity that such goals were desirable in themselves. This self-proclaimed ideology of the Indian state was a legacy of the Indian national movement, itself a rich and complex repository of ideas of which a significant part were socialism and distributive justice. The Indian national movement's struggle for freedom cannot therefore be simply negatively defined as an oppositional movement against British imperialism, but must be seen as a positive projection of a worldview that understood 'freedom' as a commitment to political, economic, and social freedom for all sections of the people—men and women—the world over, with particular reference to the dispossessed.

I would like to draw attention to this idea of 'freedom' because contemporary advertisements that I analyse later also tend to articulate a vision of freedom for the Indian woman and man, but one that is very differently anchored. In emphasising the dispossessed, I do not mean to suggest that the ideology of the Indian national movement or of globalisation is ungendered, but want to stress that the category of gender cannot be exclusively deployed to the exclusion of the myriad ways in which it articulates with class and the specific histories of non-Western post-colonial societies. I see, therefore, in the recasting of gender images in adverts, a simultaneous recreation of both a new consuming Indian 'middle' class in a globalised economy and a reorientation of the salient issues taken up by the media. I emphasise that, although the explicit focus in this chapter is the new normative Indian consumer who dons the glossy advertisements, a key argument is that these adverts implicitly but effectively eclipse the image of 'another world' of Indian men and women—poor and battered, tribal and peasant, working class and Dalit[1]—from public discourse.[2]

Apart from the construction of a 'new normative Indian man and woman', apart from the banishment of the poor and marginalised in the media in general and advertisements in particular, there has also been a shift from a widely held view in independent India that freedom from the commercial imperatives of sponsors would enable the media to function as the fourth estate of an economically poor democracy. No newspaper or magazine today, however, can be commercially viable without advertisements.[3] Industry sources[4] show a dramatic rise in the total advertising revenue. From Rs 3,000 crore (30,000 million) in 1994–95, it shot up to Rs 82,000 crore (820,000 million) in 1999–2000. Of this, 56 per cent are from the print media and 36 per cent from television. It is in this context that this chapter has been written.

Since my central contention is that there has been a shift in Indian public discourse, I will turn to history to illustrate an earlier discourse from which the shift has taken place. Indian nationalist thought was a curious mixture of disparate ideologies and worldviews, possible perhaps only in the tragic sites of colonised countries. Although the image of the traditional, Hindu, self-effacing woman was always an icon, so was the struggling Indian peasant and worker, as was the recast modern Indian woman—educated, politically aware, and yet innocent of Western cultural mores. Writings of major women activists in the nationalist period opined that, unlike in the West, the Indian women's movement was supported by male reformers and nationalists. And, in contemporary times, cultural nationalists have sought to portray the Indian woman as chaste, demure, and sexually sanitised, unlike her prurient Western counterpart.

I have discussed elsewhere that modern Indian thought on nationalism and on the woman question was a curious agglomeration of ideas freely drawn from liberalism, socialism, and cultural revivalism (Chaudhuri 1996). So, along with conflicting gender images, there was always the attempt to represent men and women from different classes. Independent India was largely dominated by a public discourse that this body of nationalist thought had shaped. Today, some of that curious admixture of ideas on gender lingers on, and is clearly noticeable even in advertisements. It would be easy, therefore, to find images of the demure, chaste Indian woman along with the self-possessed career woman. But images of either a peasant woman or a working-class man are well-nigh impossible to discover. It is well-recognised that 'society . . . requires discourse (the mapping, description and articulation of situations and processes) which by definition has the effect of annihilating and delegimitising certain views and positions while including others' (van Zoonen 1994: 40). I maintain that advertisements play precisely this role of delegitimising space in public discourse for the majority of Indian men and women.

UNDERSTANDING ADVERTISEMENTS

The focus in this chapter is on the text of the adverts themselves. I confine my study to select English-medium newspapers and magazines in the 1990s, a decade when India's new economic policy made its presence felt. The newspapers surveyed are *The Times of India*, its sister publication *The Economic Times*, *Business Standard*, and *The Hindu*. The magazines consist of women's magazines such as *Femina*, *The Women's Era*, *Savvy*, *The New Woman*, and popular general weeklies like *The Sunday*, *The Week*, and *The Outlook*. I have been following these on a regular basis, subscribing to some and borrowing others from a local lending library that is a regular feature of middle-class colonies in Delhi, often functioning from what are narrow rooms built as garages for two-wheelers. I mention this because although a *Savvy* is more expensive than a *Week*, and could therefore be targeting different socio-economic segments, the daily lending rates are such that women and men can in practice read a wide range of weeklies. I also make the point because I am *not* making a comparative analysis of advertisements that appear in different publications.[5] I am instead arguing that I discern a wider pattern despite the differences. I attempt here to read the ideological meanings of the adverts, locating them against the concrete historical instance of liberalising India. I favour, therefore, a causal logic of determinacy, but also pay deference to the internal logic of arrangement, of internal relations, of articulations of parts within a structure.

I understand advertising as 'the necessary material production within which an apparently selfsubsistent mode of production can alone be carried on' (Williams 1977: 92–93). The product is not separable from the act of producing (Marx 1976: 1048). The analysis of adverts cannot, therefore, be separated from the economic processes of liberalisation. I take the decisive relationship between the media and monopoly capitalism as given (Murdoch and Golding 1979). Scholars have extensively dealt with this as with the impact of advertising on mass media (Curran 1981; Williams 1980). This relationship between the media and adverts gets further compounded in 'Third World' media, for here the issue is not just about media being profit-driven, but driven by 'international capitalist interests' (Reeves 1993). The international is more often than not Western, which has its own set of cultural implications for an erstwhile colonised society such as India. India has a long history of self-reliant development and fierce defence of 'national sovereignty'. Fears about the impact of liberalisation in general and on the media in particular persist. We thus have not only adverts, but also features in defence of advertisements and what they portend for a free society, now that the long years of independent India's tryst with 'planned development' are over (Chaudhuri 1998b, 2000).

A concerted ideological campaign thus has to be carried out to establish the legitimacy of the new economic regime, to which advertising contributes. Adverts have been likened to myths, in that they frequently resolve social contradictions, provide models of identity, and celebrate the existing social order. As Barthes (1977) puts it, myth consists in overturning culture into nature with the quite contingent foundations of the utterance becoming Common Sense, Right Reason, the Norm, and General Opinion. That this is the way dominant ideology functions has had its share of adherents and opponents. Adherents very broadly draw their understanding, however mediated, from Marx (Marx and Engels 1984a).

The suggestion that the ideas of the ruling class are the ideas of society has undergone periodic refurbishment. Gramsci (1971: 245) used 'hegemony' to refer to the process by which general consent is actively sought for the interpretations of the ruling class. The dominant ideology becomes invisible because it is translated into common sense, appearing as the natural, apolitical state of things. Clearly, advertisements are the contemporary mediators of hegemony. In Althusserian theories of ideology, the individual is interpolated by the dominant ideology. Advertisements would, we can infer, act as ideological apparatuses.

Not surprisingly, then, adverts have a key role to play in the ideological transformation of public discourse. And within modern advertising, gender is probably the social resource that is used most (Jhally 1987: 135). The obsession is said to spring from the 'signifying power' of gender. 'Something that can be conveyed fleetingly in any social situation and yet something that strikes as the most basic characteristic of the individual' (Goffman 1976: 7). Thus, the extremely condensed form of communication in advertising lends itself exceptionally well to an examination of the cultural values, beliefs, and myths connected to gender. I argue that it also lends itself to an examination of the desirable values and practices of the normative Indian—man and woman—in a post-liberalised era.

THE NEW-GENERATION INDIAN MAN AND WOMAN

The reader may understand by now that my intent is to show a shift in the dominant representation of the normative Indian, and hence my periodic reference to the colonial past. The colonial period witnessed dramatic social transformations, region-specific histories of middle-class growth, and region-specific responses of this class to articulate a modern normative Indian. Although different ideological responses contested their way through, it may not be wide off the mark to claim that they were united in their commitment to the wider Indian society—to questions of inequity and justice. Collective concern defined their notion of selfhood. If I were asked to describe the 'new Indian' that adverts depict today, I would identify a typical corporate-sector executive, an upwardly mobile professional who travels a great deal, works hard, and unwinds during weekends and holidays. This, I contend, would hold true for both men and women, with the difference that images of a traditional woman homemaker coexist with adverts of female high achievers, while for men, images of high achievers are always at the forefront.

The entry of a large number of transnational companies at the beginning of liberalisation led to a real possibility of young men and women entering the corporate sector at salaries that their parents could not dream of even at retirement. A new work ethos entered Indian public discourse as India's middle class learned to exchange safety and security for success and upward mobility. What I am arguing is that certain changes are taking place in the ideas and ways of life of the middle class. My discussion here is non-gendered to the extent that I emphasise certain new, 'universal' characteristics of the middle class; but in a gendered society, many of these characteristics are operationalised in a gendered fashion. Thus, we have a redefining of middle-class virtues at home, with the household actively redrawn as a site of consumption. Within this context, the Indian woman learns that 'thrift' is no longer a virtue and 'shopping' is a legitimate pleasure (Chaudhuri 1998b), while Indian men learn that looking good is not a woman's privilege. I will focus first on the 'general' impact of adverts on Indian society before moving on to gender differences in the next section. Adverts both depict new trends and accelerate them. Adverts also obliterate other trends. This raises the contentious question of the relationship between 'reality' and 'representation'. A central debate among feminist media scholars concerns the 'distortion' theme; that the media does not represent the 'real' picture of women. The epistemological basis of this transmission model of communication is two-fold. One is that 'there is a reality and then after the fact, our account of it' (Carey 1989: 25). The second is that the role of the media in modern societies is bardic: by definition, the media cannot simply 'reflect', for the bard's task is primarily to render the unfamiliar into the already known, or into 'common sense' (van Zoonen 1994: 38).

The analysis below demonstrates how obviously adverts seek to create a branded self. My method of analysis avers that a reading of meanings from texts alone is guilty of internal fallacy, and that cognisance should be given to the author's intention. In the case of adverts, the intent of the sponsor is mediated through the advert maker. Before looking into the texts of adverts themselves, therefore, it is useful to explore how the advert maker understands the emergence of the 'new Indian'. The 'reader' is the 'customer', and today the advertising industry is brainstorming about who the customer is. 'What drives Sybil?' is the name for a market survey conducted by the advertising firm Lintas to study consumer profiles. 'The AP Lintas universe[6] prefers to slice Indian consumers into survivors, savers, enhancers, and splurgers. The urban and rural poor are survivors, and savers are the middle classes. Enhancers are the urban upper class, and splurgers the rich' (*Brand Equity, The Economic Times*, 16–22 June 1999).

Not all can afford to buy what the adverts seek to sell. Not all those who can afford to will buy. But they can desire and aspire to possess them and thereby be like the new Indians the adverts project. A new normative Indian is being established. I find David Chaney's observation of interest, where he tries to show how 'the new social form of lifestyles was coloured by some of the broader narratives of the cultural forms of consumerism', summarised under the headings of 'fantasy, excess, spectacle and citizenship' (Chaney 1994: 19). The first three features are reasonably self-evident. The last, citizenship, is not. Chaney's reason for using it is that he found no better way of putting the idea that mass marketing, as with other forms of mass democracy, offers the illusion of equal participation, and indeed even the glory of 'national culture' without much of its substantive powers. This, I think, is a useful way of understanding advertisements and the images they extend. Most people can look at and hear adverts. Few can read adverts. Fewer still can read English adverts. The numbers that can actually possess the goods advertised are smaller still. But theoretically, everyone has access to adverts, to the pleasure of looking, to desiring.

It is widely known that product advertisement has generally given way to lifestyle adverts. Hence, the language of advertisements is more about the consumer than the object to be consumed. The adverts themselves provide overt profiles of the new generation. Adverts demand that the media seek an audience who are 'hedonists'—who like to 'experiment' and have an attitude of spending. I attempt below to identify some key features of the new Indian, but before that, a few words on what it is that the new Indian is breaking away from.

Colonial societies underwent dramatic and often violent social, cultural, economic, and political changes. In response, these societies produced a whole range of social movements. A key component of these movements—reform, nationalist, radical—was a redefinition of what constituted the Indian. The dominant nationalist rhetoric suggested that the Indian be modern, rational, and rooted in India's past. His vision was embedded in a collectivist vision where the growth of the nation meant equity and justice, and a modest and low-key lifestyle was a desired code in public life. The erstwhile maharajas, ostentatious displays and spectacle were not part of legitimate public discourse.

The old 'new Indian' was internationalist. Non-alignment, close ties with the former socialist bloc, and fraternity with the nationalist struggles of Asia and Africa were the creeds of public life. Here, too, internationalism meant an imagining of collective struggles of the dispossessed. It is important to make this point to distinguish the internationalist from the globe-trotting Indian.

I would like to argue that liberalisation has broken down a more traditional system of marking identities within the middle class. The middle class has expanded and markings have changed. The sensualist has replaced the intellectualist paradigm. 'The shift from producer to consumer capitalism has meant its disruption, which . . . has brought the transience of new styles, the introduction of a new flattening temporality and the reduction of the self to the mere politics of presentation' (Lash and Friedman 1996: 18).

THE NEW INDIAN IS GLOBAL AND COSMOPOLITAN

A premier builder in India makes an offer to the non-resident Indian (NRI) that is splashed in almost all newspapers: 'Would an Elite NRI like you really need any other Residence more luxurious in India?' than 'Ansals Celebrity Homes—the international class country township.' VIP Skybags, with a half page picture of its luggage visible in *Outlook* and *India Today* (but not the women's magazines), writes: 'He treats his export business like sport. And airport lobbies, like racing tracks.' Skybag Luggage asks: 'Where next? Seven wonders of the world. Five Great lakes in the States. 4 days–3 nights in Seychelles. Two semis in England. One mother-of-a-trek in the Himalayas.' The advert for Mercedes-Benz, which appears in magazines (except women's magazines), says: '1. This is when he promised you his love, his hand, and a Mercedes. 2. This is when he gave you his love and his hand (pity not the Mercedes). 3. You are here now. Isn't it time?'

I had never seen an advert for Mercedes before mid-1999. Perhaps here is the contentious issue of 'equality' of access, in form if not content. The relative democratisation is not entirely illusory. Liberalisation has led to the emergence of a much larger very rich section of the population than before. The juxtaposition of love and Mercs needs no elaboration. Significantly, the advert is addressed to the woman. The potential buyer is a man. The reason for buying—the woman.

It has been argued by some that this new Indian is cosmopolitan and unmarked by the divisions (ethnic, religious, caste) that have plagued India in the past decade or more. Some have argued that a kind of secession has taken place within Indian society whereby the middle classes, whom the market seeks, no longer have even the appearance of commitment to the larger Indian populace mired in poverty and distress. Others have sought to show that many of the 'young' with an attitude of spending were among those who cheered at the demolition of the Babri Masjid (the mosque in the town of Ayodhya, Uttar Pradesh, which was torn down by Hindu fundamentalists in December 1992), and therefore the new Indian is very much marked by class, caste, and religion. My own reading of adverts suggests that for the splurgers and enhancers, the thrust is to cultivate an image of an international look and international lifestyles. For the savers, more overt statements of cultural specificities are made. *Elle*, an up-market magazine, carried on its cover page Indian model Sheetal Mallar, who had been picked up as the face of Maybelline cosmetics. Images such as hers are truly 'international', marked only by the rules of the fashion business, which are still very West-centric. When the 'traditional' or 'ethnicised' Indian is presented, therefore, the construct is a Western one. What has become a clichéd observation perhaps needs repeating in a different context. The Orient is an invention of the Occident.

THE NEW INDIAN IS BODY CONSCIOUS

There is a column on health in almost every magazine and newspaper. To illustrate, 'A toast to good health' has an assortment of recipes, with the introductory commentary saying: 'You are what you eat. So why not take a break from relishing fried food and oily fare that is unhealthy. Here's an assortment of low calorie salads that not only promise to keep you healthy, but also tickles your taste buds. You don't need to think twice here. So go ahead and indulge' (*New Woman*, March 1999: 121).

'The prospect of stretch marks may seem scary to a woman of today who is conscious of herself and her body.' But today, 'Stretch Nil', a herbal stretch mark preventive, 'is available with the local chemist' and stretch marks 'are no longer the dreadful nightmare they used to be' (*The Outlook*, 4 May 1999). The advert further mentions that 'one always tends to concentrate on the baby more than oneself during pregnancy. Though this may seem the right thing to do, it is imperative the mother takes as much care of herself too.' This new body consciousness cuts across gender, as an article on the 'slimming craze' seeks to show: 'The demand of today's young men and women to keep fit and remain attractive spawned a multi-billion industry all over the world' (*The Hindu*, 16 November 1998).

A VIP luggage advert with a woman's face (three-fourths of the page) has just this line: 'You don't have to be good-looking but it helps' in bold. Another of 'Ever Yuth; collagen and elastin'—an anti-wrinkle cream—screams: 'STOP THAT CLOCK'. This premium on youthful appearance is certainly a break in a society where age used to mean authority. I will explore the implications of this new awareness of the body in the concluding section.

THE NEW INDIAN IS 'FREE'

Advertisements have contributed to the dismantling of a public discourse where social equity was as critical as, if not more important than, growth, and have legitimised the pleasures and ethos of the free market. 'Freedom,' according to a caption of an American Express advert, is 'knowing just how far you can go and then getting there.' 'It's all about living without ambiguities. Including the facts about your credit cards.' Another claims: 'You want more from life, because you give it your best.' Both adverts have full-sized silhouettes of a young figure in a stretching-out gymnastic posture. Significantly, one of these is a man, the other a woman. Credit cards have made their presence felt in the market only in the past decade and acquired prominence in metropolitan cities in the past five years.

Then there is the family,[7] cycling into the sunset on the sea shore, celebrating 'freedom'. 'I am *free* to appreciate what I have–, to look into the future–, to open new doors for my family. I am *free* because I have one of the largest financial organizations behind me' (emphasis mine). The sponsor is Hong Kong Bank, the advert visible across the selection of non-women's magazines.

THE NEW INDIAN IS ETHNIC, NOT 'DESI'

One feature that has been commented upon in contemporary culture is 'hybridisation'—the mixing and matching of styles and artefacts from different cultures and a general stylistic promiscuity and playful mixing of codes. The argument is that hegemony is passé and hybridity is the state of being. I would differ and argue that while the fashion industry's appropriation of the ethnic may be in, the Indian still cannot be just native or 'desi'.

In the face of competition, Amrutanjan, a traditional healthcare company, is going in for a complete face-lift and taking the war right to the multinational companies. 'The balm is no longer being advertised as the quintessential grandma's home-treatment, or the secret recommendation of one housewife to another; the *target segment now is the hip, smarter set—the younger no-oil-in-the-hair generation*' (*Business Standard*, 7 January 1998; emphasis mine). The American, though, is clearly of a different order. Petal Smooth, a ladies hair shaver, is 'the fastest, cleanest, easiest way to remove unwanted hair', for it is 'made only in the USA' and it is '*the great American way* to feminine grooming' (emphasis mine).

GENDER IN ADVERTISEMENTS

Mention of a typical Indian woman invokes set images. It is culturally loaded, filled with allusions. The dominant discourse of social reform, nationalism, and independent India's state policies explicitly sought to create a model of womanhood that was deemed authentically Indian. Much has been written on India's recasted culture, tradition, and women in the colonial period (Chaudhuri 1993; Sangari and Vaid 1984), and how the woman question became a site for redefining what constituted India's tradition and culture. This entire process, which was both exclusive and hegemonic, wherein a specifically upper-caste gender norm was imposed as the 'Indian' norm, has been extensively documented. My purpose in referring to the past here is to underscore the fact that, while the Indian women's image was actively recast, we do not have a parallel portrayal of what the desirable Indian male ought to be. There are inferences (often contradictory) that we can draw from, but no deliberate exposition in the writings of Indians. What is implied is that he is 'the Indian'. The woman is 'the Indian woman', the companionate figure, but by no means the central actor. He is the upper-caste family patriarch. He is the rationalist social reformer, the nationalist with a scientific temper, the fierce cultural revivalist, desirous of the more manly virtues of the Western imperial man. For the colonial rulers, he was simply the effeminate babu, the grovelling native, or a loyal soldier from the deemed martial races (Sinha 1997: 15–16). Although colonial descriptions of the native male are explicitly articulated, the Indian (male) account can be inferred from Indian men's recasting of the Indian woman. The Indian woman has an image when the man does not because while she is the cultural emblem of the national, he *is* the national (Chaudhuri 1996). If colonialism ushered in an epoch of recasting of Indian femininity, liberalisation, I argue, has been redefining ideas about dominant representations of Indian masculinity. I analyse below how far the new male images break with patriarchal attitudes and usher in more gender-equitable times.

WHAT IS NEW IN THE INDIAN MAN

Liberalisation has heralded a new effort to make the Indian male more like a 'man', and less the 'native slob'. A portend of this trend is the appearance of the male in a large number of adverts. As argued earlier, there seems to be a shift from an intellectual paradigm to a sensual one, where the politics of presentation is what matters.

THE NEW APPEARANCE OF THE INDIAN MAN

Today, 'male models have come a long way from the days of being props for the more popular women' (*The Week*, 30 March 1997: 40).

It would be a difficult choice to make even for the beautician, considering that the market has seen an influx of male commodities. From designer underwear to men's cosmetics, they are all available now. The size of the men's toiletries market is Rs 150 crore. There are shaving foams, aftershave lotions, moisturisers, deodorants, eau de toilettes, colognes, hair cream, styling gels, talcum powders, shampoos, and soaps (*The Week*, 30 March 1997: 40).

Choice is a key word. 'Ten years ago there was just Old Spice. Now you have many choices,' said the deputy general manager of Menezes Cosmetics, which has fifteen products like aftershaves and colognes from Blur Stratos. 'The market has grown because men have realized that it is high time they looked and smelt good' (*The Week*, 30 March 1997: 41). Businessman Ketan Mehta agrees: if Indian men are becoming choosy, it is because they have a choice that was not available earlier. 'Ten years ago if I wanted a pair of suspenders even hunting I would not get a good choice' (*ibid.*: 40). An interesting figure of a man titled 'The branded man' (*ibid.*: 41) has an accompanying chart with arrows indicating 'hair', 'glass', 'face', 'body', 'shirts', 'ties', 'suits', 'trousers', 'underwear', 'belts', 'socks', 'shoes'. Against each part we have a list of relevant branded products; for example, 'socks' has 'Louis Philippe, Reebok, Nike, Proline, Bata, Lacoste'.

Men also feature as 'catwalk kings':

> THE CONTESTANTS are topless and their polished and chiseled bodies glisten in the light. Amid loud catcalls and whistling they walk gingerly down the ramp, unnerved by the ogling and leering. They are the male beauties of India, participating in an all-male beauty contest. The leers and jeers are obviously from women.
>
> Nowadays beauty conscious men, too, are getting plenty of opportunities to exhibit themselves and have silly questions thrown at them for equally silly replies. And the women just love it. (*The Week*, 30 May 1997)

An up-market fashion magazine, *Gladrags*, launched 'The Gladrags Man Hunt' contest in 1994. Maureen Wadia, the proprietor, contends that: 'It's a fun context and it's also serious' for 'it will make Indian men figure conscious and they should be. Why should we settle for pot bellies? We also work in offices but we take care of our figures.' 'They can't be sloppy and bad mannered. Etiquette is important to succeed with women or in one's job' (*The Week, 30* March 1997: 40).[8]

Men, Power, and Success

Power has belonged to men in patriarchal societies. Power as an attribute may be seen as an 'old' characteristic of men. My survey of adverts suggests, however, that while 'power' is projected clearly as a male quality, the image of 'power' that most adverts communicate is the very specific power of the successful executive in the corporate world. This is power at work, not at home. The 'native' had power at home, not at work. The image here is not that of the authority exercised by the household patriarch; it is the 'power' of the corporate world.[9] It is the power of achieved status, not of an ascribed one. As a men's wear advert says, 'Because you know you deserve your place in the sun.' The enormous possibilities that liberalisation has offered to the metropolitan middle class are dramatic. This affirmation of the 'self' as potentially capable of reaching high places also means an ideological distrust of those who do not go places, or go anywhere. Adverts have played an important role in bringing into parlance a language of 'success' and 'power'. The following text of an advert selling Contessa cars is illuminating:

> We had never met before. I decided to size him up over a game of golf. But *when he pulled up his car; I knew I'd found my business partner.*
>
> There was a *spring in his step*, a *firmness in his handshake* when he stepped out of his Contessa. They complement each other so well. Both of them are comfortable in the power they wield. Assertive but not arrogant. *Distinguished*, not deliberate.
>
> *Unflappable and in control. It is easy to know a man from his car.* So when you are looking for fine men, just look inside a Contessa. (emphasis mine)

The above text can be held up for closer scrutiny on two grounds. One, that there is an overt affirmation of power as a desirable quality of men. Two, that there is an unabashed association of the person (here male) with material objects. Descriptions of the car and the men are interchangeable. Western feminist writings have dwelt on the ways that adverts affirm traditional male qualities. My contention is that 'power' and 'success' as defining attributes of malehood in India is a post-liberalisation phenomenon. It has already been stated that colonialism unleashed a process by which the Indian male had to either masculinise himself or remain content with being the stereotypical effeminate native. For how male can you be without power? Independent India, with its policies of growth with equity, did little to encourage excess of any kind. Although power may still have been an attribute, the process of democratisation of 'power' had clearly not taken place. The hypothetical possibility of anybody accessing the power of a corporate executive was absent. I randomly draw upon adverts to illustrate the deployment of the image of 'power'.

'He exudes power, good looks and an ease with international corporate life style. He is the much sought-after Organization Guru. Those who can't afford him can study his luggage,' says an ad for VIP Skybags luggage. For 'if Skybags in general speaks volumes about its owner, Skybag Infiniti, one can say, speaks with the *authority* of a much sought-after consultant' (emphasis mine). You see adverts with 'him' working at the computer, in the boardroom, at the airport. Microsoft invites the 'new man' to 'increase productivity at office' and also 'do less work'. It is noticeable that on the very next page, Microsoft has a woman looking harassed at work with the words: 'It's not a holiday you need: It's a new office.' In smaller print, the words go on: 'Overwhelmed by work? Before you check out the nearest holiday spot, we suggest you check out Microsoft's new office suite: Office 97.' Could the contrasting images of the male and female executive be accidental? As a young male professional speaks over the cellular phone,

Infosys Technological Limited enquires, 'A college campus? A software hotshop? A professionals' powerhouse?'

> When it's Denis Parkar, *clothes make more than the man.* Creations of mastercraftspersons, they make his future. They widen the horizon of his progress. And they add a whole *new power* to his personality. That's why when you're in one of Denis Parkar's unique line of high-class BUSINESS SUITS or distinctive ETHNIC OUTFITS or elegant PARTY SHIRTS, you're sure to stand out. At home or abroad. (emphasis mine)

'The power of a perfect suit' from Bombay Dyeing, 'with a fall, feel and comfort that spells luxury', shows a Caucasian-looking male dressed in a black suit. 'You travel with a purpose and we appreciate that. Ours is a hotel which speaks your language. The *universal language of professionalism.* So take a deep breath and plunge into your schedule. You will be surprised at how refreshing the deep end can be,' reads an advert of Oberoi Hotels (emphasis mine). The accompanying picture is again a Caucasian in the pool.

Meet Navroze Dhondy who, when he 'isn't chasing deadlines, deadlines are chasing him. Everything is wanted yesterday. Airlines meals. Late nights. Dinner diplomacy. It's difficult to cope with all this. Even more difficult for the stomach. While Navroze is fine tuning the art of crisis management, stomach management is something he delegates to Pudin Hara.'

A Wipro advert, too, has the executive in a chair, phone in hand, a computer facing him, and the words: 'We know how valuable your time is. That's why we have ensured that our responsive computer maintenance service is just a keystroke away from you.'

'Some people say pay in gold. Doors open to you. Extra hands attend to you. Ask for anything and the answer is always yes. It's amazing how the flash of BOBCARD GOLD can turn a shopping trip into an unforgettable experience. After all, it's a reflection of *financial power* that only a few possess' (emphasis mine).

The new mantra for the Indian male is power and success. He has to be rich and glamorous. He has to be at the top of his job early in life. But along with this consolidation of a Western male model, we also have an affirmation of gentler qualities in men. He is no brute, a point evident in a whole array of adverts sponsored to create an image of the complete man. Significantly, it is the up-market male who is now attributed with softer qualities.

The Complete Man

The complete man has to be rich and successful. But to complete the persona, he has to be caring, tender, and endowed with what traditionally women alone were capable of. He bathes his baby and changes the nappy. He talks to his children and worries about stains on the tablecloth. He goes for long walks in the forests. Raymond, specialists in men's wear, has been bringing out a steady stream of adverts projecting the new gentle, soft, caring man. Below I cite some of the descriptions:

> Indifference is out, involvement is in, hearing is out, listening is in, selling is out, relationships are in
>
> Get real
>
> It's-not-my-job is out, sharing is in, control is out, nurturing is in, authority is out, responsibility is in
>
> Get real
>
> Hierarchy is out, collaborations are in, rule models are out, role models are in, efficiency is out, effectiveness is in
>
> Get real.

What is Old in the Indian Man

The new Indian man may have acquired some new dimensions to his personality. But on the whole, he is still involved in the public world, doing important things. He has no time for trivia. The cigarette industry has had a long-held practice of emphasising men's rugged nature and virile world through cigarette smoking. With the growth of the anti-tobacco movement in the West, Third World countries like India have been especially targeted. The following is the text of one such advert: 'He has no room for trivia. No designer crystal. No fancy champagne, No pictures of vacations in Seychelles. Just the deep satisfaction of the world's finest smoke. For the man who has no room for trivia. A very private luxury,' reads an advert for the cigarette INDIA KINGS.

He has to give his daughter away: here is an advert with an interesting combination of the old and the new. The practice of patriliny and patrilocality within much of north Indian kinship and marriage implies that the daughter of the family has to be married out of kin and village. This departure of the bride is an emotional moment for everybody. She now no longer belongs to her natal family. She can only visit when her husband's family permits it. It was part of the upper-caste Hindu male's dharma to marry her off. The advert cited below has a picture of the traditional ceremony of a daughter's departure at marriage, with the father discreetly wiping away a tear, and the words:

> Raymond Suitings
> Like a million fathers you knew from the moment she was born it had to happen. Like a million fathers you thought you would be prepared for it. It's okay, real men cry.

WHAT IS NEW IN THE INDIAN WOMAN

The myriad beauty contests that have sprung up all over the country reflect the way the Miss India/Miss World contests have captured the imagination of the people. My contention has been that adverts and features merge until boundaries are hard to discern. Just as Palmolive rests its advertising campaign on Miss India winners, we have features interviewing the various winners and aspirants in the media, as well as the hairdresser, the costume designer, etc. *Femina* carried a piece on 'Why we need MISS AMERICA.' The blurb told us: 'Jill Neimark speaks to psychologists to unravel the appeal of the Miss America Contest. We could draw some parallels here in India, too' (Neimark 1999: 50).

The modern Indian woman knows how to 'dare' and to 'dream'. For a while, NEPC Agro Foods Limited brought out weekly insertions from 'today's woman' ('aaj-ki-nari'). One such advert carries the image of an athletic young girl in shorts, who announces:

> I'm here again. The aaj-ki-nari. And your Sunday fitness friend. Sharing today's women's concerns for their menfolk. Ready for your weekly dose of goodness. PRESSURE CHECK. Your body is only human. Overwork, mental fatigue and undue work tensions can take their toll. Premature greying (or balding), dark circles around the eyes, insomnia are only too common .... You'll find that physical exercise actually takes away mental weariness ... so a good game of shuttle or squash in the evenings is not a bad idea. How about some TM? Spare 20 minutes every day religiously for just yourself. And you'll be ready to take on the world. ALL WORK AND NO PLAY .... If you don't have a hobby, a passion, get one ... quick!

> Because a man without an absorbing extracurricular life is indeed a dull boy! Read a lot more . . . as a general rule, it takes your mind away from day-to day worries and keeps depression at bay. And while I won't say ban all late nights, smoking and social drinking, it really helps to know where to draw the line.
>
> That's all from this aaj-ki-nari . . . this Sunday. See you same time, next week. It's a date!

Today's woman is old-fashioned enough to care and modern enough to tell him what she likes. She has the standard suggestions for the overworked, ambitious corporate executive. The male who is not these things is clearly a loser—a term that was alien to Indians even a few years ago. Alien too were ideas of space for oneself or meditation for healing.

WHAT IS OLD IN THE INDIAN WOMAN

THE FAMILY WOMAN

Sushmita Sen, the first Indian woman to win the coveted Miss Universe title, was stated as reiterating the new post-feminist ideology when she said, 'The essence of a woman is motherhood and teaches a man to love and care' (*The Times of India*, 16 June 1995). The woman remains the mainstay of her family; she is the one who rears and nurtures. Not surprisingly, then, it is the woman who is targeted in adverts selling pressure cookers. The pressure cooker came into Indian housewives' lives in the 1960s and never really left. It made cooking quicker, simpler, saved fuel, and was a more nutritious mode of cooking. It represented the Indian urban, middle-class housewife. This is one lineage with which the millennium woman has not broken. A smallish, black and white picture of a young woman with a Hawkins pressure cooker and an older woman (mother-in-law/mother) touching her arm in an expression of approval and support accompanies a text in largish print, which reads: 'Because my family depends on me, I depend on Hawkins'. In smaller print, the text goes on:

> Looking after this dear, demanding family of mine isn't easy. The children, my husband and his parents all need my time—sometimes all at once! And all of them want their food cooked just as they like it, on time, every time. Truly, I don't think I could manage without my Hawkins. It cooks

> so fast and never lets me down. I have had it for so many years and I have had no problems with it. It's reliable—just as I am, my husband says!

One of India's oldest manufacturers of traditional Ayurvedic medicines invokes an image of eternal Indian womanhood. Chyawanprash, a product common to India's middle-class households, is 'prepared the Dabur way: Authentic Ayurvedic principles matched with modern standards of hygiene and quality. A tradition helping over 25 million users build a strong immunity for more than 112 years. One day at a time.' It is not difficult to discern the parallel between the qualities of authentic Indian womanhood and Dabur—both incorporating the best of the modern and the traditional.

'Somewhere between breakfast, dinner, and history books is a subject called Motherhood. The story of a woman who wants to mean everything to everybody. Hundred questions. Million demands. No time for herself. No time to fall sick. Will an ordinary health tonic do the job?' (advertisement for Dabur Chyawanprash)

Kelvinator Refrigerator asks the question: 'Why do some women need the extra room in the New 165 litre Corona Deluxe?' Below a picture of a mother, daughter/daughter-in-law, and granddaughter, the answer reads,

> We believe it has something to do with the extra room in their hearts.
>
> The joys of children, parents and grandparents all living together, are many.
>
> Perhaps that's why some families refuse to abandon this way of life. Even though houses today are becoming increasingly small.
>
> Which only shows that it shows that it does not necessarily take a larger house to accommodate a large family. It takes a large heart.
>
> And it's for women with such hearts that our engineers built the 165 litre Corona Deluxe.

WOMEN LOVE 'SHINGAR'

Women's love for clothes and jewellery are part of India's folklore. An advert of a silk shop is titled 'The Ultimate Women's Paradise', while a jewellery shop claims, 'We capture the fires of passion that lie in the deep of a woman's heart.' Yet another sari shop exhorts women to 'unravel the woman in you'. While for women, beautifying themselves lies in their very essence, adverts for men celebrate men's looks, but do not invoke any 'natural' reasons for doing so. Women still save, but not just money. Although up-market Indian women are visible in the adverts, the more traditional middle-class woman is also present. Reminiscent of an earlier era, we have a typical middle-class urban Indian woman smiling alongside a text with the caption—'Women of Today Excel Everywhere': 'Women of today have a distinct presence in every aspect of life with an inherent instinct to SAVE for safety and security.' But in another Hong Kong Bank advert, the word 'save' is given a twist. For now 'I save more than just money . . . I save precious time.'

Conclusion

I began this chapter on the note that the Indian national movement and the public discourse that independent India inherited were marked by a stated claim of social responsibility to goals of equity, justice, and 'freedom.' Written into the Indian Constitution was a pledge to battle against discrimination on grounds of sex, caste, community, class, and tribe. Although serious gaps existed between the stated intent towards social equity and both class and patriarchal claims on social privileges,[10] only the very naïve would dismiss the tangible significance of the intent. Perusals of the English language print media in the 1990s embolden me to claim a break, if not a discernible shift, in the dominant discourse. What comes across is the heralding of a new epoch, a celebration of a new Indian man and woman who shape their own destinies and are unabashed about their pursuit of the good life. What is conveyed also is an adroit deployment of words familiar in the earlier discourse. 'Freedom' and women's 'liberation' are two examples. The print media appears to have given vent to a collective feeling of the nation (read 'middle class') that at last the individual (read 'consumer') is *free to choose*. But it is important to recall that the language of the freedom struggle, of self-reliance and non-alignment that Indian men and women articulated in an earlier epoch, also stemmed from a desire for freedom and dignity.

The crucial difference is that freedom, choice, and assertion of autonomous selfhood were earlier linked to broader issues of social justice in the collective nation (the poor and the marginalised). Significantly, the onset of liberalisation has accompanied a concerted expression of the values of individualism and untrammelled selfhood. Furthermore, successful (often corporate) superwomen are too often posited as models from whom the women's movement could learn a lesson or two (see Chaudhuri 2000). Accompanying this has been a questionable suggestion that the increase in male models in advertising, the practice of holding male beauty pageants, and the presence in some adverts of a more gender-sensitive image of malehood spell the onset of a gender-equal era. Crucially, these new discourses and gender images effectively displace the largest section of Indian men and women from the public eye.

NOTES

1. Dalits have been traditionally regarded as the lowest in the caste hierarchy. Significantly, the Dalit movement in contemporary India has been very strong, and has also increasingly been making its presence felt in both domestic politics and academic research.

2. In the construction of the norm, the whole and the national have always been hegemonic and exclusive. But the dominant discourse on gender in the past had never quite so systematically excluded the poor and dispossessed. Indeed, some may argue that the working-class woman was privileged in discourse, even if not in action.

3. 'Today, publications are almost mortally dependent on advertising revenue. The cover price of publication brands move within a narrow band. While the material cost and news gathering cost of newspapers have gone up (several have folded up in the last few years), the cover price has remained stagnant. So the bottom line of any publication business can be pushed up only in advertising revenue.' (Ansari 1999)

4. Personal interview with the Senior Economist of the Investment Information and Credit Rating Agency (ICRA).

5. I have done a more comparative analysis elsewhere (see Chaudhuri 2000).

6. The Lintas advertising company conducted a market survey of target customers.

7. If the West talks of the break-up of the nuclear family, in our part of the world, it is the break-up of the joint family and the emergence of the nuclear family that is discussed.

8. In my fieldwork among Asian-Indian Americans, I found that a common complaint among the girls was that the Indian man just did not know his manners. He did not know how to court a woman. A Western man did.

9. Interestingly, my friends and acquaintances within the ad world and the corporate world actually mention 'power' as a 'high'. Both men and women do so.

10. I have dealt exclusively with this tension between these two trends elsewhere (see Chaudhuri 1996).

CHAPTER 5

'Feminism' in Print Media

Introduction

Twenty-five years ago, the Indian media tended either to ignore women altogether or confine its attention to the problems of middle-class domesticity. But when women's organisations initiated major movements against gender violence in the late 1970s, the media had its own role to play.[1] In the 1990s, we not only had a much greater visibility of 'women', but also explicit deployment of the term 'feminism' in the media. The women's question today is part of public discourse. As Butalia notes, 'At the national level today, it is no longer possible to ignore women. Whether it is with regard to planning documents, policy decisions, electoral politics and so forth, the question of the specific needs of women has to be addressed' (1993: 590).

I agree, but would like to suggest that today, along with greater visibility, there is also greater hostility. In the 1970s, the feeling broadly was that since the women's question had been so far neglected, it was entirely in order that redressive measures be taken. For it was widely believed that in India, 'the national legacy' was one where men fought along with women for women's rights. This is not the place to dispute this, or offer instances where the demand for women's rights did meet with substantive opposition.

The point that I seek to make is that there was an overt stated position of consensus and agreement that gender equality was desirable on the agenda of both the national movement and the state. As the women's movement intensified, and as the Indian state re-awoke to the women's question when the United Nations declared the International Women's Year and Decade in 1975, there was no expressed resistance or hostility at the national level. This was quite unlike the United Kingdom at the turn of the century, when feminism was 'ferociously attacked' (Walby 1997: 165).

Today the story is different. A comparison with the backlash in the US (Faludi 1991) and the UK (Faludi 1992) is in order.[2] Alongside the strength of the women's movement in India, we now have a more vocal opposition. The most dramatic instance of this has been the repeated failure of different governments to steer the Women's Reservation Bill through parliament. Less dramatic but equally clearly discernible are the negative views expressed in the popular media. This chapter takes note of the wider spread of feminist ideas, but believes that this dissemination is both complex and mediated. Academic/expert discourse and popular discourse intertwine and refashion themselves, often in an unintended form. I also contend that there is an intended resistance, but almost invariably this is couched not as direct opposition, but as alternative formulations of 'feminism' and as 'reasoned' calls for 'restraint'.

The two important social processes within which any meaningful reading of popular media and feminism can be attempted today are the women's movement and the process of economic liberalisation initiated in India. The two have very different geneses and very different trajectories. But as is the wont of history, there are times when disparate social processes meet and new social forms take shape. While the Indian state heralded the policy of liberalisation and the opening up of the Indian market in the 1980s, the tangible impact on the media, on the lifestyle of a new middle class, and on urban life in general made its presence felt only in the 1990s. Increasingly visible now are the more up-market magazines' projection of a post-liberalised post-feminism, where the individual corporate woman is the icon. And more middle-class magazines' enunciation of an authentic and traditional 'feminism' criticises 'so-called feminism' on the grounds that it portends ill for the family and the Indian woman—apart from being a Western luxury that a poor country like India can ill afford. The newspapers carry both versions.

I begin with an interpretation of 'feminism' understood essentially as a matter of 'choice', an articulation more visible in the up-market magazines. I seek to locate the rhetoric of choice within the larger process of economic liberalisation and its particular effect on the media. The second kind of representation, the positing of false versus authentic or traditional versus Western feminisms, I turn to later. I am less certain of where I ought to locate it. There are three possible contexts, all of which bear upon it. The first is a 'national' legacy of 'traditional' feminism articulated over the years by the nineteenth-century social reform movement and the national movement, which sought to distinguish itself from Western feminism and brought in new forms of patriarchy while allowing for new spaces for women. The second is the rise of the Hindu right with its call to return to 'tradition' and its aggressive defence against 'outsiders'. The third is a backlash opposed to the achievements of the women's movement and a general fear that feminism will destroy the extant patriarchal family, society, and culture. All three could coalesce in the popular voicing of 'traditional' feminism, although analytically and politically the three historical strands need to be addressed separately.

This chapter seeks to survey popular writings and their use of the term 'feminism'. I confine myself to a small slice of the print media, that is, some English popular magazines,[3] with an emphasis on women's magazines, and newspapers, apart from the newly emergent residential magazines of the large urban colony that I live in. I have followed these almost continuously since January 1993, apart from a break between 1995 and 1996. The two newspapers I perused are *The Times of India (TOI)* and *The Hindu*. *TOI* was an early starter in this process of commercialisation. It underwent dramatic transformations with the management deciding on increased circulation, a cut in prices, an explicit thrust on procuring advertisements, a shift from tenured editorial staff to contractual—to a point where they only had a managing editor. As the paper took on the looks of a tabloid, the circulation figures also soared.[4] *The Hindu* remains more conservative, but at the same time seeks to construct a profile for itself through advertisements marketing it as a serious person's newspaper, where the successful corporate executive would find the information he requires in these globalised times.[5]

The magazines I covered extensively were *Femina, Women's Era, Savvy, Cosmopolitan,* and lately, *Elle*. *Femina* was among the first women's magazines in India with the upper-middle-class urban woman as its intended audience. After a market research agency study in 1989, the management of *Femina* decided that the reader's interest had shifted from family and home to personal care. In the editor's words, '*Femina* worked to establish a genre of superwomanhood in India, so that nothing would stop ordinary women from achieving and acquiring extraordinary success' (Srilata 1999: 67). Yet, unlike *Savvy*, which the management of *Femina* defines as aggressively feminist, '*Femina* takes a balanced position' (ibid.: 66). *Femina* thus seeks to locate itself between the very up-market *Savvy* and the middle-class *Women's Era*.

Cosmopolitan advertises itself as 'Honest. Sexy. Smart' and is priced at Rs 50, as compared to *Femina*'s Rs 25. *Elle* targets an even more up-market audience with a thrust on glamour, fashion, and sex, and with features often taken from the Western media. Thus, liberalisation led not only to a massive growth of the media business, but also to increasingly differentiated market needs and distinct target audiences. As in the West, feminism tends to be represented to target audiences more in keeping with various publications' highly specialised market needs, which affirm the existing social order determining those needs (McDermott 1995).

LIBERALISATION, MEDIA, AND THE MATTER OF CHOICE

The print media underwent dramatic transformations with the onset of liberalisation. The term 'liberalisation' refers to the opening up of the Indian market by the Indian state to enable it to be more integrated into the global economy. As the commercial imperatives of the media intensified in an unprecedented manner, at the beginning of the new millennium we are in a better position to judge the impact of these changes on the Indian media. The central debate within the media world today is about the impact of liberalisation. A special issue of *Gentleman*, India's oldest magazine for men, carried this debate. As Vice-President of Bennett and Coleman & Co. Ltd. Bhaskar Das puts it, commercial imperatives have clearly gained central ground.

> The advertiser, thus, becomes the primary customer of the print media .... So, I, *the print media am not trying to get readers for my product, but I get customers, who happen to be my readers,* for my advertisers. My target audience becomes those whom the advertiser wants to reach out to .... People who have the disposable income, who have the attitude to buy and to spend ... readers who are successful, who celebrate life, who consume, who are early adopters, who believe in experimentation, who are hedonists. (Das 1999: 58; emphasis mine)

The 'trouble with print media is the high gestation period for returns and the high cost of production' (ibid.). The newspaper's or magazine's 'cover price alone doesn't cover these costs and ... print media cannot do without advertising as it accounts for 80 per cent of your revenue' (ibid.).

Journalists of a pre-liberalised era had viewed the role of the media differently. The print media in independent India had envisaged a constructive role for itself in the establishment of a successful fledgling democracy and the alleviation of poverty. The Director of the Press Institute of India, Ajit Bhattacharjea, bemoans the change:

> The responsibility of the media in a democratic developing country is not the same as in affluent advanced countries, where there is less of a gap between the privileged few and the under privileged many, and society has stabilized. Until the few, who include the policy makers and executors, are made aware constantly of the condition of the rest the gap will widen until the system breaks down. (Bhattacharjea 1999: 48)

The overall transformation of the media lies in the fact that today it is the sponsors who lay down the rules. It is not just advertisements that I am referring to. My survey of the English print media since 1993 shows that it is not only ads that are witnessing dramatic growth, but also features on ads, sales, and market strategies. Accompanying this are frequent write-ups on childrearing, housekeeping, domesticity, professional attire, and demeanour that are presented as news items or researched pieces, but are really sponsoring certain products. Articles on the lifestyles of the rich and famous, interviews with models and fashion icons, and cover stories on the consumption patterns of the new-generation Indian fill an increasing section of the English print media until we no longer know where the advertisement ends and the news begins.

I draw attention to this because it has a direct bearing on the manner in which a rising trend within the English print media represents women and 'feminism'. Feminism here mostly refers to the ability of an individual to make choices. I use just one instance to show how this blurring (of ads and features) takes place on the one hand, and how feminism is invoked on the other. The first is an article titled 'CORPORATE Elegance' in *eLAN: The Magazine for Successful Women* (August–September 1999). A piece on 'women at work' initiates the discussion by suggesting that 'dressing for work must rank high in the list of life's arduous-but-inescapable chores ... a dilemma', but suggests that better days are here now, for,

> Savio Barretto *presents workwear that will ease your journey into the boardroom* .... Women over the ages have learned to use their ingenuity, creativity, even daring to adapt .... So, is the Indian woman condemned to a lifetime of endless inevitabilities? .... Not really. Especially not if designer Anita Dongre has her way .... *And while what you choose to wear is really a very personal choice ... it's up to us designers to cater to that* .... Today's Indian woman ... is more comfortable with herself and her body .... *She is not afraid of trying new things, even what the close-minded*

> *call 'western'. And what's more, she is doing it all looking good.* (eLAN, August–September 1999: 62; emphases mine)

The idea of being unique in modern consumer societies suggests that one is fundamentally 'different' from everyone else. This, however, can be questioned. For while you seek to be different from those whom you consider your 'others', you seek to be the 'same' as those whom you identify with and aspire to be like. The phrase from the above quote that reflects this is: 'what you choose to wear is a very personal choice', but 'it's up to us the designers to cater to it'. The concept of identity is therefore necessarily defined by two opposites: sameness and difference (Heckman 1999: 5). As a proposition, this would be generally valid across time, but it needs to be reiterated that an individual identity understood as a self-conscious, *choice-filled*, reflexive project defines the existential terrain of late modern life.

This point needs elaboration. No culture eliminates choices altogether, yet tradition or established habit orders life within relatively set channels. Unlike the West, in India a colonially-mediated modernity followed by a Nehruvian model of development with a public stress on thrift and austerity offered not too many choices to the middle class. Liberalisation brought in its turn a public discourse redolent with ideas of 'choice'. It has been argued that modernity confronts the individual with a complex diversity of choices, but offers little help as to which options should be followed. A central consequence of this is the primacy of *lifestyle* and its inevitability for the individual agent. It is true that the term 'lifestyle' need not be solely associated with consumerism. In India, however, the association is obvious, for the entry of this entire package of ideas had a sudden and deliberate character. The corporate sector, advertising copywriters, management gurus, and media barons worked towards the dissemination of a concept of selfhood defined by choice and consumption.

The point that I seek to make is that a lot of financial and professional investment goes into the construction of an ideology of consumption, individualism, free choice, the good life, and 'feminism'. Yet this process of organised deliberation, production, and circulation is rendered invisible, further buttressing the idea that these ideas are natural and self-propelled. The new ideology celebrates the burgeoning growth of the market and also reminds the Indian middle class of the long years of denial under Nehruvian socialism. Both ads and features articulate the upper- and aspirant upper-middle-class desire to break away from a past public discourse that spoke of thrift and obligations to society—now perceived as an obstruction to the individual's desires and potential.

Surveys on new customer profiles, another new facet of the media, confirm this. I quote from a 'Response Feature' in *The Times of India* as an illustration:

> Some of the answers by the middle-income respondents to a recent indepth media survey conducted by India Today (April 15 1995) were 'at least buying a washing machine will make us feel like we have achieved something' .... '*living is not just a question of income but also of attitude*', get educated not just about your purchasing power, but instead about your choice over the purchase .... It emerges clearly ... that, apart from the metropolitan cities, even in the rural areas, and in emerging metros ... there exists a need to possess more as much as the simple need to try and keep up with the price curve. (*TOI*, 16 June 1995; emphasis mine)

I argue that liberalisation broke down a more traditional system of marking identities within the middle class. The sensualist replaced the intellectualist paradigm. 'The shift from producer to consumer capitalism has meant its disruption, which ... has brought the transience of new styles, the introduction of a new flattening temporality and the reduction of the self to the mere politics of presentation' (Lash and Friedman 1996: 18). I would hazard that this politics of presentation of the self can be evidenced in the corporate feminism of choice that I discuss below.

Feminism is 'Choice', Women's Activism is Imposition

Concepts like 'autonomy', 'freedom', and 'choice' can be read only within the historical context of their utterance. It is important to recall that the language of self-reliance and non-alignment of a pre-liberalised era also stemmed from a desire for freedom and dignity. There is a clear break with this notion of 'freedom' in the collective feeling today of the nation (read the middle class) that at last, the individual (read consumer) is free to choose. This break, I argue, also holds good for the manner in which the women's movement and feminist scholarship in India visualised freedom for women.

Issues of class, caste, tribe, poverty, and social justice formed an intrinsic part of feminist struggles, both in colonial and independent India. Autonomous women's groups which emerged in the 1970s debated with women's organisations of the left the centrality of class in the latter's formulation, a matter which tended in their view to obfuscate the specificity of the women's question. Both groups have moved a long way since then. While left groups have played a visible role in the women's movement, autonomous groups have increasingly taken up questions of economic deprivation and matters of class. The Dalit women's movement, in turn, expressed dissatisfaction with upper-caste women activists in both the left and the autonomous women's movements. But the core concern with social justice and inequity, however defined, has remained constant.

In contrast, the popular representation of feminism in the media reflects a retreat from questions of class, caste, and social justice. Quite clearly, feminism is read here as a matter of the individual woman's right to choose. The woman concerned is either the corporate woman or the high-powered consumer.[6] A deliberate break is sought to be made with the women's movement, but the language used for the construction of her image is, however, often appropriated from the women's movement. And this works, as all co-options do, 'as simultaneously a form of sharing in the spoils and a displacement' (Sunder Rajan 1993: 132).

One noticeable and significant example is the way that International Women's Day itself is marked in the media. International Women's Day has been traditionally celebrated by women's organisations and other political forces that aligned themselves quite unambiguously with democratic and progressive forces. We now have a riot of ads with the specific day's messages appearing on 8 March every year. Ponds has an ad titled 'The Millennium Miracle: A Curtain Raiser', with an image of a woman's mask, an hourglass, and some paintbrushes. The text reads:

> As we are poised for a flight into the year 2000, what does it portend for women? A closer look at the trend-setting explosion on the careers, fashion, fitness and beauty minefields .... She's what makes the world go round. Yesterday. Today. In the new millennium. And for eternity.

We then have the logo, with 'there's tomorrow because there's you'; 'Woman's Day—A Celebration of Womanhood, March 8th'. The ad is representative of high-powered beauty shows that have been marketed over the 1990s as matters of choice, upward mobility, success, and agency.[7] For,

> Girl who had the looks, the intelligence, the right style and confidence realized that it was possible to dream of fame and fortune ... the show has become a festival ... devoted to the quest of the complete woman .... Over the years the Miss India title has been the glitzy razzmatazz world outside—both nationally and internationally. (Patil 1992)

A very similar process took place with a host of ads celebrating India's fifty years of independence. The legacy of the freedom struggle was appropriated and endowed with a completely new set of meanings. Beauty pageants are presented in a historical continuum with the women's movement. By association, therefore, the goals of the women's movement and the goals of women participating in the pageants become one. It is not surprising, then, that protests by women's organisations and right-wing groups against the Miss World pageant held at Bangalore in 1996 evoked negative responses. It appeared illogical for the women's movement, which had been demanding the 'liberation' of women, to oppose pageants that were actually offering them avenues for unprecedented success and wealth. Even the local *Vasant Kunj Times* (December 1996), one of the neighbourhood magazines of the vast new urban middle-class colony where I live, carried an article titled 'The Miss World Contest: A Missed Opportunity':

> Remember the ecstatic moment when Aishwarya Rai was crowned Miss World 1994—the whole country was proud .... Then where did this ecstasy disappear when India decided on hosting the event on November 23? *Suddenly the women's lib activists sleeping from the day of their origin, woke up. They saw this even as the ideal moment to gain world wide publicity and TV coverage. Why don't these activists protest when a wife is battered badly by her husband? A girl is barred from getting education? When a bride is burnt to death and her parents-in-law acquitted? A woman made to abort her child?* (p.10; emphasis mine)

The *Rashtriya Sahara* (December 1996) wrote:

> When the big 'B' [actor Amitabh Bachchan] took the cudgels [*sic*] of bringing ... [the] Miss World Contest—to India *desi* feminists and the women's organizations were all out to stop him. This was taken [as] an

> attack on the Indian culture and even linked to the 'culture imperialism' [*sic*] .... [W]omen's organizations declared the contest a joke with a woman's body and chastity .... (p. 29)

Further, the report stated:

> Those supporting it argued that in this era of Bay Watch [sic], Cybersex, *feminists the world over are redefining their agendas and are looking at their exploitation as a systemic factor* .... Some put it differently, '*beauty contest may be degrading to the body and soul but the degradation is certainly less obnoxious than sati and rape*'. (p. 32; emphasis in the original)

Bachi Karkaria, a well-known journalist, attacked feminist arguments stating that 'the deification of glamour makes suckers of women', saying:

> *There is an authoritarian ring to these arguments because they are made by our appointed liberators and our anointed protectors. One couches its prejudice in the language of liberation, the other in that of morality.* But both end up endorsing a stereotype that, in fact, has vanished like yesterday's pimple.... To start with, it's arrogant in the extreme for feminists to insist that empowerment can be measured only against their authorised, approved, ISO-rated parameters .... *Alas, protesting* mahila mandals *don't further the cause of women; they further male-driven repression .... Yes, the status of women remains a cause concern.* But ... our indignant do-gooders should ... attack the real demons instead of tilting at the glamour-miles .... (Karkaria 1998; emphasis mine)

The objections to women's organisations appear to be three-fold: that there are more serious issues that women's organisations ought to take up; that beauty pageants are legitimate and viable modes of empowerment; and that women's organisations have no business to be 'appointed liberators' just as others have no business to be 'anointed protectors', thus blurring distinctions between defenders and opponents of patriarchal control. The new self-propelled woman belongs to the wider nation of unfettered selfhood discussed earlier. This, I would argue further, is antithetical to the concept of organised collective action. Women's movements (and I would think all collective movements) violate the idea of untrammelled selfhood and choice that late capitalism endorses. I would like to extend this argument by suggesting that the rhetoric of the liberalised 'self' coincides with certain recent trends in both Western sociological and feminist theory.

Sociological analyses of the self in production-centred capitalism identified 'discipline, control, "clock time", deferred gratification, and calculative rationality and the related values commonly understood as the Protestant Ethic' (Wearing 1998: viii). In more recent times, the 'pursuit of selfhood in such a society has been theorized as equally dependent on the complementary consumption-centred, hedonistic ethic that encourages the pursuit of selfhood through self expression, leisure, consumer goods and pleasure' (ibid.). Trends within feminism project 'leisure' as a 'heteropia', 'a personal space for resistance to domination, a space where there is room for the self to expand beyond what it is told it should be' (ibid.: 146). While this formulation of leisure challenges the idea of non-work as leisure, I would argue that in the Indian context, possibilities of 'resistance' are undermined as leisure itself is engulfed within the agenda of liberalisation. In practice, we have a mockery of liberation where, as Editor of Femina, Sathya Saran, says: 'Now men are grooming themselves, they're turning sensitive to what women expect of them .... Finally the new male gaze has surfaced because the female gaze has surfaced' (*Outlook*, 9 July 1997).

If organised movements are abhorred for denying choice, women's movements are loathed because they usually breach the normative order, the taken-for-granted reality. This taken-for-granted reality refers to the world of daily life known in common with others, and with others, taken for granted. These 'natural facts of life' are through and through moral facts of life (Garfinkel 1967: 35–37). For a patriarchal society, the patriarchal arrangement, norms, and behaviours are therefore both natural and moral. The women's movement, by questioning this, can thereby only be unnatural and immoral. Representations of feminism in the print media surveyed are therefore replete with terms like 'unnatural', 'excessive', 'irrational', and 'berserk'. It could be argued that it was only during the 1970s, when a significant new phase of the women's movement came into being, that a distinct 'allergy' attached to feminism grew (Desai, cited in John 1998a: 4). This is perhaps true to the extent that the more radical modes of protest and a more direct attack on patriarchy may have alienated a section that would feel more comfortable with a 'patriarchal' version of women's issues. But even a cursory examination of the Hindu Code Bill debate in the 1950s, the right to vote debates in the 1930s, the Age of Consent Bill debates in the 1890s, or the widow remarriage debates in the 1850s[8] would show that patriarchal resistance to change in the social order is severe and singularly unimaginative.

To return to the broader question of middle-class hostility to organised movements, I would like to claim that India's colonial history of struggles, whether by reformers, nationalists, peasants, workers, or women, were seen as part of the large anti-imperialist struggle and perceived as inherently moral and worthy. Therefore, unlike in the West, in India a formal consensus existed about the legitimacy of oppositional movements and organisations. Concern for the dispossessed formed part of the rhetorics of nationalism and entered the consciousness of independent India's middle class. Liberalisation ushered in the new Indian who disassociates himself or herself from movements, unless it is a question of celebrity endorsements of causes. The strength of dominant ideologies lies in their 'naturalness'. Where advertisements defining how we ought to live appear natural and celebrate choices, a campaign by a women's organisation to oppose this would appear as a violation of choice and a killjoy attack.

This aversion towards the women's movement and its protagonists finds more than an echo in the editorial comments of *New Woman* (October 1999), a popular women's magazine edited by film star Hema Malini: 'There has been so *much talk about economic empowerment for women lately*. It's a big difficult word, which many of *our simple women folk in the interiors* would hardly understand, a ubiquitous term *in all feminist jargon that is thrown about from Beijing to New York in all women's conferences* (p. 5; emphasis mine).

Another editorial (*New Woman*, February 1999) comments on the case of a woman who had charged the former advocate of Orissa of molestation:

> First, her husband deserts her, next she is branded insane, some dismiss her as a publicity monger, and still others gang rape her .... After a studied silence over the issue, it took a gang rape for our women activists to wake up to the issue .... Isn't that a shame? ... *On March 8, this year, most* Mahila Aghadi *leaders will cut ribbons, stage token protests, make speeches laced with new fangled jargon, because it would be politically correct to do so. Post gang-rape, it may now seem 'politically correct' for them to also add Anjana to their agenda.* (p. 5; emphasis mine)

A recent study that had interviewed media personnel found a similar aversion to the women's movement:

> Papers are very anti-women organizations. My boss ... says *that these people are all publicity conscious* and like themselves to be photographed. Most ... senior people look at these activists as shrill *women who keep screaming, and call them devious ....*
>
> Feminists are rabble rousing, dogmatic, West oriented, not rooted in [the] reality of India, not open-minded, anti-family and pro-divorce (Bathla 1998: 124–25; emphasis mine).

Women's mode of campaigning is seen as '*unnecessary ... shouting and screaming and jumping* over gates'. And:

> I found all these women wearing very good saris, all collected together, smoking cigarettes and *discussing women's issues* and holding rallies to get some publicity, that's all. (ibid.: 126; emphasis mine)
>
> Every day water goes, electricity goes and we do not make an issue out of it. So *why on a vague issue like women?* ... I do not think these are women's issues and sooner you remove the gender bias ... the better. (ibid.: 129; emphasis mine)
>
> I am more keen on how people have been treated by law and society as human beings and not as men and women .... *In fact society does not need feminism as much as the inter-relation of both men and women into humanism.* (ibid.; emphasis mine)

Feminists of 'choice' criticise women activists for their 'self-appointed role as liberators' and their 'protest mode'. However, unlike middle-class critics, they do not criticise feminism on the grounds that it is 'Western'. The more middle-class opposition, however, is made on the grounds of 'elitism', 'Westerness', 'cultural rootlessness', 'publicity seeking', and the alleged failure to take up 'real' issues.[9] I have argued earlier that concern for the poor was part of the nationalist discourse. Repeated mention of 'real' issues can therefore be read as part of a legacy of a society so marked by poverty and despair that any demands other than that of amelioration of poverty may be viewed askance. This, however, would be untrue, for this plea for 'real' issues is usually pitted against women's issues.

Of traditional and Authentic Feminism

In the representation of 'feminism as choice' and 'corporate feminism', we discern the more tangible impact of liberalisation.[10] At the other end of the representation, which speaks of 'a false (Western) against a true (Indian) feminism', we come upon a mix of attitudes. I have suggested at the very start that I am less sure of offering any one social cause as an explanation for 'traditional' feminism. I would like to understand it within a contemporary Indian context, which is informed by many factors: twenty-five years of a growing women's movement; a colonial history wherein the women's question was also articulated as a return to an authentic and ancient tradition of liberated Indian womanhood and not an aberration;[11] and finally, the rise of the Hindu right-wing, which has accompanied the processes of economic liberalisation. It is important to emphasise that Indian public discourse has been altering dramatically with the onset of economic liberalisation on the one hand, and a concomitant process to contain its cultural fallout by a call to return to an authentic/traditional Indian culture on the other. This culture can of course be saved and nurtured within the authentic/traditional patriarchal Hindu family by the Hindu mother and wife. It can certainly be argued that this ideological current of cultural revivalism has always been part of Indian public discourse. And so it has. I would, however, maintain that it is the relative ascendancy, the historical specificity, the emergence of new forms, and finally the hegemony of a particular ideological trend at a particular historical moment that need to be identified. The change in public discourse therefore does not mean that the constituent ideas themselves have radically changed; rather, it is the relative placement and endowment of new meanings.

I have contended elsewhere that the three distinct ideological tendencies in the nationalist discourse were liberal, socialist, and cultural revivalist (Chaudhuri 1996; see also Chapter 2, this volume). At an earlier period, the main contest was between the liberal and socialist vision, with cultural revivalism playing a more muted and also a benign role. We now have a very clear demise of socialist ideas. Public discourse is dominated by an aggressive cultural revivalism and a liberal worldview increasingly underwritten by consumerism, community politics, and the assertion of marginalised groups, be it caste, tribe, or women. We also have in our public discourse an unprecedented role for the media, an industry that has seen rapid growth since the mid-1980s. The increasing prominence of the media, it has been argued, signalled 'an industrialization of not only material cultural goods but also of "culture" in general' (Rajagopal 1994: 1660). The desire to splurge is accompanied by a consumerist celebration of 'Hindu' culture. In this vision, the 'women's movement' and 'false feminisms' are the villains responsible for the erosion of the qualities of traditional Indian womanhood.

Therefore, just as we discern a hedged response articulating *fears of a backlash* against the 'extreme' positions that feminism takes, its Western roots, and cultural alienation, we can actually sense a recoiling, a more overt fear that feminism is endangering the family, motherhood, and culture. It can well be argued that 'liberalisation' is responsible for the growth of an unbridled individualism that alters the parameters within which Indian women have always learnt to behave. We are therefore witnessing a worked-out attempt to redefine simultaneously a more traditional (read family-oriented) and market-friendly 'feminism'.

Through India's colonial history, an attempt was made to construct a lineage of feminism that was traditionally authentic and derived its roots from an ancient past. Academic feminism and feminist movements may have interrogated the idea of an unsullied glorious past. But this is one area of 'expert' knowledge (see the next section) which seems to have passed by the popular media.

The editorial of an issue of *Parenting* (February 1999) applauds a Supreme Court ruling in favour of women's empowerment thus:

> Women were revered in this country when our ancient civilizations led the world. Writers, thinkers, reformers of this century are again urging the same lost focus—women's uplift. In fact the *contemporary need is to celebrate the Rig Vedic times, who had the choices and reveled in her complete liberation* [*sic*]. A society that respects its women is twice blessed—as nurturer and mother she brings to it a sense of emotional and social well-being. Now with documented assertion of women's rights and emphasis on the development of the girl-child, we can hope to dream again. (emphasis mine)

The overriding view expressed is that while feminism is an acceptable ideology, some of its inadvertent or deliberate misuse ought to be condemned. This kind of writing is more evident in middle-class women's magazines, but is also found in English-language newspapers. *Women's Era* (2 February 1999), which claims to make 'happy homes', argues that '25 years ago, feminism'—which is defined as 'a change in the traditional role and image of women'—was 'comparatively well advanced in our country—but only as far as the highest levels of society were concerned'. Today, 'though feminism has spread much further ... the emphasis on the upper echelons persists'. But there is still 'a deeply ingrained male resistance to the granting of parity of women .... Men seem extremely reluctant to change their views about women' (p. 34). This may be in part

> because there are too many educated girls who think feminism means freedom to smoke, drink, wear vulgar clothes and indulge in free sex .... This is wrong. Women have certain functions (such as motherhood) which men cannot perform, and without which the race would perish. *Therefore feminism today should mean making women realize they are different from men, but not inferior to them* .... This can only be done by constantly exposing the hollowness of anti-feminism in males. (ibid., emphasis mine)

Modern India has witnessed the 'metamorphosis of a submissive, oppressed and uneducated Indian woman into an independent and able administrator'. Earlier, 'the Indian woman' was looked upon as the epitome of love, patience, and endurance, but also as a 'frog in the well with little general awareness and personal feelings'. Education 'played a vital role in bringing about a change in her physical attire and mental attitude' (*Women's Era*, 2 February 1999). However,

> there are always 2 sides of a coin. The *development of [a] questioning attitude has reduced her capability to adjust [to] her surroundings which in turn has been one of the causes of the rise of nuclear families*. As a result, many a senior citizen is compelled to lead a lonely life or put up in an old age home. Similarly, children of working mothers also long for her attention and care. *Ironically, her confidence and economic independence have only helped her come out of an incompatible matrimony to lead a solitary life*. (*Women's Era*, 2 January 1999: 38; emphasis mine)

Other articles are more forthright about the male backlash. 'Even as women fight gender bias and role stereotyping, men are forming organizational fronts to fight *aggressive females. Are we heading for a backlash from men whose efforts to help are being rebuffed by feminists?*' (*TOI*, 9 December 1998; emphasis mine). Speaking of the double burden that women labour under, the article points out that the aim of gender justice is to show that this sort of sexual division of labour is unfair because it places an unequal burden on women. But,

> *the trouble is that, in order to put this point across, a section of women have gone to [the] extreme. There was even a phase when being a mother and wife was decried. They bashed you on the head with extreme ideas, and came across as man-haters* ... we were regaled with stories of women attacking men with knives .... *It is as though feminism is suddenly going berserk.* The shift from passive victim feminism to power feminism is welcome; yes but who is to draw the line between rational and irrational? Obviously women themselves .... (ibid.; emphasis mine).

Warning of backlashes, it contends that '*the trouble with too much feminism is that it says little of women who routinely harass husbands and children; and, short of rape, perpetuate every sort of torment*' (*TOI*, 9 December 1998; emphasis mine). We saw that even self-professed voices of feminism expressed dissociation with women's movements. With the more cautious views that laud women's improved status in society and also address the issue of male resistance to change, we find a concern for what they term the 'other side of the coin' of feminism. Others are overtly hostile and actually caricature the idea of women's liberation itself.

Another article sharply attacks 'warped feminists' and contrasts them with 'authentic feminists'. We are told that 'the Wist [warped feminist] is "bold" and 'beautiful"', but are warned to 'look out for the guile behind':

> The Wist ... a woman in limbo ... her entrepreneurial ventures sometimes work, sometimes bomb .... her dad foots ... her bills .... *The ... idea of having a child is offensive* .... Marriage ... appeals to ... Wists ... it can lead to ... a lifestyle overhaul .... will not tolerate imposing in-laws or their kids ....
>
> ... The working-woman-Wist will rely ... on feminine wiles than ... hard work ... *they indulge in petty, sexual politics .... A straight feminist is .... in touch with the real implications of female roles .... to bear children, to shape young personalities, can also be considered the highest power ....*
>
> ... The availability and affordability of servants actually creates a unique condition for Wist_liberation. (*Society*, September 1994: 112; emphasis mine)

In contrast, we have the Bharatiya Janata Party's (BJP) high-profile leader Sushma Swaraj, an icon of what a modern Hindu woman ought to be, presenting herself as a role model in a write-up titled 'Wife, Mother, Politician: A Woman of Our Times'. She says:

> I was never discriminated against [for] being a woman and I have never been a victim of intrigues. The party has never denied me anything because I am a woman .... For two years, I took a break when my daughter was born because I did not want to keep an ayah .... The complete supervision was done by me and my mother-in-law .... I always feel that if one is dutiful towards the family then they will also support you. When I see the happiness on my devar's [brother-in-law] face if I give him a gift it fills me with happiness. If I give some thing to my father-in-law, ... his age gets lessened by two years. (Bal 1999: 12–13; emphasis mine)

Sushma Swaraj emphasises the fact that she faced no obstacles from any quarter—family, community, or party—to her success. She in turn has given time, labour, and devotion to her family, community, and party. Significantly, no mention is made of 'feminism' or the women's movement, or of any attempt to link her fortunes with other women.[12]

A recurrent feature in many of the writings is an attempt to suggest that there is an acceptance of real feminism. But it is not hard to discern the cynicism and denunciation of feminism. Derogatory asides are made even when feminism is referred to only in passing. A review of the film *Woh Chokri* remarks, 'That both the casualties of the politician's ambitions in the film happen to be women is purely chance. The director has gone on record to say that *he is no feminist (nobody is any longer)*' (*TOI*, 20 October 1994).[13] *Women's Era* (2 January 1999) carried a story recalling how 'during the 60s, there were several lovelorn students in our college but they did not have the courage to have a love affair openly' (p. 18), but 'now some decades later, the love scenario of the college campus has undergone dramatic changes' with 'permissiveness in sex relationships, *women's liberation and also the (bad) influence of candid, sex-oriented films and TV Programmes*' (ibid.; emphasis mine). A story titled 'Other side of the Coin' narrates the frolics of 'wives' and 'kitty parties', and recounts how one such woman was initially taken in, but 'finally she comes to realize that *women's lib has been thoroughly misinterpreted by the modern woman. Aj ki nari, kitty party main bhagidaari*' (today's woman, holders in 'kitty parties') (ibid.: 49; emphasis mine). Yet another article titled 'Emergence of a New Khalnayika' (anti-heroine) decries the interference of the girl's mother in her married life, and blames both women's organisations and the media for the 'direct onslaught on the very basis and foundations of this hitherto sacrosanct relationship: that of the husband and wife' (*Women's Era*, 1 August 1994).

HOW FEMINIST IDEAS HAVE TRAVELLED

A premise that informs this chapter is that ideas of feminism have entered public discourse, but that 'ideas' and 'concepts' tend to change their meaning and emphasis as they travel. Academic and/or expert discourses of all kinds do filter into popular discourse,[14] and the popular also influences the academic.[15] Both feminism of choice and traditional feminism are replete with such instances. This was evident also in a mix of writings: reportage of new lifestyles, which were informed by more gender-equitable concepts of marriage, parenting, and work; a frequent invocation of 'feminist expert knowledge', and caricatured depictions of feminists.

The significance of lifestyles in late modernity reflects itself in a growing genre of writings about changes in the notions of marriage, family, and parenting. With voluntary childlessness emerging as a reality, Pinki Virani investigates the alternative family pattern. She finds that there is a growing acceptance of the fact that maternal instincts do not come naturally to women. Citing experts, the report argues: 'Childless women don't feel motherly because there is no such thing as maternal pangs and ... nature initiates the maternal instinct only post-pregnancy in a woman so that the offspring is instinctively looked after' (Virani 1998). 'A Father's Touch' suggests different ways in which fathers can get involved in parenting and discusses how 'gender myths' can be 'destroyed' (*Parenting*, February 1999: 78–79). 'Men Behaving Broodily' reports on how 'males succumb to ... nesting urges' as 'today's females choose to put careers first' (*Gladrags* 1999: 122).[16]

On occasion, all three trends (lifestyle, expert knowledge, and caricature) would coexist. An instance of this is a debate on 'women bosses'. The critical male view states that 'male bosses have schedules and goals by which their competence can be judged', but 'female bosses have an additional agenda—propagating the ideology of feminism in management'. The female boss 'has a designer chip on her shoulder .... If she fails in her task, it was a male conspiracy that did her in. It's win-win situation'

(*The Sunday Times of India*, 7 February 1999): 'Female bosses have two excuses for their bouts of bad behavior—their body and their mind. Their body—which makes them *females and feminists*—is [a] hindrance, they claim' (ibid.; emphasis mine).

Labelling women bosses as 'among the most graceless creatures in nature', the article goes on to say:

> A feminist can succeed only if she becomes a pseudo-male. That's hilarious. I love it. *The ancient Amazon warriors must have given some such justification when they cut off one breast, so that they could hold a bow and arrow comfortably.*
>
> *Female bosses are like ideological or religious fanatics* .... Managing has little to do with the sex of the boss, except in bordellos where a feminine touch is necessary. (ibid.; emphasis mine)

The defence, written by a woman 'boss', anticipates a response where a woman boss conjures up images of 'a command-spewing dragon', a 'woman with a cigarette holder dangling between her lips', 'a feminist flag-raiser'. She argues that since in 'a male-dominated world, they constantly have to apply their emotional faculties to succeed', this 'makes them more stress friendly than men'.

> The so-called pinstriped wearing gruff chairman, presiding over an industrial empire may never have to stretch himself emotionally. For, at home he goes back to a pampered and cushioned existence. While the woman boss who hardly wears the pants at home, and sits gently on a swivel executive chair, might have survived *a day of no-gas, sick child, errant domestic, and a major deadline*! (*The Sunday Times of India*, 7 February 1999; emphasis mine)

The woman writer, who happens to be the editor of *Verve* magazine, invokes a feminist analysis of the public and private split. The male columnist brings the biological cycles of female bosses centre-stage. Feminism is posited as an unnatural, ridiculous, and fanatic ideology. The passing reference to Amazonian women cutting off one breast is a particularly powerful deployment of an image of feminists that sticks long after the article ends. Contrast that with the alternative image of the woman boss who has 'survived a day of no-gas, sick child, errant domestic, and a major deadline!'

An article by Visa Ravindran (1999), 'The Two Sides of Femininity', explores why 'successful women in public life are branded aggressive' and answers by saying that 'research says that masculinity and femininity are not a matter of social conditioning but biology'. She quotes, among others, Betty Friedan, who says, 'It is not easy for a woman to transcend or question the masculinism of a powerful, successful male institution. The first woman there will necessarily try to succeed according to the male model.' In an interview with the New Femininity group, one woman says: '*We have special qualities that belong to us as women*, and we do not intend to suppress those special qualities in the rat race for equality with men. We think the world would be a much poorer place without femininity, and we are worried that the world is going that way' (Ravindran 1999; emphasis mine)

Approvingly, Ravindran observes:

> This warning not to discard the feminine values in the name of a false equality was sounded by a clinical psychologist who considers the break-up of the modern family one of the sad outcomes of the race to achieve this false equality. *It must be pointed out here that encouraging feminine values in a world getting overly masculine would bring a better balance and replace the masculine with the feminine.* (ibid.; emphasis mine)

A letter talking of 'women's power' articulates the same point: 'Women have every right to choose the profession they want to pursue and their enthusiasm cannot be undermined. Yet, besides displaying an interest in such jobs one wonders if another reason that eggs them on is simply to prove that they are on par with men (*Savvy*, October 1998: 12).

The theme that women are 'equal but different' is a recurrent one. It has been argued that 'while the logic of aggression that governs the market including media cannot be wished away', 'there's no denying that *the female agenda is reconciliation rather than conflict*, for when men swagger into battle, it is the women who die' (Karkaria 1999; emphasis mine). An article titled 'Gender Talk' mentions that 'involvement is a quality which men could learn from us, women' (*New Woman*, May 1999: 42). Yet another, titled 'Politics: Women's Domain?', champions the participation of women in politics as 'this profession suits women eminently because they are *nurturers by nature*' and 'this work is part time and endowed with a definite purpose' (ibid.: 26; emphasis mine). On International

Women's Day, the *TOI* asked six 'high profile men why they'd like to be a woman'. The men reaffirmed that 'women have many innate qualities like endurance, determination, resilience and the capacity to give more love than they receive. Women's strength lies in softness' (*The Sunday Times of India*, 8 March 1998).

Liberal feminist ideas of equality have been counterposed to radical feminist ideas of 'difference'. Significantly, this appears more acceptable to both feminists of choice and traditional feminists. The reason for this is the double-edgedness of the concept itself. The tendency to gloss over 'difference' has been a problem in feminist thought that cannot be easily dismissed. But radical feminist assumptions of essential differences between women and men, and their call for separate women's spaces and communities, are equally problematic. They imply a return to an ontological explanation of human differences, introducing a tyranny of biological destiny historically used to circumscribe women's place in society. Not surprisingly, then, traditional feminists read in it an affirmation of the traditional gender division of labour, while corporate-sector feminists celebrate 'feminine' qualities of caring and sharing that have been traditionally marginalised in patriarchal societies. Feminist philosophers and historians have pointed to the historical specificity of the idea that men are political and rational, while women are more personal, emotional, and inclined to nurture. Landes (1988) locates the origin of these ideas in the work of Rousseau, Montesquieu, and other philosophers of the French Revolution, who inspired Republicans to banish women to the home and call men to their supposedly natural fulfillment in the world of politics. Thus, it could be argued that not only had the French Revolution banished women to the family, but it had also succeeded in imprisoning feminist theory and politics in its philosophical framework (van Zoonen 1991).

I would go further to argue that management theory itself is deploying ideas about women's 'emotional' nature for its own purpose. Part of the corporate sector's familiarity with feminist ideas generally, I suggest, is mediated by management literature.[17] The West has seen (as India is seeing) an unprecedented growth of the service sector, which is characterised by a very large female workforce. In this changed context, service-sector employers have been not only recognising, but also privileging 'emotional labour'. In a way, this means the acknowledgement of values traditionally associated with women, but marginalised in a patriarchal culture defined by other skills. 'Feeling management, as part of the valorization process, is a predominant aspect of the new service sector workplace' (Taylor 1996: 84). Total Quality Management (TQM), a widespread service organisational restructuring mechanism, argues that it 'empowers' employees to employ emotional autonomy during interaction with customers. Studies have shown that the management has devised intrusive supervisory and evaluative systems, which attempt to *prescribe* this 'natural' manner in line with *perceived* customer expectations (ibid.).

Occasionally, an article can be more unabashed about power, arguing that powerful women are like powerful men. 'Difference', in such cases, is clearly set aside. 'The Phenomenon of the Younger Man' in *Elle* (October 1999) narrates how 'the younger man is increasingly becoming the perfect accessory for powerful, older women'. And how it 'isn't a whatever-guys-can-do-we-can-do-better game but *a question of choice*, and whether one exercises it with freedom and a complete lack of self-consciousness'. While most of the stories covered are drawn from the West, we have a specific entry for India:

> *Feminist* Writer Sonal Shukla points out that the younger man, in a more basic version, has always existed in India. 'In certain villages in North India it was a common practice for a younger brother to marry the wife of his brother, if his brother died. The age gap between the two could very often be quite a bit.' She believes that what is happening in cities is only a more globalised version of the same phenomenon. 'But let's not forget *it's also a power-thing*. Just as younger women would look towards an older man for security and patronage, a younger man would do the same with a woman in power.' (*Elle*, October 1999; emphasis mine)

This invocation of a 'feminist' writer is disconcerting. The oppressive nature of levirate practices is well-known (Chowdhry 1994: 12). Academic discourses therefore do filter down, but often in a quite unanticipated manner.

While acknowledging that there is no one pure definition of 'feminism', and also that it is to the credit of the women's movement that many demands once thought of as feminist are no longer considered so,[18] I do not think that distinguishing between feminisms and anti-feminisms is too difficult a task. While feminism of choice does offer new spaces for some women, its attempts to disassociate itself from the women's movement in particular, and democratic movements in general foreclose any collective possibilities. 'Traditional feminism', while seeking legitimacy through invoking 'tradition and 'history', also prefers to render invisible India's history of women's struggles and progressive movements. I contend therefore that the affirmation of feminism evident in what is clearly anti-feminist writings in the media could perhaps be explained by the apparent 'national consensus' that exists about commitment to women's equality. Such a formal avowal of commitment to a principle while substantively reworking the principle itself is a strategy that the BJP has used very successfully with the concept of secularism. The coining of the term 'pseudo-secularism' rendered the secular project itself suspect. Few would disagree with the proposition that 'secularism' can be interpreted in either of two ways: the state's non-interference in religious matters or equal treatment of all religions. But this does not mean that the ideological hegemony of the majority religion becomes self-evident. And yet such a successful displacement has taken place. I fear that denigration of the collective feminist enterprise and hostility towards the women's movement in a language of 'authentic' feminism may lead us on to a similar path. As Winch puts it: 'The world is for us what is presented through ... concepts. This is not to say our concepts may not change; but when they do our concept of the world has changed too' (1958: 15).

NOTES

1. The media has had no mean role to play in bringing about the stream of legislations, a new sense of judicial, prosecutorial, and police accountability, and an increased demand for preventive and support services.

2. Both Faludi and Walby have shown that one of the features of the contemporary backlash is that it works by reversal. The feminist movement is blamed for the problems of women's lives, rather than being considered a potential solution. Instances of this are common in the Indian media, too, as are strategies of ridicule, trivialisation, and demonisation. But what cannot be overstressed is the specificity of our history—the legacy of colonialism, our difficult relationship with the West, the concerns of Indian women's and national movements, and more recently, the rise of Hindutva forces coupled with economic liberalisation—which shape the nature of the backlash.

3. According to the Indian Readership Survey conducted between July 1997 and June 1998 by the Media Research Users Council in collaboration with

ORG-MARG, only 6.6 per cent of readers accessed English publications (*The Hindu*, 19 October 1998).

4. An ad in the Brand Equity supplement of *The Economic Times* (a sister publication of *TOI*) reads: '[We] hate to admit it, but there's hardly any difference between *The Hindustan Times* and *The Times of India*.' A graph of comparative circulation figures accompanies the text, which reads further: 'Not editorially, of course. What we are talking about are the numbers': 546,212 copies in circulation. In 1993 the *TOI* figures were 171,079, as compared to *HT* at 343,763.

5. *The Hindu* (12 November 1999) has an ad depicting a young male executive saying:

> My days are so packed that there's no time for shopping. This is where living-room shopping comes handy. Through the pages of my newspaper, laptop, microwave or the stereo system. I first found them in the columns of *The Hindu*, before seeing them on the showroom shelves. So if you can't buy time, I suggest you buy *The Hindu*. It's a one-stop-shop for news and information.

According to the NRS 1997 findings, people with higher purchasing power have found a popular showroom. So have advertisers. A showroom that opens at sunrise.

6. For instance, well-known socialite and columnist Shobhaa De has a weekly column, 'The Sexes', in the magazine *The Week*. A typical column would be: 'Be Smart and Shut up a la Hillary Clinton' (De 1999).

7. For extensive discussion, see John (1998b).

8. For details, see Chaudhuri (1993) and Southard (1995).

9. Interestingly, Madhu Kishwar's (1990) argument about why she is not a feminist articulates similar issues.

10. For a detailed discussion of the transformation of India's post-liberalised middle class, see Deshpande (1997).

11. This understanding expressed itself in the recent controversy about Congress (I) president Sonia Gandhi's foreign origin, when the Shankaracharya of Prayagpeeth argued that 'Sonia is as pure as Sita in the Ramayana and the BJP was committing a grave sin by raising doubts on her being Indian'. Quoting an instance from the epics, he said, 'Those who had disrespected women in history, like Ravana, Kansa and Duryodhana, have had to pay dearly for their sins' (*The Hindu*, 15 September 1999).

12. In the 1999 Parliamentary elections, Swaraj contested against Sonia Gandhi on the basis of the slogan *desi* vs. *videshi* (national vs. foreign).

13. The declaration of a premature demise of feminism and the women's movement has been a recurring theme in the West (see Rhode 1995).

14. By way of examples, genetics, psychoanalysis, and feminism.

15. This chapter itself can be read as such, and is a good example of the over-determination of academic and popular discourse.

16. *Gladrags*, run by Maureen Wadia, wife of a leading industrialist and herself a well-known socialite, also conducts a very high-profile 'Man Hunt'.

17. *Ascent*, a supplement of the *TOI* which advertises jobs, often carries features reflecting this. A feature on 'a brave new world' thus claims that companies of the twenty-first century will have to offer more progressive policies that will understand key family issues. And prospective employers are warned that the future employee may legitimately ask questions about 'how women progressed in the company and what care the company had for them' (*TOI*, 16 August 1995).

18. For instance, equal wages in the West (Walby 1997: 163). Walby also makes the interesting point that there are women who say, 'I am not a feminist but', and then say and do things usually identified with feminists. So feminism is not dead, even if the word is not used in some quarters.

CHAPTER 6

A Question of Choice

Advertisements, Media, and Democracy

India is widely seen as the world's largest democracy and increasingly also as a major economic player, a role attributed to India's new economic policy of liberalisation initiated in the late 1980s. Proponents of both democracy and free market economy speak in the language of individual freedom and choice. A principal tenet of liberal democracy is that of a free media. Exponents of modern market economies argue that advertisements create the necessary conditions for 'free choice', a pre-requisite for a successful functioning of democracy. It could, however, well be argued that the media's financial dependence on corporate advertisements logically erodes its autonomy and thereby its role as the fourth estate of democracy. This is an old debate, but one that has acquired significance in India more recently with the onset of liberalisation.

The Context

Indeed, this chapter has to be read in the specific context of liberalisation, the rapid growth of the advertisement industry, and its impact on the media. Central to the rhetoric of advertisements in this period have been the concepts of choice and freedom that I seek to interrogate in this chapter. We have seen major and dramatic changes in both the print and electronic media from the mid-1990s to the mid-2000s. The most evident of these changes has been the number of channels on television, the additional supplements of newspapers, and the increasing presence of new and glossy magazines. The more obvious of the changes has been the apparent proliferation of 'choices' that an individual has. The less obvious of the changes has been the control of corporations on the media through ownership, and indirectly through advertisements. I seek to explore in this chapter the contradiction between the very visible surfeit of choices that the media consumer has today and the much less visible constraint that the market wields over the media. This constraint decides both the range and limits of choices, but operates in a manner that renders this control invisible. This it does through the closed circle of ideas with which advertisements operate. These ideas suffuse the media, blurring the boundaries between what is recognisable as an advert and that which may well pass off as a feature, news, or even an editorial (Inglis 1972: 101).

I argue here that advertisements in media have functioned as rhetorics of India's project of economic liberalisation to alter the central motifs of Indian public discourse. The new Indian state in 1947 had stressed on growth with equity, not only as a model of development but also as a critical slogan that defined independent India's public discourse. Development was projected as an important goal of the state, for growth alone was seen as the answer to feed, clothe, and provide shelter to India's poor. The poor, the peasant, and the worker were imagined as the significant people that the nation constituted itself of and whom the state had to address itself to. Gandhi's choice of apparel dramatised the social concerns of the national movement. Socialist reservations about the fallout of a free market for India expressed itself in the formation of the National Planning Committee by the Indian National Congress way back in 1938, an early precursor of India's path towards a state plan-oriented development.[1] This is not the place to talk about India's experience of a mixed economic development. Many would be sceptical of the nature of state licensing that it spawned. But few would perhaps deny that the state had to keep in its rhetoric a commitment to an expressed concern for the social security of the poor. The state itself now speaks of equity with efficiency;[2] the earlier slogan was growth with equity. While the state therefore finds it difficult to shift its rhetoric entirely, the actual contents of its policies speak the language of the market. Advertisements are freer to speak an unabashed language of individual consumption, freedom, choice, leisure, and privileged pleasure.[3]

My questioning of the concept of 'choice' is therefore linked to the concept of the 'individual' and 'individual freedom', increasingly evident in the context of today's ascending ideology of market liberalism. Furthermore, the relationship between the apparent freedom of the individual and the freedom of the press in a market-dominated context is fraught with the contradictions between the freedom of the consumer/ reader to choose and the market control on the media, which erodes the 'freedom of the media'. This addresses the thorny question between representative democracy and capitalism. As Therbon (1977) points out, capitalism as an economic system implies a society in which the imperatives of capital accumulation are dominant. This 'rule of capital', as he calls it, runs counter to the 'rise of democracy', which implies a form of state in which electoral power has been equally distributed on the democratic principle of 'one person, one vote', and where the basis of representation is not wealth and influence, but universal suffrage and the 'sovereign will of the people'. Can these two principles coexist? Are they compatible or will they always be in conflict? And if they are in conflict, which will win? These are questions that have been intrinsic to the debate on liberal democracy.[4]

Therbon's central contention that the 'rule of capital' necessarily runs counter to the 'rise of democracy' was turned on its head by the rhetoric that arose after the quick and dramatic collapse of the existing socialist states. A euphoric sense of the inevitability of capitalism and its supposedly necessary corollary, democracy, marked global discourse after 1989, the year that saw the beginning of the dismantling of socialist states. It is important to emphasise that it is in this global context, at the same point in time, that India's own tryst with liberalisation began. In India itself, an adequate appreciation of the sense of 'collective relief' of the middle class to the opening up of the market has to be understood not only by the sheer logic of the availability of a large range of consumer items previously unseen, but also by the belief that the state had monopolised the media, particularly the state-owned television and radio. I write 'collective' in quotes for it is the articulated opinion emergent in the media that 'voices' and 'frames' this collective. And a legitimate wariness existed about the centralised control of information.

THE ARGUMENT

A significant point of departure for us here in India is the fact that while the media opens up, while corporations actively recast the media, the state prerogative and primary importance accorded to issues of 'national security'—itself a highly potent and possibly contested concept—continue. It is therefore even more pertinent to explore what exactly 'choice' means, and pose the question: Are we overemphasising the power of advertisements if the state does exercise almost absolute power in some spheres? This in turn leads us to the question of spheres itself and the kind of ranking and prioritising that the state accords to different issues like 'national security', 'development', 'freedom of expression', and to different sections of India's populace—the poor, the middle class, the rich. Such an exercise may help to clarify the concept of choice itself.

I would argue that as the state's agenda shifts away from a professed commitment to the real 'mass' of people—workers, peasants, tribals, students, women, the less mobile middle class—the rhetoric of abstract 'national security' gains ascendance. It is an abstract commitment to 'national security' rather than a tangible accountability to its people that the state spouts forth. One of the seamier sides of globalisation that we stand witness to is the coupling of aggressive market liberalism with revanchist cultural nationalism.[5] Finding the enemy of the state becomes the prerogative of the nation. Alongside this obsessive concern with the security of the state (also read as the free way of life), manifest most grossly in the United States of America's policy of war against terrorism, runs the debate between market liberals and their critics.

In the past few years, India has seen the opening up of the media to the private sector. Market liberals such as Murdoch have forcefully tried to put forward their argument that 'market competition is the key condition of press and broadcasting freedom, understood as freedom from state interference, as the right of individuals to communicate their opinions without external restrictions. Market-led media ensure competition. Competition lets individual consumers decide what they want to buy' (Keene 1991: 52). State-protected media are also criticised for ignoring the interests of advertising. It is argued that the media should simultaneously provide two services, supplying programmes to audiences and audiences to advertisers. Other criticisms levelled by market liberals concern the paternalism of state-protected media and the fact that it squeezes, confines, and reduces choice (ibid.: 53–56).

Critics of market liberalism, on the other hand, have been appalled by the systematic envelopment of human consciousness by corporate speech:

> Following Adorno and Horkheimer, they condemn advertising for universalising false images of abundance, novelty and freedom of choice. In reality, says its critics corporate advertising encourages individuals to fling themselves onto the treadmill of commodity consumption .... *Advertising deadens the nerves of civil society.* It seduces citizens into using and discarding some things and into disregarding others. Private desires stifle public spirit: nobody cares a nickel about anybody but

> themselves. Profanity, mindlessness, glitz and waste triumph (Keene 1991: 84; emphasis mine).

The point in question is that a sociological understanding of advertisements ought to steer clear of assessing the impact of an advert by its immediate fallout in terms of an increase in the sale of the object advertised. What is of far greater significance is that as a whole, advertisements create a culture of entitlements that make the notion of a good life marked by ideas of a just and free medical system, common and equal education, and a wholesome and lovely environment both dull and silly.[6] Or worse still, they create an atmosphere that forecloses such questions from being asked. It thereby 'manufactures a product of its own: the consumer, perpetually unsatisfied, restless, anxious, and bored. Advertising serves not so much to advertise products as to promote consumption as a way of life' (Lasch 1978: 72). This is what is meant by 'the closed circle of ideas' or 'the magic system'. Once these ideas suffuse public discourse, the possibility of dissent itself is threatened.

My study is based on my almost regular perusal of some English newspapers and magazines, namely *The Times of India* (*TOI*), *Hindustan Times* (*HT*), *The Hindu*, *Women's Era*, *Femina*, *India Today*, *The Week*, and *Outlook*. The scope of such an exercise is limited to the English medium and the metropolitan cities. The English readership in India, although insignificant in terms of percentage, wields an influence that cannot be accounted for by numbers. Their self-proclaimed exclusiveness and their simultaneous claim to have an all-India reach are an essential part of a pattern of development intrinsic to globalisation, which is integrally a topdown and exclusivist process. The logic of such a process leads to a development that is uneven and fragmented, at the international, national, and the local levels. In this entire process, advertisements play a critical role, making one world of people and things more visible and rendering another world invisible. As we thumb through the glossy pages of these magazines, pages of advertisements beckon us into a world of the rich, the famous, the successful; their work and their leisure, their public and private images.

I do not deal here only with the images that these advertisements beckon us with. I have dealt with this aspect exclusively elsewhere (Chaudhuri 1998b, 2001). I address here the broader question of the relationship between advertisements and the media on the one hand, and between an advertisement-driven media and democracy on the other. Critical to this discussion is the question of how one identifies an advertisement. It has been suggested that recognising an advertisement is an easy business, something which audiences 'routinely accomplish'. The implicit intention to sell seems the deciding core that differentiates advertisements from other kinds of messages conveyed by the media (Pateman 1983). In fact, advertisements differ from each other in significant ways that can lead to three distinct kinds of advertising: direct advertising, shared advertising, and indirect advertising. Direct advertising refers to advertisements commissioned by manufacturing companies and produced by agencies. It is what we most commonly understand as adverts. Shared advertisements is where the expense of an advertisement may be shared by two or more interested companies, or, in the case of 'advertorials', by the magazine and the manufacturer. Indirect advertising refers to the support that successful promotion or marketing can provide, upon which all forms of advertising depend. My own study of the English print media suggests that this is a form that has acquired salience.

Manufacturing companies or hired agencies and public relation services work to provide magazines with up-todate product information. This kind of promotion aims to encourage journalistic attention in the hope that it will reap favourable 'free' advertising benefits. The scale and significance of indirect advertising is hard to detect, as it may be incorporated into a magazine article or consumer advice page at the discretion of journalists and editors (Myers 1983).

I attempt therefore to peruse the more indirect manner in which commerce makes its presence felt in the pages of the media. However, I confine myself to the text of the media with the intention of recording: (*a*) the debate within the media world on the need for and impact of advertisements; (*b*) the case that the advertisement industry itself makes for its own increasing role in the media; and (*c*) the imprint of the language of sponsors in the advertisements themselves. The last is a methodological point for all too often, we discuss advertisements in such a way as to almost empty them of sponsorship. This trend has acquired greater salience with studies that have demonstrated that the consumer is not a passive entity but a creative agent, who can both subvert and transform the meaning that sponsors inscribe on the adverts. This may well be the case for one or the other advert, of one object or another. Advertisement companies know that. The effectiveness of a particular campaign is not our concern here.

It is the generalised impact of advertisements as a whole that alter public discourse. Subversion, as we all know, operates within the paradigms laid down by the dominant section.

In the next section, therefore, I attempt two things: (*a*) draw upon writings by people who are in the business of selling, of promoting advertisements, and media managers; (*b*) draw attention to the increasing volume of features which are about advertisements in the media. Both processes reflect a proactive role played by the advertisement industry to argue out their case in the media. Central to their discourse are the core ideas of choice and freedom, individual liberty, and the free market economy.

ADVERTISERS AND THE LANGUAGE OF MARKET LIBERALISM

This chapter, as will be evident by now, rests on the assumption that advertisements are a vital component in the organisation and reproduction of capital. I have argued that the ideological role of advertising in society extends far beyond this limited commercial extent. The significance of advertising cannot be gauged only by looking at how effective a particular advertisement is in terms of selling the intended object, even though that may well be the yardstick of the copywriter. The sheer power of the advertisement industry ought to be gauged by the simple fact that no newspaper or magazine can really be commercially viable without advertisements. An analysis of advertisements in the print media therefore has to be located in the context of the overall transformation of the media, where advertisements that you booked and paid for were really old stuff; the real thing was what you got through ordinary news (Williams 1980).

Public discourse has ceased to talk about issues of social justice.[7] Instead, the media regales us with the 'happening' places and people. The Page 3 phenomenon is now also part of the electronic media. These are not advertisements as we commonly understand them, for no product is being promoted. Instead, what gets reported and talked about in the media tends to encourage a condition of unbroken purchase and prodigality. It redefines the 'good life'. I quote a typical instance from a leading newspaper. The 'news' item titled 'Bhang, Booze and Bonhomie: Holi Menace Sweeps City' reports, among other happenings, a party planned at the home of a journalist: '"We're having a Holi bash for the consecutive year" informs

Shukla, who has ensured that his "family-and-friends affair" turns out to be the talk of the town. "I'm expecting my politician and bureaucrat friends, besides those from the TV industry and the fashion fraternity"' (Arora 2001).

What to me seems significant is that proponents of this change in India, while arguing for a decisive role of the market, move beyond a defence couched only in the language of sale. They also articulate a worldview. They state that the long years of independent India's tryst with planned development is passé. And today, India is a society that has become 'plural'. 'And in a plural society, if you try to impose one opinion, a difference of opinion starts' (Das 1999: 58). Plurality here does not refer to India's fabled diversities—ethnic, religious, economic. What it does refer to are individual differences in taste and choice. This change in meaning accompanies many others, the concept of social commitment for one, which itself is posited against individual choice. 'You can't be an isolated island thinking that you have a responsibility of changing society's heart. People are aware of things .... We are not a homogenous lot .... Every individual is unique ....' And, 'there may be violence in the front pages of newspapers but the reader may not be interested in it any more. He may go for sunny side journalism only.' The tale that hangs thereby is: 'If you manage to help your reader in becoming successful, then he will stay with you. Also, when he's successful he celebrates, and when he celebrates he consumes more. And when he consumes the advertiser is satisfied. That is the cycle' (ibid.: 60).

What we have is a simultaneous focus on 'selling' and a construction of an ideology of consumption, individualism, free choice, and the good life. We are therefore flooded not only with advertisements telling us to buy, but also with messages that rearticulate how the Indian middle class ought to think.

As mentioned earlier, the media has been witnessing not only advertisements, but also proliferating features on advertisements and the good life. That the American public relations magazine in India, *Span*, carried special features on advertisements in 1998 reflects the sense of optimism in an ascendant capitalism, both globally and in India. The gist of the articles was that, 'Advertising can drive down prices in a competitive market. It offers us a variety of choices. It can also help us to vicariously fulfil our fantasies of freedom and adventure without having to play basketball like Michael Jordan' (Hood 1998: 8). Most significantly, advertisements are part of a discourse on the free market and democracy. It is denied to those who live in other kinds of societies. The post-1989 public discourse has increasingly veered towards a position which states that unbridled capitalism alone can ensure democracy.

> *Commercial advertising,* at *least,* is *found only in societies where individuals have the right* to choose *their own goods and services* from competing suppliers. Ads convey critical information about price, quality and availability. Furthermore, in many cases ads are indistinguishable from the product; to consume is to express yourself through the symbols that ads have invoked .... As in other areas of our lives—such as *family* or *faith—free enterprise is a means by which we seek meaning and enjoyment.* The extent to which advertising contributes to that function is greater than is usually perceived. (ibid.: 8–9; emphasis mine)

This conjoining of family and faith with free enterprise is immensely significant in suggesting both the naturalness and the sanctity of a market economy. What else could be more sacred, more important to a person than family and faith? For our purposes, how much more evident can the ideological role of advertisements be? Images are powerful in advertisements. Referring to the power of these images, John Hood, president of the John Locke Foundation, a think-tank based in North Carolina, writes:

> Whatever the source, it is obvious that in these cases the advertising becomes, in a way part of the good being purchased. To some extent, the buyer of a new mustang convertible is buying the feeling that the advertisements for the convertible have expressed ....
>
> .... The desire for goods and services to make our lives safer, cleaner, easier and more enjoyable is already implanted deep within us. What advertising does is merely to bring that desire out into the open, and give it a distinct form. (Hood 1998: 10; emphasis mine)

The argument that Hood makes here is two-fold: *one,* that advertisements play a crucial role in the making of a free and democratic society; and *two,* that the desires that advertisements articulate are yearnings that are deeply embedded in humankind. Stated differently, it implies that consumerism is natural, neither socially constructed nor historically specific. It is important to note that the extracts that I quote are not advertisements, but from a carefully crafted essay legitimising advertisement as both essentially fair and virtuous. Hood approvingly cites James Twitch, who observed;

> Advertising is simply one of a number of attempts to load objects with meaning. It is not a mirror, a lamp, a magnifying glass, a distorted prism, a Window, a trompel'oeil, or a subliminal embedment much as it is an ongoing conversation within a culture about the meanings of objects .... *It is language not just about objects to be consumed but about the consumers of objects* (Hood 1998: 10; emphasis mine).

Readers will notice that my sources are from the popular media in India. I did not have to do a search to locate articles on advertisements. Indeed, my study started with a concern for the images in the 'real' adverts, but I found out soon that something else was happening here. A self-conscious attempt seemed underway to build a discourse on advertisements in the popular print media. The 1990s had euphoric articles on advertising, for it is 'the life-blood of modern business'.

> Liberalization hasn't catered to any other sector as it has done to the Indian advertising Industry. The pace of its growth kept scaling up since then and attained propositions for the market watchers the world around. With near stampede of products in the market it was inevitable. Gone are the days when you had the choice of selecting products from the limited national brands. Today the multinationals seem to have penetrated into almost every consumer product range. (Badal 1997: 110)

The ideological role not only celebrates the burgeoning growth of the market, but also reminds the Indian middle class of the long years of denial under Nehruvian socialism. Men and women depicted in the advertisements speak for the entire upper and aspirant upper-middle classes' desire to break from a past where public discourse spoke of thrift and of obligations to society—now perceived as obstructions to the individual's desires and potentials. Along with the dismantling of red-tapism, licences, and restrictions, Indian men and women have also been 'freed'. I present below a very typical reminiscing of the 1980s:

> If a style guru ensconced in some temperate clime deemed tight (Guess!) jeans in ... I had to be seen in a pair .... That meant, in those

> pre-liberalization days a visit to the friendly neighbourhood smuggler's. Since I was a student and my father wasn't Dhirubhai .... that meant also parting sorrowfully with the grimy notes saved from a meagre allowance. All for that pre-washed, light blue work of art. Or beseeching letters were sent off to American cousins. (*Saturday Times*, 12 December 1998)

My central contention has been that an analysis of adverts alone is not enough. One has to bring to notice the proactive manner in which the corporate sector and the advertisement industry themselves make their presence felt in the media. Integral to this is the increasing number of opinion polls and surveys conducted by the corporate sector on the readers/customers/audience. The distinctions between these categories necessarily blur. The 'reader', you will recall, is really the 'customer', and today the advertisement industry is brainstorming about who the customer is. I draw on just one or two such reports of surveys conducted. These surveys make explicit the rationale on which advertisers operate, but which disappear from the text of the advertisement itself.

'What drives Sybil?', a lead article in *Brand Equity* (a supplement of *The Economic Times*), debates on possible Indian customer profiles. 'The AP Lintas universe prefers to slice Indian consumers into survivors, savers, enhancers and splurgers .... The urban and rural poor are survivors and savers are the middle classes. Enhancers are the urban upper class, and splurgers the rich' (*Brand Equity*, 16–22 June 1999). It is widely known that product advertisement has generally given way to lifestyle advertisements. Hence, the language of advertisements is more about the consumer than the object to be consumed. The advertisements themselves therefore provide overt profiles of the new generation. Advertisements demand that the media seek an audience that is 'hedonist', likes to 'experiment', and has an attitude to spend.

There are two points that I wish to make. *One*, that an entire commercial apparatus, equipped with high-end technology and trained researchers, has been engaged in recasting the image of an Indian as a consumer who is seriously engaged in the business of spending. *Two*, the category of 'splurger' is of special interest for marketers, and therefore for advertisers. Not all can afford the wonders that advertisements project. But they can desire and aspire to be like them. A new normative Indian has slowly come into being. I find David Chaney's observation of interest, where he tries to show how 'the new social form of lifestyles was coloured by some of the broader narratives of the cultural forms of consumerism', summarised under the headings of 'fantasy, excess, spectacle and citizenship'. The first three are reasonably self-evident. The last is not. Chaney's reason for using it is that he found no better way of putting the idea that mass marketing, as with other forms of mass democracy, offers the illusion of equal participation and, indeed, even the glory of 'national culture' without much of its substantive powers (Chaney 1994). This, I think, is a very useful way of understanding advertisements and the images they extend. Everybody can look at and hear the advertisements (although many in India still do not have access to TV sets or radios). Few can read advertisements. Fewer still can read English advertisements. The numbers that can actually possess the goods advertised would be smaller still. But theoretically, everyone has access to advertisements, to the pleasure of looking, of desiring.

While the advertisement industry has its own research apparatus to explore changes in the new Indian (customer), there are other sponsored surveys also conducted on different segments of society. One such survey of college students conducted in the major cities affirms that this new generation of students is unapologetic about its competitive attitude to life and unabashed self-interest (Pathak 1994). Such attitudes, the survey suggests, were markers of the 'maturity' of the New Generation, as opposed to their 'honest but immature' predecessors who swore by Che Guevara and looked for 'causes' to uphold. While 'this generation is probably the most lonely, calculating, overstressed generation of youngsters that India has ever seen', it is optimistically concluded that this singular emphasis on 'individualism' might well lead to a collective good. 'The New Generation might well be the harbinger of a social revolution.' With the collapse of the socialist world, 'social revolution' takes on new meanings. And the advertising world has been quick to seize the lexicon of an earlier era of movements and radicalism towards their own ends. The women's movement has been no exception to this process (Chaudhuri 2000).

We have thus been witness to a constant process of new meaning making in advertisements. Further, we have also been seeing a sophisticated deployment of what scholars have understood as distinctions between the functional and emotive function of words. In the former, one applies what is called a 'linguistic rule', the role of which is to stabilise responses to a word. Definitions hold good for the functional or cognitive function of words. But for the emotive, the suggestive there is no linguistic rule to stabilise meanings. In Stevenson's system, therefore, emotive meaning is something non-correlative to and independent of descriptive (or cognitive) meaning. Wondering about the meaning of ethical terms, he asks how 'an ethical sentence acquires its power of influencing people—why is it suited to suggestion? He answers that ethical terms are emotive; that is, they 'produce ... *affective* responses in people. It is an immediate aura of feeling which hovers about a word. Such tendencies to produce affective responses cling to words very tenaciously' (https://credoinunumdeum.wordpress.com/2007/07/21/c-l-stevenson-on-the-emotive-meaning-of-ethical-terms-a-review-and-critique; accessed 17 April 2017). The words 'license' and 'liberty' are good examples of how meanings change, a point that Lodge makes (Lodge 1978), and one illustrated more recently in a media article (see http://www.thehindubusinessline.com/todays-paper/tp-opinion/when-liberty-becomes-licence-dictatorship-is-near/article2168908.ece; accessed 17 April 2017). Bakhtin (1992) had stressed that contexts are already textualised.

The new-generation Indian, I argue therefore, steps into a world rich in new meanings and allusions. Words have histories embodied in them. For instance, the word 'freedom' needed to be appropriated and given new meanings in a changed political-economic context. Advertisements, I argue, have been crucial in the story of appropriation and reinventing in a liberalising India.

Is this an Ad? The Blurring of News, Interviews, and Adverts

Features and write-ups on the advertisement industry and reports on various commissioned surveys are not the only ways in which the new ethos of commerce makes its presence felt in the media. My survey of newspapers and magazines since 1993 indicates that while *The Times of India* moved in the direction of commercialising early (with its price cut, dismissal of tenured editorial staff, its range of supplements, city editions dealing almost exclusively with lifestyle articles), it was really the forerunner of a practice whose presence can be felt in almost all publications. A number of national newspapers now regularly publish business supplements that report on the progress of important industries, be it fabrics, tourism, telecommunications, steel, information technology, or advertising. The spread and success of such supplements are themselves a measure of the deep penetration of the communication system by the corporations.

Newspapers and magazines are increasingly awash with columns on changing lifestyles, the social circuit of industrialists, diplomats, and socialites. In all, an entire ethos and structure of beliefs are created, which comprise the ideology of advertising and of its sponsoring system. A typical feature in *The Saturday Times* (supplement of *TOI*), titled 'Take A Break This Sunday', reads:

> Today we find ourselves in the midst of a cataclysmic change. The work place is metamorphosing into an intensely competitive, consumerist, sometimes savagely professional environment, where every yuppie is competing for a foothold on the career ladder for fat pay cheques, fatter perks and fancy titles. It was bound to happen when the economy opened up. Undeniably, the multinational way of life is here to stay. (*Saturday Times*, 17 December 1994)

The reader gets to know what people do to have a break. Yoga, music, the 'Once a month I fly down with my family to our farmhouse in Bangalore' all tell us the kind of things we can do or dream of. Advertisements build on this, telling us further what to do with our workplace, our leisure, our family and privacy. There is a feeling of boundless new possibilities to be explored through the boundless new products that arise every day. The articles, the focus, the advertisements form a continuum. The reader, in a very real sense, can move from an article like the one above on 'weekend breaks' to an advertisement without any sense of rupture. It is a curious fact that a sense of continuum is conveyed in the print media, newspapers in particular, between very disparate kinds of writings. For instance, we have a medley collection of news, advertisements, and features side by side. What helps them appear indistinguishable, I argue, is the growing practice of insertions of interviews with 'celebrities'—whether from the field of sports, business, or the performing arts. It is not irrelevant to mention here that the very term 'celebrity' gained currency in India very recently. But the broader point I make is that such interviews blur the categories further. One can ask, 'How may I categorise such an interview?' Can one describe it as sports news if the interview is with a celebrity tennis player? Or a paid feature if the star discusses his/her preferred brands?

The print media also carries a large number of features on the changing lifestyle of the new generation Indian. While articles on the new emerging norms of families, marriages, career choices, and gender relations are common, there are also explicitly sponsored features which deal with profiles of 'the new Indian'. For instance, *The Economic Times* describes in a feature titled 'Outsourcing comes home' the new needs of 'specialized providers' for 'Indian metro professionals who are as time-poor as their American counterparts' (19 October 1999). A 'Response Feature' titled 'White Goods and Woman: Consumer Durables and Finance' (*TOI*, 16 June 1995) writes on 'catering to her changing needs'. Beginning with Sushmita Sen's words, that 'the essence of a woman is motherhood and she teaches a man to love and care', the feature goes on to say how, while 'motherhood is associated with the word "housewife"' and 'evokes the traditional concepts of feminity which holds good even today', cognisance has to be given to the fact that 'women have confidently assumed a new role, that of a professional'. The demand for consumer goods is placed in this context.

Since homes become the central sites of consumption in capitalism, we not only have many adverts on kitchen designs, but also have researched pieces on kitchens themselves. *Saturday Times* thus carried an article on workable designs for homes: 'A good kitchen has to be well designed with comfortable work areas. All research about fatigue and inefficiency on account of work areas not being close together in offices, applies to kitchens as well. Added to it is the concern for safety .... Good storage space is essential to any kitchen' (17 December 1994).

Significantly, the print media itself has to advertise its own self. All images have to be cultivated and a segment of reader/consumer/audience has to be identified. *The Times of India* and *India Today* in particular use their image as publications with a high-profile readership to attract advertisements. *The Times* thus carried an advertisement on the front page with a big black blurb saying 'Last 3 days' with the following write-up:

> The front page of *The Times of India* carries an air of distinction about it. In fact, it can make sure that there are no last three days.
>
> As advertising professionals will agree, the front page solus ad gets pride of place. It is the first ad in the reader's day, and has the best chance of making a sale. The solus ad is the only display ad on the page, with very little to distract. (25 February 1995)

Newspapers and magazines thus have a profile that is carefully cultivated. There has been a remarkable increase in the exclusiveness and specialisation of newspapers and magazines in the past few years, facilitating the catering of advertisements to likely purchasers. For example, a cursory comparison of advertisements in *India Today* and *Women's Era* suggests different target groups. A comparison of the nature of advertisements in different publications is not our concern here, though. I refer to this aspect only to emphasise the concerted effort of the advertising industry to reach every potential reader who is also a potential customer.

I have understood advertising as a commercial activity that is firmly locked into a total structure of communication system. What I mean by this is that the logic which governs the making of advertisements is internal to the communication industry—to the demands and codes of marketing. It is therefore impervious to any critique which arises from outside it. It is the certainty with which it operates that makes it so effective. This perhaps is the key to understanding the effectiveness of the ideological transformation that an advertisement-driven media has brought about in Indian public discourse. It has rendered new ideas of choice and freedom as both natural and desirable. In the previous two sections, I have attempted to show that advertisements have managed to do this not only through the content and form of the 'real' adverts (important as they are), but also by the new style that has transformed media, blurring distinctions between news and advertisement. Important to my core argument has been the understanding that mass communications groups interweave a national structure of values and attitudes. The significance of advertisements lies therefore not in one advert or another, but in the closed circle of ideas that it creates, where even a suggestion that adverts are constraining would be laughed at. What I am arguing therefore is that it is not the loss of this or that advertising client to a newspaper or magazine that would be important. These things would happen in the normal competitive run of things. What cannot happen is a wholesale shift from dominant codes of management and editorial styles.

The Print Media on its Redefined Relationship with the Market

It is widely accepted today that:

> ... *publications are almost mortally dependent on advertising revenue.* The cover price of publication brands move within a narrow band. While

> the material cost and news gathering cost of newspapers have gone up (several have folded up in the last few years) the cover price has remained stagnant. So the bottom line of any publication business can be pushed up only in advertising revenue. (Ansari 1999; emphasis mine)

A market-driven media has 'to capture the advertiser', for which 'the media must attract the right reader .... If you have to get advertisements, you have to get the audience to stay in your publication. And if you want him to stay it has to be for him, because today's is the "I" generation. So, if your offering doesn't help him become successful, if it doesn't entertain him, he's not interested' (Das 1999: 57). This matter of fact tone, the recourse to pragmatic market sense, all effectively constitute the new rhetoric.

> The trouble with print media is the high gestation period for returns and the high cost of production. The newspaper's or magazine's Cover price alone doesn't cover these costs .... Naturally, you have to depend on advertising cost to cover your cost .... But the fact is that the cover price has to go up, because as more of the advertising revenue gets divided between television, direct marketing, the Internet etc., ... advertising may not Cover the print media's costs. *For the moment, print media cannot do without advertising* as *it accounts for 80 per cent of your revenue.* (Das 1999: 58; emphasis mine)

From the perspective of the media manager who wants to be commercially viable, the options seem to be closing down. As Das goes on to elaborate:

> The advertiser ... uses the print media as a vehicle to reach his customer .... So, I, *the print media, am not trying to get readers for my product, but I get customers, who happen to be my readers, for my advertisers.* My target audience becomes those whom the advertiser wants to reach .... *Advertisers like to reach readers who are successful, who celebrate life, who consume, who are early adopters, who believe in experimentation, who are hedonists. In this respect, youth* is a *strong reference point, representing what's modern and trendy.* (ibid., emphasis mine).

Such commercial imperatives of liberalisation made their presence felt most dramatically in the changes that *TOI* underwent, until the whole paper took on the appearance of a tabloid. Of course, circulation figures soared. The alleged 'reader friendly' approach of *TOI* was most evident during an interview with the then editor of the *TOI*, Dileep Padgaokar, which appeared in the Metro Channel broadcast on 26 June 1999. The programme was discussing the inadequate coverage of the Northeast in the media. His response was that perhaps the reader may not be interested. This perhaps captures what Bhaskar Das described as the sunny side of journalism. This is probably also what Inglis sought to put across about an instance of a business supplement which argued that 'the fundamental challenge of democracy' is that people 'don't always want what is good for them'. The unexamined assumption is that the sales curve is the measure of the rational choice and unsolicited desire of consumers in a free market economy (Inglis 1972: 55).

Journalists of an earlier generation in India saw their role quite differently. The print media in India played a historical role in the anti-imperialist national movement, and in independent India saw for itself a role in the establishment and running of a fledgling democracy and a poverty-stricken country. Ajit Bhattacharjea, then Director of the Press Institute of India, wrote:

> For several weeks I have been going through mainline English-language newspapers looking specifically for field reports and feature articles on ... rural parts of our country, small towns and growing slum colonies. Some 70 per cent of our people live in these areas which, to my mind, comprise the 'real India'... the national press, ... are expected to serve as watchdog over the system of governance, a role traditionally described as that of the 'Fourth Estate'. (1999: 47)

Bhattacharjee's views are clearly not in sync with the 'sunny' journalism advocated by Das. A shift in accountability is clearly taking place, the moot question being: Is the media accountable to the corporations by providing them with eventual consumers? Or is the media responsible for making policymakers aware of the conditions of the dispossessed?[8] Our study of an advertisement-suffused media shows that the concerns of the poor and the lower-middle class are either rendered invisible or framed in a manner that makes them look responsible for their own plight. The mantra of market liberalism states that were they of any mettle, the market would have rewarded them. For the market is both fair and free.

CONCLUSION

I had proposed at the start that the relationship between the apparent freedom of the individual and the freedom of the press rests on a basic contradiction between the freedom of the consumer/reader to choose and the imperatives of market control on the media. I have sought to explicate this by analysing: (*a*) how the text of the advertisements and features within the print media speak the language of the sponsors; (*b*) how the advertisement industry itself makes a case for its own increasing role in the media; and (*c*) how the media itself understands the change. While contextualising the chapter within the broader debate of democracy, media, and capitalism, I locate it in the particular context of India's new economic policy. A central contention has been that advertisements in the print media have sought to make a break in the public discourse in India during this period.

Another point that I have stressed upon is that the role of advertisements cannot be gauged by looking at 'real' adverts alone or by the prospects for a single product: 'The institution must also generate a moral as well as an economic climate which controls attitudes towards consumption, modes of perception, linguistic conventions and changes. To sustain real inquiry into this process we must also notice how powerfully the ethics of advertising suffuse the whole system of communication (Inglis 1972: 9).

Even a cursory look at the English print media in India would show that the attitudes and ethics of advertising promoted are that of an idea of good living characterised by an aspiration at once wistful and familiar vis-à-vis the lifestyle of the very rich; the ostentatious display of wealth and worldly success; and the acquisition of objects (including beautiful women) in order to secure one's social identity. Apart from this generation of a moral as well as an economic climate that advertisements produce, it is critical to appreciate the fact that advertising is locked firmly within a total structure of communications. This is the point that this chapter has sought to make. We have gathered from the stated position of media barons and the management that the first intention of a newspaper or of commercial television is to gain advertising revenue. A newspaper's relation to its advertising backers therefore varies according to its circulation and its readers' social habits. We have also seen how newspapers and magazines carefully cultivate their image in consonance with the image of the reader/customer (Chaudhuri 1998b).

This dependence on sponsors, however, does not imply that a particular organisation will necessarily dictate its editorial policy on some line or another (although it may), but rather that the more elusive result will be that the topic and tone of a publication will be deeply coloured by its place within the commercial structure. What we have found is that there is a harmonious interaction of advertising and editorial styles, styles which consistently reproduce and endorse the consumers' way of life. As I have argued in the course of this chapter, one can barely discern the line between fact and fiction, news and advertisements. A new style of presentation has emerged. It blends editorials with advertisements, features with news in an effortless manner. It asks no inappropriate question about the need to try and distinguish facts from opinions, nor does it offer any contrary version. This new style is no happenstance. It is a code of manners and it follows a structure of values.

Simply put, the central values are extreme wealth, sexual attractiveness, and rapacity and competitive success. Attainment of these values is signalled by acquiring the appropriate objects, using them, throwing them away, and acquiring replacements. At the same time, the circle of advertising information is tightly closed to the intervention of such questions as 'Who goes short while you produce more?', 'Do we need what you produce?', 'Who pays for you, anyway?', 'How do advertisements constrain the freedom of the media?', 'How can an individual be "free" to "choose" when the information available is entirely suffused with corporate speech?' Such questions cannot of course be asked, because it is in the nature of total systems to close the circle against alternatives. For:

> The whole concept of democracy is bound up with this concept of rational argument, and the democratic concept of equality partly to be elucidated with reference to the fact that rational argument appeals to criteria which entail a verdict that is irrespective of persons. If, however, I change your views by giving you injections, or by causal manipulation of any other kind, then I destroy this equality, for I see you as manipulated, myself as manipulator (MacIntyre 1962: 68).

The democratic concept of equality presumes an idea of public good, a 'criteria which entails a verdict that is irrespective of persons', as MacIntyre argues (ibid.). Capitalism aided by the advertisement industry both creates and responds efficiently to what people want as individual consumers. Democracies, on the other hand, have struggled to perform their own basic functions: to articulate and act upon the common good, and to help societies achieve both growth and equity. Contemporary India is witness to this tension. Advertising rests and operates on the criteria that persons are differentiated. And adverts have to target segregated categories (as the study by Lintas mentioned earlier stated about splurgers and enhancers). What advertising does is to embody its way of life as normal, natural, and rational. It does so by talking about prodigal consumption as an intrinsic way of being and of freedom of choice without perceiving the alternatives that remain neglected or suppressed, and without naming actual suffering and scarcity. These are critical freedoms for any society, but for India, where the majority is poor and dispossessed, the freedom to choose too often simply does not exist. The choices we make are thus limited in number and largely empty of social significance. The second is done often by overtly defending advertisements as the instruments of democracy. We have seen how the media has, over the past few years in India, carried features in defence of advertisements.

Views on the relationship between democracy and private aggrandisement are intensely contested. They also rest on alternative understandings of both the content and the motor of democracy. I have shown how an increasing control of the market of Indian media has been accompanied by a vigorous campaign stating that the market alone ensures freedom, democracy, and happiness. I have also sought to show how the meanings of key words like freedom, democracy, choice, and collective responsibility are being redefined. Indeed:

> ... there is a structural contradiction between freedom of communication and unlimited freedom of the market, and that the market liberal ideology of freedom of individual choices in the marketplace of opinions is in fact a justification of the privileging of corporate speech and giving more choice to investors than to citizens. It is an apology for the power of king-sized business to organise and determine and therefore to censor individual's choice concerning what they listen to or read and watch (Keene 1991: 87).

NOTES

1. I am not suggesting that the Nehruvian model was socialist. Indeed, I have elsewhere analysed the First Plan Document on Women to argue precisely

the contrary (see Chaudhuri 1996). But an attempt to mitigate the harsh impact of corporate capitalism and protect the Indian economy from the vagaries of international capital was certainly present. Significant for our concern in this chapter is the fact that the media was entrusted with a social responsibility for India's less privileged section.

2. Yashwant Sinha, the Finance Minister of the National Democratic Alliance (NDA) government, presented the annual budget on the slogan of equity with efficiency (*The Hindu*, 1 March 2002).

3. It is in a sense ironic that between the writing of this chapter and its [first] publication, the United Progressive Alliance (UPA) came to power, while the NDA led by the BJP, which had conducted a blitzkrieg campaign of 'India Shining' advertisements, had been defeated. Prime Minister Manmohan Singh, widely seen as the architect of India's liberalisation policy, remarked that 'We are not going to pursue privatisation as an ideology'. And the Congress-led UPA had addressed the concerns of the peasants, a category that had been virtually eclipsed in the media in the past decade.

4. A recent article by Harish Khare in *The Hindu* addresses this in the context of the entry of extremely rich members in the Rajya Sabha, whom political parties have felt obliged to accommodate. Khare terms this the 'Silvio Berlusconi phenomenon' (2004: 10).

5. This is an issue that seems to be occupying space in the public discourse after the defeat of the NDA.

6. This point is important in the background of an increasing tendency within sociological literature to argue that the consumer is no passive entity and responds autonomously to adverts.

7. Once again, after the 2004 elections, which were seen as evidence of the disenchantment of the poor and marginalised with liberalisation, the English print media has been carrying pieces that reflect this.

8. This is a point that has resurfaced in a big way after the 2004 national elections. The many opinion and exit polls simply failed to gauge the resentment of the marginalised against the NDA. The media was unable to identify the issues that were of central concern of those who are now being termed, even within the media, as belonging to a 'non-shining' India.

CHAPTER 7

Nationalism is not What it Used to be
Can Feminism be any Different?

This chapter examines some of the new challenges facing democratic movements in general, and the women's movement in particular, in the context of globalisation. The vantage point from which it seeks to do so is the idea and practice of nationalism and of the nation-state in India. There are three reasons for doing so: (*i*) The history of the Indian national movement and the women's movement have intersected at many points, and diverged and contested at many others. If indeed we are faced with a post-national condition, as some have argued, how are we to now conceive of either the nation or the state, or the women's movement? (*ii*) Given the close linkages between Indian nationalism and the Indian nation-state with the women's movement, it is not surprising that there is an important and rich body of Indian feminist scholarship on the idea of the Indian nation and Indian womanhood. Much of this critique has veered around the gendered and caste nature of cultural representations of the nation and of women. The political economy of nationalism retreated, even as the hegemonic nature of Indian nationalism and the Indian state featured in feminist scholarship. The challenges of globalisation have perforce brought back an overt engagement with questions of political economy. This engagement often comes from unexpected quarters: sections within the Dalit and feminist movement on the one hand, and from proponents of globalisation on the other. How does this engagement help us understand gender and its connection with nationalism and the state in a globalising context? (*iii*) New critiques of nationalism have emerged, particularly within the Dalit movement. This has been accompanied by a linked rethinking of British colonialism, against which Indian nationalism arose. Significantly, such rethinking is not confined to a section within the Dalit movement, but has been echoed in quite another quarter by (former) Indian Prime Minister Manmohan Singh, who articulated a new assessment of British colonialism at a talk at his alma mater, the University of Oxford. It is not beside the point, therefore, to recall that Manmohan Singh is widely perceived as the architect of India's present tryst with globalisation. How do we read this congruence?

My contention in this chapter is that any effort to address the above questions demands an analysis of the transformed structures of power in contemporary India. *I argue that the key to understanding this transformed structure are two disparate developments that together and at once impinge on the structural and ideological formations of contemporary India. One pertains to the assertions of subaltern groups, the other to the changing nature of capital. While the first interrogates the exclusive and hegemonic character of the 'nation-state', the other seeks to redefine a national order more in sync with the imperatives of global capital and a now transnational Indian capitalist class. This would help us to fully appreciate why neither nationalism nor feminism nor the state is quite what it used to be.*

The two social forces *embodied in the 'assertions of subaltern groups' and 'the changing nature of capital' are constitutive of each other,* but with different pasts and different trajectories. The first pertains to the dynamics of contemporary India, the assertions of Dalits, backward classes, tribals, and religious communities, which can also be read as a fallout of the intended and unintended measures of the 'national' and 'developmental state'. Sixty years of affirmative action, land reforms, and green revolution have led to new middle classes and powerful middle castes. If this can be read as success, then the failure would be the large sections who have been unable to avail of any benefits of 'development' but have been the 'victims' of development, displaced from land, home, and livelihood. The second pertains to the far-reaching changes initiated by a neoliberal globalisation that has ushered in momentous social changes, a growing middle class, and an altered public discourse. But importantly, it has had its own consequences for the aforementioned local movements with their own internal dynamics. The Dalit movement and an increasingly visible Dalit diaspora would thus rally globally to ensure that the Durban Conference recognises Dalits as victims of racial discrimination. International institutions would play no mean role in this (Lerche 2008). Likewise, the tribal movement in India would have a stake in being recognised by the Indian state and globally as indigenous people. This connection between the local/national and the global is of course nothing new. The story of the Indian national movement with its diverse linkages with an international anti-imperial movement is only one of many obvious cases. The women's movement in India has similarly had close links in the colonial period to global movements. In 1975, the Declaration of the International Women's Decade by the United Nations was in many ways a marker, for it began a period of institutionalisation of the women's movement and women's studies. And I would like to argue that it is this matter of institutionalisation which alters the nature of the linkages between the global and the national.

I argue that while ideas and movements in the modern period have often crossed borders, never more than in the period of colonialism and the heydays of liberalism, socialism, and nationalism, *what has altered has been a concerted move to harness social movements by both states and international agencies.* A quick reference to India's Tenth Five-Year Plan (2002–07) may be in order here. With 'the acceptance of market liberalism and globalisation', the Five-Year Plan states how

> it is expected that the state yields to the market and the civil society in many areas where it, had a direct but distortionary and inefficient presence ... It also includes the role of the state as a development catalyst where, perhaps, civil society has better institutional capacity. At the same time, with the growth of markets and the presence of an aware and sensitive civil society, many developmental functions as well as functions that provide stability to the social order have to be progressively performed by the market and civil society organisations. (Tenth Five Year Plan 2002: 181).

Both the state and international institutions, as we shall shortly see, envisioned what I would like to call an institutionalised role for social movements and civil society organisations. Poor women, as both agents and recipients of development, fit very well into this scheme of things.

The term *institutionalisation* is widely used in social theory to denote the process of something being embedded within an organisation, social system, or society as an established custom or norm within that system. If the Tenth Five-Year Plan is any indication, quite clearly the state saw in social movements a partner rather than an antagonist. It is also reasonably certain that not all political movements would be seen in such a light, which brings us to the question of the nature of a social movement or even that of a social organisation. Some would be more amenable to a partnership, some less.

At this point, I would like to make a distinction between the nature and mode of institutionalisation itself. One agrees with the contention that in the case of peasant movements (and the argument could very well be extended to all social movements), there have been processes of transformation of social movements from that of the intensive phase of radical action to institutionalisation (Singharoy 2005). What this chapter would like to focus on, however, is not the general process of routinisation, but the *large scale and specific form of institutionalisation of civil society organisations and social movements by the state, by international institutions (IIs), by non-governmental organisations (NGOs), and importantly, by the corporate sector that has been underway with globalisation.* One instance is the link between women's reproductive health and population stabilisation, made explicit in the Cairo Conference, reaffirmed in the Beijing Conference, and now the mainstay of developmental strategies, part of the given working knowledge which states, NGOs, and research institutions function with (Dube and Jabbi 2009). Likewise, the manner in which micro-credit has come to be the buzzword for women's development, equally at home among grassroots organisations, corporate boardrooms, finance ministries, and major banks.

This matter of institutionalisation is further compounded by the logic of professionalisation of social movements and research institutions, even when committed to action research. There would be funding protocols, agendas, targets, standard modes of evaluation for projects built in, which over time would necessarily alter the manner of functioning, whatever be the original intent. As academics, one increasingly encounters a sense of being rapidly converted into service providers, not very different from the wide range of civil society organisations (Chaudhuri 2010d). There is an increasing impression that research necessarily means evaluations (Krishnaraj 2005), and that such research alone can be useful. Both the content and form of the ongoing process of institutionalisation have a tangible impact on the practice and theory of feminism. And that this altered pattern of institutionalisation is our key to understand what is it that is redefining nationalism and the manner in which the state functions today.

The implications of institutionalisation on social movements, NGOs, and the academia are profound. One gets trained to work within given guidelines. Questions outside either cease to arise, or if they do, tend to get dumped as irrelevant, impractical, and meaningless. The entire task of researchers and project executives become that of technicians and managers. The agenda is taken as given. It is in this context that I find it particularly useful to return to some core aspects of institutions.

'Institutions are the foundations of social life. *They consist of formal and informal rules, monitoring and enforcement mechanisms, and systems of meaning that define the context* within which individuals, corporations, labour unions, nation states and other organisations operate and interact with each other' (Cambell 2004: 1).

To recap my central contention, there are two forces at work: one a model of corporate globalisation, and the second, increasing assertions of marginalised sections which perforce raise new issues and new ways of thinking about them. Further, while the latter has very deep local/ national antecedents, globalisation (both the corporate and the global civil society models) has impinged on their content as well as mode of functioning. And further still, a distinct logic of institutionalisation through the state, through the IIs, through NGOs, through new practices in the academia is at work, redefining both nationalism and feminism. This perforce has to take into account the changing dynamics of capitalism and the interests of capitalists to invest and profit from anywhere in the world sans territorial/national restrictions. Indian capitalists have been particularly adventurous in global acquisitions. If they no longer have stakes in economic nationalism, neither do Dalits, nor women, nor the poor, as one line of argument goes.

The *structure of this chapter* would roughly correspond to the manner in which I have articulated my argument. Feminism has had a very close and also a very uneasy relationship with nationalism. The chapter veers around this. In the next section, I begin with a very discernible and once dominant strand within the Indian women's movement, which saw its goal as inextricably linked to the nationalist project, and move on to the diverse feminist interrogations of colonialism, nationalism, and globalisation from very different locations. This, as the next section will show, is of great relevance to contemporary responses to globalisation. The third section therefore looks at two broad responses to both the nationalist framework and the globalisation model from within the women's movement: one discerns clear possibilities in globalisation, the other a loss. I also seek to analyse the convergence of positions between pro-globalisers and a section of the Dalit movement and strands within feminist articulation. The conclusion returns to my key contention—that contemporary India is witnessing a fusion of the dynamics of a globalising India, with its brand nationalism and 'corporate feminism' on the one hand, and concerns of social movements on the other. In the dominant discourse of civil society, the appropriation is tangible.

THE NATIONALIST FRAMEWORK, FEMINIST LINKAGES, AND INTERROGATIONS

Early scholarship on gender in India often highlighted how 'feminism and nationalism were closely inter-linked'. The 'goal of independence became the only concern for both men and women' (Basu 1976: 40). Likewise, as the narrative of a pioneer of women studies in India, Vina Mazumdar, suggests:

> [T]he independence of the country and of women had become so intertwined as to be identical. What had been mainly an individual woman's effort at 'managing' the demand of professional and family responsibilities changed into a collective and ideological struggle for *rediscovery of the nation*, the world, the past, the present and the future—*from the perspective of India's hidden and unacknowledged majority, i.e. poor working women in rural and urban areas* (Mazumdar 2001: 135; emphasis mine).

Poor women as icons of the nation were one way of imagining the nation, with obvious implications for nation-building. The independent nation-state saw as one of its central tasks an effort to address itself to their needs. That this vision of the poor could be faulted as being largely caste-blind is a matter that is being increasingly raised by the women's and the Dalit movement.

The first Plan on women, one of twenty-nine subcommittees set up by the National Planning Committee (NPC), 1938, titled significantly *Women's Role in a Planned Economy* (*WRPE*), therefore did highlight women workers, both urban and rural. But the logic of the developmental model that was adopted was unable to address them (Chaudhuri 1996; see also Chapter 2, this volume). It was not long before the language of women's welfare overrode that of women's and worker's rights. The 1950s and 1960s saw the re-emergence of 'women' in the community development programmes (financed by the Ford Foundation), whose projects were geared to enable village women to become, in the words of the director of the Women's programme in 1959, 'a good wife, a wise mother, a competent housewife and a responsible member of the village community'. Women's work and labour were not alluded to (John 1996: n 6).

A question often raised is: How did the left-oriented *WRPE* disappear completely from the public discourse on development and gender in independent India? Why did the transformation of gender relationships disappear when the other aspects pertaining to social equity and state planning, characteristic of *WRPE*, persist? I offer two sets of explanations. One is specific to gender. There was a clear retreat from more radical questionings of sexualities and sexual division of labour of an earlier period to a time when the Hindu Code Bill was being opposed, not just by the conservatives, but by many within the Indian National Congress (Chaudhuri 1993). Significantly, one should recall that much of the nineteenth-century middle-class social reforms were seeking to refashion the family into an ideal typical modern, Western bourgeois family with a male breadwinner and a domesticated, genteel mother and wife (ibid.; Sangari and Vaid 1989). The challenge clearly stemmed from a patriarchal notion of social order, identity, and tradition, heightened in the aftermath of the unprecedented violence of partition. A committee for abducted women was formed and feminist scholars have etched out from the tragic narratives how women's voices were violently brushed aside, preceding the decisions of the state and nation (Butalia 2000; Menon and Bhasin 1998). This period also marked the confrontation of the Nehruvian Congress government and the Communists with the Tebhaga and Telangana Peasant Movement, and a little later by the 1962 war with China. It is important to recall the historic peasant movements, for they bring to the fore the conflicts, glossed over today, that the nationalist framework faced. Relevant to this chapter is also the fact that a section of the communist movement read the nationalist framework as one that belied the 'freedom' that people fought for. It would be interesting to compare the present Dalit critique and the old left one of a nationalist framework that necessarily marginalised the subaltern.

A point that this chapter seeks to communicate is that it is important to simultaneously analyse both the local/national and the international context. For, at one level a great deal of the manoeuvrings of the state often happens vis-à-vis strategic moves with a global order that has its own objectives. Locating the Community Development Programmes in a Cold War-era India is not inappropriate (Singh 1986: 9–10). Indeed, in the contemporary period I argue that Women's Studies can provide a vantage point to understand these moves of global politics and the dominant global frames of development, be it in the rapid growth of micro-credit and self-finance groups, or in shifts in higher education policies, or in new discourses of choice and autonomy. As it happens, violent interventions are often defended on the grounds that they were liberating women.

If one were to identify a core critique of the nationalist framework from the rich body of Indian feminist scholarship and the women's movement, it would be the tendency of a nationalist framework to conflate the dominant group with the nation and the state. A great deal of feminist theorising in India, therefore, has interrogated the imagining of a nation that conflated itself with a sanitised image of upper-caste women. While writings on modern India have explored the recasting of women in colonial India (Chaudhuri 1993; Sangari and Vaid 1989; Uberoi 1996b), scholars of ancient India have interrogated the Altekarian vision of the high and noble status of women in ancient India (Chakravarti 1989; Roy 1996).

One of the more significant critiques in recent years has come from the Dalit movement and scholarship. As V. Geetha puts it, a visit to the past is imperative for the progress or retardation of the women's movement in India. But 'such an understanding cannot merely veer between the elite and subaltern versions of Indian nationalism, but would have to actively engage with the histories and ideologies of social and political movements whose founding premises were not, in fact, definable within the terms of Indian nationalism' (Geetha 2004: 156). In a similar vein, Sharmila Rege observed that 'the non-brahmanical reconstructions of the historiography of modern India ... have underlined the histories of anti-hierarchical, pro-democratising collective aspirations of the lower caste masses which are not easily encapsulated within the histories of anti-colonial nationalism' (Rege 1998: WS 41).

In fact these histories, Rege contends, have often faced the penalty of being labelled as collaborative. But Dalit interrogations are quite clearly not the only ones for new narratives of nationalism. When former Prime Minister Manmohan Singh spoke of the benefits of colonialism for a modern Indian nation, he was clearly engaging in reframing nationalist history, for global capitalism would surely require new global histories, just as nationalism did. At this point in time global histories are being rewritten on two registers: one of global capital and the other of the previously marginalised and excluded. And on occasions they coalesce, while on others, they do not (Guru 2005; Patnaik 2005).

ADVERSE NATIONALISM, ADVANTAGEOUS GLOBALISATION

I argue that there are two very distinct locations from which a pro-globalisation position is being articulated: *one*, from within social movements, whether Dalit, women, or the political left; and *two*, from the ideological adherents of neo-liberalism itself, as well as from the beneficiaries of the process. We start with the first set and look at the views strongly articulated by the Dalit movement. The Durban Conference was the first big event. Many other global initiatives have been taking place. To mention but one, a concurrent bill was introduced at the 110th American Congress Session on caste and untouchability. It was then referred to the Congress Committee on Foreign Affairs. And as I write in 2009, the debate about caste as race has hit the headlines again. It brings back to the fore the crisscrossing of issues, the significance of the global agenda, and the persistence of nation and the state. The review of the World Conference on Racism (WCAR), which addressed the issues of 'racism, racial discrimination, xenophobia and related intolerance', states:

> India is also fighting a related battle, of giving tribals the status of 'indigeneous people' .... *Given the huge presence and profile of NGOs in global human rights discourse, India can expect a battering from organisations like Human rights Watch, international dalit organization etc. Analysts of the UN process said these little inclusions in official documents make a big difference on the field—in terms of funding to social activists organisations. This could be channeled to organisations with a strong caste basis.* (*TOI*, 18 April 2009; emphasis mine)

Evident in the debate about racial discrimination is the fact that sections within the Dalit movement understand the nationalist framework as limiting and globalisation as a historical point where the Dalit can have access to capital and become players in the game. For, as Chandra Bhan Prasad argues, 'dalits have no stake in India's wealth but are expected by progressives to protect India's wealth and business interests from the forces of imperialism' (Prasad 2002). Kancha Illaiah makes a distinction between economic and cultural globalisation, arguing that while the former has created 'a nightmarish' situation for the poor, cultural globalisation has opened up 'a new channel of hope for historically suppressed masses'. While the nationalist framework after colonialism had imposed a Brahmanic culture denigrating the productive culture of the

Dalit Bahujans, globalisation has reopened 'channels' to integrate global culture with this productive culture (Illaiah 2002). It is significant that in the nationalist framework, women figured prominently as cultural emblems. Both Dalit and feminist critiques would view this 'national culture' as hegemonic and exclusive.

Gail Omvedt, from a Marxist Dalit position, contends that 'being anti-globalisation' has become the standard of political correctness (Omvedt 2005). She agrees with Rohini Hensman who argues that in a globalised world, 'if capitalism is acting as midwife at the birth of a borderless world, shouldn't we be ready to nurture the new arrival and imbue it with our values of justice and love instead of trying to push it back into the womb of history?' (Hensman 2004: 1030). She wonders, 'Why is there such a passionate opposition to the undermining of national borders?' 'Imperialism and its world war' grew organically out of European nationalism. Chandra Bhan Prasad's stance is clear: 'we want a bourgeoisie to emerge from the Dalits for without a Dalit bourgeoise, dalits can hardly claim total emancipation' (Prasad 2002). Omvedt argues in a similar vein: 'the only meaningful question is, for a Marxist (or dalit, or feminist) activist, what advances the revolution, that is, the movement towards a non-caste, non-patriarchal, equalitarian and sustainable socialist society?' (Omvedt 2005: 4881).

But Omvedt's and Hensman's ideological grounds are not the only ones upon which possibilities can be discerned in globalisation. There is quite another generation and quite another stance. One had mentioned earlier the iconic nation of the poor and dispossessed in various strands of both nationalism and feminism in India. An Omvedt, a Hensman, a Mazumdar with sharply variegated stances vis-à-vis nationalism veer around the centrality of the poor in their political visions. In some feminist articulations today, a break emerges with that vision, whether of a socialist feminist kind or of a nationalist feminist one. Scholars have argued the grounds on which feminists are sharply divided are about their relationship to the state (Sunder Rajan 2003).

In 1997, India had witnessed protests by the women's movement against beauty contests on the grounds that 'these contests both glorify the objectification of women and serve to obscure the links between consumerism and liberalisation in a post-globalisation economy'. Processions were held in Bangalore with mock 'queens' crowned as 'Miss Disease', 'Miss Starvation', 'Miss Poverty', 'Miss Malnourished', 'Miss

Dowry Victim', etc., in order to *highlight the issues of poverty,* and lack of nutrition and healthcare in the country (Phadke 2003: 4573). Shilpa Phadke argues in this context that 'the focus on women as "victims" could well serve to erase images of women as subjects with agency, sometimes suggesting that *feminism is a movement devoid of joy*'. She further notes that 'the contestants' insistence on the voluntary nature of their participation was ignored by women's groups' and they were seen inevitably as 'victims in the thrall of a false consciousness'. '*Not only did the context and content of the arguments made by women's groups serve to deny agency to the contestants,* they also could not contribute to addressing *the increasing aspirations and anxieties built around the desire for beauty or sexual success*' (ibid.; emphasis mine). The nation and women's own aspirations and sexualities were posited as opposed, quite dramatically in contrast to the positions articulated by Mazumdar. Phadke further contends that 'the women's movement critiques of the 1997 Miss World Contest in India could potentially be read as an effort located in the protection of the nation conceived in terms of desexualised womanhood'. Phadke's break from the past does not stop with the necessary and happy break between 'nationalism and feminism'. She argues that the market, rather than the state, is better as 'a potential turf for negotiation'. For

> unlike the state, where the citizen is largely a client, for the market the individual is first and foremost an actor-consumer. Can the women's movement use the strategies of the market to re-sell itself to a larger audience and reclaim its right to speak on behalf of a larger constituency of women? Can we reclaim the language of choice and restore its radical edge? (ibid.: 4575)

Not all would agree with the contention that the market is an 'actor consumer'. The idea of citizenship as both hegemonic and potentially liberating has been argued time and again (Roy 2005). Many Indians persist with the idea of a benevolent Leviathan chartered to bring about growth or to eliminate poverty. Neera Chandhoke, drawing evidence from a survey, found that most respondents continued to perceive the state and political parties, rather than the market or NGOs, as responsible for their 'basic needs', and they approached either the government agency concerned or political parties when they needed resolution of any problem (Chandhoke 2005). In another context, in the immediate aftermath of the Mumbai terrorist attack of November 2008, the Indian media witnessed unprecedented bashing of the state and political parties by the well-heeled; there was just one gentle reminder that while the great Indian middle class may not need the government, the vast majority of the poor do. More recently—and readers will note that this is after the global meltdown—there have been write-ups welcoming the 'corporate take over'.

The key contention around which this chapter is framed is the importance of appreciating the contemporary juncture as one that contains both the top-down dynamics of globalisation and the bottom-up dynamics of grassroots organisations, many of which have also liberally dipped into the language of international institutions and sometimes into the neoliberal discourse itself. Contemporary feminisms in India in turn often reflect the dominant academic traditions in North America.

If there are voices that see globalisation as progressive, many within the women's movement are not just uneasy, but distinctly critical. A quick way to focus on this is by addressing how the informal sector is looked at, given that in the neo-liberal framework it is the heart of the market economy and represents its prime model (Kalpagam 1994). Feminist scholars were quick to indicate the manner in which the new model was appropriating feminist findings and deploying them for its own use. One of the crucial texts to come out of the 1980s was the 1988 *Shramshakti* report on self-employed women and women in the informal sector. The World Bank Gender and Poverty Report followed only a few years later. It focused on 'the incredible range of tasks poor women perform, their often greater contribution to household income despite lower wage earnings, their ability to make scarce resources stretch further under deteriorating conditions ...'. But a crucial shift in signification takes place, as 'these findings are no longer arguments about *exploitation* as much as proofs of *efficiency*' (John 1996). So the 'poor', once the icon of Indian nationalism, reappear in a new avatar.

Given the centrality of this model, a great deal of development gender discourse is now exclusively addressed within the micro-credit framework, premised upon the idea that women are efficient managers and can be trusted to repay. The rationale of micro-credit is based on the hypothesis that the poor can be relied upon to return on time the money that they borrow. The poor are encouraged to save and practise thrift, while the growing body of middle-class Indian women are encouraged to spend (Chaudhuri 1998b, 2001). In the discourse of micro-credit and self-help groups, the categories of class and production relations disappear. The 'poor' and 'poverty' appear to be self-contained entities with no structural connect with production relations. Naila Kabeer argues that 'the "financial systems" approach which offers a commercially-oriented, minimalist package of financial services for the economically active poor—with subsidised job creation or charity for the rest' is run on the 'imperatives of cost-recovery and financial sustainability' that 'clearly resonate with neo-liberal orientations to market principles'. 'It is not surprising therefore that it has come to assume a hegemonic position in international development thinking about micro-finance as a tool for poverty reduction' (Kabeer 2005: 4709).

The political implications of making the informal sector, where the greater proportion of women workers are clustered, the hub of the new economy is, as Breman argues:

> ... the informalisation of gainful employment which has become a major trend especially in developing countries in this late phase of capitalism hampers steady increase in the wretchedly low wages and regular employment with casual, spasmodic work arrangements, paid not in time-based wages but on piece rates. *An economic regime of this kind discourages militancy and obstructs the mobilization of the labouring poor into other unions and other representative organisations.* (Breman 2004: 3872; emphasis mine)

In this unwieldy account of responses to globalisation, there appears little that holds it together. If Breman speaks of the obstructing logic of flexible labour on any possibilities of collective struggle, others speak of the immense possibilities that globalisation ushers in. One can hazard the claim that there has been a shift from a language of liberation to a language of stakes.

Many registers removed from the debate on the working-class and Dalit woman are the moves by the corporate sector to operationalise feminist concerns. Today, the nation itself is often referred to as India Incorporation or Brand India, and there has been an incredible move towards corporatisation in all spheres, including that of the academia and other centres of knowledge production. Advertisements and sponsorships have played a huge role in refashioning the dominant public discourse. The very term 'feminism' has undergone a shift that moves it away from a collective emancipatory project to a lifestyle statement of choices (Chaudhuri 2000).

There are other moves within the corporate sector to implement what they perceive as a more gender friendly work space. An example of what could be described as the corporatisation of gender rights would be the advert that I refer to below from the January 2008 issue of the magazine *India Today Woman*. A two full-page advert with three shelves of shoes, placed some distance (space) from each other, has a brief write-up titled *Match Point*. '*Gender inclusivity aims at creating work spaces to entice a college graduate, a career woman and a mother*. Recognizing this change, Nasscom and *India Today Woman* announced winners of the corporate awards for *Excellence in Gender Inclusivity*, recognizing companies that have implemented outstanding practices in promoting gender empowerment' (*India Today Woman* 2008; emphasis mine).

Another small advertisement may help us to further appreciate gender in the corporate vision. This is about a Workshop on Work-life Balance for Working Women in Delhi.

> *Across generations, gender, industries, and international borders, work-life balance is surfacing as a common concern*. What is the high price of a life that is out of balance? Within the past decade or so, the *global workplace* has seen increased numbers of working women; dual-career and single parent families, and increased numbers of employees with eldercare responsibilities; a decrease in job security; and a blurring of work-family boundaries due to technological change. (India Habitat Centre Notice 2007)

What we see at work above are two sets of assertions: *one*, that of an upwardly mobile middle class, and *two*, that of women from a certain section within the corporate sector. What is also discernible is a model of a 'fulfilling life', a 'balanced life', and of course, a more obvious affirmation of the new individuated self. Many issues raised by women's movements and women's studies have indeed entered public discourse and the new everyday common sense. On occasions, we see a crasser version of how gender has travelled in public discourse. For instance, a case was registered against a leading telecom firm under the Pre-Natal Diagnostic Techniques (Prohibition of Sex Selection) act for 'displaying an advertisement on its website pertaining to sex determination of the foetus with a suggestive "Better Rs 500 now than Rs.5 lakh later"' message (*HT*, 1 February 2005).

In conclusion: The logic of doing the 'doable'

I have argued at the outset that we need to locate some recent developments in two contexts, which are increasingly constitutive of each other, but in many ways with different pasts and trajectories. The *first* pertains to the dynamics of contemporary India, the assertions of dalits, backward classes, and tribal and religious communities. The *second pertains* to the far-reaching changes initiated by globalisation, a growing middle class, and an altered public discourse. Globalisation had its own impact on local movements, notwithstanding their own internal dynamics. In part, this global impact is linked to the increased role of International Institutions (IIs) and their reworked relationship to states on the one hand, and a reworked relationship of states to NGOs on the other. A certain institutionalisation and routinisation of social movements took place, even as the goals of social movements were recast as 'doable' aims of NGOs. This focus on the 'doable', the 'manageable' fit in with the given state and II policies, which were governed by a neoliberal development agenda as it unfolded in the 1990s. This new ideological approach was both flexible and capable of recasting the practices and meanings of social movements. Many programmes on gender and development were recast in this new spirit of capitalism. The contours of the Dalit movement, likewise, were redefined in this global context.

It is important to make the point that neo-liberalism appears to be simply a set of prescriptions that are practical, that make self-evident sense, that are innocent of ideologies and politics. However, as has been shown, it is deeply ideological, and like most ideologies has a tendency to be actualised, simply because it is expected to work. In India, the ascendancy of neo-liberalism as a vision coincided with the dismantling of an earlier consensus around what goes into the making of the Indian nation and state.

My contention in this chapter is to locate the travels of feminism in this swirling melting pot of very diverse sets of ideas and practices. What I would like to argue is that this ideological shift has to be understood in the broader matrix of structural and ideological changes in this late stage of capitalism. The stakes are high. If a demand exists for Dalit capitalism, so does a view that the women's movement is better placed to negotiate with the market rather than with the state. That the state is expected to facilitate the process of licenses for Dalit business is part of the story of the constitutive nature of the relationship between the state and market. Understanding nationalism has to take note not just of transnational labour, as Hensman does, but also of the transformation of an earlier era of national capitalist to a transnational capitalist class, for quite clearly, the role of the bourgeoise—whether Dalit or indigeneous—remains pertinent.

What is also discernible in the dominant ideological paradigm in India is that an earlier relative privileging of workers as nation-builders has been replaced by an almost entirely capitalist or 'captains of industry' nation-builders. The finance minister and prime minister of India have been routine participants in award ceremonies to captains of industries in recent years. In one, the finance minister made an interesting distinction between what he called an earlier era of organic development of capitalism, where Indians built industries, and the present stage, where they should buy off already established industries in a major global takeover. NDTV broadcasted live its awards for the Indian of the Year 2008, hosted at the Taj Mansingh Hotel on 17 January 2008 and attended by, among others, industrialists, politicians, the prime minister, and the finance minister. The anchor introduced the event by mentioning that 'India's best and brightest have come together in the room', and that today it is economics, not politics, that drives the world. I think both statements emerge as the apparently unproblematic common sense of the neoliberal era. Indeed, politics is seen as disruptive to development. Not surprisingly, 'women's empowerment' is viewed as constructive, and 'women's unionization and political movements' as obstacles to the furthering of neoliberal policies, now termed 'reforms'. Yet, at this very juncture there are restless claimants to the party. Indeed, Indian nationalism is now broader than ever before, with more sections engaged with it. Yet, at the same time, the language of nationalism has changed because both the nature of capital and the social base of capitalists have changed. The globe is the playing field, even as the regions and marginalised groups stake claims.

CHAPTER 8

The Indian Media and its Transformed Public

After decades of sedate existence, the Indian media universe has witnessed a 'big bang' of sudden and gigantic expansion. The most spectacular changes have been in television, where 24x7 news channels, reality programmes, chat shows, sting operations, celebrity weddings and birthdays, beauty pageants, award functions, sports events, natural disasters, political crises, music channels, tarot readings, stand-up comics, and competing religious discourses jostle for space and attention. There are in all 622 TV channels either already operating or planning to commence operations in India.[1] The growth in the print media has been no less remarkable (Jeffrey 2000; Ninan 2007). The two most widely read Hindi newspapers, *Dainik Jagran* and *Dainik Bhaskar*, together recorded a total of 89.8 million readers in 2008, while the most read English daily, *The Times of India*, had 13.3 million readers (Indian Readership Survey, 2008).

This chapter argues that these momentous changes in the Indian media world have transformed the idea of the public and the public sphere (Rajagopal 2001). It is divided into three parts: the first introduces the basic stance of the chapter and outlines the overall argument. The second part looks at the transformations that the 'public' has undergone. The final part analyses the ideological role that the media seems to have appropriated for itself in shaping the dominant public discourse.

The empirical material presented here is based primarily on the content provided by several TV channels (including *Times Now, CNBC, NDTV, Sony TV, Zee TV*, and *Star TV*) and one newspaper, namely *The Times of India* (*TOI*),[2] over a period of one month between 24 May and 23 June 2007. However, the argument about a transformed 'public' that I seek to put forward has emerged from a longer study of the media since the early 1990s, the beginning of the period of liberalisation in India. I contend that this argument may be sustained from a scrutiny of the media, even when the period is a random month in a random year, as is the case here.

The Argument

Standard civic textbook learning suggests that the expansion and transformation of the media can only lead to greater democratic participation. However, it is now widely recognised that the relationship between free media and deliberative democracy is not so straightforward (Habermas 1989; Macintyre 1962; Therbon 1977). I argue, therefore, that the very idea of the 'public' in standard classical liberal theory has undergone a transformation. I argue further that this three-fold transformation is evident in the *ideological content of the media*, the *membership of the public sphere*, which now stretches beyond the territorial nation to include the increasing presence of the Indian diaspora, and the interactive *form of publicness*. A central argument of this chapter is that the media plays a crucial ideological role in legitimising neoliberal capitalism in contemporary India. This point needs to be emphasised precisely because the dominant language of the media is apparently non-ideological and apolitical. Likewise, corporate control or market censorship becomes more difficult to discern because it is expressed in the language of choice and freedom (Chaudhuri 2005a). Not surprisingly, when the draft Bill to prevent monopolies through 'restrictions on accumulation of interest' was sought to be passed, it was condemned by the media industry as 'anti-consumer, anti-choice and anti-market' (Joseph 2006).

I find it useful to draw from Conrad Lodziak to buttress my stance that the form (and not just the content) of ideology has to be looked at in order to appreciate how it works. Lodziak argues that ideologies do not generally motivate people, who are motivated by quotidian, everyday realities rather than abstract explicitly articulated doctrines, such as socialism, liberalism, neo-liberalism, religious fundamentalism, and so forth (Lodziak 1995: 40), I concur with Lodziak that the media today does communicate 'a range of popular expressions' through news, features, stories, adverts, and expert views.[3] However, I also argue that the media actively promotes explicitly articulated neoliberal doctrines on the market and the state, and further, that there is a synergy between the substance and style of contemporary media. Thus, racy language and combative anchors with a weakness for scandals and conspiracies are an integral part of the ideological discourse. For 'entertainment and media industries increasingly rely on gossip to stay ahead of rivals'.[4]

I turn now to the second aspect of the transformed public, namely its interactive nature and the greater presence of the ordinary and the local. This presence of the ordinary public is most visible in the burgeoning growth of talk shows, reality shows, and various singing and dancing contests (such as *Indian Idol* on Sony TV, *Sa Re Ga Ma* on Zee TV,

Star Voice of India on Star TV, *Nach Baliye* on Star Plus TV, and *Zara Nach Ke Dikha* on Star One), where public votes decide the winner. Most channels also have a current issue on which the audience can mail their opinions. Newspapers, too, have regular opinion polls. The numbers who participate are often staggering; for example, *TOI* reported that *Kaun Banega Crorepati-II* received over 130 million and *Fame Gurukul* received 50 million responses through SMSs. An ordinary SMS costs just 50 paise, while that sent for voting on a reality show costs between Rs 2–3, depending on the arrangement with the TV channel hosting the show (*TOI*, 29 October 2006). In print media there is more local news—the staple of success for Indian-language newspapers—which publicises people and issues that would have been ignored in the past. Does this 'publicity of the public sphere', as Jeffery (2000: 210) puts it, change politics?

Do the compulsions of commerce imply that there is no longer any merit in the classical liberal defence of the freedom of the press as being necessary for the cultivation of opinion beyond the state (Thompson 1995: 239)? I think the state remains critical, central as it is in navigating the entire set of market transformations that this chapter deals with. What is important, however, is to appreciate the changes that the state has undergone and the ensuing changes in its relationship with the media. A brief reference to the past may be in order here. If the state was the defining institution against which the free media was defined in nineteenth-century England, in colonial India public opinion was nurtured and channelised by the nationalist press against the colonial state. In the first four decades of independent India as well, it was the state that expected the media to spread the spirit of self-reliance and national development among the people. And except for the nineteen months of the Emergency declared by the Indian state in 1975, the press *did* enjoy relative freedom. However, as Purnima Mankekar notes, most people were well aware that news about domestic politics on All India Radio and Doordarshan was censored by the state (Mankekar 1999: 354). The opening up of the media to private channels in the early 1990s was thus widely seen as freedom from state censorship. This perception is not unique to India. For the early liberal thinkers, the main threat to individual liberty did stem from the state. The Indian state, for a good four decades after independence, was indeed the central actor.[5]

These assumptions can no longer be taken for granted almost two decades after the Indian state introduced the new economic reforms. With the transformation of media organisations into large-scale commercial entities, freedom of expression is threatened not from state power, but from the commercial concerns that govern media organisations. The assumption of a media that is 'national' is also difficult to sustain with the development of transnational networks, leading to the globalisation of communication as well as to the emergence of a global or transnational capitalist class (Robinson and Harris 2000; Sassen 2002). As a consequence, the configuration of issues that confront us is qualitatively different.

I am not arguing that the state is no longer important or that the hegemonic 'national imaginary' has ceased to exist. I argue instead that the Indian state has been transformed and that Indian nationalism is not quite what it used to be. This is a point that has been widely noted, albeit in different ways. In a pre-liberalised India, even studying the middle class 'may have seemed an "unworthy" or self-indulgent topic', for the social scientist's mandate was to act on behalf of the 'people' who constituted the nation (Deshpande 2003: 128). Today, the nation and the public are increasingly being appropriated by the middle class. In the context of gender and development, Mary John has argued how production was no longer a definitive identity for a liberalising Indian nation, whereas at another time the working-class woman was a national icon (John 1996). If the rhetoric of globalisation in the early 1990s was about the reinvention of the thrifty Indian housewife as a profligate woman consumer (Chaudhuri 2001), today the national icons are the women CEOs who are lauded as 'India Inc crashes through the glass ceiling' (*TOI*, 18 January 2009).

Very significant class and gender reconfigurations accompany this recasting of the nation. The rhetorics of globalisation initiate, accompany, and legitimate the changing nature of capitalism, nationalism, and the idea of the 'public'. It has been argued that nationalism is no longer what it used to be, for there is a 'visible ascendency of the transnational fraction of capital in India even if the contest with other fractions is as yet not a foregone conclusion (Bhattacharya 2005: 10). Another contention has been that the erstwhile hegemony of an essentially nation-based capitalist class has been replaced by a transnational capitalist class (TCC), which is the fraction with the greatest influence on the international institutions that today have an increasing say in the running of nations. This network of high-profile corporate executives, bankers, brokers, financial management experts, media managers, academics, and bureaucrats use the most modern means of communications to create a new world of ideas (Chimni 2004).

I seek to locate both the transformations of the public and the visibility of the diaspora in the Indian public sphere in this context.

This often strident appropriation of the nation and the Indian 'public' by a middle class ideologically aligned with the project of liberalisation is most evident in the media today. I argue that this is done in two ways: by an overt ideological defence of an unbridled market and an attack on the very idea of an interventionist and welfare state; and by the everyday quotidian features and news that inscribe corporate speech, create a new imaginary of a global Indian, and a global Indian middle class.

THE TRANSFORMED 'PUBLIC': VISIBLE, INTERACTIVE, ORDINARY, AND DIVERSE

This section examines what I identify as key elements in the transformation of the media and of the 'public': the increasing visibility of political personages, its growing interactive nature, the inclusion of the ordinary and diverse representations. At an apparent level they all suggest greater public participation. However, while there is indeed greater interactivity, inclusion, and visibility of both political personages and the ordinary public, they do not add up to a more critical public sphere.

One of the features of this transformed visibility of the media is the 24x7 phenomenon with its continuous flow of information, entertainment, and 'breaking news'. The most momentous news is 'broken', only to be replaced by yet another momentous story. This 'communicative abundance' (Keene 1991) does not necessarily lead to an informed and engaged public. For the media channels, this abundance means severe competition to survive and be the centre of news for the day. Most TV channels now preface their news with 'Times Now has reliably learnt', or 'NDTV, in an exclusive interview, has found' ... or 'thanks to the exposure made by *Times Now* [or NDTV or CNBC] some action has been taken ...'. Each newspaper and channel is also a brand that has to compete hard to be in the news.

For both the 'media' and the 'public', there is a certain urgency that captures the restless spirit of the times. Research by advertising agencies shows that the maximum attention span of the audience is measured in seconds. In this scenario, 'politics' is essentially about events and personages, the more sensational the better. There is also a very clear break between mass politics and a new generation of political leaders, whose style and approach are in sync with the media functionaries. Assembly elections in Uttar Pradesh held in May 2007 were an interesting pointer. The media had been conducting various exit and opinion polls, but the results belied the predictions of all political pundits. After her victory, the Bahujan Samaj Party (BSP) leader Mayawati commented on TV that unlike others, she had given no interviews since the media appeared to be busy and she did not want to 'disturb' them. The point she was making was that political leaders are more visible in the electronic media than in parliament or public rallies.

It is in this context that one wonders about Thompson's claim that 'whether they wish to or not, political leaders today must be prepared to adapt their activities to a new kind of visibility which works in new ways and on an altogether different scale. And they ignore this new visibility at their peril' (Thompson 1995: 120).

The former Speaker of the Lok Sabha, Somnath Chatterjee, was often seen pleading with the Members of Parliament (MPs) to behave themselves for they were being observed by the people at large, thanks to the live telecast of Parliamentary proceedings. Thompson's view seems to hold little ground in the Indian context where politicians have the benefit of this 'new visibility' with little at peril. The most obvious instance of this was the cash and vote scandal in Parliament in 2008 where MPs, during the voting of the Indo-American Nuclear Bill, upturned bags full of money in full view of the national public to expose an alleged attempt to purchase support for the bill. The bill was passed, an enquiry instituted, and no truth was found in the accusation. Such visibility, apart from eroding the already weak trust of the urban middle class in the political system, does not seem to act as a tangible deterrent.

In the period covered by research for this chapter, there were two major events involving mass public participation that made the headlines, namely the Gujjar agitation for inclusion as Scheduled Tribes and the sudden sectarian controversy in Punjab. Headlines with the term 'caste wars', accompanied by visuals of rampaging mobs breaking and burning, interrupted for a brief while the routine of a media that seemed more comfortable with sound bites of politicians and the usual quota of glamour and Page 3 news (*TOI*, 30 May, 1 & 2 June 2007). The issues that these movements raised remain unresolved. Yet they disappeared almost completely from the media with the cessation of rioting and killing.

The heightened visibility of political personnel for the public at large is also accompanied by a greater presence of the public, the *aam janata*. Many reality shows harp on the 'ordinary' background of the participants, that is, their marginal regional, ethnic, or class background. People who in an earlier era could never have shared the stage with national-level celebrities, whether from politics or the film and music industry, now actually do so. Indeed, at one point the extension of representation of the ordinary in documentaries or social realist films was a subversion and critique of mainstream media representations. The ordinary is now co-opted as a badge of professional authenticity, a sign of the proximity of the professionals, including stars and celebrities, to the vernacular and the plebian. This is one master strategy of containment in which class is simultaneously acknowledged and conjured away in one stroke: the ordinary is valued precisely because of its contrast with the elites (Wayne 2003).

I would like to argue that what the 'ordinary' is to the 'elite', the non-Western is to the Western. I do so to allow a more critical take on the considerable celebration of how Indian cuisine, fashion, clothes, films, and music have made visible inroads into Western societies. As an illustrative example, I take the case of Shilpa Shetty who won the *Celebrity Big Brother* (UK) contest. Is this a victory for multiculturalism and cultural hybridity or for global India? Perhaps it is a bit of both. But what is more intriguing for me is precisely the use and appropriation of progressive ideas and movements within the corporate structure, yet another add-on to maximise profit. It is perhaps relevant, therefore, to spend a few lines on the conscious diversity of the contestants in *Big Brother*:

> [W]hile there is class, ethnic, gender and sexual diversity in the selection of the contestants, *this only becomes converted into elements of their media performance* .... For the audience this social diversity works in a contradictory fashion. On the one hand it offers multiple points of identification, on the other, the text encourages the social or political basis for that identification to be converted into an individual's media performance. (Wayne 2003: 152; emphasis mine)

The idea of a more 'inclusive and interactive public' has to be analysed along with the idea of fragmented audiences and the political implications of 'narrowcasting'. On the one hand, as is obvious, a great many new things are happening in the media. On the other hand, there is a curious repeat of what has already happened in the Western world a great many years ago. Similar processes were underway in the late nineteenth-century American media. The pressure to increase circulation led to the growth of sensationalism and emotion-laden features to increase readership (Leighley 2004).

A RECONFIGURED PUBLIC SPHERE: THE DIASPORA COMES HOME AND THE DESI[6] GOES GLOBAL

Benedict Anderson's nationalism of the 'imagined community' that the print media helped to construct at another time is being recast before our very eyes. A preconfigured idea of the 'national media' is difficult to sustain, both because of the globalisation of communication and the emergence of a transnational capitalist class. I want to push this argument further to emphasise that the increasingly influential media presence of the Indian diaspora has to be placed in this context. Not all sections of the diaspora can vie for the kind of space given to steel tycoon Lakshmi Mittal or economist Lord Meghnad Desai. Patricia Uberoi was not only one of the earliest scholars in India to fully appreciate the importance of studying popular culture, but was perhaps also one of the first to note the significance of 'the diaspora coming home'. While analysing two immensely popular Hindi films of the mid-1990s, *Dilwale Dulhania Le Jayenge (DDLJ)* and *Pardes*, she argued that:

> Indians 'at home' have had quite contradictory attitudes to their own diaspora. So long as the diaspora was constituted largely of the descendants of indentured labour in the ex-colonies, of farmers and lumberjacks in Canada, or—by the 1960s—of working class immigrants in Britain, the diaspora could be both out of sight and, mostly, out of mind. But with professional middle-class emigration in the 1970s and 1980s, and the Indian community's attainment of a 'model minority' status in the North American context, the diaspora could no longer be ignored. Simultaneously, *a new role was discovered for emigrant Indians as patriotic investors in their country's future*. (Uberoi 2006: 181; emphasis mine)

Since neither nationalism nor capitalism is quite what they used to be, the emigrant Indian does not necessarily act as a 'patriotic investor'. Nor do the resident-Indian captains of industry speak the earlier nationalist language of protecting Indian industry and sovereign economic space. Instead, Indian capitalists are feted for buying up foreign corporations. Former Finance Minister Chidambaram made an interesting distinction between what he called an earlier era of organic development of capitalism, where Indians built industries, and the present stage, where they should buy up already established industries through global takeovers.[7] Significant alliances are being forged between the resident and non-resident sections of the Indian TCC.

Delhi Times, a supplement of *TOI*, carried a feature titled 'India, the Land of Wealth Churners'. A cartoon of a prosperous-looking Indian man dressed in Western suit and tie, sitting cross-legged, wearing a turban, and playing a snake charmer's flute, with a basket not of snakes but electronic cables, captures the reinvented global and corporate Indian. The accompanying text reads:

> Indians ... featuring prominently in the list of high net worth individuals in the world today .... Lord Swaraj Paul features as the second richest Asian Briton with a net worth of $750 million .... India had the biggest contingent of billionaires from Asia .... India's 36 billionaires pipped Japan's 24 to the post.

Lord Meghnad Desai, who is also a celebrated economist, says, '... Indians now offer to the world a heady mix of wealth and intellect .... Global Indian takeovers have not gone unnoticed .... We are not only creating wealth here, we are also ... chipping in with the welfare and development of these developed countries' (*Times Business*, *TOI*, 31 May 2007).

The diaspora appears in both full-fledged write-ups as well as news reports like 'British curry fix just got spicier', about the British firm ABF acquiring Indian food brand Pathak's (ibid.). It appears on television programmes like the IIFA Awards event in Yorkshire, where Bollywood personalities were present in large numbers. And the greatest applause was for Bollywood actor Upen Patel, a British Indian, who thanked all British Indians and hailed the United Kingdom.[8] Being Indian acquires new meanings as presumed notions about the coterminous nature of culture and territory are challenged.

The shift away from an essentialist to a contingent idea of culture has been a welcome development. However, this delinking of culture and nation from the territorial and political may not have the same implications in all situations. It may mean that in a multicultural USA, Diwali is celebrated in the White House. It may mean that the Indian media can now take up some of the difficulties that the Indian diaspora faces. For instance, when British immigration minister Liam Byrne ruled out any change to the controversially amended Highly-skilled Migrant Programme, *TOI* carried a report on 'disenfranchised Indians in UK' (Lal 2007: 15).

Sunday Times (TOI) actually has a regular column, 'Indiaspora', by Chidanand Rajghatta, who is based in Washington. He had an interesting report on the immigration debate in the US which highlights what Patricia Uberoi described as the 'contradictory attitude' of Indians towards the diaspora: one for the affluent 'model minority' of the USA, and a quite different one for working-class emigrants elsewhere.

> The fate of tens of thousands of high-skilled Indian professionals waiting to be permanent US residents is being sidelined in an immigration debate that is heavily tilted in favour of illegal workers ....
>
> ... the ongoing debate centres mainly on the 12 million mostly illegal immigrants, who, ... will jump ahead of high-skilled Indians and qualify to become US citizens. (*TOI*, 25 May 2007: 11)

Some Indian Americans have sought to link themselves to the first working-class migrants who came to the West Coast in the early 1900s, with whom they have little in common. On the other hand, the same group was also rewarded with higher rates of interest for investments in India (Chaudhuri 1998a: 196). The argument I am making here is that the transnational Indian middle class defines its 'national' interest almost exclusively in terms of its class interests, regardless of the state or nation concerned. The idea of India becomes almost entirely cultural, and excludes the political ideas that seemed so central to the making of a modern and free India. While the modern nation was always a class project, it was not permissible to speak of it as though it belonged solely to the capitalists and the middle classes.

In another of his columns, Chidanand Rajghatta writes: 'Typically, jokes about Indians now center around outsourcing and tech-support, in which they come out as smart-assy, if accented brainiacs .... Indians are now providing so much material for humour that half a dozen Indian-

American comedians are milking it till it moos' (Rajghatta 2007a, b).

It is not just diasporic Bollywood actors such as Upen Patel and resident-Indian Shilpa Shetty who are visible in the Indian media (*TOI*, 25 May 2007: 11). Significantly, diasporic Indians also find space in Western films; for example, the 'Desi Diva' Sheetal Seth, the original ABCD, known for her role as the 'tempestuous Nina' who struggled to find her identity in the film *American Born Confused Desi* (*TOI*, 2 June 2007). This is significant for the broader argument about the emergence of a global middle class of resident and non-resident Indians (NRIs), whose 'national' interest and imaginary will necessarily be different.

EXPLICIT IDEOLOGY AND EVERYDAY CORPORATE SPEAK IN THE MEDIA

My central argument has been that the media has been both extraordinarily visible and deliberate in refashioning the public discourse of India. Key to this recasting has been the construction of a new global Brand India. This has been done in two ways: by an overt ideological celebration of the market and an undermining of the welfare state, and a more covert transformation of public discourse through its assortment of features, stories, reports, news, gossip, and advertisements. Common to both is the new interactive approach and the representation of the 'ordinary' and the 'diverse'. I touch upon the media's self-articulated role for itself, address the instances of overt ideological campaigns, and then move on to the quotidian features that help in the recasting.

The centrality accorded to the ideological role of the media goes against two influential arguments in media studies because it often assumes that people are passive victims—rather than autonomous agents who often read against the grain of the text—and reduces the complex working of society to a conspiracy (Liebes and Katz 1993).[9] I disagree with this view because while readings may vary, the broad parameters within which they are expressed and debated are laid down. And more importantly, some issues are rendered invisible. It would be rash to set aside the fact that the media industry is located within the complex of corporate capitalism, and that serious business interests are at stake.

The media appears to be engaged in a brazen projection of its own role as some kind of knight in shining armour at the forefront of civil society, its last hope since the three organs of the state—the executive, legislature, and judiciary—have failed the system. This includes voicing the apparent disenchantment of the 'public' with the government, and more broadly, with political parties and politicians. An interesting instance of running down state welfare measures is evident in the report titled 'Why Some People Want to be Poor':

> The perks of being Below the Poverty Line is making some people do desperate things, like demolish their toilets, to achieve the status .... So valuable is the BPL status that all across impoverished, lawless Bihar .... Influential landlords managed to get their names on the BPL list by showing poor people's huts as their own. (Wajihudin 2007: 23)

This is a good instance of how discourses render some kinds of policy measures illegitimate. This is in keeping with the fact that 'society ... requires discourse (the mapping, description and articulation of situations and processes) which by definition has the effect of annihilating and delegitimising certain views and positions while including others' (Van Zoonen 1994: 40).

Yet another instance that highlights the media's self-appointed role as the only institution which the nation can trust pertains to a sting operation carried out by NDTV into what is widely described as the BMW case (29 May 2007). The case pertains to the mowing down of a number of people by a BMW car, driven by rich young revellers returning from a party. The lone witness who had not turned hostile, a man named Kulkarni, gave *NDTV* the sting tapes showing both the defence and prosecution lawyers offering him money. However, Kulkarni himself has repeatedly changed his statements (*TOI* 2007c: 2). Indeed, in many such instances like the Jessica Lal case (where a well-known model and woman bartender, Jessica Lal, was murdered), the media did help in bringing punishment to the guilty. At the same time, a tendency of trial by media has also led to very unfortunate and dangerous trends. To mention one instance, a woman teacher was lynched by parents and then summarily sacked by the school authorities, thanks to a fraudulent sting operation that suggested that she used her students to run a sex business. No action was taken against the media.

I move now to a dramatic case of overt ideological engagement that erupted in the media over a rather innocuous remark by former Prime Minister Manmohan Singh to corporate India. He suggested that corporations ought to avoid paying large salaries to their CEOs and should also move away from a culture of ostentatious display. On its front page, the *TOI* reported the prime minister's speech thus:[10]

> … Manmohan Singh … asked big companies to 'resist' paying large salaries to their top executives as rising 'inequities' … could lead to social unrest. In his speech to CII, PM proposed *an unusual model of austerity* …. The PM's formulation may well have taken his audience by surprise as Singh has always praised India's growth story …. But Singh's remarks were clearly out of sync with his own model … which laid stress on unshackling individual enterprise to encourage wealth creation …. (*TOI* 2007a: 1)

Apart from the front page report, *TOI* also commented on this in its lead editorial:

> … Indians know … that the most profligate and wasteful institution … is the government …. poverty owes … to the failure of the government's policies and welfare programmes …. to generate wealth … Indian companies need the best CEOs … for which globally competitive salaries and perks will have to be offered …. The more the rich consume, the more it's possible to tax them and create resources to help the poor …. The prime minister … chose to rehash the old political wisdom of the establishment, which turned India into the sick man of Asia …. (*TOI*, 25 May 2007: 22)

Clearly, an overt ideological campaign is at work here. The government is run down, the diaspora heralded, corporations felicitated, and a model of economic development prescribed. *TOI* covered this the following day too. The headline read, 'India Inc says no to CEO salary curbs', and went on to state: 'The Prime Minister's call to India Inc to trim salaries of top executives has got a thumbs down from industry' (*TOI* 2007b: 1, 22). Swaminathan Anklesaria Aiyar wondered whether the PM would 'extend this same principle to the political sector' and demand of them avoidance of conspicuous consumption (2007: 24). Two weeks later, Shobha De returned to the issue (De 2007: 24).

The themes remain the same. The CEO's accountability is seen as the model to be emulated, while the wider understanding of the democratic accountability of the state to its citizens is given short shrift. This ideological offensive sounds a bit over the top in the light of the global meltdown in 2008, the incredible bailing out of bankrupt corporations, and our own fraud by Satyam, a once iconic IT corporation of India.

Full-blown debates on models of development, such as those generated by Manmohan Singh's speech, are not as common as the overwhelming presence of corporate news and views. The latter are woven through the media and are far more difficult to identify as tangible ideological elements. I argue that it is these that transform the content of the media and thereby of public discourse. And here, sponsors lay down the rules. Even as I come to the end of my month-long scrutiny of *TOI*, I find its 25 June issue with a blank front page containing only a blue 12-inch square with the line 'Now imagine 1,121 lacs' below. And in small print, 'Please refer to page 2'. Page 2 carried a full-page advert of the Housing Development and Infrastructure Development (HDIL) corporation.

However, it is not just advertisements that I am referring to. As Raymond Williams stated decades ago, paid advertisements are old-fashioned; the real thing is corporate coverage obtained through normal news reporting. My survey of the English print media since the early 1990s has shown that it is not only ads that grew dramatically, but also news features on subjects like ads, sales, and market strategies (Chaudhuri 2000). Regular corporate market studies are reported in the newspapers. I quote from two that appeared in the *TOI* during the period of my study. One is a study by a global market intelligence firm, iSuppli: '... India is fast emerging as a key driver in the global TV market both as a consumer and manufacturer .... In a country where nearly 70 per cent of people earn less than $ 5,000 a year, the nation has shown remarkable interest in buying TVs. And this includes even the expensive flat-panel TVs ...' (Dutra Sachdeva 2007).

A study titled 'Country of Consumers' by McKinsey Global Institute reported that Indians are already spending big. But the next twenty years would see them spending bigger. A new upwardly mobile middle class will be responsible for reshaping global consumer markets. The study categorised the new emerging classes as the deprived, aspirers, seekers, strivers, and Global Indians (*TOI* 2007c: 22).

The rhetoric of Global Brand India clearly dominates the media discourse. The nation is surely being reinvented. The media is central in this transformation of the 'public'. The most challenging part of this transformation is its apparent democratising of form and content, which conceals the hollowing out of a more critical public discourse.

FIGURE 8.1 VISUAL FRAMING: 'Incredible India' on the move at the World Economic Forum 2012 at Davos. The photo is from fieldwork conducted in 2012.

Source: © Ravinder Kaur/University of Copenhagen. Reproduced with the permission of Ravinder Kaur.

EPILOGUE

This chapter was based on a study of the media for one month in the summer of 2007. Mid-2008 saw the collapse of Lehman Brothers, which heralded the global economic meltdown and intruded unexpectedly into the unabashed celebration of corporate capitalism by the media. On 26 November 2008, terrorists struck Mumbai, and we had a minute by minute, often hysterical, coverage by the media even as the killings were on. A great deal of discussion followed about the role of the Indian media. Some attacked it for its over-the-top jingoism, others for endangering the lives of people still held hostage, yet others for its obsession with the rich and the famous under attack in the Taj and Oberoi Hotels, while the people killed at the erstwhile VT (now Chatrapati Shivaji) station were given a miss. All the while the channels were engaged in an unseemly competition with their 'breaking news' of the ongoing tragedy. The media then took on the responsibility of awakening the nation. Channels invited celebrities who took over the mantle of the public, the voice of the nation, and announced that 'enough is enough'. On *Times Now*, two days after the event, Suhel Seth, well known in the public relations and ad world, advocated sacking all politicians (the 'jokers') and replacing them with CEOs who would know how to be accountable to the public. That many of these 'jokers' did not share the same social background as the older urban middle class is another well-known story of Indian public life. The shrill media rhetoric that followed the attack resonated with the themes that are part of the newly dominant rhetoric. The government and politicians are run down, and corporate professionals are seen as the saviours who will run an efficient and global nation.

The key contention of this chapter has been that Indian liberalisation has changed the idea of the 'public' in many ways and the media has been a central agent of this transformation. I have sought to understand this shift in terms of the changed form of global capitalism and the nature of the ascendant capitalist class, the transnational capitalist class. I have argued that new cultural forms are constitutive of the reinvented political and economic order. We now have the rise of a new set of public personages who fit the bill better, like the ones whom Thompson wrote of, who interact with the public through blogs and emails. But unlike Thompson's 'transformed public', they connect only with some. A recent cover story, 'Pop Goes the Icon', is worth a careful read.

> ... we seem to be ... witnessing the rise of a 'poster boy politician' cult .... There's a generational shift in politics and there are regular well-educated guys you can idolise. They are just like any other professionals ... the 30-something pin-up netas are grabbing eyeballs with their suave looks and impeccable sound bytes .... (*Times Life, TOI*, 25 January 2009)

NOTES

1. See www.Scatmag.com, January 2009 (accessed 20 January 2009).
2. *The Times of India (TOI)* has been a pioneer in introducing the new forms and content that have transformed the media.
3. I have, in an earlier piece, argued how both strategies have been at work in the context of the media's representation of feminism (see Chaudhuri 2000).
4. See 'Gossip!', *Times Life, TOI*, 30 July 2006.

5. This was true in all fields, be it gender, culture, or development (see Chakravarty 1987; Uberoi 1996a, 1996b; Vasudevan 2000). Ravi Vasudevan observes that most articles in his volume on Indian cinema have 'the state as a prominent factor in the shaping of cultural forms ...' (2000: 14).

6. The global growth of what was seen as a regional film industry is an interesting example (see Ghosh 2007: 10).

7. He was speaking at a function to present the Indian of the Year Award 2008, at the Taj Mansingh Hotel on 17 January 2008 (NDTV broadcasted this live).

8. The IIFA Awards were aired on Star TV, 20 May 2008.

9. I have discussed this issue at greater length in Chaudhuri (2005b).

10. This was a theme that the *Hindustan Times (HT)* also took up in a major way (see Thapar 2007).

CHAPTER 9

Gender, Media, and Popular Culture in a Global India

The context

Gender is a pervasive presence in contemporary Indian media and popular culture. There are three grounds upon which this visibility of gender rests: *one*, India's new economic policy, *two*, the Indian women's movement, and *three*, the prominence and reach of media in contemporary India. The first two developments are historically distinct and apparently ideologically incommensurate. However, as are the curious ways of history, their paths have intersected and found myriad expressions in a proliferating and converging media. The unprecedented growth of the media and communication industry, our third context, owes as much to revolutionary technological innovations as it does to a political economy where communication, representation, and publicity increasingly define contemporary public culture (Chaudhuri 2010b). A consequence of this intersection is the hyper-visibility of gender in a loquacious and intensely mediated popular culture. A brief elaboration of the three contexts within which this chapter rests is therefore in order.

India's new economic policy towards greater integration into global capitalism was formally initiated in 1991. This marked a radical break from a long period of state-initiated development based on import substitution and a focus on equity rather than growth. Until then, the spirit of austerity was seen as a virtue that drew moral sanction from Gandhi's lasting impact on Indian nationalism. This was to change quickly and dramatically over the next two decades. The media played a decisive role in making profligacy socially legitimate and even a 'national' duty (Chaudhuri 1998b). In this entire process of recasting the 'nation', the constituent elements of Indian nationalism were reconfigured, as choice rather than constraint and extravagance rather than thrift became the new rhetoric of globalisation. What did not change from an earlier period is the deployment of gender as a key icon of public discourse.

Public discourses on gender since liberalisation have been shaped in significant ways by the second phase of the Indian women's movement (since the 1970s). In earlier decades, one of the central issues that the movement addressed was the cognitive invisibility of gender. The emergence of women's studies, its expansion, and steady institutionalisation over the next three decades in India has to be located in this context. The 1980s saw the beginning of the academic institutionalisation of women's studies in colleges and universities on the one hand and in the developmental sector on the other, and in good measure, within the media as well. Issues such as dowry, rape, and legal rights raised by the women's movement were also increasingly covered in the media and debated in public discourses from the 1970s into the 1980s. From the 1990s, we discern a shift. Gender becomes even more visible now, but the tenor has shifted, although it is by no means unidirectional. The issues raised by the women's movement do not recede entirely. What happens is that in the increasing glossy features and advertisements, collective ideas of women's liberation and freedom become reconfigured as essentially individual desires and goals, which the new opportunities offered by the growing market could gratify. Instances of backlash to feminism exist, but this is by no means a visible presence in the media (Chaudhuri 2000). Feminism and gender, albeit redefined, enter the lexicon of public discourse and are deployed widely by the state, civil society, and the market. In the media, they become a preferred choice to anchor their stories and images, to represent both themselves and the 'global nation'.

The third ground for the pervasive presence of gender is the logic of a culture in which self-representation, image construction, brand-building, and communication are extremely important. This process is aided by the old and new media, which are also the central sites for the making and dissemination of the dominant ideology. In such a culture, what matters is how you appear and present yourself, whether as an individual, as a company, as a political party, or as Brand India. In the initial years after liberalisation, the rapidly growing advertisement industry's influence on the media was the driving force in publicising the new rhetoric of globalisation (Chaudhuri 2001). In more recent years, the media and the public relations industry have become critical, not only for corporate institutions but also for political parties, the government, and social movements. Publicity about Brand India was important for global investment, as well as for its own citizenry. Both the nation and its people were to be refashioned economically and culturally. The *industrialisation of representation and communication* that began with the modern era has acquired an unprecedented scale, convergence, and speed in contemporary India. Speed is critical for effective communication today. Therefore, catchy phrases, smart sound bites, powerful visuals, sexual images, hidden cameras, sting operations, and incessant exposure are indispensable for communication. An idea of discursive persuasion, once deemed appropriate for the public culture of a modern liberal democracy, is simply too time-consuming to be effective. Gender and sexuality as basic categories of identity form an extremely condensed but effective mode of communication in such a circumstance.

THE ARGUMENT

My central argument in this chapter is that any discussion of gender, media, and culture in contemporary India needs to recognise these three contexts that I have outlined: the constitutive influence of three decades of institutionalised feminism; the imperatives of neoliberal economic policies; and the scale of the media and communication industry[1] in the making of popular and public culture. I argue further that this constitutive influence has been largely made possible through knowledge produced by a new set of firms specialised in market research and communication, which are interested in understanding the Indian market. I draw upon the analysis of major firms like Ogilvy and Mather, Mudra, Erickson, and TMRC. These firms function across the media industry, developmental, advertisement, and management sectors. They reflect the changed nature of the media industry—a proliferating site of media and communication studies. Thus, the firms are linked not just with each other, but with the academia as well (Chaudhuri 2010a). The thick-and-fast flow of images and ideas on gender, which I focus upon in this chapter, has therefore to be understood not as free-floating and self-propelled—an unintended consequence of new technologies in a globalised world—but as products of these agencies. For instance, as we will see, marketing agencies take cognisance of the impact of feminist ideas of 'freedom' and 'autonomy' on the new Indian woman consumer, and further reconstruct these ideas in alignment with neoliberal ideas of self-realisation through achievement and pleasure. In my argument, I draw on a conception of neo-liberalism as a radicalised form of capitalism based on deregulation and the restriction of state intervention characterised by an opposition to collectivism, a new role for the state, an extreme emphasis on individual responsibility, flexibility, and a promotion of freedom as a means to self-realisation, which disregards any questioning of the economic and social conditions that make such freedom possible (Hilgers 2011: 351).

I also focus on the significant influence of the West, undeniably in the corporate world of media and advertisement, but also in academia. While there is a new focus on India in Western academia, including a new attempt to provincialise the West, the influence of theoretical paradigms generated in the West is paradoxically more insidious in sectors of Indian academia. While I cannot develop this point at any length here, I would like to buttress my argument by drawing upon a recent survey of decadal trends in Indian sociology and social anthropology in the past decade, and an observation by the editors of one of the foremost sociology journals in India.[2] When I draw attention to this new phase of Western influence, my effort is to show, first, the altered yet powerful nature of this influence, and second, a certain convergence of ideas between market strategy and academic theory. Postmodern theory, and its deference to recognising diversity and 'other cultures', has been influential in many humanities departments within Indian academia since the 1990s. Significantly, during the same time we have had an increasing deployment of 'local' cultures in the advertisement of products by Western companies such as Coca-Cola or Pepsi-Cola, or, for that matter, McDonald's with its pure vegetarian burgers. I develop this argument later through a discussion of post-feminism and the growing market for chick-lit fiction in India. Post-feminism has been variously defined and is a contested term veering between signalling an epistemological break with second-wave feminism, a historical shift, and a regressive stance. I prefer to use it in the mode that appears to be popular in Indian media—understood as a distinctive sensibility, made up of several interrelated themes such as an emphasis on individualism, choice and empowerment, subjective desires, and a resurgence of ideas of natural sexual difference. Chick-lit was defined as a 'genre that went beyond female as to include the breadth of female experiences including love, courtship and gender' (Wikipedia; accessed 7 December 2012). While Western audiences today are more familiar than ever before with the Indian culture industry (for example, with Bollywood, Indian fashion, music, and cuisine), I still hold that in the broader institutional and ideological apparatus—through which this familiarity is produced and transmitted—gender, sexuality, cultural diversity, and race are usually configured as elements in the business of consumption in a global market. The questions I pose therefore are: How does the idea of feminism get redefined in neoliberal times? How does gender travel? How do we look at the hyper-visibility of gender from a critical feminist perspective?

MEDIA, GENDER, AND MARKET RESEARCH

A dominant view of popular culture in a globalised world is that of a free-flow movement of images and ideas, arbitrary and hybrid, fusing rhizome-like in unexpected fashions (Probyn 1998). My argument is that this flow is neither free-flowing nor arbitrary. New and old ideas of gender are researched and deliberated upon before they are deployed by the wide network of communication and market research agencies that form part of post-liberalised India's popular culture. Gender became very visible, but perhaps in ways not anticipated by the women's movement of the 1970s when it raised the question of the physical invisibility of women in the public sphere and cognitive invisibility in extant conceptual frames. What strikes one most about these marketing and communication agencies is the refreshing straightforwardness and candor with which they explain the reason for using gender so extensively in marketing. I begin with an analysis of the nature and purpose of research by marketing agencies.

A paper commissioned by Mudra, one of the biggest advertising firms, 'to delve into the practices of the urban youth to give insights to the Marketer' observes that gender has been a major focus of investigation by market research and 'has been widely used in brand communications to achieve better segmentation and targeting of consumers' (Jetley 1998). Further, the paper spells out the reasons why market research found it effective to simultaneously use from both the 'domain of feminism' and 'gender stereotypes':

> The domain of marketing communications not only deals with effectively connecting the brand with its consumers but is also responsible in reflecting and shaping the perceptions of the consumers at large .... The *goal is to provide the marketers with updated literature, which may help the brands understand the perceptions of its consumers better .... It is not unethical for the media to reflect any stereotype that exists in the society. However, ... certain stereotypes, which are regressive for any gender, can be avoided.* (Chaudhuri 2009; emphasis mine)

Such adroit use of 'feminism and chauvinism', with a very specific purpose to shape the perceptions of consumers, is far removed from the 1970s when, as Indian feminists argued, the media used stereotypical projections of women. This stereotypical approach was criticised by Indian feminists since it had not taken 'into consideration the other realities of a woman's life', nor had it considered the validity of 'a woman's way of thinking, expressing and feeling' (Rao 2001). Consumer research has been responsive to this critique, as the comments of a consumer insight director, McCann Erickson, suggests: 'Advertisers and market researchers tend to look at consumption patterns and accordingly straitjacket women as traditionalists or hedonists or sophisticates. They're missing the basic point. Women are human beings first, then consumers, you must know how they think, feel, respond and react in real life situations' (McCann Erickson 2000).

Notwithstanding the fact that both feminists and consumer analysts seek to recognise the validity of women's way of thinking and feeling, the dilemma remains as to how and where one draws the line between discriminating stereotypes and the authentic, subjective desires of women. The matter is further compounded because:

> *often feminist arguments that analyze this internal conflict are appropriated by market forces to create messages that successfully establish recognition and identity between the text and the receiver.* The consumer insight team of McCann Erickson came up with a profile of new-age Indian women after a series of focus group discussions with a cross section of urban middle class women. In an assessment of the felt need of these women, in what they call the 'wish list', the market research team highlights 'the strange but easy coexistence of traditional values and a modern outlook evident in the urban Indian woman.' (Rao 2001: 45; emphasis mine)

These firms have been able to capture the complex mix of ideas that form part of the lived reality of middle-class Indians. Chauvinism and feminism may thus both be deployed. Relatively new ideas of the metrosexual and recognition of female sexuality can be appropriated to target new social segments. The Axe Body Spray advertisements have made popular sexually charged images. I draw here on two examples. One is an image of a chocolate man literally being 'eaten' by a woman, the other of a formally dressed man in an office, similarly 'attacked' by women in various states of undress. Both these examples are overt expressions of women's sexuality, a taboo subject for much of modern India's history. Feminist writings on colonial India have specially addressed the imposition of Victorian mores, the nineteenth-century Indian middle-class aspiration to fashion a normative model of domesticated and sexually sanitised women, and the reinvention of the purported traditional, virtuous Hindu woman (Chaudhuri 1993; Sangari and Vaid 1984). The latter has been a continuous, albeit muted, strand in modern Indian ideological thought, which acquired a re-energised stridency with the rise of Hindutva since the 1990s. Not surprisingly, the Axe advert drew expected disapproval from right-wing Hindu groups, which in turn evoked mocking responses to such moral policing:

> Ever since they started allowing kissing in Bollywood movies, boy, India's morality is going straight to hell. The cow-filled conservative nation is seeing its Victorian standards of sexuality crumble in the face of racy foreign advertising. The prime offender? You guessed it: Axe Body Spray. *Of course.* The Indian government recently banned Axe's infamous 'Chocolate Man' ad, which it sees as a symptom of cultural decline, along with all the new sexy billboards popping up across the country. (http://gawker.com/5047155/axe-body-spray-ads-destroy-indian-culture)

My central concern here is, however, not the varied ideological responses to the advertisement. My point is to call attention to the informed deliberations that go into the making of advertisements. TMRC, 'an innovative consumer intelligence company operating across Asia' with a 'team of experienced specialists' who 'possess keen minds and the professional skills required for gaining a deep and comprehensive understanding of consumer experiences, their deep psychologies, their perceptions, and motivations', and knowledge of 'what actually drives consumer behavior', writes:

> Axe has always used the basic insight—in fact, the very basic animal instinct—of the male species' attraction towards the opposite sex to position and sell the brand. And quite successfully. *They have never been shy of stating their 'get laid' message in most explicit insinuation in their advertising campaigns. India is an important emerging market for male deodorants, and a number of new players are trying to copy Axe's positioning by jumping on the 'get the girls' bandwagon.* (http://www.tmrcresearch.com./; emphasis mine)

Such uses of sexuality and gender are new in the Indian media, and, one could argue, are *at once* reflecting new mores and actively reshaping them.

The broader point that I seek to make through this exposition is the industrial scale of regular monitoring, research, and analysis that goes on in the convergent industry of media, communications, public relations, and advertising to make possible the idea of the self-responsible individual. Consider the following example of a story in an advertisement for a skin-lightening app. The following quote is one of the many stories in advertisements available on the web, more often than not presented simply as a free-floating piece of objective 'reporting'. 'A *Facebook application* that pales the skin of darker men has been launched. The Vaseline app is targeting *India's* fast-growing *'metrosexual'* marketplace. In India, a multibillion pound industry provides creams to lighten complexions. The campaign is fronted by *Bollywood actor Shahid Kapur* .... The response has been pretty phenomenal' (http://www.dailymail.co.uk/news/article-1294649/Facebook-app-Indian-menusers-look-paler-ace.html#ixzz1vxr0Vdmn; emphasis mine).

This is one of many examples in the media of individuals who are depicted as completely free to make her/his choice—to lighten their skin tones or go for a nose job. We need to take note of the fact that such advertisements do not operate in isolation but in tandem with a surfeit of sponsored features, news, editorials, and interviews with professionals such as doctors, beauty specialists, hair stylists, sports icons, CEOs, etc., to promote new ideas of 'self-realisation', aspirations, achievement, and pleasure.

Thus far I have discussed the role that market and communication research agencies play in mapping new and old gender constructions with the clear and evident purpose of effectively seizing on what the potential customer desires. A related but significant point that also needs to be taken into consideration is that the media industry itself is a major site for communication research. Like the marketing agencies discussed earlier, the media industry too is very aware of its new role in shaping public discourse. It is also very alert to the competitive need to advertise and promote itself as a commercial entity. The boundaries between these roles are increasingly blurred.[3]

My discussion reveals that we need to take careful cognisance of the changes since the early 1990s, when India witnessed a rapid growth of the advertisement industry. What was novel in advertisements twenty years ago has become commonplace and routine, part of the landscape of popular culture. A rich corpus of 'studies' generated by advertising agencies on advertisements exists. Discussions on new gender norms and its cross-cultural variations are carried on within the industry on questions such as whether 'male and female roles in Indian ads have changed over the past decade'. Referring to a study published in the November 2000 issue of *Sex Roles: A Journal of Research*, Chatterjee mentions that some of the common stereotypical portrayals are less prevalent in Indian ads than in British magazine ads.

> Indian ads are being presented in a much more macho-dominant manner than they were before .... today ... you may see a cricketer like Mahendra Dhoni as often as you see Mirza .... Women in Indian ads are being presented in less dependent roles than they were before. An ad for a leading women's fortnightly recently carried a delightful image of an ageing woman in bridal attire. It later transpires that her daughter is getting her married again! *This is an example of positive advertising that subtly carries a social message.* Many mother-daughter ads in recent times bear out female bonding, in effect, subtly marginalising the role of men. (Chatterjee 2006; emphasis mine)

The body of research and analysis that goes on within the media and communication industry should make us wary of any blanket claim that the audience and customer are 'selfresponsible' subjects who are not passive victims of ideology. The discussion thus far suggests a far more complex working of how dominant ideas are constructed, not in gross opposition to what subjects feel, but informed about and sensitive to it. The contention, therefore, that they are no 'passive victims, but resistant actors' needs more careful attention (Chaudhuri 2005b). My engagement with the functioning of communication and marketing research is also to dispel a very widespread claim in globalisation and culture studies about free-floating images and ideas. Consumer research, as we saw, seeks to project this very message of 'self-propelled' individuals and freedom. They do so after studying the potential consumer at great length, scale, and sophistication, so as to target consumers with 'what they freely' choose and desire. Having identified the agencies that are central in the business of gender and media communication, I move on in the next section to an analysis of some recurring gendered ideological motifs that the contemporary Indian media and popular culture appear to promote, namely an ideology of self-realisation. This, I argue, is done at two levels: self as enterprise which one can build up, and a cult of self-expression. If the first finds its way in stories of women bosses, the latter is in the growing visibility of sexuality in the media and popular culture.

OVER-COMMUNICATIVE ABUNDANCE, CONTESTING IDEAS, AND THE MAKING OF A NEW SELFHOOD

The aim in this section is twofold: to capture the pervasive sense of over-communicative abundance, and to focus—albeit in a limited fashion—on an ongoing new construction of selfhood which draws elements from disparate ideological sources. It is by addressing two central motifs which define selfhood that I seek to capture the effortless ease with which disparate ideologies such as post-feminism and neo-liberalism coalesce in the construction of a selfhood that celebrates self-enterprise, pleasure, and sexuality, and posits them as women's empowerment. The idea of self-enterprise as central to selfhood is of course not delinked from the idea of pleasure as self-realisation. It is important, however, to distinguish between two related but different ideological strands in neo-liberalism in contemporary India: one strand more closely tied with the visible and hegemonic presence of the corporate world in public life, manifest in stories on women bosses; the other with the salience of consumption and hedonist pleasure in the media and popular culture, apparent in the hyper-visibility of sexuality in the public sphere. Significantly, both are seen as markers of women's empowerment and are therefore most visible during the yearly celebration of International Women's Day.[4]

I started with a notion that the idea of self as enterprise may have emerged from neoliberal ideas, while the idea of pleasure as self-realisation may have been influenced by post-feminism. One cannot push the point of sources too far. What, however, one can affirm with far greater certainty is that there is considerable overlap. We have already seen the considerable acumen of market research in deliberately and selectively drawing from those feminist ideas that appear most conducive to neoliberal reconstruction (Chaudhuri 2010c). Earlier in the chapter I referred to the neoliberal idea of extreme emphasis on an individuated selfhood, flexibility, and a promotion of freedom as a means to selfrealisation that disregards any questioning of the economic and social conditions that make such freedom possible. An analysis of the rhetoric of globalisation in India, however, suggests that projection of the 'unfettered' self in the immediate decade following liberalisation was equally a projection of economic liberalisation, the concerned social context that made this 'freedom' possible, a freedom once unimaginable in the Nehruvian epoch of license raj and state control (Chaudhuri 2001). Celebration of this new-found 'self' of Indian women was therefore a simultaneous celebration of India's economic reforms. In recent years, however, we have witnessed the celebration of the new selfhood, rather than the celebration of reforms.

As mentioned earlier, there are two aspects to this 'new individuated selfhood' that appear to recur in the media: the joyous celebration of

FIGURE 9.1 Consumption Comeback: Consumers are willing to splurge once again on a range of products. This is just what the doctor ordered for the Indian economy.

Source: http://media2.intoday.in/btmt/images/stories/come660_101816121146.jpg.

sexuality, evident in films, advertisements, fiction, and popular culture at large; and laudatory accounts of success, evident in stories about women achievers such as corporate bosses. In both images the unstated, and sometimes stated, assumption is that women are now free to both achieve and enjoy. Keeping the convergence of the distinct contexts, it is therefore not surprising that ideas informing marketing strategies and post-feminist ideas of selfhood articulated within the academia merge seamlessly. It is in this context that one begins with an abstract on post-feminism for a conference organised by a department of English in India. It reads:

> *Post feminism is a new form of empowerment and independence, individual choice, (sexual) pleasure, fashion, hybridism and the renewed focus on the female body can be considered fundamental for this contemporary feminism.* Post feminism might be seen as critique of 'second wave' feminism, as being, for example, too white and middle class. Some post feminists use the term 'third wave' to avoid the usage of 'post', which could be taken to imply 'anti-feminism'. *Media discourses play a crucial role in the representation, evaluation and development of this new feminism.* (Taghizadeh 2011; emphasis mine)

It is of some significance that the above abstract makes special mention of the crucial role that the media plays in the 'development of this new feminism'. My own survey of the English media also suggests that it has widely covered both the emergence of post-feminism and the new genre of chick-lit, described as the latest and most irreverent entrant into the world of English-language fiction. Publishers and critics alike have heralded it as a reflection of the growing confidence among women in the cities.

> *She is single, has a career and is willing to have fun, take risks and find a man her way, not necessarily her family's way.* It is a woman we have only read about in books from the Western countries and now, suddenly we are finding her on Indian roads ....
>
> A generation ago, marriage was the only route to independence from parental control in India. Now women are working, living alone in the cities, hanging out with women friends, drinking, dating and having fun in spite of the enormous social pressure to get married. (Lakshmi 2007; emphasis mine)

This laudatory account by no means goes unchallenged, but it does not occupy the centre-stage that the former does. If congratulatory pieces on chick-lit as post-feminism occupy the front pages of major newspapers, critical comments by feminists (such as the one below) are restricted to blogs or, at the most, sound bites in the electronic media.

> [I]f you are a woman you have to walk a certain way at a certain hour. If you begin transgressing, you are marked and your vulnerability increases manifold. I have tried and I know it is so difficult to be oblivious of the space one inhabits or perambulates. To proclaim that it is neutral is to ignore reality. (Subramaniam 2007)

If post-feminism sits at one end of this burgeoning discourse, overt anti-feminism too vies for space in this communicative clutter that marks popular culture. As in the case of the abstract on post-feminism, here too the media finds mention, once again indicating the hegemonic space that it has come to occupy in recent times.

> It is a common perception [through the media hype about women's torture and anti-patriarchal propaganda] that only men are the torturer and women are victims .... The legal torture of men is not an issue of physical strength or abusive behavior of one party, it is an issue of a legal system .... Such a nazist legal system created by feminist groups is making feminism synonymous to Nazism in India .... The *feminazis* in India is well recognized by International media and other countries and is disgust to the national pride. (http://travel.state.gov/travel/cis_pa_tw/cis/cis_113 9.html)

Such blatant attacks on women in general and feminism in particular are a visible presence in contemporary Indian popular culture, although it does not share the legitimacy that feminism or neo-liberalism does within the public discourse. Yet, on many occasions we see such sentiments in statements made by important public personnel.

Sexuality is certainly out in the open, although the intention with which different agencies seek to sponsor this hyper-visibility may be quite different. For instance, in the thick traffic of ideas that mark the contemporary culture of communicative abundance, the advertiser, the feminist, and the public health activist may intertwine unexpectedly in making sexuality visible in discourse. Thus, as I surfed the Web, I found a write-up on the construction of masculinities by researchers associated with the Population Council in the *Journal of Family Welfare*, which begins a discussion on the role that gender perspectives have played in the study of Indian masculinities, so necessary for the 'health and well-being of women' (Verma and Mahendra 2004: 71). A click of the mouse later, I found an advertisement on vagina bleaching.

> Do your ladyparts need some sprucing up? Like, color-wise? .... But a new ad for an Indian skin lightening product called Clean and Dry Intimate Wash, spotted by Jezebel seems to answer that question with a big fat 'DUH.' In the commercial, a couple lounges in their house, the man idly reading a newspaper while the woman pouts to herself because, clearly, he's ignoring her due to her dark-colored privates. Luckily, she gets ahold of Clean and Dry, which makes her vulva a few shades lighter, and her husband is happy-go-lucky again. Whew! Divorce averted. (http://article.wn.com/view/2012/04/12/vagina_Bleaching_Ad_Sparks_ Controversy_Over_Who_Needs_A_Pale; accessed 25 May 2012)

There is a pervasive focus on sexuality evident from even a cursory surfing of the Web, and on television, in films and radio programmes, on billboards, and in the relentless text messages on cell phones. In this regard, I would like to draw from two recent requests that I received from journalists whom I have never met or known for my comments on 'acceptance of sexual humour' and women with 'facial hair', respectively. I quote from both, since they reveal the issues that young journalists are encouraged to work on, and the kind of subjects an academic working on gender issues is expected to be familiar with.

> I am working on an article on the increasing *acceptance of sexual and toilet humour as part of modern Indian pop culture.* Merchandise with kinky themes and toilet humour has suddenly become popular in India :... illustrations with references to sex are becoming increasingly commonplace. These brands are all homegrown and they don't seek to titillate so much as to poke fun at sexuality .... What does this tell about Indian society? Is this sexual playfulness a marker for sexual openness and coming-of-age? (personal communication, June 2012; emphasis mine)

> I am a Delhi based journalist presently working on an article that discusses how facial/body hair is still a hurdle for women to get accepted or termed beautiful in our society. Studies say women are rated as less sexually attractive, intelligent, sociable, happy, and positive compared to hairless women. We do see the effect of this mind set in metros, where

> women are already slave to various depilatory practices, but now even small town and rural India is hooked.
>
> Also as Breanne Fahs, an associate professor of women and gender studies at Arizona State University, in an article titled 'Dreaded "Otherness": Heteronormative Patrolling in Women's Body Hair', says depilation affects women's attitudes towards themselves giving rise to 'body disgust'.
>
> Wanted to discuss how this affects women in India, both in metros, towns and villages. (personal communication, 16 October 2012; emphasis mine)

Such approaches by journalists are routine, since I too am just a click away, like the sites I surveyed here for this chapter. These requests obviously emerge from the kinds of demands and expectations with which the media industry operates. Stories on the body and sexuality are therefore important. I find the last communication significant not only for its attention on the body and on sexual desirability, but also for the telling reference to the American professor of women and gender studies, which takes me back to my point about the persisting Western influence, whether in Indian academia (as in this case) or the advertising sector, whose links of course are more direct.

If the overt flaunting of one's *sexuality* is one element in the construction of the new individuated selfhood, the other element is an *ideology of self as enterprise*, manifest in the surge of stories on women achievers and women bosses. If sexual expression forms one end of self-expression, the other end is achievement. If academia and various Western feminisms are one source of influence, Western corporate research is another. The body of market research, which we discussed at some length earlier, quite clearly draws on both, apart from finding out more about the 'real feelings' of the Indian man and woman. In other words, a concerted attempt exists to promote neoliberal practices and representations, which are produced and disseminated on a global scale. I have earlier referred to this drive towards the self as enterprise as a major principle of the neoliberal art of governing. The corporate world, with its hegemonic presence in the media, has to be recognised today as a central site of ideological production and dissemination of neoliberal culture. An example is the *McKinsey Quarterly*, which anyone can subscribe to online and which carries features such as 'Moving Women to the Top'. In this example, a survey shows that a majority of executives believe that gender diversity in leadership is linked to better financial performance, but companies take few actions to support women in the workforce (Prabhudesai 2000). Within the dominant celebratory rhetoric of India's growth story, the theme of women bosses is important. We have seen a series of pieces on this in the recent past.

> About a decade back, this discussion about women bosses in the Indian workforce may have been irrelevant. Today, India Inc. has woken up to a *surreal surge of women executives taking reigns of companies, departments and organizations* and are slowly clawing back on the apparent gender gap that has been the buzz for many years. (http://trak.in/tags/business/2012/03/30/women-bosses-indian-corporates-growth/; accessed 1 May 2017)

The expanding sports business in India, too, has been marked by the rise of women bosses, a development widely reported in the media. 'In a male-dominated sportsworld, some females have outshone their male counterparts. MSN India takes a look at some of the top female bosses who've broken the glass ceiling in sports ... Gayatri Reddy is the face of the Deccan Chargers' (http://sports.in.msn. Com/gallery/female-bosses-in-sportsworld; accessed 23 May 2012).

These examples reflect one more dimension in the wider cultural milieu marked by images of abundance, talk of information overload, and cornucopias of communication (Keane 1999) that I have been analysing. This is also a milieu where ideas from the West flow with greater ease, whether within academia, or the marketing agencies, or the social sector. Finally, this is a milieu wherein individuality, gender, sexuality, empowerment, cultural diversity, and race are configured as elements in the business of consumption in a global market.

CONCLUSION

My aim in this chapter has been to plot the hyper-visibility of women in the media and contemporary Indian popular culture against three contexts: the women's movement; India's economic reforms; and the unprecedented reach of an over-communicative and, importantly, largely audio-visual, often interactive media. In such a context marked by institutionalised feminism, a neoliberal ideology, and the logic of a publicity driven culture, the lines between the real and the reel blur. A surfeit of images and information appear to float freely and randomly as they relentlessly make their presence felt through 24/7 radio and television, internet and cell phone. It is this idea of a fusion of free-floating images buttressed by certain theoretical perspectives that this chapter has sought to question. My argument is to see them as intended consequences of the myriad professional organisations of market, media, and communication research that today are central sites for the ideological production and dissemination of global capitalism. I do not for a moment doubt that many of these efforts have been democratising, opening up spaces for self-expression that has for too long been forbidden. I would also argue that contemporary media and popular culture offer 'potential access', a 'promise to entry for other social segments' to the post-liberalised middle class[5] (Fernandes 2011: 71). I do not question this, but would like to locate this matter of access in the broader context of an India where there are more mobile phones than toilets (Vishnu 2012). My questions are simply: 'What could be the possible impact of post-feminism jostling alongside anti-feminism on democratic politics, other than catering to potential market segments'? 'Does the "liberating individual creativity" empower the market to tame emancipatory politics' (Fraser 2009: 108)? Perhaps Marcuse's observations are not so out of date.

> All points of view can be heard: the Communist and the Fascist, the Left and the Right, the white and the Negro, the crusaders for armament and for disbarment. Moreover, in endlessly dragging debates over the media, the stupid opinion is treated with the same respect as the intelligent one, the misinformed may talk as long as the informed, and propaganda rides along with education, truth with falsehood. (cited in Wolff, et al. 1969: 108)

However, must we be so pessimistic, or should we concur with the view that 'feminist analysis offers the fundamental epistemological tools necessary to understanding ICTs, as it does to all fields of enquiry', notwithstanding the communicative abundance? Perhaps it does make sense to understand 'the global digital technological architecture and advanced capitalism' as 'the warp and weft of the social fabric through which our subject positions are shaped; yet it is in the new spatiality and mobility of the digital realm that the possibility of egalitarian change lies' (Gurumurthy 2011: 144).

NOTES

1. The number of internet users in India—currently estimated at around 140 million—exceeds the number of TV sets in our homes. Facebook, with its 44 million Indian members, reaches more of us than any single TV channel, Doordarshan included, while YouTube, with over 31 million Indian viewers a month, is far and away our largest English television channel. Meanwhile, Twitter and Google Plus each get to about 14 million of us in a month—a number that is twice the circulation of India's largest newspaper (Murthy 2012).

2. Significantly, at the fiftieth anniversary celebrations of the *Contributions to Indian Sociology* (CIS), a real fear was expressed that non-resident Indians (NRIs) or foreigners writing about India would soon outpace the number of Indians researching themselves (Baviskar, et al. 2008: 4). See also Chaudhuri and Jaichandra (2014).

3. The proprietor of *The Times of India* (TOI) recently described his company, Bennett and Coleman (which publishes *TOI*), as an advertising company.

4. The horrific case of the young woman named Nirbhaya, or fearless, by the media, who died after being brutally raped and beaten in a moving bus in December 2012 in New Delhi, has elicited responses ranging from child marriage to banning skirts for schoolgirls. This in part appears as a backlash to the visible sexuality in the media, a point that needs careful engagement rather than a cross-fire between misogynist attacks on women's sexuality and a celebration of sexuality in a society deeply marked not only by gender inequality, but also by gross class and caste inequality (http://indianfusion.aglasem.com/ban-skirts-in-schools-safety-of-womenl; accessed 21 January 2013). See also http://www.thehindu.com/news/states/other-states/ child-marriage-as-remedy-for-rape-sparksfurore/article3984623.ecen (accessed 21 January 2013).

5. The rush of middle-class and lower middle-class parents to push their children into the mushrooming reality shows across channels is indicative.

CHAPTER 10

National and Global Media Discourse after 'Nirbhaya'

Instant Access and Unequal Knowledge

On 16 December 2012, a 23-year-old physiotherapy student was brutally gang-raped and assaulted by six people in New Delhi, the capital of India. The victim, who came to be known as 'Nirbhaya' (one without fear) died thirteen days later. The ghastly incident evoked widespread protests. The national and global media covered this extensively. It was the cover story in Indian media for a few weeks and never quite dropped out of national discourse, unlike other issues. This was unprecedented. But given that it happened in the Indian capital and the Indian media's own past in engaging with women's issues, it is more easily understandable. The widespread coverage of this incident in the international media calls for greater explanation, given India's traditionally low visibility in it. One possible explanation is that Delhi has emerged as one of the important nodes and switches, in Castell's language, of the global network society, and that without the massive mediatisation of this critical event in the Indian media, the Western media would hardly have become aware of it (Castells 1990, 2000).

While this is an undeniable fact, I would argue that any attempt to understand this has to also pay careful attention to the historically specific context within which the discourses were played out. The context, I argue, is new. Both globally and nationally, it is defined by neoliberal globalisation, India's own economic ascendency within it,[1] the rise of a host of international organisations fitting norms of global governance; new technology, media convergence, and the unprecedented role of a mediatised public discourse. This chapter argues that although there is a growing convergence between 'national' and 'global' discourse, important differences persist between the content and tenor of the two sets of discourses. It is through a comparative study of the two on 'Nirbhaya' that this chapter seeks to examine how and why they differ.

This chapter therefore argues that an imperative need exists to bring in history and political economy for a better understanding of the contexts, commonalities, and differences between 'national' and 'global' discourse. Neither the logic of media nor the mandate of proliferating project-based research would explain this. Yet, it is evident that India's past bears heavily on the present 'national' discourse. And the history of Orientalism cannot be wished away entirely from global discourse. The latter, one can argue, stems from 'the inequality of ignorance' that Dipesh Chakravarti pointed to many years ago, which persists between First World and Third World scholars (Chakravarti 1992). Academic centres of global excellence such as Harvard University, too, are not free of this 'bane of unequal ignorance', as Prabha Kotiswaran's remarks in the context of 'Nirbhaya' imply. She argues that 'circuits of feminist scholarship and activism have become so inter-disciplinary and transnational that maintaining and policing turf is an utterly useless endeavour'. The problem, however, lies in the fact that 'Some Western feminists ... barely care to become familiar with the context in which they are trying to intervene',[2] even as their 'particular versions of American legal feminism[3] have been propelled out of their provincial contexts into international law and policy making'[4] (Kotiswaran 2013: 1).

I would like to argue that the observation holds true not only of the academia, but also of most key sites of knowledge production, such as IIs, global think-tanks, corporate research institutions, and non-governmental organisations (NGOs). These institutions hold great influence in the contemporary global order and we shall see how they also form key sources of information for contemporary media and for the emerging global public sphere (Chaudhuri 2010b). While this asymmetry of knowledge has perhaps been long true, what is new is a potent convergence of 'ignorance' and 'instant access' that new technologies have made possible. It is within this configuration that I attempt to analyse both the content and the form of the mediated discourse in the aftermath of the gang-rape.

This chapter is based upon a thematic analysis of public discourse in the aftermath of the 'Nirbhaya' rape. I followed discussions in newspapers, on television, and the internet on a daily basis in the immediate months after the event, and have continued to follow them since. Television channels followed have been primarily English and Hindi, and occasionally Bengali, while my study of the internet and print media has been in English.

The Argument and Approach

My emphasis on a historical and political economic perspective stems from a certain unease with the manner in which the media is often seen as a discrete entity that can be analysed, either in terms of its texts/ images or their reception and resistance by people who are also treated as bounded empirical beings, rather than an ensemble of social relations. My argument is that it is important to distinguish between the concrete economic and legal structures of the global order from the logic of new media technologies and their almost magical possibilities. I make this claim, fully aware that the latter is played out within the ambit of the former. This section therefore first elaborates how my distinction between 'national' and 'global' discourse rests on a political economic understanding of contemporary capitalism. And second, it explicates the nature and consequences of new media technologies and the reason for my use of the term 'mediatisation'.

THE POLITICAL ECONOMIC

The transformed relationship between the 'national' and the 'global', I argue, has to be seen in the way states and markets have been recast in contemporary capitalism. I am not using 'national' and 'global' to refer to empirical regions or entities alone. However, fundamental to this chapter is the idea that in the current stage of capitalism, the state and the nation as we have understood them since Westphalia have been reconfigured to take on board the play of global capitalism and transnational capitalists. My argument is that although distinctions are apparent between national and international media in the Nirbhaya case, it is equally true that significant processes of transformation are already underway. Important structural changes mark the relationship between Indian and international media. The collaboration between *India Real Time* and *Wall Street Journal* is one example.[5]

My contention is that states have been major players in laying the terms of public discourse in modernity. In India, where civil society had not emerged in the way that it had in Western modernity, the state had an even more important role in setting the agenda for public discourse (Kaviraj 1991). The media did play a significant role in the growth of Indian nationalism, and later in projecting state policies. A greater role, however, was played by the engagement of political leaders and organisations with people through direct interaction at different levels. Public meetings held in different corners of India, even in a period when travel entailed considerable time, defined the story of India's nation-building project. Stories of how the news of protests travelled through word of mouth to different parts of India are also part of this history. In the current context of global capitalism, however, the state is no longer the only player. Social movements leverage the media and the media itself no longer simply 'represents' but 'sets' agendas. This would be evident in both the national and global discourse, which I examine below. The media does not act alone in this regard, but along with a host of national and new transnational players within which the media as an industry is implicated.

In the 'Nirbhaya' case, we see within the national discourse the role of: Indian feminists; civil society organisations; political parties representing different ideological positions; and the Indian state. In the global discourse on 'Nirbhaya', we witness a greater role of: international institutions; international nongovernmental organisations (INGOs); consultancy sectors such as risk assessment organisations; and the tourism industry. The pervasive presence of the global discourse draws its legitimacy from the hegemonic position that IIs occupy in this new order. However, this omnipresence would be impossible without the technology that makes media convergence possible. As stated earlier, this chapter therefore at once privileges both political economy and media logic. If the former reflects the compulsions of capital, the latter provides information of a 'format' of 'how material is organized, the style in which it is presented, the focus or emphasis on particular characteristics of behavior, and the grammar of media communication' (Altheide and Snow 1979: 10).

MEDIA LOGIC, NEW TECHNOLOGY, AND MEDIATISATION

This chapter acknowledges that the extraordinary speed with which 'Nirbhaya's' tragedy travelled would have been impossible without the new configuration of media technology brought about by the digital revolution and the birth of the World Wide Web. This ushered in paradigmatic changes in creating, delivering, and consuming content. The emergence of new media, widespread use of multimedia, and an inevitable transformation of traditional media has ushered in a world of instant access to people and institutions globally. Notwithstanding the magical possibilities of new technology, instant access does not necessarily spell either equal or informed access to content. For content remains constitutive of a host of historical, political, economic, cultural, and social forces.

In this regard, I would also like to make a point about media convergence, which is often understood as post-ideological, for convergence speaks of a cultural shift where consumers seek out what they want, making discrete connections among the scattered media (Jenkins 2006). The claim is that people are no longer 'passive media spectators' but participate at all three levels of production, selection, and distribution. I disagree, for there is a clear ideological content that is emerging from specific sites of knowledge production and decision-making in the new global order. This chapter develops this argument at some length. Jenkins also contends that the digital divide is less about access and more about the 'participation gap'. I agree with this for even in a country like India, where inequality is sharp and the digital divide[6] large, a significant section of people, literate or illiterate, rural or urban, do watch and listen to the media, and then discuss what they saw and heard. They are not 'passive victims', but the script of their debate is also not entirely theirs.

A key approach that informs this chapter is the intersection of the political economic and the new multimedia technology. This is most evident in the increasing cross-ownership[7] in the media sector and media convergence. Cross-ownership of the media has been a matter of some concern as India is one of the few countries where there has still not been any regulation in place, although it is in proposed policy discourse. Strong opinions have emerged in the media industry—both for and against—concerning the Telecom Regulatory Authority of India's (TRAI) initiatives regarding cross-media ownership in the country.[8] It has been defended by associations representing the print media on the grounds of attaining economies of scale, for 'Cross-media operations can reduce the cost of news gathering, news dissemination, while also providing affordable access to international news' (Kumar 2013).[9] My concern here is neither about the need for economies of scale nor for economy of access, but the trend towards less diversity of sources.

It is within this convergence that I seek to capture the themes that emerged in the multiple discourses in the aftermath of the December Rape. The case of 'Nirbhaya' is an early and dramatic instance of 'modernisation' in India, where the media appeared to shape and frame the processes and discourses of political communication (Lilleker 2008). Different actors in the event 'adjusted to the demands of the mass media' in the manner that Kent Asp had described as the 'mediatization of political life' (Asp 1986). I use the term 'mediatised' therefore to enable one to see the media not as an external institution that affects social life, but as entangled in almost all spheres of economic, political, social, and cultural life.

KEY ASSUMPTIONS

There are a couple of assumptions that flow from my understanding of the political economy of twenty-first century global capitalism on the one hand, and media logic on the other. The first is that some key tropes that define the dominant global discourse—governance, development, gender, and human rights—are broadly crafted by IIs such as the World Bank, World Trade Organization (WTO), the United Nations (UN), and a host of human rights agencies. Crucial in the dissemination of this script have been the large number of international non-governmental organisations, new and critical sites of knowledge production which actively engage with the media. There is a dominant presence of a global human rights discourse in the responses to the 'Nirbhaya' case. Admonishment at India's human rights violation is evident in travel advisories issued by foreign states; statements by international institutions; commentaries in international media; transnational feminist academia; sundry blogs; and corporate commentaries.

Second, in the national discourse, there is greater intervention by different sections located within the Indian nation, such as social movements, women's organisations, the legal fraternity, courts, and conservative patriarchal sections of Indian society and the state. Hence, my contention is that the 'national' does continue to matter, even as 'global' discourses impinge upon the 'national'. It gets transformed, but is not entirely subsumed within the global.

Third, my use of the term 'national public sphere' is deliberate. I am acutely aware of India's 'internally differentiated publics' in view of language plurality and the manifold asymmetries within the public sphere in India. However, empirically, as would be evident from this chapter, there is a basic difference in the intense and variegated discourse within the country and the reactions of institutions and people located outside India (irrespective of 'national' or 'ethnic' origins) to the case. I would also stand by the term 'national public sphere' to counter theoretically the idea that the 'fragments' of the nation, or in this instance the various 'publics' within the political entity India, are discrete, bounded entities that operate independent of each other. This view has widespread academic currency in postcolonial theory, but is questionable on grounds that are both theoretical and empirical. Theoretically, it looks at the 'publics' as 'bounded' entities, in the manner in which traditional Western anthropology studied 'native' 'communities' and 'villages' as though untouched by macro processes even of the scale of colonialism. Historically, it belies the fact that politics outside the dominant Indian 'nationalist framework' had to engage to counter and critique the former.

Empirically, we know that there has been a long tradition of Indian newspapers being read aloud and discussed in village teashops, among people both literate and non-literate. The last quarter century has witnessed the ubiquitous television set in city barbershops, which again functions as a 'public' and shared site of consumption and discussion. Nothing brought this more to the fore than the 2014 General Elections in India,[10] where '*chai pe charcha*' (discussion over tea) became a key campaign strategy of the Bharatiya Janata Party (BJP) after its prime ministerial candidate Narendra Modi was mocked for his humble beginnings as a tea seller. He won the elections. In other words, the idea of a 'split public' (Rajagopal 2001) appears to make both the role of the political state and an expanding market inconsequential in the making of everyday life. Significantly, the past few years have seen a greater expansion of Indian language media than English language ones.[11] More recently, we have had English-language television channels conducting interviews in Indian languages with English subtitles.[12] Further, media logic has increasingly transformed Indian language media along lines that mirror the format and content of English media, once again raising questions about whether one can hold on to the idea of split publics.

My fourth contention is that the purported boundaries between old and new media seem to collapse as we witness in the multiple discourses a seamless continuity in both content and form. One of the profound ways in which the internet and new media change the public sphere is through a change in temporality—our relationship and experience with time. Information and images travel the world instantly. The internet is a highly mediated and highly capitalised form of circulation organised in the 24x7 instant access. The consumer has instant access, but the processes and structures within which messages are constituted and multiply mediated remain invisible to the consumer (Warner 2002). This makes it difficult to fully understand how people read a text or image in specific locales. Further, we know little about how this 24x7 instant access, coupled with abbreviated and context-innocent messages, shapes opinions and propels political agency.

This matter of localised readings gets further skewed because, *one*, there are unequal levels of global knowledge and ignorance within which both the making of media content and instant access takes place; and *two*, while the internet is global, its use is still defined by communities and culture that could well be spread across the globe (such as diasporic communities), but are essentially bounded in specific cultural groups. The WhatsApp messages, whether of virulent or banal content, in circulation are evidence of this. There is, in other words, a dissonance between content as well as transmission, reflecting a deep-seated hierarchy and a form that expedites instant uploading and access.

In this regard, my fifth contention is that we need to take history into account to appreciate that the women's question has been central in modern Indian public discourse, and this past that has been rendered invisible in media gender discourse. A historical perspective is therefore more important than ever before, as we race an increasingly dominant, homogenised, and effectively mediatised narrative[13] that can travel instantly and spread everywhere, even as 'unequal ignorance' in key sites of knowledge production persists.

The sixth and final contention of this chapter, therefore, is that in a mediatised and publicity driven world, we have to recognise that the role of talking, discourse, and communication acquires a different order of centrality.[14] As a sociologist, I am aware of the limits of seeking to understand the 'social' through a study of media discourses. However, what I would like to underscore here is that we need to take cognisance of the fact that the 'social', in a fundamental sense, has been redefined. The volume of information and images, their scale and reach, speed and persuasive power marks a new era. This redefines the meaning of 'experience' as a commodity form that mediates people's relationship to both their pasts and presents. There are a couple of theoretical and methodological issues that this observation raises with regard to any attempt to study the events pertaining to the case of 'Nirbhaya'.

Can we study this particular event sans its media discourses? How do we look at the matter of commodification of experience in the media? Did the personal 'experience' of the victim or her family or her friend get commoditised in the media? The broader political question that arises is whether this commoditisation cancels out the expansive potential of democracy, contained in the sheer scale of public protest and the wide-ranging debate on core feminist questions even within mainstream media. A more careful examination of the responses may provide an answer to the limits and possibilities of mediatisation for democracy. The structure of this chapter flows from the argument articulated above. It is broadly divided into two parts: the *national* discourse and the *global* discourse; that there will be inevitable overlapping is part of the story that I seek to tell.

National Discourse: Bringing in History

Historically, gender issues have often been central to modern India's public discourse and even as gender remained a pivot, it tended to spawn discussions on a whole range of issues that do not directly pertain to gender. My decision to overtly refer to history is to counter the current obsession with the 'contemporary', if not the 'immediate'. Few would disagree that this is widespread in the media, with its 24x7 logic and 'breaking news' syndrome. I, however, contend that this focus on the immediate and an orientation towards a checklist of 'problems' and a readier checklist of 'solutions' increasingly inform social science academia too. It is not surprising, therefore, that there is a widely prevalent view in gender global discourse, now spilling into the 'national', that gender rights in India are a fallout of the United Nation's Declaration of International Women's Year and Decade in 1975 and the initiatives of IIs and INGOs since.[15] A social science analysis of media discourse therefore has to bring in history, political economy, and the minutiae of everyday life,[16] apart from the specificities of media logic and its form of presentation.

From the early beginnings of modern media in colonial India, various issues pertaining to women have occupied centre-stage: sati,[17] widow remarriage,[18] child marriage,[19] age of consent, and education for women (Chaudhuri 1993). Debates in the then young Indian media (ibid.) and within women's organisations such as the All India Women's Conference (AIWC, 1926), Women's India Association (WIA, 1917), and others have in a fundamental sense been debates on Indian modernity and its uneasy relationship with tradition; nationalism and democracy; culture and individual rights, inequality and citizenship; public and private spheres; west and east; gender and sexuality; progress and backwardness. This is how it was during the nineteenth century and this is how it is in the twenty-first century.

There was a retreat of the women's question from public discourse after independence in 1947 and a resurgence with the Indian women's movement in the 1970s (also termed the second phase of the Indian women's movement), triggered by the Mathura rape case that led to sustained efforts by the women's movement to change the law.[20] The range of issues raised in the second phase of this movement, as in the first, were carried widely by a media increasingly engaged with questions of women's equal rights as citizens (Kumar 1997; Sen 1990; Shah and Gandhi 1992).

The 1980s witnessed the Shah Bano[21] and Deorala Sati[22] cases, which once again brought back many of the old contestations, such as cultural versus gender rights and community versus state, to the centre-stage (Chaudhuri 1993; Sangari and Vaid 1989; Sunder Rajan 2003). The media played an active role in raising questions of gender justice with regard to this case (Chaudhuri 2000). However, the nature of the media during this entire period was different. It did not have the broader political economy set up by neo-liberalism, nor did it have the technological sophistication of an interactive media or a publicity driven culture, which are constitutive of the media today. It is this transformed media that was both an actor and a central site for representing the public outcry against the gruesome rape and murder of a young woman in Delhi in December 2012.

Sixty-six years of Indian independence, development, affirmative action by the state, and social movements have all contributed to both a deepening and expansion of democracy. There is an increasing presence of marginalised sections in the public sphere (Rege 2006). In the immediate years preceding Nirbhaya's death, India had seen the rise of a strong anti-corruption movement and a growing presence of what has been termed civil society organisations. This movement has drawn huge support from the urban middle class and it has used the social media extensively. This movement was actually being covered in real time. At its peak, it was a media event, drawing more audience than even the most popular soaps.[23]

The anti-corruption movement, drawing heavily from the transparency and governance discourse of the World Bank, was primarily directed against the ruling government. The state, and not the corporate, was the object of critical scrutiny, as the media had actively projected since the early 1990s that the 'market' was more accountable and responsive to the 'public' than the 'state' (Chaudhuri 2000, 2001, 2010b). More recently, however, in the campaign for the 2014 general elections, the Aam Aadmi (common man) Party (AAP), whose leading members were part of the anti-corruption movement, has been attacking the major political parties for being in cohort with big business houses who now have a major say in state functioning.

With the emergence of new media and media convergence, recent practices of an interactive 'public' have become possible. A significant convergence of a political mood of the 'public' and the technological possibility for enhanced public interactivity has taken place. In the aftermath of the December 2012 rape, the dominant media rhetoric was that the 'public' has risen. The 'public', the media pontificated, will no longer 'take things lying down'. Significantly, it was the word 'public' that was increasingly being used, even in Indian-language media discourse. In everyday parlance, it meant 'everybody'. The spontaneous outburst was triggered by what had happened to 'Nirbhaya', but it had happened at a point where there was already a growing anger against the government which was seen as corrupt, cut off from and unresponsive to the ordinary person, the 'Aam Aadmi'.[24] It is worth mentioning here that it is a common sight on Indian television these days to watch a news broadcaster breaking off in the midst of debating live with a range of people[25] to read from a purported SMS, or attend to a caller, even as the television screen has audience responses on a ticker below.[26]

MULTIPLE SITES, MULTIPLE DISCOURSES

I have already stated in my initial observations that in the national discourse, the central actors are members representing different sections located within the Indian nation, such as social movements, women's organisations, the legal fraternity, courts, conservative patriarchal sections of Indian society, and the Indian state. In my schematic account of the national media discourse on the Nirbhaya case, the role of these actors will become visible. Readers will also notice how the Indian media took on an aggressive position, became a spokesperson for the protests, and sought to set the agenda for both public discourse and the state.

In the initial weeks, 'Hang the rapists' was the strident cry of the media.[27] Nothing less than capital punishment would assuage the collective grief and anger of the 'public'—so went the dominant discourse. As the crowd surged, demanding justice for 'Nirbhaya', remembering the 'daughter of India', the government appeared unsure of its response. Police attempts to disperse the crowd through the use of water cannons further fuelled public anger. The media was shrill, demanding instant justice. The active intervention of women's organisations and feminist lawyers in media discussions mitigated this stridency.[28] This shift in focus has been described as one from a 'retributive public', where the death penalty or castration became a 'vocabulary of protest', to a 'passionate reasoned' public intent on 'what the government needs to do to be accountable to rape survivors' (Baxi 2012). The active intervention of women's organisations and feminist scholars appeared to have persuaded the media to change track from hysterical ranting to more reasoned debates (Agnes 2013; Geetha 2013).

However, there did emerge a new '"public in solidarity" which has "informed, provoked and supported" a "determined fight" against sexual violence anywhere in the country' (Baxi 2012). Women's groups of diverse ideological persuasions, students' organisations, individuals with no political affiliations, and housewives came together on the streets with a common intent to fight for gender justice. In response to this public demand of Indian citizens, the Indian state set up a committee headed by Justice Jagdish Sharan Verma,[29] a retired Chief Justice who passed away in April 2013. Representatives of women's and human rights groups, lawyers, and activists from across the country who had for decades fought for reforms on rape and sexual assault welcomed several provisions of the Criminal Law (Amendment) Act 2013, and the Criminal Bill 2013 that was passed by Parliament in response to the Verma Committee recommendations.[30]

If the women's movement, alongside many ordinary citizens from diverse walks of life, was anguished at the incident, there were others who raised quite different kinds of questions. Political parties appeared divided. Their responses ranged from dominant liberal views to communist critiques to cultural Hindu nationalist statements. It is pertinent to mention here that for the first four decades after independence, a conglomeration of left of centre liberal ideas had defined the dominant discourse. This has been changing over the past two decades with a growing articulation of Hindu nationalist ideas, pitted against what they describe as pseudo-secular politics. It is therefore important to take note of the observations of Mohan Bhagwat, chief of the right-wing Rashtriya Swayamsevak Sangh (RSS),[31] who opined that rapes are an urban crime shaped by Westernisation, and are not a matter of concern in rural India where traditional values are upheld. 'Mohan Bhagwat doesn't know either India or Bharat,' said Brinda Karat, a Communist Party of India (Marxist) politburo member and a leading member of the All India Democratic Women's Association (AIDWA), for 'the largest number of rapes occurs in rural areas on Dalits, tribals and rural workers' (Ghosh 2012). Asaram Bapu,[32] a popular Hindu guru, said that the New Delhi rape victim could have saved herself if she had simply 'held the hand of one of the men and said, "I consider you as my brother"' (Harris 2013). In yet other sites, debates of a very different order were carried out on Marxism and gender (Chauhan, et al. 2013). Yet others commented on the differential response to rape committed against poor Dalit women, which often went unreported and unremarked upon in the media.[33]

A string of administrative measures was launched by the government, even as parliamentarians made offensive, sexist remarks during the debate on the anti-rape law. Sharad Yadav, a legislator of Rashtriya Janata Dal (RJD), justified 'following girls' for 'when you want to talk to a woman ..., you have to put in a lot of effort'. Mulayam Singh Yadav, leader of the Samajwadi Party (SP), the ruling party in Uttar Pradesh, wanted to stop co-education while Lalu Prasad Yadav, head of RJD, a regional party in Bihar, called on the government to cover up ancient erotic sculptures in Khajuraho and in Konark—both of which are UNESCO world heritage sites.[34] Sumitra Mahajan, a member of the BJP, criticised Indian reality television for 'throwing young boys and girls together [...] and [...] dancing together to all kinds of love songs' (https://blogs.wsj.com/indiarealtime/2013/03/20/in-anti-rape-debate-indian-mps-reveal-sexism/; accessed 4 May 2017).

Advertisements since Nirbhaya have often addressed questions of gender and sexual harassment.[35] Popular television serials dealt with training women for self-defence,[36] even as other TV programmes discussed gender-related issues, including the glass ceiling for corporate women. In this entire process the news channels in particular took on the role of spokespersons, speaking to and on behalf of the 'nation'[37] and the public. What cannot be ignored, however, is that gender justice did become a key issue in public discourse, something that every political party had to contend with in India's 2014 general elections.

GLOBAL DISCOURSE

The previous section provided a glimpse of the diverse discourses that covered an entire range of perspectives—Marxist, liberal, Dalit, patriarchal, feminist—in the different languages that constitute the national public sphere. I had earlier stated my reservations about the idea of a 'split public' and would like to once again suggest that there does appear to be a mutually comprehensible, albeit diverse, conversation going on across the nation.[38] In this section, I look at the global discourse whose focus and tenor do appear to differ. The significant differences are: *one*, global media's condemnation of the Indian state's failure to live up to India's global brand image as an economic power, expressed variously in tones of horror, dismay, shock, and mockery; *two*, greater dependence on specific sources for information, which I elaborate upon below; and *three*, a broad brush treatment of India as one monolithic entity.

A central contention of this chapter has been that any analysis of the media has to take into account the new structure and functioning of transnational capitalism. Linked to this is my contention that this new economic order is accompanied by the emergence and growing influence of international institutions, global think-tanks, corporate research organisations, a new regime of international human rights and women's rights laws that inform the practice not only of states, but also of big business houses that want the minimum norms of gender justice, law, and governance in place. Likewise, we have the rise of the tourism industry as an essential element of the new global architecture. New organisations like global risk assessment firms have emerged to facilitate both global investment and tourist flow. They monitor social risks such as violence against women. A whole corpus of reports has emerged from these sites. They are readily available sources on the web, not just for the media but, as I have documented at some length elsewhere, also within the practice of social science (Chaudhuri 2010b). As of now the international media's dependence on these sources appear to be greater than in the national media in the 'Nirbhaya' case. As things stand today, this is bound to grow in the near future, cutting across both national and global discourse. These are significant producers and disseminators of 'knowledge' today, and it may not be inappropriate to see them as the new ideological apparatus for governance.

Before I go any further, I would like to make a clarification regarding my take on these new developments towards better global governance. I would like to reiterate that while at one level, international human and gender rights are commendable and enabling; there is a need for caution. I do not wish to engage with the dangers of an II-based governance here, except to mention two points: *one*, a point often ignored in the buzz on 'global governance', that they are sites of power and work in tandem with other centres of strategic power; and *two*, that while democratic states are accountable to citizens, IIs are not. Elections provide citizens the right to vote against a government if they wish to. However, similar mechanisms do not bind the citizens of a state to transnational entities such as IIs. This was a major point of debate in India when the country acceded to the WTO regime.

My focus in this chapter is, however, on their role as media sources and I return to that here. There are issues with both the content and format of these studies. The content, apart from reflecting 'unequal ignorance', also suffers from the logic of writing 'reports' and 'project evaluations', which have a set motif that defines the questions, indicators, and mode of data analysis. The rise of the global index as a measure typifies this. This trend is further compounded in the media by the limits of the form of communication that contemporary media practice deploys—sensational stories, sound bites, and set-up controversies programmed to convey flattened, easy-to-consume information.

This straitjacketed treatment of social issues is also reflected at the ground level in the everyday functioning of myriad NGOs, with its mechanical dissemination of buzzwords and tropes that fit in with the managerial mode of much of professional grassroots activism. This, in combination with deepseated ignorance of histories and contexts, cannot further either critical awareness or democratic rights, which in a fundamental sense is the task of the media in liberal democracies. But liberal democracies in the past rested on an institutional base of the nation-state and national public discourse. How, then, do we imagine a democratic 'global public sphere'?

International Media

As mentioned earlier, one significant way in which the national media discourse differed from the global was the focus on India as an economic power and its poor showing in its social indicators. The *New York Times* observed how '*India is a rising economic power* but the world's largest democracy can never reach its full potential if half its population lives in fear of unspeakable violence' (Ghosh 2012; emphasis mine). Claire O'Sullivan in the *Irish Examiner Reporter* asks: '*What is going on in the world's ninth richest economy* that women are now increasingly scared of being brutalised on the streets, that they can't board a bus, stay in a hotel alone, or camp with their husband?' (O'Sullivan 2013; emphasis mine).

A central marker of Orientalist discourse has been the 'barbaric' treatment of women.[39] A 2013 report on the Global Slavery Index carried in international media and in *The Times of India* reveals a convergence of twenty-first century human rights discourse and nineteenth-century Orientalism.

> Sixty-six years after independence, India has the dubious distinction of being home to half the number of modern day slaves in the world. The first Global Slavery Index has estimated that 13.3 to 14.7 million people live like slaves in the country .... The index, published by the Australia-based Walk Free Foundation, ranked 162 countries based on three factors that include estimated prevalence of modern slavery, a measure of child marriage and a measure of human trafficking in and out of a country [....] (March 2013).

'Nirbhaya's' case was seen as a major dent on India's image in global business circles. A media report on a visit by then Prime Minister of India Manmohan Singh to Germany after the incident observed that '*India ... found itself once again in the dock on its high maternal and child mortality rates. The embarrassment happened in full view of the world press,* which had assembled to hear ... the outcomes of the Indo-German Inter-Governmental Consultations' (Subramaniam 2013; emphasis mine). The report saw this as a serious 'human rights violation', as the state could be seen as complicit in 'murdering' its women and children.

I would like to draw attention to the assortment of keywords in the above news report: 'Indo-German bilateral ties, Bilateral Investment and India-EU Free Trade Agreement, maternal mortality, child mortality, gender insecurity, and crime against women'. They indicate how closely matters of trade and commerce have been intertwined with human rights issues[40] in the new global order. While few would have any quarrel with the extension of human rights, the problem has been that this has often been used selectively by IIs and Western states.

O'Sullivan's piece in the *Irish Chronicler* displays the same media practice of using available statistics (from a UN source in this case) and select interviews with NGO personnel. In this instance, it was one Paul Healy who was working as Programme Manager to a local partner INGO Trocaire, run by the 'National Alliance of Women in Odisha' (NAWO). What is discomfiting is that O'Sullivan's account of women in India virtually rests on this very limited source of information. This actually exemplifies what I mean by the potent convergence of 'instant access' and 'unequal ignorance'. The quotes from the report below may help to make my point clear.

> Baby girls and young girls are also more at risk in India than anywhere in the world, according to the *United Nations. The Indian child rights organisation CRY estimates say that about 12m girls are born in India every year, however, one million of these girls die by the age of one* [....] Dowries are still engrained in Indian culture. (O'Sullivan 2013; emphasis mine)

The dismal account does not stop here as it recounts horror stories of the rampant practice of dowry without a mention of either the anti-dowry campaign that marked the second phase of the women's movement, or the whole gambit of laws that were put in place, or any reference to feminist scholarship in the field. '[...] *Sometimes what they do is poison her; they can kill her with weapons, throttle her or bride burning—is common .... Then with one wife killed, they can get another girl and another dowry*' (ibid.; emphasis mine).

In a world of instant access, one can assume that older distances, hierarchies, and misrepresentations have been done away with. This quote suggests otherwise: '[...] According to Paul Healy [...] the victim of *the Delhi bus gang rape was savagely killed as she dared to go out with a boy and at 8.30 pm* [...]' (ibid.; emphasis mine).

Wall Street Journal posted an article on the website of *India Realtime* (whose tagline is 'The daily pulse of the world's largest democracy') on whether it was safe for foreigners to travel in India. Stancati, the author of the piece, provides a compilation of information through interviews with foreign tourists, members of the Tourist Bureau, as well as information gleaned from the websites of different states. I present below a quote from the piece to highlight the sources that she uses.

> [...] What is happening here is a little bit worrying but when you are travelling, ... it's important to have your wits in place,' said Ms. Beard, who is traveling with a *tour group*.
>
> [...] Delhi representative of the *Travel Agents Association of India*, ... says that the December rape case has not affected the tourism industry ... the industry is now more aware about the need to help prevent sexual crimes against tourists.
>
> [...] director at the Delhi-based *Sadhana Tours*, says he hasn't received any questions from clients on women's safety in recent months ....
>
> *Guide books* and *foreign governments* have long warned women to be careful when traveling in India.
>
> 'U.S. citizens, particularly women, are cautioned not to travel alone in India,' says a note from the U.S. Department of State [...].
>
> ... a woman traveling in India ... should respect local dress codes and customs and avoid isolated areas [...] says .. the website of the British foreign office. (Stancati 2013; emphasis mine)

Before I end, I would like to refer to one particular debate on the Age of Consent that was covered extensively both within the global and national media—old and new. I quote illustratively from this to make the point of unequal levels of ignorance. All intense public debate on the Age of Consent Bill had divided public opinion in the late nineteenth century.[41] More than a hundred and a quarter years later, the central actors were different. The colonial state had long since gone. It was the Indian state that was being addressed by the women's movement and other groups to bring in a more effective law.[42] Stating that the Bill is a step forward for women's rights in India, activist and lawyer Vrinda Grover said:

> [...] this Bill seeks to protect our entire society from the scourge of sexual violence. *This is not a bill against men; it is a Bill against criminals; it is a Bill from which all citizens stand to gain pence of mind against the mindless violence that stalks us* [....]
>
> Farah Naqvi, women's rights activist, went on to say that this stand is not a moral endorsement of teenage sexual activity. *We must recognize that 'criminalising as rape' the consensual acts of young adults will make most vulnerable our young men, particularly those from marginalized communities* (RINA 2013; emphasis mine).

The government's decision to fix the legal age for consensual sex at eighteen from an earlier agreement by the Cabinet on sixteen was seen by women's organisations and feminist scholars as succumbing to pressures from conservative leaders who believed that the move would encourage young people to experiment with sex. The police felt that the move could make it harder to secure rape convictions in cases where the victim was between sixteen and eighteen, as she would be asked at trial to show that she had not consented. The fault lines of Indian society were clearly in play.

Globally, however, this dimension was not reflected. The caption of a report read: 'India which has more child brides than any nation in the world did not sign a United Nations initiative to end child marriage.' This report had to be corrected shortly after.

> *Correction: an earlier version of this story and headline said that India failed to 'sign' the resolution. In fact, it chose not to co-sponsor it. The story and headline have been edited to reflect this.*
>
> Syed Akbaruddin, a spokesman for India's foreign ministry said that although the government was not a co-sponsor it nonetheless 'supported the objectives of the resolution'. (Stuart 2013)

But Avert, a UK-based charity group, was quick to conclude that 'by raising the age of consent to 18, India last year became one of the most conservative countries in the world, according to data compiled by Avert ...'. The global average on the legal sex age, according to Avert, is sixteen.[43] This same report refers to the All India Democratic Women's Association (AIDWA), which has an organisational presence in twenty-two states in India and a current membership of more than nine million, of which several state units came into existence during the 'freedom struggle',[44] as a New Delhi-based 'non-profit organization'. This may appear a trivial point to make. However, it demonstrates the ignorance of the history of social movements in India. For in this global discourse, all movements for gender justice are seen as off-shoots of efforts by well-meaning global NGOs, charity groups, and IIs.

CONCLUSION

The questions that I raised at the start of the chapter were: Does greater visibility in the media means greater democratisation and gender justice?

And did the logic of media practice and commoditisation cancel out the expansive potential of democracy evident in the public protest and wide-ranging debate on feminist questions after 'Nirbhaya'?

A year and a half after 'Nirbhaya's' death, one can say that the campaign against gender violence and rape has been sustained by the media. News reports, TV serials, blog discussions have all kept the pressure on.[45] But violent incidents of this kind remain and seem to be growing. It is undeniable that the media was critical in drawing attention to violence against women after 'Nirbhaya' and in making gender justice a key issue in the General Elections of 2014. But it is also true that the media is not a magic institution that would solve all problems, although this is an impression that has been gaining ground. It is only concerted action by social movements, political parties, the state, and society at large that will help to usher in changes that will not allow such incidents to take place. Indeed, legal changes have taken place. But it is important to recall that India is a country where historically, laws have usually been far more democratic than social norms. This gap between the two reflects the fault lines in Indian society. It can be legitimately asked: Why, despite all the movements, is sexual violence becoming a norm? Or is it? We, as social scientists, need to answer that.

However, neither the tropes of Global Indexes nor the here and now sensationalism of media logic would be able to understand the complexities involved. This, in combination with 'unequal levels of ignorance of histories and instant access', cannot further either critical awareness or democratic rights. The problem gets compounded when liberal 'global governance' and 'governance feminism' redefine nation-based democracies. How do we then address what ought to be the nature of a democratic 'global public sphere'?

NOTES

1. This was an oft-repeated theme in global discourse, but absent in the national media.

2. Kotiswaran (2013) observes:

> So it is not surprising that a couple of years ago, Catharine MacKinnon after urging the Indian government to pass a law criminalizing customers of sex workers, was stumped when asked an innocuous question on what she thought about the ban on bar dancing. And lest we forget, this

inequality of ignorance matters! Western feminists have access to Indian institutions in a way that Indian feminists do not. Indicative of this is the profuse thanks that the Justice Verma Committee offered to Diane Rosenfeld of Harvard Law School in their mammoth report.

3. This approach has been termed 'governance feminism'.

4. See Halley et al. (2006) for more detail (available online at http://www.law.harvard.edu/students/orgs/jlg/vol292/halley.pdf).

5. '*Real Time* offers analysis and insights into the broad range of developments in business, markets, the economy, politics, culture, sports, and entertainment that take place every single day in the world's largest democracy. Regular posts from Wall Street Journal and Dow Jones Newswires reporters around the country provide a unique take on the main stories in the news, shed light on what else mattered and why, and give global readers a snapshot of what Indians have been talking about all week.' INDIAREALTIME is a blog operating from India, but with some understanding with *Wall Street Journal* and Dow Jones.

6. There are indeed more mobile phones in India than toilets (Jagannath 2013).

7. Even as I put the last touches to this chapter, it has been reported in the media that 'industrialist Mukesh Ambani's Reliance Industries Ltd (RIL) is acquiring a majority stake in Raghav Bahl's Networks 18 Media and Investments and its subsidiary TV18 Broadcast through Independent Media Trust (IMT) of which RIL is a sole beneficiary. Network18 Media and TV18 control a suite of broadcasting channels like CNBC-TV18, Viacom 18 and CNN-IBN, besides a bevy of e-commerce business and digital Internet sites' (BS Reporter 2014).

8. It may be recalled that TRAI had organised an open house discussion with stakeholders on 29 June 2013 regarding the ratings issue and cross-media ownership (see Hasan 2013).

9. Tilak Kumar, President of the Indian Newspaper Association (INS), pointed out that although print media continued to register growth in the country, advertising was steadily getting directed to electronic media. Recognising that the internet was fast emerging as a potent force in today's multimedia environment, Kumar said, 'Any attempt to bring in restriction on cross-media ownership in India will almost certainly stop any further investment in the print media industry, which currently operates on fragile profit margins. The horizontal cross-media ownership is important to attain economics of scale.' (Kumar 2013).

10. This was also an election where the role of social media and new technology, such as the widespread use of holographs of Narendra Modi, was unprecedented.

11. The Indian Readership Survey (IRS) is the largest continuous readership research study in the world, with an annual sample size exceeding 2.56 lakh

(256,000) respondents. The IRS collected a comprehensive range of demographic information and provides extensive coverage of consumer and product categories, including cars, household appliances, household durables, household care and personal care products, food and beverages, finance and holidays. The IRS is not restricted to the survey of readership alone, but is synonymous with both readership and consumption across various FMCG (Fast-Moving Consumer Goods) products throughout India. It covers information on over 100 product categories. The IRS is conducted by MRUC (Media Research Users Council) and RSCI (Readership Studies Council of India).

12. Narendra Modi's public speeches are either in Gujarati in his home state, or in Hindi elsewhere. His interviews in English-language TV channels such as *Times Now* were conducted in Hindi.

13. On 1 June 2014, Rajya Sabha Television held a discussion on why we need to bring in history in media discussions, which are usually obsessed with the immediate.

14. 'Almost every leading newspaper and magazine in India these days seems to think it is necessary to organize an "intellectual" event. They call these events summits, conclaves, or conferences. The organizers project these events so as to appear on the side of "thought" or "ideas," as if seeking credibility and justification for their existence. But these gatherings are nowhere close to the brainstorming sessions they are cracked up to be. *Basically, they are huge "talking" extravaganza in which every participant is a performer before an audience, and like any other performer, craves its approval*' (Krishna 2012; emphasis mine).

15. Ph.D. theses on gender, for example, invariably begin with the WAD, WID, and GAD debate.

16. Inhabiting the world you study offers what anthropologists call a worm's eye view of your object of inquiry.

17. The Sati Act was passed in 1829 (Chaudhuri 1993: 20–24).

18. The Act legalising the marriage of Hindu widows was promulgated in July 1856 (ibid.).

19. The age of marriage for girls was of central concern with child marriage being common across many parts of the country. The first Age of Consent Bill was passed in 1860 (ibid.: 72–78).

20. Mathura, a teenaged tribal girl, was raped by two policemen in a police station in 1972. The legal battle began when a woman lawyer took up her case, but the Supreme Court of India held that Mathura had given consent. A nation-wide anti-rape campaign demanded the reopening of the Mathura rape case and amendments in the Rape Law. Prominent lawyers took up the issue, as did the national and regional-language press (see Patel 1985).

21. The Shah Bano case (1985 SCR [3] 844) was a controversial maintenance lawsuit in India (see Sunder Rajan 2003).

22. Roop Kanwar, aged eighteen, immolated herself on 4 September 1987 in Rajasthan. Several thousand people attended the sati event. The event quickly produced a public outcry in urban centres. The incident led first to state-level laws to prevent such occurrences, which till then had been under the central government's Commission of Sati (Prevention) Act. See http://en.wikipedia.org/wiki/Roop_Kanwar.

23. See Udupa 2014 for an analysis of the Aam Aadmi Party, which spearheaded the anti-corruption movement as a media creation.

24. The emergence of the Aam Aadmi Party bears significant resemblance to earlier political events in recent Indian history. An Emergency was declared in 1975 by Prime Minister Indira Gandhi. All democratic rights enshrined in the Indian Constitution were suspended. The large coalition of political parties that fought this and finally won the General Elections in 1977 was tellingly christened the Janata Party (translating to People's Party). More recently, the anti-corruption movement initiated by Anna Hazare and led by others such as Arvind Kejriwal chose to form a political party titled Aam Aadmi, meaning literally the 'ordinary man', figuratively the 'everybody'.

25. This usually comprises the spokespersons of various political parties, other veteran journalists, and 'experts' and 'celebrities' from various fields.

26. These are the everyday minutiae that I referred to earlier.

27. Le Monde reported: 'New Delhi roars of emotion and anger. The crowds are out in the street, candle in hand, to honour the victim or the more virulent call for hanging attackers' (Ghosh 2012).

28. Flavia Agnes welcomed the nation-wide protest but hoped that 'for the sake of quick and easy solutions', the discourse 'will not flatten out the complexities involved in issues concerning violence against women' (Agnes 2013).

29. See Justice Verma Committee Report Summary (Kalra 2013).

30. Acting on the recommendations of the Verma Committee, the parliament passed the Criminal Law (Amendment) Act 2013, which widened the definition of rape and also provided for the death penalty in rape cases that cause the death of the victim or leave her in a vegetative state. It also created several new offences, such as causing grievous hurt through acid attacks, sexual harassment, use of criminal force on a woman with intent to disrobe, voyeurism, and stalking.

31. The RSS is a critical element of the BJP-led Indian government, which took over at the end of May 2014. What the RSS public position will be now is yet to be seen. It is too early to take a final call, even as possible changes may be expected. The RSS recently agreed to take a fresh look at homosexuality.

32. Asaram Bapu has since been arrested on charges of sexual assault.

33. '... Dalits who suffer alone when their daughters are raped and murdered with impunity are annoyed by this sudden burst of concern for rape victims' (Teltumbde 2013: 10).

34. The RJD and the SP have fiercely opposed the Women's Reservation Bill (see Chaudhuri 1993: Preface).

35. A ready example is that of a Gillette advertisement, which states that we need soldiers not for warfare but for standing up for women. It has been appreciated by some and condemned by others.

36. The long-running popular serial *Balika Badhu*, on child marriage, had the protagonist Anandhi run a campaign on sexual harassment and ways to fight it with her screen husband (*Colours*, 17 September 2013). In 2014, we saw the same serial depict one of its central protagonists as a rape survivor.

37. Indian television anchors increasingly invoke the 'nation' on a daily basis. Arnab Goswami of *Times Now*, modelled along Fox Television lines, initiated a combative style, appropriating the voice of the nation.

38. Many experts participating in debates move from one TV channel to another, across Hindi and English-language channels.

39. Katherine Mayo became notorious for her polemical book *Mother India* (1927), in which she attacked Hindu society and religion, and the culture of India. The book created an outrage across India, and it was burned along with her effigy. It was criticised by Mahatma Gandhi as a 'report of a drain inspector sent out with one purpose of opening and examining the drains of the country to be reported upon. The book prompted over fifty angry books and pamphlets to be published to highlight Mayo's errors and false perception of Indian society, which had become a powerful influence on the American people's view of India' (see http://en.wikipedia.org/wiki/Mother_India_%28book%29).

40. Core labour standards are inserted into an article within the WTO Agreements. If a member state violates the social clause, the breach could become subject to WTO scrutiny, through the usual WTO dispute settlement provisions. At the request of the complaining party, retaliatory trade measures could be taken against the offending country.

41. While the orthodoxy had criticised this on grounds of religious sanction, a section of nationalists had opposed it on the grounds that the British state had no business interfering in the domestic matters of Indians when they had turned a deaf ear to other pressing issues raised by Indians.

42. A Criminal Law (Amendment) Bill 2013 was passed and women's groups persisted with their campaign to ensure that the law passed by the Union cabinet was approved in parliament (*The Hindu*, 17 March 2013).

43. See 'Age of Sexual Consent', available at http://www.avert.org/age-sexual-consent.htm.

44. The AIDWA is an independent left-oriented women's organisation committed to achieving democracy, equality, and women's emancipation. AIDWA members come from all strata in society, regardless of class, caste, and community .... About two-thirds of the organisation's strength is derived from poor rural and

urban women. AIDWA was founded in 1981 as a national-level mass organisation of women. However, several state units of the organisation came into existence in the crucible of the freedom struggle, each with a commendable record of anti-imperialist and pro-working class actions (see http://aidwaonline.org/).

45. Two young cousins were raped and hanged in Badoun, Uttar Pradesh, which once again has become a prime event on national media. Political parties, the National Commission for Women, the media have once again rallied around the case. The United Nations has issued a condemnation. It may not be easy to ignore this terrible crime any longer as an aberration (NDTV, 2 June 2014).

CHAPTER 11

The 2014 General Elections and Afterwards

A Churning Public Discourse and the New Hegemony

The focus of this chapter is on the 2014 General Elections and the three years that followed with a new Bharatiya Janata Party (BJP)-led government in power. I had not planned to have a chapter on this, for this book—as is evident—has been a work in progress literally over the quarter century since the new economic policies of the Indian state were initiated in 1991. The chapter in that sense is sheer happenstance, because some of the key processes that one had been addressing through the book acquired a larger-than-life presence, first in the run-up to the elections, during its six-week duration, and then in the first years of the new government (2014–17). The processes that I allude to are: the extraordinary role of media and communication in politics; the new hegemony of managerial language; initially a concerted unsettling, then a direct assault on the idea of a democratic, inclusive, and diverse India; and the persisting visibility of gender issues in public discourse. I also return here to the central contention that has run through this book—that public discourse, increasingly mediatised, is a key site wherein a nation-state's identity is made and remade. Linked to this is also the understanding that nationalism is both a cultural construct and a social formation that is deeply imbricated with the story of capitalism and the adaptive possibilities of its contemporary avatar, neo-liberalism.

This chapter is divided into two parts. **Part 1** has two broad objectives: *one*, it focuses on the 2014 election campaign—the unprecedented role of media and communication, its rhetoric and images; the commercial and technological apparatus deployed; and the centrality of gender rights as an electoral issue. *Two*, it seeks to portray the changing relationship between the media and the new government; the initial rhapsody and enthusiasm that turned from bonhomie to disappointment in sections of the media in the first year. **Part II** maps some major events and the ensuing media debates in the three years since the 2014 General Elections. The list of events is long and the attempt here is not to describe them in any detail. I identify only some issues to underscore two points: the ideological assault on the Constitutional identity of India, the assertion of a vacuous nationalism, and the rise of the media as a central actor in this process. *Essentially descriptive, the schematic account in this concluding chapter rests verbatim on media reporting and commentary. This is to convey both the content and tone of media discourse.* I also use extensive footnotes (where too I draw verbatim from the media) for two reasons: *one*, to very quickly provide the bare details of some key events; and *two*, to offer a media feel of the times and the concerted efforts, most often successful, engineered by the ruling party to fuel primordial emotions and passions in public discourse. In part the success of the BJP is based on many long years of work at the ground level, which then was accelerated and amplified through the use of the media to create and legitimise a rhetoric of 'hate-based nationalism' at its worst, and vacuous 'feel good nationalism' at its best. That the BJP ideology is uncomplicated, with a central 'other' to hate and an aggressive 'self' to champion; that it was early to use the language of corporate advertisement on an unprecedented scale; and that it is economical with the truth, all helped. A concerted attempt by the ruling party to legitimise a new majoritarian hegemony was underway. There was considerable criticism in the first two years. But as the third year drew to a close, as the ruling party won one election after another, the very legitimacy of critique was at stake. All dissenting voices were deemed anti-national. India appeared to be at a point where the old nationalist rhetoric of composite culture, secularism, internationalism, and social justice (see Chapters 1 and 2, this volume) was turned on its head (also see https://scroll.in/article/831621/uttar-pradesh-2017-how-modi-and-the-bjp-beat-the-politics-of-social-justice-at-its-own-game; accessed 1 May 2017). This is the ongoing churning of a public discourse—sometimes overtly vicious, sometimes covertly venomous—that this chapter seeks to capture. The narrative is arranged in a present continuous fashion, hoping thereby to seize that 'rapidity of change' which I flagged off early in the Introduction.

This chapter is *based on a daily tracking of the media, primarily English print and electronic media,*[1] *through the campaign, the results, the subsequent media analysis, and the unfolding story of mediated politics over three years.* This daily engagement with the media helps to capture the heady spirit of those months. The mood in the past three years has changed so fast that the chronological ordering in this chapter offers a look at the quick shifts—a glimpse of unprecedented hope among many, fearful anticipation among some, rapid disillusionment, and fresh excitement. This also highlights a striking feature of contemporary times, starkly evident in the breathless excitement of media reporting; what anthropologist John Postill has called the 'dilemma of the present continuous'. It could also be phrased as the 'tyranny of the imminent, with little if any historical perspective. We seem to be constantly imagining a near future that rarely happens' (Hemer 2013: 1–2). That unprecedented scale and glitz of a media-driven campaign, the promise of a brave new future in 2014 faded in one year and became fodder for ridicule and criticism by 2016. The defeat of the Congress in the state elections in May 2016 and the BJP victory in Assam ignited a fresh bout of enthusiasm for the BJP in the media. Everything else that had happened before seemed to disappear.[2] Then there were the surgical strikes, followed by demonetisation.[3] Then followed the spectacular victory of the BJP in the Uttar Pradesh Assembly elections. In the language of the day, 'the Modi chariot was unstoppable'[4] and 'unbeatable' (see http://giveandgain.shop/news/the-huge-uttar-pradesh-win-was-pm-narendra-modis-unbeatable-one-man-show/; accessed 27 April 2017).

The chronicle is premised on a broader argument about the salience of media and communication in the making of public discourse, which in significant ways have refashioned democratic politics[5] and the representation of India's 'national' identity. The question of India's identity was raised in the 2014 elections, but did not become the central point of debate. The Indian National Congress (INC) sought to contrast its idea of a plural India versus the BJP's parochial vision.[6] But as we shall see in this chapter, Narendra Modi, who spearheaded the BJP election campaign, did not wish at that point to enter this debate.[7] The strategy was to focus on development and governance. A slew of buzzwords was deployed: minimum government, maximum governance; *sabka saath, sabka vikas* (collective efforts, inclusive growth); India First; government has only one holy book—the Constitution (http://www.narendramodi.in/sabka-saath-sabkavikas-collective-efforts-inclusive-growth-3159; accessed 2 May 2016). The message was defined and the task was to convey this through a well worked-out and expensive communication apparatus.

THE CAMPAIGN: IMAGES, MAKEOVERS, AND THE APPARATUS

In early May 2014, newspapers carried a report that the three American social media giants—Facebook, Twitter, and Google—had emerged as major players in the ongoing general elections in India, with political parties and candidates competing with each other in breaking news and spreading their message through these outlets, in addition to those via the traditional media.[8] In March 2014, another report had forecast that India's upcoming general election would break many records as the largest democratic event in history, with more than 814 million people entitled to vote to decide the country's sixteenth government. This, however, was not the only record that was to be broken for, according to the Centre for Media Studies, Indian politicians would be spending as much as $4.9 billion during the electoral contest. The estimate suggested that the 2014 general election was the second most expensive of all time, behind only the 2012 US presidential campaign in which, according to the US presidential commission, $7 billion was spent (http://www.scoop.it/t/indian-general-election-2014; accessed 26 May 2016).

Modi himself was described as the first social media prime minister,[9] an outstanding orator with a keen sense of communication and the possibility of media-driven politics. More significantly, Modi had to *re*-present his image. A makeover was necessary to reach out as a statesman-like leader, and not one whose name was associated with the Gujarat riots. One media analysis, for instance, highlighted that Modi, the 'new face of India', heralds 'sinister' times, for he stood for what was antithetical to the core principles that defined what the nation stood for: 'Modi is a lifelong member of the (RSS) ... a ... organisation inspired by the fascist movements of Europe ... his ... devotees on Facebook and Twitter ... render the air mephitic with hate and malice, populating the paranoid world .... with fresh enemies—'terrorists', 'jihadis', 'Pakistani agents', 'pseudo-secularists', 'sickulars', 'socialists' and 'commies' (Mishra 2014).

The same commentator observes that Modi's own electoral strategy as prime ministerial candidate, however, has been more 'polished' (ibid.). A careful decision had obviously been taken to step away from exclusivist ideas of cultural nationalism and focus on 'governance' and 'development'. This decision, once taken, had to be publicised, and what we witnessed was the most aggressive mediatised campaign ever. It was not just that the media and Modi were omnipresent, but that there was a self-conscious recognition of this presence. 'Television and other forms of social media are now far more pervasive than ever. Mr. Modi has cleverly used them to his advantage while *the Congress is floundering about like a technological dinosaur*' (http://www.hindustantimes.com/comment/how-modi-is-winning-friends-and-influencing-people/article1-1217586.aspx; accessed 25 April 2014, emphasis mine).

Communication, publicity, and presentation of the self became buzzwords.[10] Narendra Modi, the Indian public learnt, was a master communicator. His skills as an exceptional orator could not have come at a better time, given that Prime Minister Manmohan Singh's silence was seen as a key reason for the defeat of the Congress. Modi, however, did not rest on his oratory alone, but managed to magnify its impact through a 'blitzkrieg of well-planned use of technology that included new and old media'. This skill of oratory, combined with 'enormous resources, meticulous planning and understanding of the use of different media and technology', was unprecedented, as was its high-impact use of symbolism. Media reports stressed how Modi fine-tuned his style in accordance with the form of media used. 'When addressing rallies, he tailored his speeches to suit the audience'; for example, 'the references to Lord Ram in Faizabad, to development in Kolkata, to the markets in Mumbai and so on'. This was his 'spin-masters' at work. That 'much thought' had gone into Modi's appearances in the media is clear from the fact that 'it is he who controls the whole show, taking all questions howsoever uncomfortable head-on'. The communication apparatus of Modi 'realised early on that there has been a high involvement of the middle classes in this election', and so we had the 'carefully interspersed television interviews, interviews to newspapers and tweets'. The tone would change for different audiences. When addressing the middle class, '... there are no flourishes'. Here, he 'presents a statesman-like figure, talking of national issues, transcending caste, class and religion'. Here is 'the face of Modi that the world wants to see—reasonable, inclusive and progressive' (http://www.hindustantimes.com/comment/how-modi-is-winning-friends-and-influencing-people/article1-1217586.aspx).

It was widely recognised within the media that he was putting on this façade for the benefit of the viewers, but was iterated time and again that *politics is all about communication*. The UPA-led government, the media alleged, was 'characterised by an icy silence from its top leaders. The prime minister, always awkward in public, hardly ever gave interviews.' And the Congress president and vice-president 'did little to engage with people using the plethora of mediums available now, including social media' (ibid.).

Just as advertisements cater their messages to target diverse groups, a similar modus operandi was at work here. Both content and style are tweaked to cater to the sensibilities of a concerned audience. Veteran journalist Mark Tully described Modi as a 'pugnacious orator' who 'revels in his power to sway massive audiences ... delights in punching a point home, pouring scathing scorn on his opponents, while making grandiose commitments himself'; switches tone 'effortlessly' from 'the bruiser on the campaign trail' to 'the conversationalist when in front of the radio microphone' (Tully 2014).

The 2014 elections witnessed the widespread use of holograms or 3D images of Modi. Significant as the use of such images is, what is of equal significance is the array of organisations that make this possible, bringing in new actors into the thick of the electoral battle. I draw attention, therefore, both to the images (the symbolic product) and to the corporate organisation and finance that made this possible. An accurate indication of the logistics of such an exercise is best provided if we look at the website of the British company hired for this task, Musion, 'the world leader in holographic technology' (http://musion.com/?portfolio=narendra-modi-campaign-2014; accessed 16 May 2016).

The caption, titled 'Narendra Modi embraces Musion's hologram technology once more in bid to lead India', states how the leader of India's main opposition (the BJP) is using Musion technology in a mammoth and carefully orchestrated campaign designed to 'amplify his appeal and maximise his reach'. And how 'Narendra Modi is again moving electioneering beyond the traditional rally', choosing Musion to 'consult, design and manage these holographic addresses'.

> ... Narendra Modi will be using our holographic technology to address multiple audiences .... A 3D life-like hologram of the politician will be projected onto stages at a staggering 3500–4,000 events in just 45 days .... The events ... provides multiple opportunities to appear before his electorate in 1,500 locations and ... personally address 100 million voters. (http://musion.com/?portfolio=narendra-modi-campaign-2014; accessed 16 May 2016)

An HQ studio was built 'at the Narendra Modi campaign HQ from where, speeches were filmed and broadcast live via a satellite uplink to the stages at each day's events'. There was also a 'GSM camera car at each location beaming back images of the venue construction and the address in real time, which is then simultaneously displayed on a massive screen at the HQ' (ibid.).

I have gone into some detail to highlight both the business-like approach and the finances involved; both aspects are rendered invisible to the consumer citizen whose vote was being wooed. The scale of the money spent was widely commented upon in international media. 'Indian politicians', Reuters reported, were expected to spend around $5 billion on campaigning for elections, seen as 'a sum second only to the most expensive U.S. presidential campaign of all time' (http://in.reuters.com/article/india-election-spending-idINDEEA2804B20140309; accessed 23 June 2016).

Widely commented on also was the range of professional expertise, often from an overseas Indian community, whose services had been called in.[11] I have discussed the implications of a national public sphere informed by the concerns and interests of non-nationals in the Introduction (also see Chapter 9). As if this were not enough, we also had a 48-page glossy comic book titled *Bal Narendra*, depicting the incredible deeds of Modi as a child. The book contains seventeen stories that recount what is described as the 'life shaping experiences that moulded Bal Narendra into Narendra Modi of today'. There was a story about 'his bringing home a baby crocodile one day only to be told by his mother how painful it's for a child to be separated by its mother. Narendra promptly went back to the river to put the crocodile back in the water.' Another story, with 'brilliant animation talks of how Modi set up a tea stall with money given to him to enjoy a carnival so that he could collect funds for victims displaced by floods' (http://www.news18.com/news/buzz/bal-narendra-in-pics-comic-book-shows-fearless-young-narendra-modi-saving-drowning-boy-taking-on-crocodiles-bullies-676841.html; accessed 21 June 2014).

GENDER IN THE ELECTION CAMPAIGN

If the centrality of the media and communication was one aspect of these elections, the focus on gender issues in the campaign was the other. I have argued through the book how gender has been a key element in India's public discourse: from the colonial period to the early days of nation-building; through the second phase of the Indian women's movement to a complex process of institutionalisation of gender by the state and international institutions; to the more recent hyper-visibility of gender in a corporate-led globalised India (see Chapter 10). The 2014 elections saw a mandatory reference to gender questions. For instance, women's issues were part of the election manifesto of the major political parties.[12] Further, the media actively campaigned for the rights of the homosexual communities, and of the transgender community.[13] Despite the media support to the BJP election campaign, there was some anxiety expressed about the ideological dispositions of the party (see Parashar 2014). Overtly, women's empowerment was the buzzword of the campaign. What accompanied it at the ground level were frequent obnoxious public remarks about women by political leaders at worst (http://indianexpress.com/article/india/politics/tunch-maal-to-sanvli-ten-sexist-remarks-by-politicians-on-women/; accessed 3 June 2015), and a patronising attitude at best.[14] These were most likely views that many of India's public figures felt deeply about. Yet the fact that they had to retract from them indicated that such views were no longer deemed legitimate in public discourse, and most certainly not before elections. Such comments, however, acquired distressing frequency in the year after the elections. There was a BJP MP who asked Hindu women to bear more children (http://www.thehindu.com/news/national/sakshi-stokes-another-controversy-asks-hindus-to-have-4-kids/article6763837.ece; accessed 3 May 2015), and a minister who thought marital rape was alien to Indian culture.[15] The well-known yoga guru Ramdev's ayurveda firm was reportedly manufacturing pills to enable women to bear male children.[16] The list of such issues is long.

A point that I would like to emphasise here, and one that I return to in the concluding section of this chapter, is the anomaly in the BJP's stated commitment to women's rights. It sat uneasily on a party whose forbear, the Hindu Mahasabha, had fiercely opposed the Hindu Code Bill (see Chaudhuri 1993). I have already flagged the many anti-women stances, but am tempted to quote the Rashtriya Swayamsevak Sangh's (RSS) chief Mohan Bhagwat who, while addressing RSS workers, stated that 'women should restrict themselves to doing household chores, according to what he calls the theory of social contract' (http://www.ndtv.com/india-news/women-meant-to-do-household-chores-another-shocker-from-rss-chief-509519; accessed 26 May 2016).

A perceptive commentary during the election campaign recalls a BJP advertisement on women's safety and observes:

> However, *in action, the BJP has shown that the ads are conceived in the cool, air-conditioned publicity agencies by clever, imaginative and well-paid*

copywriters and directors, far from the grime and dust of real political exchanges .... It has gone ahead and 'welcomed' Pramod Muthalik, chief of Rashtriya Hindu Sene, ... whose members 'raided' a pub in Mangalore in broad daylight in 2009, chasing, pushing, shoving and beating up women to make sure they are reminded of their place in the world. (http://www.firstpost.com/election-diary/pramod-muthalik-in-bjp-is-this-modis-idea-of-womens-rights-1446577.html; accessed 27 May 2016, emphasis mine)

The Results, Media Strategy, and the Analysis

The Narendra Modi-led BJP's victory with an absolute majority in the elections was variously described as a juggernaut, a democratic 'asteroid' that wiped out old habits (Khilnani 2014), and a veritable tsunami that relegated the Indian National Congress to a mere forty-four seats, a number so low that it did not qualify to be recognised as the leading opposition party in Parliament. Both the BJP and the INC had planned their media strategy for the results.

As the results came in, a tweet stating 'India has won! Good days are coming'—in a mixture of Hindi[17] and English—was the confirmation that Narendra Modi was to be India's next prime minister. Modi's victory message became the most re-tweeted post in Indian history—more than 70,000 and counting—confirming the role of social media alongside conventional political campaigning in the 2014 electoral battle (Chilkoti 2014).

That the Congress had failed badly in communication strategy was repeatedly raised in the media.[18] Just before the results, it was reported that the Congress party was keen 'that a uniform, coordinated stand is taken by Congress spokespersons while addressing the media' to face the 'media onslaught on the 16th and defend the party in the best manner possible' (Choudhury 2014). Post-election analysis returned to the question of oratory and communication. In a longish article written by an adman, Santosh Desai, this point of 'an unequal oratorical contest' between Manmohan Singh and Narendra Modi was highlighted. 'There are many reasons why Manmohan Singh is not demitting office in a blaze of glory, but *his failure as a communicator is probably the reason that will be remembered by most* .... being a poor speaker is a disadvantage *in these media-fuelled times* ...' (Desai 2014; http://www.outlookindia.com/article.aspx?290702' emphasis mine).

Others were more critical about the role that the media had played in going out of its way to project Modi as the one who '... could steer the country out of the crisis by providing strong leadership' (Hasan 2014). The contention was that the media had moved from 'manufacturing consent' to 'manufacturing dissent' (ibid.). This was not a stray view for even before the elections, the question had been raised: Was there a wave for the BJP's prime ministerial candidate, Narendra Modi? The answer was:

> Certainly yes, if you watch television channels that day-after-day and night-after-night showcase a man who has been projected as decisive and charismatic, with plans to rid the country of corruption and has already drawn a road map to take India to higher economic growth .... The question however remained whether this is for real or just *media hype* to create a *mirage of a man* .... (http://www.india.com/loudspeaker/lok-sabha-elections-2014-modi-wave-or-media-hype-24535/; accessed 23 June 2016, emphasis mine)

MEDIA AND THE GOVERNMENT: THE YEAR AFTER THE ELECTIONS

Barely 100 days later, there was a dramatic shift in the story. Prime Minister Modi preferred to stay away from the media and use his own Twitter account to say what he wished to. It is in this context that veteran journalist Mark Tully wrote:

> Prime Minister Narendra Modi ... reportedly treats his ministers as schoolchildren, telling them what to wear, who to meet, and what to say .... *the prime minister believes that the media should merely report what the government says and not question it.* So he, his officials and his ministers communicate with the media through Twitter .... *India doesn't have a listening prime minister.* (Tully 2014; emphasis mine)

Narendra Modi's 'aversion for the media' was variously commented upon. It was 'very evident during his trip to Japan', where he did not meet the media. Instead, 'the MEA simply prepared a brief resume of the PM's daily activities in Japan and e-mailed it to correspondents'. The MEA also produced a propaganda video on Indo-Japanese relations. In addition, Doordarshan and the official media put out several videos on the internet of the PM at a tea ceremony, feeding fish, visiting the Akasaka Palace, and so on. Modi also 'changed his outfits several times a day, conscious that in this new age, *visual impact can be more important than sound byte*'[19] (Kapoor 2014; emphasis mine). A year later, this very strength seemed to turn against him when Prime Minister Modi wore a suit with his name emblazoned all over during President Obama's visit to India as the guest for Republic Day 2015. It drew considerable flak from the media for its narcissist insensitivity and 'socio-economic audacity' (http://www.firstpost.com/living/narendra-damodardas-modi-suit-was-a-pm-sized-fail-heres-why-2067815.html; accessed 3 May 2015. Also see Chapter 1, this volume). The suit was finally auctioned off, but the story refused to die down. Rahul Gandhi, the INC leader, drew attention to it as the opposition rallied together to target the BJP government as anti-poor over the Land Ordinance Bill.[20] The same media which had hailed Modi's oratory now started to agree with a journalist's early observations in May 2014 that although 'Modi has a wonderful way with words, true, ... it comes with a fondness for reduction and empty wordplay' (Patel 2015). And the same silence for which Manmohan Singh had been ridiculed was seen by Patel as 'famously intellectual to the point of being boring and taciturn, and it is a quality that some of us like in prime ministers. It indicates he is aware of the complexity of the world and of India's problems' (http://www.hindustantimes.com/analysis/take-a-closer-look-at-moditva/article1-1220632.aspx; accessed 23 June 2016).

The story line regarding the Modi-led government's attitude towards the media appeared to again shift eight months down the line. Media reports suggested that 'Government communication could be in for a sea change with information and broadcasting (I&B) minister Arun Jaitley asking his ministerial colleagues not to shy away from the media while cautioning bureaucrats against propaganda'. For 'we live through the media, we communicate through the media' (http://timesofindia.indiatimes.com/india/Dont-shy-away-from-media-Jaitley-tells-mantris-babus/movie-review/46101309.cms; accessed 30 April 2016).

The Indian media that had predominantly favoured Modi prior to the elections[21] appeared to be turning away. And Modi, who had gone out of his way to launch his mediatised campaign, consciously retreated. But one saw overtures, as in Jaitley's speech. There were shifts, but as the months rolled by there was evidence of open hostility. In the 2014 Delhi Assembly elections, Prime Minister Modi called the media '*bazaru*' for conducting opinion polls that favoured the Aam Aadmi Party (AAP). And one of his ministers, General V. K. Singh, called the media *'prestitutes'* (Ghosh 2015). What we increasingly witness is the blame game by politicians vis-à-vis the media on the one hand, and a talking back by the media, as evident below.

> BJP says journalists are pro-Congress, Congress counters that the media's sold out to the ruling party .... Are reporters reduced to only porters carrying too many agendas? ... But India's Fourth Pillar is not just paparazzi, it's also creating the culture of argumentative Indians and keeping alive the democratic dictum of 'shout don't shoot', even if some of us are shouting too loudly. (ibid.)

Ghosh goes on to underscore the fact that 'PM Modi shuns uncomfortable questions but has great media strategy'. Further, 'those who live by the media die by the media as Aam Aadmi Party recently found out'.[22] The point she makes is that 'a huge, diverse, chaotic, clamorous and largely uncontrollable media' still provides a rough check (and not a blank cheque) on the system. Santosh Desai contrasts this present clamorous state of the media to a time when 'regard for journalism bordered on the reverential', as if 'the world spoke directly to us through the medium of news' that was 'a force of nature'. It was a world where 'the newspaper appeared everyday like the sun, slipping under our doors as yesterday folded neatly into newsprint'. He then makes the important point that 'the idea of news being a distilled representation of reality' 'without any prejudice or bias being exercised was an illusion', but 'made real by the idealism that fueled journalism and the safeguards that were built into its practice' (Desai 2015, http://blogs.timesofindia.indiatimes.com/Citycitybangbang/manufacturing-bias/; accessed 21 June 2016). This 'mental model of journalism has changed radically as media has become a deliberate player in the fashioning of reality as we understand it'; it amplifies events and views and 'create our sense of the present'. Opinion trumps news, and increasingly this opinion is designed to create a specific effect (ibid.).

BATTLING INDIA'S IDENTITY: THE FIRST YEAR

I had begun this book with a certain understanding: *one*, that modern public discourse can be fruitfully understood as 'presentation of the nation's self', its identity, and image; *two*, that the mutually imbricated economic, political, and cultural articulations are embedded within specific contexts; *three*, that the central site of ideological production varies in different contexts, for instance, the state at one juncture and the media at another; and *four*, that national identity is deeply gendered and 'gender' itself as a concept acquires new meanings in new contexts. I had further sought to argue that a dominant, if not general, agreement had evolved through the national movement—that Indian civilisation was plural and, in spite of periods of intolerance, a distinct and internally differentiated composite culture had emerged. The Constitution enshrined these principles.

The Indian state after 1947 sought to project this idea along with the idea that since the vast majority of Indian people were poor and the nation, as it were, lived in villages, democracy and freedom would mean little unless the needs of the poorest were addressed. I further argued that both domestic and foreign policies of the state are integral to the making of the identity of a nation. The foreign policy is the image of the nation that the state presents to the world. The policy of non-alignment pursued by independent India sought an equidistance that was not founded on hard realism but on an idea of a third world, morally grounded in a shared past of colonial exploitation and a universal striving for a just world order.

What one witnessed in the year after the 2014 elections was a concerted challenge to this identity. This is not to suggest that there were no challenges earlier. The introduction had noted that exclusivist ideas promoting religion-based nationalism were always present. However, they were neither pervasive nor endorsed. These ideas were muted in the dominant national discourse. I use the word 'muted' with care. For communal politics were pursued in the everyday world; but only when communal politics 'grabbed headlines', in events such as the destruction of the Babri Masjid, the Bombay riots, or the Gujarat riots, did they break into dominant discourse. In most such instances, the role of the state was critical. In that sense 2014 indeed marked a departure from the past. The complete majority that the ruling BJP had in the Union Government meant that for the first time in independent India, the ideology of the BJP was getting to be played out aggressively and unmasked in India's public discourse. In contrast, the central refashioning of public discourse that ensued since 1991, which most of the chapters (Chapter 3, 4, 5, 6, 7, 9, 10) focus on, are about challenges to the ideas of state commitment to equity and socialism; a focus on profligacy and consumption as virtues;

rethinking austerity as an obstacle to economic growth at one end, and the denial of desire at the other.

Another story unfolded through these years, a point I have underscored in the introduction and exemplified in Chapters 9, 10 and 11. That is the new hegemony of managerial language, or, as I argue in Chapter 4, the growing dominance of 'the universal language of professionalism'. It marked a 'new social form of lifestyles', coloured by some broader narratives of the 'cultural forms of consumerism'—'fantasy, excess, spectacle and citizenship'. I argue that viewing the 2014 elections and its aftermath, including the spectacle of the government's two-year celebrations in May 2016, through this lens is productive. Mass marketing in the long decades since 1991 transformed the middle class and, importantly, mass democracy. It has been argued that in late capitalism, the sensualist replaced the intellectualist paradigm. In such times, as we saw, communication acquires central place and 'optics' and 'perception' become key words in political analysis. There is a new flattening temporality and reduction of the self to the mere politics of presentation, a world that is defined by 'impoverished absolutes' (Vishvanthan 2015).

What occurred after the 2014 elections is significant, for the BJP had never shared the dominant 'ideological consensus' of the idea of an India whose bedrock was a commitment to diversity and pluralism. As stated earlier, one cannot engage in any detail with the many events that marked the BJP's first year in government. I would, however, mark the following: early attacks on churches and then the declaration of Christmas as Good Governance Day;[23] a campaign against 'love jihad';[24] banning of beef and the Dadri lynching;[25] assaults on the autonomy of educational institutions such as the IITs and FTI;[26] and the campaign against the growing intolerance.[27] I seek to provide a glimpse into media responses to these events. I begin with Gopal Gandhi on why he thought the year was so extraordinary for the Republic.

> The change has been symbolised in statements made by three Union ministers .... The original alternation between 'halal' and 'haram' to distinguish what was unlawful from what was lawful was now replaced by one which distinguished *what was Hindu from that which was not, conflating the sacred-in-religion with the sacred-in-law* .... The next ... came in a comment on the *2013 floods ... a divine chastisement* .... The third ... was about *the Gita*.[28] (Gandhi 2015; emphasis mine)

The three statements formed a 'triptych of religious assertion inconsistent with our Constitution, incompatible with our inner "core" as a secular Republic'. Soon came the suggestion that 'learning Sanskrit should be made compulsory', then 'ghar wapsi for reconverting', and then 'the most important "improbable"', in the shape of adulation for Nathuram Vinayak Godse's act of murdering an unarmed 79-year-old man as one of indomitable courage (Gandhi 2015). Gopal Gandhi was not alone. Well-known television anchor Barkha Dutt wrote: 'The word in the BJP is that Prime Minister Narendra Modi is angry ... the truth is that for the first time since the Modi government took charge, its rabble rousers have ensured it is not in control of its own political messaging .... the cacophony drown out a previously cogent communication policy' (Dutt 2014).

According to Dutt, the PM has a '*canny instinct for communication* and, unlike his predecessor, is also a masterful orator [which] makes the present stand-off even more ironic'. A key reason for the electoral success of the BJP has been 'its intuitive understanding that *in an age of hyper-information and shrinking attention spans, silence is the language of political obituaries* .... both as candidate and PM, Modi has often by-passed the traditional media to talk directly to his constituents in a communication strategy that has worked very well for his government thus far' (ibid.). The reader will notice the repeated reference to 'media' and 'communication strategy'.[29]

Dutt goes on to say that 'if it is indeed aspirational India that gave a thumbs up to a strong leadership and economic resurgence in voting the BJP to power, then for its own sake, manufactured controversies around religion and identity need to be relegated firmly to the periphery'. This is a significant point, for increasingly one witnesses a tension between the cosmopolitan imperatives of global capitalism and the parochial impulses of the BJP. I return to this point later to ask whether there is a contradiction or whether the two can cohabit reasonably comfortably.

President Obama's visit, which was seen as a minor *coup d'état* for Modi, turned out to have more than a bitter aftertaste. All the attention on Modi's suit[30] and bonhomie on television could not prevent Obama from commenting on the attacks on minorities in India. As the months rolled by, the matter of India's core values was increasingly debated in the media. Shiv Viswanathan wrote: '... majoritarianism is a challenge to democracy .... As a Hindu, I loved Christian festivals and enjoyed Sikh *langars* .... the BJP's Hindutva now makes our culture uniform, politics majoritarian and citizenship, a matter of loyalties' (Vishvanthan 2015).

He goes on to say that the 'BJP government speaks like corporate companies' and shows a 'preference for the Indian abroad than the resident Indian', because the latter is capable of reworking identities while the diaspora has limited choices. And 'in the inclusive vision, culture is all about the availability of alternatives, while for Hindutva, it is about a space that needs to be policed'.

The parochial vision of the government appeared to offend a large and ideologically diverse section of the Indian public. It disappointed those who had seen in Modi one who would usher in economic reforms, maximise governance, and minimise government. *The Times of India* which, as we saw early in the book, had taken up the ideological task of championing the new economic policies, carried an editorial after the repeated attacks on minorities. It highlighted the fact that 'Prime Minister Narendra Modi won the national election on a platform of modernity, good governance and economic change—which is at significant variance with the cultural as well as economic agenda of RSS and affiliated far right organisations'. It welcomed the PM's 'speech reiterating freedom of religion' and observed that RSS chief Mohan Bhagwat's statement that 'our mothers are not baby-making factories' and VHP leaders cautioning their followers to make 'balanced statements' which won't 'trouble the government' suggested concerted messaging. The editorial, titled 'Modi minus RSS', identified two sets of tensions: one between 'pushing forward on the second wave of economic reforms and ending socially divisive rhetoric', and the other between contending visions of economics.

Concern remained, however, that 'some Sangh-related outfits are even joining hands with the Left to agitate against what they call the government's "anti-poor" and "anti-farmer" policies'. Basically, there appeared to be a fundamental dichotomy between the promise of a modernist, aspirational India that drew so many new voters to the BJP in 2014 and the obscurantist and Luddite notions of society and economy that typified most of the Sangh (http://blogs.timesofindia.indiatimes.com/toi-editorials/modi-minus-rss-time-for-bjp-to-ditch-social-as-well-as-economic-agenda-of-hindu-right/; accessed 23 June 2016).

The Hindu had a different take on the tension, suggesting that economic reforms are 'riding piggyback on the political appeal of Hindutva under the Narendra Modi government', and that Hindutva is being 'smuggled into a discourse in which growth and development alone matter'. Therefore, 'the Bharatiya Janata Party's reforms agenda seems inseparable from—even if not organically linked to—the Hindutva project'. If that were so, the *TOI* dream of a Modi minus the RSS is intrinsically unrealisable. But the tensions are palpable and, as evident, those in support of a right-wing economic agenda would '... want to rescue the BJP from regressive Hindutva politics, and make it the foremost right-wing neo-liberal party of India, the challenge is to keep the two sets of agenda separate: to isolate the religious lumpen elements and not allow them to discredit the economic reforms (Nambath 2015).

Within the media, a view began to be espoused that Indian public discourse, long dominated by left liberal ideas, had virtually no space for right-wing ideas, unlike Western democracies. Even as a united opposition sought to stall the BJP government's ordinance on land (http://www.news18.com/news/india/land-acquisition-bill-the-main-points-of-debate-and-controversy-969424.html; accessed 23 June 2016), we had views that critiqued the tendency of 'opposition members to rush out and denounce it as anti-poor or anti-farmer' once the budget was placed in Parliament. The argument is that both the government and opposition 'suggest that budgets should be prepared solely for the poor', as though 'the middle class or rich do not exist, even if they do nothing need be done for them'. And a point quite visible in the media for some time, as shown through the chapters, is that 'everything must be done for the poor because they vote in large numbers'. The commentator, Swain, goes on to ask: '... *is poverty a virtue? Does one commit a crime by earning well? "Industry" is presented as a dirty word* .... "Profit" too is a dirty word .... The Indian government should not aim to be "mai-baap", infantilising people and making them depend on it for everything' (Swain 2015; emphasis mine).

Modi himself had mocked the Congress' anti-poverty policies such as the Mahatma Gandhi National Rural Employment Guarantee Act (MGNREG), but chose two years later to change his earlier stance. The 2017 Budget was presented as a budget for the poor. Earlier, he had said that with demonetisation, 'the poor are enjoying a sound sleep while rich are running from pillar to post to buy sleeping pills' (http://www.dnaindia.com/india/report-demonetization-pm-modi-says-he-has-given-sound-sleep-to-poor-opposition-calls-it-economic-anarchy-2273494; accessed 2 February 2017).

Journalist Swapan Dasgupta claimed that this shows how 'Modi has tried to position himself above political dogma. Nominally, he may be rightwing but this is coupled with an astonishing show of flexibility that comes from doing what is necessary and what is effective .... Modi has undertaken an expansionist approach that is best described as Keynesian' (http://blogs.timesofindia.indiatimes.com/right-and-wrong/the-makeover-of-modi-and-the-remaking-of-india/; accessed 29 May 2016). There were interpretations to the contrary. [31]

TWO YEARS LATER

As stated earlier, one cannot engage in any detail with the many events that crowded the BJP's second year in government. The year 2016 saw attacks on Dalit students, such as that in Hyderabad University that led to the tragic death of Rohith Vemula;[32] and the controversy over the alleged anti-national slogans raised in Jawaharlal Nehru University (JNU), followed by the hyperbole of nationalism that ensued.[33] Accompanying this were daily accusations of corruption levelled by the BJP government on various Congress leaders,[34] including their chief Sonia Gandhi.[35] Going by media headlines, one wave of 'breaking news' followed close on the heels of another. Accusations and counter-accusations were hurled, and each was declared a groundbreaking event. The 'stunning' defeat of the BJP in Bihar at the end of November 2015 (http://www.indiatvnews.com/politics/national/7-major-reasons-behind-bjp-s-stunning-defeat-in-bihar-elections-33646.html; accessed 21 May 2016) was seen as a decisive turning point, the party's 'decimation'. Barely six months later, the victory of the BJP in the Assam state elections in May 2016 was heralded as the beginning of a 'Congress-*mukt* (free)' Bharat.[36] If the above account appears cluttered and difficult to make sense of, it is a good reflection on the state of media discourse. For even the phrase 'over-communicative abundance', which Chapters 9 and 10 refer to, falls short in conveying the crowding of media discourse. The heat, the mass of people, the pushing and jostling, frayed tempers, the shouting down, the chaos, the performances and entertainment of a good Indian bazaar is more akin to current Indian media discourse, particularly on television and social media.

> In recent years, TV viewers have observed the relish with which channels have packaged news in the hyper mould of debates .... *Aided by an arsenal of distraction—hammering tone, looping replays, ticker tapes with nano-*

> *second news breaks, graphic minefields, and an ensemble cast of speakers chosen for maximum outrage, many an anchor has created a republic of virtual reality based on the principle of naming and shaming as primetime entertainment.* (Padmanabhan 2016; emphasis mine)

The print media stands out with its catchy headlines while online media is quite another story that increasingly has become a key site for building opinions.[37] What slowly unfolded is a divide within the media: one warily critical, the other openly partisan, almost like the official propaganda wing of the ruling party.[38] Some television channels sought to carve out a more sane space, reflecting a deep awareness of the danger of the media becoming a mindless site for uninformed and hysterical rhetoric, leading to some extraordinarily powerful programmes.[39]

Within the print media, we saw forewarnings that all was not well. On 23 January 2016, Adhikari wrote: 'The thrill is gone' and ' ... *the excited anticipation* of India about to turn a corner that was evident in the early months of the Prime Minister Narendra Modi-led government *appears to have evaporated ...*'. For 'disappointment has begun to eclipse optimism about the country's medium term prospects' and '... badly necessary major reforms haven't been carried out...'. But what appears to have been most damaging is that 'on secular tolerance, on freedom of speech, on institutional functioning and on other liberal democratic markers, India's image has been damaged' in the international media and soured 'global public opinion' (Adhikari 2016).

Kaushik Basu, chief economist of the World Bank, said in an interview that 'tolerance is not just good value, but good economics'. He further opined that 'a society's development also depends on the social norms and mindsets of the people' and 'cross-country studies that show that nations in which there's a lot of trust among people do well economically', for 'people work harder and are more productive when they feel included' (http://economictimes.indiatimes.com/opinion/interviews/tolerance-is-not-just-good-value-but-good-economics-kaushik-basu-chief-economist-world-bank/articleshow/51070083.cms; accessed 13 May 2016). Closer home, the Governor of the Reserve Bank of India (RBI) spoke up for tolerance and debate and encouraged students to 'challenge all authority and tradition' at the Indian Institute of Technology-Delhi's forty-sixth convocation, held in October 2015 (http://timesofindia.indiatimes.com/india/Tolerance-essential-for-progress-Raghuram-Rajan-says/

articleshow/49606677.cms; accessed 13 May 2016). There appeared to be a 'growing crescendo of criticism both within and without, some vocal, many watching from the sidelines in silence, maybe a change in tactics is called for. Otherwise, many of his dreams, his pet projects, his vision of India zipping ahead like a bullet train will go the way of the Land Bill, discarded mid-way' (http://www.firstpost.com/politics/heres-why-pm-modi-should-not-ignore-arun-shourie-sour-grapes-jihad-2494594.html; accessed 21 May 2016).

The rhetoric of globalisation, growth, and consumption mapped through this book defined the ideological recasting of India after 1991. Those who had strongly subscribed to this vision of development, those who at one point had eulogised Manmohan Singh as the architect of a new India, now looked upon Prime Minister Modi for deliverance. As we saw above, those who had expected Modi to push the economic reforms were disappointed.[40] Those who had believed in his makeover during the election campaign in 2014, his slogan of '*sab ka saath, sab ka vikas*', were appalled at the bigotry of what the media called 'fringe elements'.

What had worked like magic in 2014 now acquired new meanings. The promised 'good days', the 'acche din', became the butt of ridicule. The hope that 2016 had generated among a wide section has been replaced by disappointment, and often anger. Then came the victory of the BJP in Assam in May 2016 and the exultation of the media evoked memories of May 2014. This was followed by the new government's extravagant celebration of two years in office in a glitzy ceremony (http://www.ndtv.com/india-news/modi-government-spent-over-rs-36-crore-on-publicity-to-mark-2-years-1474871; accessed 23 April 2017).

> While the highlight of the NDA's seven-hour-long gala celebration ... may have been Prime Minister Narendra Modi's speech at the end, the hours preceding his appearance were heavily studded with stars of both the BJP as well as Bollywood .... The show, though open to limited invitees, was beamed live on all news channels. To add a lighter touch ... cultural performances were included. (http://www.newindianexpress.com/nation/BJP-bollywood-stars-help-NDA-celebrate-2-years-in-government/2016/05/29/article3455808.ece; accessed 17 June 2016)

That night, everything that had happened earlier faded away. The disappointment disappeared from mainstream media. The next day ushered in new breaking news. A film on drug abuse in Punjab was censored.[41] The Dadri beef case, where a man had been killed, was rekindled. [42] Prime Minister Modi was hailed for his address to the US Congress,[43] where he affirmed that India's constitution protected the equal rights of all citizens and enshrined freedom of faith (http://www.brookings.edu/blogs/order-from-chaos/posts/2016/06/14-reviewing-modis-speech-congress-madan; accessed 17 June 2016). The media observed how 'Narendra Modi has endeared himself to the US Congress like no other Indian leader in a long time', and 'the Congressmen applauded Modi 64 times' with 'nine standing ovations' (http://qz.com/702983/in-numbers-narendra-modis-speech-at-the-us-congress/; accessed 21 June 2016). And then broke the Essar phone tapping story (http://indianexpress.com/article/india/india-news-india/essar-phone-tapping-in-ex-staffer-albasit-khan-scrapbook-pictures-of-snoop-equipment-suren-uppal-logbook-2863633/; accessed 21 June 2016). This takes us back to a striking feature of contemporary times—the breathless excitement of the media's reporting and the tyranny of the imminent that I noted early in this chapter.

THE THIRD YEAR

In early 2017, as Assembly-level elections were underway in Uttar Pradesh, the development plank which had swept Modi to power in 2014 gave way to issues of temple, Hindu migration, and love jihads (now renamed as the Romeo brigade).[44] The prime minister himself stepped in to further this tone.[45] And importantly, it worked. The BJP won two-thirds majority in Uttar Pradesh. Yogi Adityanath (see n44) became the chief minister. The weeks that followed saw an intensification in the attacks against Muslims by *Gau Rakshaks* (http://www.dailyo.in/politics/alwar-d muslim-murder-cow-pehlu-khan-dadri-beef-gau-rakshak/story/1/16549.html; accessed 3 April 2017). During the first year, we saw a media engaging with, and when required, critiquing, the government. The second year saw struggles by students in different parts of the country, protesting against the government. Protests against the government of the day have been part of contemporary India's history. What was new here, however, was the studied refusal of the government to engage with its protesting citizens. Instead, they were painted as the enemies of the nation, a task facilitated by an extraordinary barrage of propaganda by the old and new media alike. The 'liberal outrage factory' was stretched beyond its limits.[46] Protests were tired out—exhausted and pushed to the margins of public discourse. Once labelled anti-national, their voices are rendered illegitimate. Television debates reached new levels of shouting and invective. Reason and facts ceased to matter. Passions grew fiercer. Social media became more vicious. Images from one context were cut and pasted onto quite another.[47] Fake news became real. Seldom had we seen a mediatised civil strife, dividing people, created, nurtured, and fuelled by the government. There was no accountability, for the rules of public discourse had changed.[48] Meanwhile, security personnel continue to be killed (http://economictimes.indiatimes.com/news/defence/24-jawans-killed-in-encounter-with-maoists-in-chhattisgarhs-sukma/articleshow/58343332.cms; accessed 3 May 2017). Army men are beheaded (http://www.telegraph.co.uk/news/worldnews/asia/india/9789181/Indian-soldier-beheaded-by-Pakistan-troops-as-Kashmir-dispute-escalates.html). The government remained unanswerable while passion for revenge rent the media (http://indianexpress.com/article/opinion/columns/telescope-the-belligerent-box-indian-army-soldiers-mutilated-line-of-control-4639549/; accessed 5 May 2017). Human rights organisations and JNU were 'condemned' (https://thewire.in/131249/jnu-buddha-singh/; accessed 3 May 2017).

CONCLUSION

As I draw to the end of the book, I return to the matter of gender which, I have argued, offers a vantage point to understand the changing India. One had noted the focus on gender in the 2014 election campaign. The trend continued after the elections. In January 2015, Prime Minister Modi had launched a programme, 'Beti Bachao, Beti Padhao' (Save the daughter, educate the daughter), with the stated objectives of preventing gender biased sex-selection elimination; ensuring the survival and protection of the girl child; and ensuring the education and participation of the girl child (http://wcd.nic.in/BBBPScheme/main.htm; accessed 26 May 2016).

I wish to make a couple of points. The *first* point is that both feminism and gender, albeit redefined, entered the lexicon of public discourse and were deployed widely by the state, civil society, and the market (Chapters 10, 11). And the broader institutional and ideological apparatus through which 'gender', 'sexuality', 'cultural diversity', and 'race' are usually configured are elements in the business of consumption in a global market (Chapter 11). This, I argue, is as much the language of IIs as it is of the state, of NGOs, and of the corporate sector. Ranking on global gender indexes matters (Chapter 11). Importantly, the language is simple: a few buzzwords, a couple of acronyms, a flowchart. In a somewhat different context, I have argued in the last chapter about the 'asymmetry of knowledge' and the new but potent convergence of 'ignorance' and 'instant access' that new technologies have made possible. In such a context, words such as rights, justice, and equality are, in fundamental ways, emptied of their philosophical and political histories.

The *second* point that needs emphasis is that since the core BJP ideology sits uneasily with gender justice,[49] the party uses this plank to further other agendas. There appear to be two planks on which the BJP operates so far as gender justice is concerned. *One*, on a plank of an overt stated commitment to women's equality—understood as some buzzwords and programmes in vogue in the global circuit. In the first two years this showcasing of a 'global', 'modern' image of a prime minister committed to gender justice seemed to be a concern with the party. With a fast changing global order, where it is all right for the President of the United States of America to boast of sexual molestation (https://www.theatlantic.com/politics/archive/2016/11/election-trump-vote/507140/; accessed 27 April 2017), that need no longer seems to matter too much. The *second* plank is one that has been used for long by hegemonic powers—the use of gender to pursue other agendas. The BJP's aggressive campaign to fight for Muslim women's rights by fighting against the triple talaaq (see https://scroll.in/article/835097/love-in-the-time-of-triple-talaq-the-bjps-newfound-affection-for-muslim-women-is-that-of-a-stalker; accessed 27 April 2017) is at once to showcase its commitment to women's rights and send a message to the Muslim community to fall in line. That this fight for gender justice ought to have been taken up by 'secular' parties is another story, linked to what would have been the farcical, had it not been so tragic, play of secularism.[50]

One cannot quite anticipate what lies ahead, how, in Pratap Bhanu Mehta's words, the 'tension between the lofty aims of the government and the low politics of the party', between its 'backward-looking instincts' and 'its forward-looking mission' will play out (Mehta 2016). One is not even very sure of its 'mission'. For a 'mission' strung by buzzwords, as the smart slogans on gender shows, is necessarily hollow for it rests neither on any comprehensive understanding nor on any ideological commitment. Two points can be made here. *First,* gender equity can be read in this context as an element of the necessary professional wherewithal of contemporary managerial practices, much like 'diversity' and 'inclusion'. *Second,* sans any ideological roots, 'missions' and 'images' are eminently malleable. The more recent makeover of the BJP as a party committed to the welfare of the poor displays this flexibility, as does the party's fast changing narrative after demonetisation.[51]

One can further argue that the propensity to change narratives with impunity has been buttressed by the extraordinary role that communication has acquired. Communication strategy governs whether to project an image that promises gender inclusivity or empowerment of the poor, while whether to display muscular power and majoritarian violence is governed by ideological commitment. There is therefore a fundamental gap between the ideological core of exclusion and hegemony of the BJP and its presentation in a 'statesman-like Modi' on the global stage. The image has tended to slip once too often. At the policy level, three years after the 2014 elections, we witness a complete reversal of what was promised. A quick and obvious example would be Modi's promise of minimum government, maximum governance.[52] Interestingly, that section of the media that had decried the Indian government's tendency to 'infantilise the poor', those who had hailed Modi as one who would usher in economic reforms, are no longer so vocal. We seem to have moved a long way from the heydays of the rhetoric of globalisation, which the early part of the book dwelt on.[53]

At one point there appeared to be early inklings of an audience that might have become a bit tired of Prime Minister Modi's extraordinary communication skills, which had stood out for its impudence and stark loudness in contrast to then Prime Minister Manmohan Singh's silence in 2014. During the assembly elections in Uttar Pradesh early in 2017, there was a media comment that Akhilesh Yadav's campaign style was 'without any emotive oratory', an effective low-key style in an 'age of Trump where brashness sells' (http://www.hindustantimes.com/columns/can-the-low-key-akhilesh-yadav-win-the-high-stakes-up-battle/story-FDc9sfRmf7Xygxo1GDKRN.html).

Some of us hoped, perhaps wrongly, that the hammering tone, the shrill, designed to offend signature styles of television debates would give way to new forms, much like the way advertisement styles are recast, sensing audience fatigue. This does not seem to be happening, as the over-the-top communication blitzkrieg of the BJP seems to be working well. This communication strategy is aided effectively by a refashioned state that is putting in place regulations to 'keep a tab on its citizens'.[54] All dissent has been rendered illegitimate and anti-national. At this point, despite the valiant efforts of a few in the media to offer another way of presenting news and debate, the churning of public discourse for now seems to have succeeded in establishing a new state-led ideological hegemony.

NOTES

1. I also followed some of the Hindi news channels, but not the Hindi print media.

2. This time around, however, some sections within the media attempted a more dispassionate, fact-based analysis. See http://www.firstpost.com/politics/assembly-elections-2016-bjp-congress-amit-shah-narendra-modi-sonia-gandhi-rahul-gandhi-assam-kerala-west-bengal-tarun-gogoi-2792574.html (accessed 26 May 2016).

3. Prime Minister Narendra Modi addressed the nation on 8 November 2016 to announce the withdrawal of Rs 500 and Rs 1,000 notes (http://www.indiaspend.com/cover-story/how-modi-changed-and-changed-the-demonetisation-narrative-54391). Surgical strikes were carried out by army commandos across the Line of Control (LoC) to destroy multiple terrorist launch pads (see https://thewire.in/81440/what-is-indias-strategy-after-the-surgical-strikes-in-pakistan/; accessed 13 February 2017). Also see http://indianexpress.com/article/india/president-pranab-mukherjee-praises-note-ban-surgical-strikes/ (accessed 2 February 2017).

4. See Amit Shah's remark that 'Trinamool Congress can't stop PM Modi's chariot in West Bengal' 'Here too change will come,' said Amit Shah, assuring that Mamata Banerjee's shameless appeasement policy and politics of discrimination has crossed all limits of tolerance (http://indiatoday.intoday.in/story/amit-shah-bjp-west-bengal-trinamool-congress-mamata-banerjee-modi-wave/1/939211.html; accessed 27 April 2017).

5. 'Much of the media is dominated by corporate conglomerates that have a single goal of maximising profits. The autonomy and the independence of the media get compromised because of the corruption within. Thus, the media fails to bring about transparency in society by *not* playing an antagonistic and adversarial role against those who are in positions of power and authority. In different forms, *paid news has existed for many years; but when this phenomenon*

becomes prevalent during elections, the democratic process gets subverted' (Guha Thakurta 2014; emphasis mine).

6. The INC leader Rahul Gandhi, in an interview during the election campaign, observed,

> The core philosophy of the BJP ... seeks to perpetuate status quo which makes it impossible for the poor and the disadvantaged to rise above their stations through hard work. Under the current BJP leadership, this ideology has acquired a particularly virulent character. It has shed any semblance of respect for the democratic, secular and inclusive fabric of our nation. It is a politics of hubris, anger, and divisiveness .... Tolerance appears to have little place in their thought process. (George 2014)

7. This should not suggest that communal mobilisation was not taking place at the ground level. Sundry issues such as love jihad, the high birth rate among Muslims, beef eating, and illegal migration were very present, but had not become national media headlines as they did after 2014.

8. A typical newspaper report went like this:

> Though none of the companies are willing to discuss the advertisement revenue ... all of them have ... diverted substantial amount of their resources in the elections, *many of them working thousands of miles away from India*. Facebook started working on the Indian elections towards the end of last year .... *Twitter is a powerful way to return to retail politics. He conceded that elections have helped Twitter expand in India*. (http://www.thehindubusinessline.com/features/smartbuy/social-media/social-media-changes-the-face-of-indias-elections/article5981267.ece; accessed 30 May 2014, emphasis mine)

9. Brand Modi was created successfully through the new and the old media. In the social media, Modi already is a brand. On Twitter, he has over 3.5 million followers, while on Facebook over 11 million people like his profile. It was this US-president-like media blitzkrieg that ensured that he became the BJP's electoral mascot (http://www.india.com/loudspeaker/lok-sabha-elections-2014-modi-wave-or-media-hype-24535/; accessed 25 April 2014).

10. Readers will have noted this growing trend over the last chapters. See Chapters 7, 9, 10, and 11.

The Aam Aadmi Party (AAP) was an early starter in the use of media, but constraints of space and focus do not permit any detailed analysis in this chapter. A quote from the media in 2013 explicates this.

> As opposed to the Delhi units of the Congress and the BJP, which have just started making their presence felt, the AAP has 3.33 lakh followers on Facebook and around 1.35 lakh followers on Twitter. Party leader Arvind Kejriwal has over 5.4 lakh followers on Facebook and around 6 lakh on Twitter .... One could argue that the AAP and Mr. Kejriwal owe their very existence to social media .... (http://www.thehindu.com/news/cities/Delhi/aap-took-baby-steps-on-social-media-now-its-a-runaway-hit/article5190122.ece; accessed 16 May 2016)

11. Modi's fundraising was led by a team that included a former investment banker, who was previously with Citibank in London. This team organised an online fundraising drive in India, targeting donations from wealthy Indians living abroad (http://in.reuters.com/article/2014/03/09/india-election-spending-idINDEEA2804B20140309). A similar trend was visible in the AAP campaign (Khandekar 2014).

12. 'As India enters its second week of nationwide polls, the issue of female safety ... is coming second only to corruption .... According to a joint survey by Marketing and Development Research Associates and online campaign forum Avaaz, over 90% of Indians want tackling sexual violence treated as a priority .... many see a dearth of meaningful content in party manifestos .... 70 independent civil-society activists have launched ... Womanifesto 2014, which sets out positions on female economic empowerment, female access to education and political representation, faster administration of justice in cases of sexual violence, and better policing' (http://time.com/61122/india-womanifesto-election-women-voting/; accessed 23 June 2016).

13. '... are gay rights on the ballot? Technically, no..... In past elections, gay rights haven't even been a peripheral issue. *This time around, they are an issue.* The Indian gay community currently neither has popular opinion nor political muscle behind it. LGBT rights in western countries often became politically mainstream after an ... explosion in the number of straight allies and the gay lobby's increasing wealth and clout. For now, ... gay rights have at least entered the political conversation in India ...' (http://www.huffingtonpost.com/2014/12/01/new-delhi-gay-lesbian-march-_n_6245802.html?ir=India; emphasis mine).

14. The thrust was on 'promising safety', instead of 'guaranteeing freedoms' without moral conditions attached (http://time.com/61122/india-womanifesto-election-women-voting/; accessed 23 June 2016).

15. Commenting on the Minister of State for Home's statement that the notion of marital rape is not applicable in Indian culture, Antony (2016) wrote:

> In Indian fairy tales, the girl grows up ... fair, educated enough to understand instructions on how everyone likes their rotis and the entire

family guards her hymen while she prays and fasts for a groom. After marriage, she uninterruptedly gives birth to son after son before she dies of uterine complications, leaving husband to marry her younger sister .... Their body is to be given to whoever calls dibs on it. If they dare dream of being wooed, aroused or satiated, ... they have to fight ... gropers, an archaic law and argue with politicians ... illiterate about sex.

16. 'The yoga guru who controls a Rs 3000 Crore empire including the pharmacy and manufacturing business of Ayurvedic medicines is in deep trouble this time. The issue is related to alleged manufacturing of pills which promise the delivery of a boy' (Gandhi 2015).

17. *Achhe din aane waale hain* ('Good days are coming') was the Hindi slogan of the BJP for the 2014 Indian general election. The slogan was coined by Narendra Modi, indicating that a prosperous future was in store for India if the BJP came to power.

18. '"We could not match up to the resources of the BJP. We could not match up to their ad campaign, the full page ads they came up with ... the amount they spent," senior Congress leader Ajay Maken told NDTV.... Asked whether his party was outclassed by the BJP in the first major election that played out on social media as much as TV channels, Mr Maken shrugged, "Our social media campaign only started last June"' ('Congress Concedes Weak Campaign, Failed Media Strategy', http://www.ndtv.com/elections-news/congress-concedes-weak-campaign-failed-media-strategy-562211; accessed 23 June 2016).

19. Shiv Viswanathan, on the TV channel *Headlines Today* (Morning), 30 April 2014, commenting on Modi's 'body language' as he voted, remarked that he was 'the greatest designer' and that when you watch the pictures, it is 'almost cinematic ... this kind of visuality is exceptional'. And 'between the commentator and visuals ... a new election'. Modi's use of the symbolic was 'exceptional'.

20. 'The Congress on Sunday declared a full-scale war against the "anti-farmer" and "pro-industrialist" government over the land acquisition bill, with Rahul Gandhi accusing Prime Minister Narendra Modi of bringing an ordinance on it to pay back "loans" of industrialists (http://www.hindustantimes.com/india-news/rahul-gandhi-to-lead-protest-against-pm-modi-s-land-bill/article1-1338778.aspx; accessed 23 June 2016).

21. Narendra Modi and his BJP got more than a third of all prime-time television coverage during these Lok Sabha elections, significantly higher than any other politician or party.

Researchers at CMS Media Lab ... found that Mr. Modi got 2,575 minutes, or 33.21 per cent, of the prime-time news telecast. His closest competitor was Aam Aadmi Party leader Arvind Kejriwal (10.31 per

> cent). Rahul Gandhi, who is leading the campaign of the Congress, came a distant third (4.33 per cent). The study analysed the coverage of five major news channels: Aaj Tak, ABP News and Zee News (Hindi) and NDTV 24x7 and CNN IBN (English) in the 8 p.m. to 10 p.m. prime-time band from March 1 to April 30. (Rukmini 2014)

22. 'Delhi Chief Minister Arvind Kejriwal has accused the media of accepting a supari or contract to finish off his Aam Aadmi Party (AAP), in his sharpest attack yet on journalists. The Chief Minister also called for a "public trial" of media groups' (see http://www.ndtv.com/india-news/media-has-taken-out-a-contract-to-finish-aap-says-delhi-chief-minister-arvind-kejriwal-760306; accessed 12 May 2015).

23. 'The controversy over the Narendra Modi government's decision to observe December 25, the day of Christmas celebrations, as national Good Governance Day refuses to die down. The Christian community feels this is a deliberate attempt to dilute the importance of the day. While it describes the move as "discriminatory against minorities", political parties see it as a design of the Bharatiya Janata Party and its ideological fount Rashtriya Swayamsevak Sangh (RSS) to promote communal agenda' (http://www.firstpost.com/india/good-governance-day-angry-leaders-say-communal-design-to-target-minority-holidays-1853529.html; accessed 19 May 2016).

24. 'BJP ... bolstered its Hindutva plank for the next UP elections by accusing the Akhilesh Yadav govt of encouraging 'love jehad'—the alleged phenomenon, where Muslim boys lure Hindu girls into relationships and later marriage and conversion' (http://timesofindia.indiatimes.com/india/Love-jihad-is-BJPs-new-poll-polarizer/articleshow/40829029.cms; accessed 19 May 2016).

25. 'Mohammad Akhlaq, 52, was beaten to death on September 28 in Bisahra village in Dadri district by a mob infuriated by rumours that he and his family were eating beef' (http://www.thehindu.com/news/national/dadri-lynching-incident-meat-turns-out-to-be-mutton/article8037029.ece; accessed 19 May 2016).

26. 'The presence of Baba Ramdev with members of Vanvasi Kalyan Ashram at the meeting of the Unnat Bharat Yojana anchored by the IIT-Delhi ... where recommendations were made for research on the genetic code of bulls, cows and cow-based agriculture, was hardly an academic exercise .... The Institute wants to be a part of the establishment and those in the administration ... are not concerned about its academic reputation .... The proposal to have separate vegetarian canteens in the IIMs, IITs and other major universities was another one of those acts to sharply divide the institutions' (http://www.mainstreamweekly.net/article6331.html; accessed 21 May 2016).

27. 'Meanwhile, at least 15 renowned Indian writers have returned literary prizes bestowed on them to protest what they call the country's "rising intolerance."

Poet Ashok Vajpeyi says Hindu nationalists are using "bans, suspicion and hurt feelings" to stoke religious bigotry in the name of "tradition." "There can't be a bigger insult to the Indian tradition," he says, than this growing intolerance. "The Indian tradition for millennia has been accommodative, open. It is a multireligious tradition, a multilingual tradition. And that plurality is now being under assault'" (http://www.npr.org/sections/parallels/2015/10/13/448182574/indias-ban-on-beef-leads-to-murder-and-hindu-muslim-friction; accessed 19 May 2016).

28. See 'BJP MPs want Bhagwad Gita to be declared 'National Book' (http://www.thehindu.com/news/national/bjp-mps-want-bhagwad-gita-to-be-declared-national-book/article8014464.ece; accessed 21 June 2016).

29. In an interview, erstwhile prominent BJP member Arun Shourie made two remarks that are relevant here. *One*, that the government needs to be low profile and *two*, that even the good work that it has done has not been communicated. Both reflect, paradoxically, the significance that the media appears to have acquired in politics (http://indiatoday.intoday.in/story/arun-shourie-narendra-modi-bjp-nda-government/1/433289.html; accessed 5 May 2016). Also see http://www.firstpost.com/politics/heres-why-pm-modi-should-not-ignore-arun-shourie-sour-grapes-jihad-2494594.html; accessed 21 May 2016.

30. The PM, who had won laurels for his sense of optics and visuality, struck a wrong chord when he wore a suit emblazoned with his name. The media found the perfect story in the visual of Narendra Modi wearing 'a dark suit with gold pinstripes and check pocket square for talks'. *Mail Today* reported that it was 'a bold fashion choice to greet President Obama'. Close-up photographs revealed the words 'Narendra Damodardas Modi'. Obama praised Modi's sartorial flair, adding, 'He has style'. But a supporter of the opposition party said: "The levels of megalomania and narcissism are unparalleled' (http://timesofindia.indiatimes.com/india/Pin-code-Modi-wears-name-on-sleeve-and-suit/articleshow/46024477.cms; accessed 23 June 2016). Discussions on whether it was fine style and good form, or a thinly-disguised show of narcissism coursed through social media, even attracting global attention.

31. 'What the Modi government has done is unprecedented in the history of modern India. Even the colonial government had shown greater sensitivity to the convenience of the people ... by demonetizing only those notes which were possessed by the super-rich and not those possessed by the people at large. This "emergency measure", however, is in line with the numerous other measures being currently pursued by the Modi government which has embarked on an undeclared "Emergency": it is as fatuous as it is against the people' (http://www.thecitizen.in/index.php/NewsDetail/index/1/9151/Demonetization-Witless-and-Anti-People; accessed 13 February 2017).

32. In a letter addressed to Rohith, a fellow student wrote:

this entire country is on fire in a way that it never has been over the institutionalized murders of dalit students. You had fought for justice after each such death on the University of Hyderabad campus, ... You have touched the millions ... who read your letter because your letter reflects so many parts of you that were the way you wished the world was—beautiful, honest, full of amazement, full of humility, of magnanimity .... your letter gives people ... an inkling of what we have lost and this is why so many people are mourning'. (http://www.hindustantimes.com/india/india-is-on-fire-letter-to-rohith-from-his-first-transgender-friend/story-G22Zd8ouq0DnFzblmGryKJ; accessed 23 June 2016; emphasis mine)

33. 'JNU Students Union president Kanhaiya Kumar was arrested on sedition charges after allegations of "anti-national" sloganeering ... surfaced .... Rajnath Singh ... released a statement: "If anyone raises anti-India slogans, ... raise questions on the country's unity and integrity, they will not be spared ....." Singh alleged that JNU students had the backing of Jamaat-ud-Dawah (JuD) chief Hafiz Saeed. But, his statement was based on "fake tweet" from an unverified Twitter account ....

When contacted, a senior officer ... said, "Our domain is ... to red-flag any incendiary content on social media"' (http://www.thehindu.com/specials/in-depth/jawaharlal-nehru-university-row-what-is-the-outrage-all-about/article8244872.ece; accessed 20 May 2016).

34. 'Union minister Nirmala Sitharaman questioned the role of former finance minister P. Chidambaram in the 2G spectrum scam .... She listed "several instances of blatant corruption" by "a series of noble great leaders of Congress", who included the chief ministers of Kerala and Himachal Pradesh besides former Union ministers Chidambaram and ... the wife of Amarinder Singh, currently the Congress's deputy leader in the Lok Sabha' (http://indianexpress.com/article/india/india-news-india/bjp-on-offensive-with-graft-charges-against-chidambaram-chandy/#sthash.6zuUK352.dpuf; also see http://indianexpress.com/article/india/india-news-india/bjp-on-offensive-with-graft-charges-against-chidambaram-chandy/; accessed 21 May 2016).

35. 'Constantly seeking ammunition against Congress president Sonia Gandhi and ... Rahul Gandhi, the ruling Bharatiya Janata Party has zeroed in on the Agusta Westland helicopter bribery case to mount a fresh offensive .... The latest revelations by an Italian court over alleged corruption in the deal ... have come in handy for the BJP, which found itself on the backfoot over its decision to impose President's rule in Congress-ruled Uttarakhand' (http://scroll.in/article/807297/bjps-agustawestland-game-plan-attack-sonia-and-hope-that-the-congress-eventually-unravels; accessed 21 May 2016).

36. '... there was a sense of jubilation at the Congress being wiped out in *all* the four states. In an oblique manner, this could also be said to be a testimony

to the then prime minister-designate Narendra Modi's campaign slogan of a "Congress-mukt Bharat". Successive state elections since 2014 have only witnessed the near-total elimination of Congress irrespective of which party won' (http://www.dailyo.in/politics/congress-assembly-elections-2016-rahul-gandhi-nehru-prashant-kishor-narendra-modi/story/1/10752.html; accessed 21 May 2016).

37. The prowess of BJP on social media is legion. One report states: 'While on one level, trolls are quite simply a digital mob; on another, this kind of trolling is an ideological attack on those who would stand in the way of Modi's pet project of a "Congress-mukt Bharat"—an India free of the Indian National Congress, or a "Hindu Rashtra"—a Hindu nation—where anybody who is not a supporter of Modi or the Bharatiya Janata Party (BJP) is deemed a "Congressi"' (http://www.caravanmagazine.in/vantage/power-social-media-emboldened-right-wing-trolls#sthash.rI4OipSK.dpuf; accessed 28 May 2016).

38. Zee News, for instance, had played a critical role in the 'making' of the JNU incident. Following the event,

> a journalist working with Zee News has resigned, suggesting that the channel deliberately misinterpreted a video clip to brand some students ... as anti-nationals and trigger the controversy .... The video didn't have any 'Pakistan Zindabad' slogans at all--yet we played it repeatedly to spread madness and mayhem .... we heard 'long live Indian courts' as 'long live Pakistan' and working on the government line, brought the careers, ... hopes and aspirations and families of some people to the brink of destruction .... (http://www.hindustantimes.com/india/journalist-vishwa-deepak-resigns-from-zee-news-channel-over-jnu-coverage/story-Ov1ToVEl7DiSOZ3vYb3LIL.html; accessed 27 May 2016)

39. '... on February 19, something ... remarkable happened ... an intuitive act of journalism ... reaffirming the journalist's pact with the viewer as one of conscience and conviction .... Ravish Kumar of NDTV India came on primetime screen ... to tell viewers that television has become diseased .... first we fell ill, now you .... Has this venom in you been communicated ... by us perchance? ... then the anchor vanished ... asking viewers to ... reflect on whether they wanted to be part of the terrible world that he and his fraternity create ....

'What followed was ... bites from TV debates of the past week .... one could finally hear ... the ugly ... hatred and violence dripping from the voices ...' (http://thewire.in/2016/02/21/ndtvs-ravish-on-the-dark-world-of-news-television-22267/; accessed 26 May 2016).

40. Arun Shourie's remark, 'The Modi government was nothing more than "Congress plus a cow"', will forever remain one of the most quotable quotes in our political annals (http://www.firstpost.com/politics/heres-why-pm-modi-

should-not-ignore-arun-shourie-sour-grapes-jihad-2494594.html; accessed 21 May 2016).

41. On 4 June 2016, the Central Board of Film Certification sought a stay on the release of the film *Udta Punjab*, citing that the themes dealt with in the film were too mature for the general audience. As a result, the producers were directed to make a total of eighty-nine cuts in the film. However, on 13 June 2016, the Bombay High Court struck down the stay and gave permission for the film's national release, albeit with a single cut in the screenplay. The film was released worldwide on 17 June 2016 (https://en.wikipedia.org/wiki/Udta_Punjab; accessed 17 June 2016).

42. 'Eight months after Muhammed Aklaq was murdered, a lab report now claims that the meat sample collected from his house is of cow and not mutton .... Sanjay Rana the father of the prime accused said he will file a complaint against Aklaq's family for storing beef .... BJP and other Sangh parivar leaders have also joined the chorus demanding action against Akhalq's family. BJP MP Yogi Adithyanath ... blamed opposition parties and the media for making the lynching a big issue' (http://naradanews.com/2016/06/is-dadri-next-polarisation-pot-for-bjp-before-up-polls/; accessed 17 June 2016).

43. 'Indian Prime Minister Narendra Modi told Congress Wednesday that his nation and the U.S. have overcome "the hesitations of history" and called for ever-stronger economic and defense ties between the two countries .... "Let us work together to convert shared ideals into practical cooperation," Modi said in a speech that lauded both nations' common democratic principles and hailed two heroes of nonviolence, India's Mahatma Gandhi and civil rights leader Martin Luther King Jr. (http://www.usnews.com/news/politics/articles/2016-06-08/indian-pm-burnishes-his-standing-with-address-to-congress; accessed 17 June 2016).

44. 'The manifesto touched upon contentious issues such as the alleged communal exodus, cow slaughter, triple talaq and the Ram Mandir, while also reaching out to farmers, landless labourers, women and youth' (http://www.thehindu.com/elections/uttar-pradesh-2017/U.P.-manifesto-BJP-promises-Ram-temple-1-GB-free-data/article17108508.ece; accessed 11 February 2017).

45. '"*Agar kabristan me bijli hai to shamshaan me bhi honi chahiye. Agar Ramzan mein bijli aati hai, to Diwali me bhi aani chahiye, bhedbhav nahi hona chahiye* (If there is electricity in the graveyard and during Ramzan, it must also be available in a crematorium and during Diwali. There should be no discrimination)," PM Modi had said .... BJP leaders defended the comment by saying that he just promised equal treatment to all the religions' (http://www.india.com/news/india/up-elections-2017-heres-why-political-parties-shifted-from-development-narrative-to-nasty-rhetoric-1903829/; accessed 23 April 2017).

46. 'Cow traders were hanged from a tree in Jharkhand, but the uproar fizzled out soon. In defence of the "liberal outrage factory", it's stretched beyond

its limits. Outrageous things are as common as the polluted air we breathe ' (http://www.dailyo.in/politics/alwar-d muslim-murder-cow-pehlu-khan-dadri-beef-gau-rakshak/story/1/16549.html; accessed 3 May 2017).

47. The allegation that the death of jawans in Sukma and Kupwara was celebrated by students gained some currency when right-wing fake news sites passed off images from another event as photos of the alleged 'celebration' on campus. The students union has since filed a police complaint over the fabrications (https://thewire.in/131249/jnu-buddha-singh/; accessed 3 May 2017).

48. '... in Rajya Sabha, BJP MP Mukhtar Abbas Naqvi denies that the Alwar incident happened the way it is being narrated in mainstream and social media .... *Maybe the possession of the videos that are circulating in social media would be deemed illegal. Maybe it would be considered antinational to protest a daylight murder of a Muslim man and brutalising his partners (while sparing his sole Hindu associate) in the still constitutionally secular India'* (http://www.dailyo.in/politics/alwar-d muslim-murder-cow-pehlu-khan-dadri-beef-gau-rakshak/story/1/16549.html; accessed 3 May 2017, emphasis mine).

49. 'RSS wing has prescription for fair, tall "customized" babies. The project claims to have ensured the delivery of 450 "customised babies" so far, and its target is to have a Garbh Vigyan Anusandhan Kendra, a facilitation centre, in every state by 2020' (http://indianexpress.com/article/india/rss-wing-has-prescription-for-fair-tall-customised-babies-4644280/; accessed 13 May 2017. Also see Bachhetta 2004).

50. The hollowness of the entire discourse is evident in Samajwadi Party leader Azam Khan, who asked Uttar Pradesh Chief Minister Yogi Adityanath to reinstate 'sati pratha'. 'Who is stopping him from legislating on triple talaq? But first tell me which Muslim opposed ' Sati pratha'? 'Sati pratha' is a part of the Hindu culture. Make it applicable, first,' Khan told ANI (http://www.deccanchronicle.com/nation/current-affairs/190417/legalise-sati-first-azam-khans-shocker-on-triple-talaq.html; accessed 28 April 2017).

51. '... Narendra Modi announced the withdrawal of Rs 500 and Rs 1,000 notes on 8th November 2017 .... The Prime Minister uttered the phrase "black money" 18 times ... "fake currency" or "counterfeit" five times .... The next day, the papers termed it a "war on black money" .... and the Prime Minister left for Japan.

By the time the Prime Minister returned ... the move had been christened "demonetisation" ... The Prime Minister made six speeches across the country on the demonetisation policy .... data analysis ... reveals a shifting of the narrative .... By November 27, he used the phrase "digital/cashless" thrice as much as "black money" with no mention of "fake currency" (http://www.indiaspend.com/cover-story/how-modi-changed-and-changed-the-demonetisation-narrative-54391; accessed 13 February 2017; also see Patnaik 2016).

52. A media analysis thus observes: 'One may go back to the summer of 2014, when the current Prime Minister repeated from BJP's medley of slogans his personal favourite of "minimum government and maximum governance". Surprisingly, in 2016, we live in times where dictates of the State govern what a citizen is to produce and eat, how much of his/her own money can be withdrawn and how social welfare benefits to the poor will be made available only by fulfilling government's Aadhaar card obligations' (Chimni 2016).

53. '*We are living in the moment of chauvinism*. No wonder then that the trappings of Hindi language chauvinism should also become more explicit ... the dominance of Hindi could be made official ... we may be moving towards *a new national identity based on uniformity, rather than the promise of a national identity without giving up diversity*' (http://indianexpress.com/article/opinion/columns/the-hindi-imposition-4639534/; accessed 4 May 2017, emphasis mine).

54. 'The petitioner argued that a law abiding tax payer cannot be forced to give his Aadhaar while filing income tax return and this was like an "electronic leash" as government would keep a tab on its citizens' (see http://www.firstpost.com/business/linking-aadhaar-to-pan-its-like-an-electronic-leash-on-honest-citizens-petitioner-tells-sc-3410264.html; accessed 30 April 2017).

EPILOGUE

FROM CERTITUDE TO UNCERTAINTY

The dictionary definition of an Epilogue terms it a section or a speech at the end of a book or a play that serves as a comment on or a conclusion to what has taken place so far. It can also refer to the meaning of the book's title. Both these meanings offer a productive entry point to this Epilogue, which can indeed be read as a comment on this book. Invoking the dictionary definition, the Epilogue may refer to the meaning of the title, *Refashioning India: Gender, Media and a Transformed Public Discourse.* In this book, eleven chapters seek to map India's changing discourse after the Indian State formally initiated a new economic policy in 1991, which led to greater integration with global capitalism. While writing the first edition of this book, I had argued that it was a new beginning in the history of contemporary India, marking the advent of not just new economic policies, but new political visions and cultural imaginings. I sought to convey these new imaginings through a focus on public discourse, from the vantage point of gender as it played out in the quarter-century after India initiated economic liberalisation—or what was widely known as globalisation.

Not to be forgotten were two momentous political shifts, which acquired considerable visibility in the 1990s: the growth and rise in legitimacy of the Bharatiya Janata Party (BJP), which epitomised a radically different idea of India and social order, and a strong presence of anti-caste public discourse. The announcement of the implementation of the Mandal Commission in 1990 and the demolition of the Babri Masjid on 6 December 1992 ushered in a historically new epoch for India. The political, social, and ideological forces that made the demolition of the Babri Masjid possible have become a hegemonic presence today. The political visibility of members from marginalised castes in Indian politics reflects the visible shifts after Mandal. I argue, however, that while the anti-caste spirit did not retreat, it has morphed in unexpected forms.[1] In some ways, a comparison with the gender question may be of interest here. Both caste[2] and gender are hyper-visible in contemporary public discourse. It is important to note, though, that all too often—albeit not always—they are emptied of their democratic content and promise of social justice.

I write this Epilogue in early 2026 as war rages in West Asia, heralding a world where uncertainty and danger appear as the only certainities. It is now a good ten years after the book was first published. The central motifs of globalisation and consumption, so predominant in many of the chapters, appear to have retreated from public discourse. Today, some declare that globalisation has met its end while others argue that it needs a reset. Trade, data, and capital flows suggest that globalisation is here to stay, but even experts in the world of finance acknowledge that the rhetoric of de-globalisation is increasingly shaping the global media narrative as the world lurches from one crisis to the next.[3] As India waited anxiously to see how the Trump tariffs play out, global voices pronounced the 'funeral rites' of globalisation.[4] Prime Minister Narendra Modi has been appealing for a revival of the spirit of *Swadeshi*, urging Indians to prioritise *locally-made products* and stand united in the face of a growing global economic uncertainty.[5]

The rhetoric of India Shining (p. 151) and the India story at Davos has faded (p. 211). I therefore offer this Epilogue as a comment and not a conclusion. For, as corporate parlance suggests, 'the rapidity of change has changed' (p. 1), and we do not know what will unfold in the near future. A conclusion is difficult under such circumstances. Indeed, looking back, I notice that Chapter 8, which was based on the study of the media for one month in the summer of 2007, necessitated a short Epilogue. For even as I was working on the chapter in mid 2008, 'the collapse of Lehman Brothers, which heralded the global economic meltdown ... intruded unexpectedly into the unabashed celebration of corporate capitalism by the media' (p. 211). I had written then that Chapter 11 could also be read as an Epilogue. A decade later, one can no longer do so. However, the trends discerned in the 2014 Lok Sabha elections, which I wrote about in Chapter 11 even as it played out in real time—a mediatised campaign, larger-than-life image-building, a flurry of buzzwords, catchy phrases, and a publicity apparatus—has only grown stronger and louder over time.

What has changed is the palpable sense of uncertainty, not only in our commonsense, everyday perception, but also in the 2025 Chief Economists Outlook edition. The unabashedly optimistic outlook of the 1990s and 2000s, evident in the chapters here, has been replaced by caution, 'uncertainty' and 'extraordinary volatility'.[6] The storyline in India reflects this larger narrative. The celebratory India growth story was pervasive in the dominant discourse etched out from Chapters 4–9. Its burgeoning middle class, feted as the big spenders, was the talk of the corporate world. The upbeat report of the McKinsey Global Institute, titled 'Country of

Consumers', predicted that this middle class would grow even bigger, 'reshaping global consumer markets' (p. 201). In contrast, there are today worrying commentaries on its shrinkage and widening inequalities.[7] The larger context of globalisation has indeed changed, but neoliberalism, the scaffold on which it rested, remains , although some argue that its decline has begun.[8] I argue that not only do we need to comprehend the nature of neoliberalism, but we also need to explore its relationship with authoritarianism.

Developments in contemporary India, I argue, can be understood only within a larger framework of neoliberalism and authoritarianism, increasingly conjoined together, both of which are antithetical to democracy. This Epilogue examines the links among neoliberalism, authoritarianism, and the retreat of democracy; the shift in the official markers of the Indian State and 'nation'—the making of a 'New India'; and the unprecedented role that the media and its linked apparatus of publicity, communication, and management have played in 'refashioning India', its 'public discourse', and 'gender'. As this book repeatedly shows, these elements are all interwoven.

NEOLIBERALISM, AUTHORITARIANISM AND DEMOCRACY: MEDIA, MARKET, STATE, FAITH

Neoliberalism is a powerful set of economic policies. It is about facilitating free trade, maximising corporate profits, and challenging welfarism. Neoliberal rationality, while foregrounding the market, is not only, or even primarily, focused on the economy; it involves extending and disseminating market values to all institutions and social action, even as the market itself remains a distinctive player. This has serious political implications for liberal democracy. In a neoliberal world, it may be more accurate to contend that the market becomes the organising and regulative principle of the state and society. The state does not retreat. However, the welfare state does, and is replaced by an authoritarian and neoliberal state. This state at once openly responds to the needs of the market as well as its own ideological imperatives through monetary and fiscal policy, immigration policy,[9] its treatment of criminals, and the structure of public education.[10] A late 2025 commentary, tellingly titled 'Kanwariyas: Kings of faith and the market', illustrates well the new state-market reconfiguration in India and how well neoliberalism sits with authoritarianism. It captures the point I am labouring to make. The Kanwar Yatra is an annual pilgrimage of devotees of the god Shiva, known as Kanwariyas, to Hindu pilgrimage sites in order to fetch holy water from the Ganga. What used to be a traditional religious pilgrimage has, like many other aspects of society, been weaponised in recent years. It was reported that the 'Uttar Pradesh and Uttarakhand governments[11] had ordered eateries to prominently display their licences', purportedly as a measure of 'quality assurance, consumer awareness, and even public order', because in the past '"a ruckus" was created by some *yatris* over the use of onion, garlic, or meat products in places they chose to eat'. However,

> A group of petitioners had challenged these orders, and argued that they hampered the right to practise a profession, amounted to social profiling, and discrimination against Muslims. The lawyer for the petitioners ... invoked '*anonymity of the marketplace*' against the government orders. The SC decided not to determine these Constitutional questions and asked the eateries to display their licenses. '*Consumer is king*,' the Court said.[12] [emphasis mine]

Contrary to the long-held belief that 'modernisation' and 'globalisation' would put an end to all 'parochial' identities, the latter have actually flourished, albeit not always in the same direction. Early in the story of globalisation, we saw the celebration of the 'ethnic' in food, fashion, and music—a happy market recognition of 'identities', much like the celebration of multiculturalism in the West in the 1990s (Chaudhuri 2003, 2023). Later in the story, we witnessed unabashed political majoritarian state aggression against the 'other' culture, language, religion, race, caste, and ethnicity. Returning to the *yatris* and the court judgment that the 'Consumer is king', the commentary writes that 'the idea that the consumer is king is a secular notion', and that nothing could better express the 'decapitation of religion by capitalism in modern societies than this motto'. The consumer, 'typically seen as a soulless seeker of pleasure and gratification', has, however, now brought in faith into their 'market choices'. Faith has entered the marketplace as 'capitalism' struggles to serve 'god and mammon at the same time', for '... Muslims, Jews, and Hindus want faith-compliant products and services'.[13]

We can perhaps now understand better why the much-feted Indian middle class, instead of transforming into global citizens, has morphed so effortlessly into bigoted, majoritarian, intolerant, and digital hatemongers. In Chapter 4, written in the early days of India's globalisation, I mention that while the new Indian was 'cosmopolitan', they were not unmarked by their ethnic, caste, and religious identity. And 'many of the young with an attitude of spending cheered at the demolition of Babri Masjid' (pp. 90–91). This is not the space to dwell on whether they were always parochial, even bigoted, and whether the 'idea' of India as inclusive and democratic was a thin veneer, ready to crack. My contention is that much like the different ideological trends that existed in the nineteenth-century social reform movements and later within the twentieth-century national movement, contradictory visions of a good society and nationalism existed simultaneously. What remained muted in official discourse, such as the different forms of bigotry, continued to flourish in Indian society.[14] While such attitudes were strong, they had for long worked below the radar. However, grassroots activism had kept communalism alive and ready to spread.

This grassroots communalism is now fuelled and weaponised, and has been elevated to the official, legitimate discourse. It is normal to hear the Home Minister speaking in Parliament about the killing of terrorists and his barely veiled asides at Samajwadi Party leader Akhilesh Yadav.[15] Such instances of dog whistling now define our everyday lives, from the Parliament to the mainstream media, which has proved itself a compliant instrument, to the numerous Resident Welfare Associations (RWAs) that are integral to the new urban India.[16] Indeed, several WhatsApp messages (of RWAs and otherwise)[17] reflect the micro-disseminating and home delivery of both state ideology and consumer goods and services. Like most technologies, WhatsApp is a double-edged sword.[18] Alternate content is possible, but is narrowcast. Each WhatsApp group is usually composed of like-minded people. We hear what we wish to hear. Media no longer exposes and examines received views. It validates existing opinions. However, the stories of a brave alternate media survive and offer hope in besieged times.

Central to this book is the idea that while discourses matter in all societies, they have acquired a very distinct shape in contemporary times. I have argued in the Introduction and in several chapters that any discussion of gender, media, and culture in contemporary India needs to recognise three contexts: the constitutive influence of three decades of institutionalised feminism, the imperatives of neoliberal economic policies, and the scale of the media and communication industry in the making of popular and public culture. Further, this constitutive influence has been made possible largely through knowledge produced by a new set of firms specialising in market research and communication, which are interested in understanding the Indian market and State messaging. The question that may arise is: What role do these advertisement and management firms play in the current authoritarian times? What was novel—the PR firms and professional campaign teams—in the election campaign of 2014 (Chapter 11) is now integral to governance. The management of image and perception is the driving mantra. ven in the ongoing war this not only holds but is augmented.[19]

The market rested heavily on such methods in the early decades of globalisation in India. The State has harnessed the model and amplified it to an unprecedented degree. What has altered is the content. While earlier, marketing agencies took cognisance of the impact that feminist ideas of 'freedom' and 'autonomy' had on the new Indian woman consumer in order to reconstruct them in alignment with neoliberal ideas of self-realisation through achievement and pleasure, we now witness government policies that are packaged smartly, but invoke 'ancient Indian culture', 'sanskar', the Hindu nation, and a strong muscular State.[20] The corporate model that we mapped through the chapters holds good. However, the content of the images and ideas has altered. If scholarly plan documents defined policymaking earlier, today they are designed for fast communication. Catchy slogans, buzzwords, and acronyms inform every sphere of society, including the academia.[21] Even war and counter-terrorist operations are now named 'Operation Sindoor'[22] and 'Operation Mahadev'.[23]

It is here that we perhaps need to examine the relationship of liberalism with populism. People's sovereignty does connect populism with democracy. But an innate tension exists between the two concepts. Liberal democracy involves informing, and the political participation of, citizens, political pluralism, and the transparency of political structures and institutions (Pasquino 2008). However, populist conceptions concerning the power of 'the people' are rarely applied under such conditions. Populisms often oppose the political structures mediating between the people (such as civil society actors) and power. In fact, the exclusionary view, whereby 'the people' are represented by a certain stratum of society, based on socioeconomic class, religion, or ethnicity, creates an incompatibility with the fundamental tenets of liberal democracy. Were we to study how the Indian State has functioned, we would witness a two-fold and extremely effective strategy to silence civil society and dissent. *One,* the State acts as a repressive apparatus that punishes dissent, jails, and threatens. *Two*, the State acts as an ideological apparatus that ensures the demonising of'others' on the one hand, and the continuous publicity of the larger-than-life achievements of its leader on the other. The creation and amplification of a slew of buzzwords on which this publicity blitzkrieg rests make them part of everyday lexicon. [24]

In this book, the focus has been on India's changing public discourse, its media, and the curious ways that gender has played out in unexpected avatars over the last decade. As mentioned earlier, the chapters here were written at different points, and much water has flown under the bridge since then. A BJP-led government is firmly in power under the leadership of Prime Minister Modi, who is now into his third term. Chapter 11 can no longer be read as an epilogue, but perhaps as a breathless harbinger of things to come. We live in a refashioned India, to invoke the title of the book. 'New India'[25] is a term used widely in social media, signalling the message that the'old India' is *passe* and long gone. Everything appears changed. Everything, however, is not new; some, like the unprecedented rise of the media and a culture and industry of publicity accompanied and amplified by the new media, have been in place for a while. Likewise, alternative ideas of the nation (majoritarian) and State (muscular), which were always present but muted, have grown sharp and loud. When the brute power of the State is coupled with a dexterous use of the media for instant persuasion, with a plethora of catchy phrases and acronyms to define social justice, we have a potent combination to fundamentally recast India. The long muted idea of a majoritarian nation and strong State is now legitimised, powerful, and pervasive. Ahimsa is *passe*. The muscular State is in. The State controls mainstream media,[26] which amplifies state propaganda and permeates public discourse through WhatsApp and social media. India has the largest number of WhatsApp users, with approximately 853.8 million people using the platform.[27] The Indian middle class and its many RWAs spread the State message every day, even as they remain committed to spreading the word about new consumer goods and sales. Studies are documenting this.[28] In 2018, I had written on hate messaging and the use of WhatsApp:

> Murderous attacks on helpless victims have now become routine in India, with numerous and varied grounds for killing the victims.... The antipathy towards'outsiders' and'others' is not the only pattern. *In all these instances,*

> *rumours fuelled by Facebook and WhatsApp have been the immediate triggers. But what is far more ominous and important to recognise is that these triggers rest on an ecosystem of fear and hate, which has been nurtured with care and clear intent.* There has been a careful dissemination of such messages (text message forwards) in the works. Hate has been the central motif. (Chaudhuri 2018; emphasis mine)

It is not that 'hate' among communities is new to India. The horrors of Partition and successive riots have too often brought to the fore the ugliness of society beneath its veneer of civility. But what *is* new is its scale, pervasiveness, and tragic acceptance. What is also new is the systematic dismantling of institutions—of education,[29] media, judiciary[30]—and the stripping off of the veneer of civility.

We live now in an authoritarian populist regime, a hardwired regime that has been recasting every aspect of the public and private spheres, harnessing a well-oiled, technologically-enabled ideological refashioning of society. This has been supported by the repressive machinery of the State, now in its smart avatar. In the Indian context, the ideological task of making both authoritarianism and neoliberalism the commonsense of people has rested predominantly on the media (print, electronic, and new media across all its platforms—WhatsApp, Twitter, Facebook). This book has extensively documented the changes in the media—the early post-liberalisation days of advertisements and advertorials, its over-communicative abundance, its narrow casting, and media convergence. Twelve years is a long time. The 'new' is now settled. Eminent journalists are now YouTubers; some have exited the field while a few have been killed. Attacks, meanwhile, have mounted.[31]

RECASTING INDIA: HOMEGENEOUS, MUSCULAR, ALL-ALIGNED

The past several years have seen new campaigns: 'One Nation, One Election', 'One Nation, One Examination', 'One Nation, One Subscription'. The emphasis is on the 'oneness'. A key contention of this book has been that a nation and its State are founded on a very self-conscious, articulated notion of identity, and that 'India first encountered the question of national self-definition in the course of its anti-colonial struggle' as it engaged in the historical task of creating a new India (pp. 5–6). I had then attempted to discern some of the motifs that became central to the image and idea of India.

First, the idea that India was plural, and that, in spite of periods of intolerance, a distinct and internally differentiated composite culture had evolved over time. I had emphasised that sharp disagreements persisted at the ground level. 'The ideology of fanatic Hindu nationalism, the kind that inspired the assassination of Gandhi, has been a recurrent theme within the many contending ideas of India. The idea of religion as the defining marker for nationhood, evident in the making of Pakistan, likewise challenged the idea of a composite culture' (p. 6). Such visions have occasionally been strident, but remained muted for the most part, even—surprisingly—appearing to retreat almost wholly from the dominant national public discourse, only to reappear with renewed vitriol.[32] This has been most evident since the formation of the NDA-I government in 2014. This idea of plurality and composite culture has been systematically eroded by ideological recasting, in which mainstream media played a significant role. The rhetoric and policy of 'One...' is a self-evident shift, accompanied by State violence against minorities in particular and dissenters in general. Textbooks for children have been rewritten, erasing the history of the Mughals.[33] It has also deleted facts about Gandhi's assassination and Gandhi's role in fighting communalism.[34]

Second, an acknowledgement that since the vast majority of Indian people were poor, democracy and freedom would mean little unless the needs of the poorest were addressed. During the celebration of the first two years in power, the prime minister reiterated his commitment to the poor.[35] This attitude towards the 'poor', however, underwent interesting policy shifts, reflecting the profound neoliberal recasting and the powerful idea of a patron-client relationship. Two events should be mentioned here. One is the sudden announcement of demonetisation on 8 November 2016, at 8 PM, which commentators suggested was a political act to rebrand the BJP as a pro-poor party. 'Once seen as the "Brahmin Bania" party of the Indian town-square, the BJP was now a pro-poor party that saw the rich with suspicion.'[36] Justifying demonetisation, the prime minister said that as a result of the move, 'the poor were sleeping in ease and those who have stashed ill-gotten money are running from pillar to post, buying sleeping pills'.[37] That the poor ultimately suffered the most did not seem to matter.

Four years later, the poorly implemented coronavirus lockdown in March 2020 revealed that the BJP remains in its disposition a Hindu, upper-caste, middle-class, urban party. It *thinks* like one, even if it sometimes *manages* to act differently to woo the voters.[38] The emphasis on 'thinks' and 'manages' is important, for two key arguments that run through the book are that the 'managerial' approach is both the dominant ideology and practice, and 'publicity' is both an ideology and an industry. The quote below explicates the gap between what the regime 'thinks' and what it 'says':

> Only an *urban middle class-minded government* would decree showing *Ramayan* and *Mahabharat* on TV as a solution to the people's lockdown woes, because it *presumes that people are just bored at home*. But the poor weren't facing boredom. They were facing hunger, homelessness, unable to find daily work.... And since the Modi government has suspended all public transport, they don't know how to get home.[39]

The lockdown, the commentator writes, was 'undoing that image' of being pro-poor that the BJP had tried to convey through demonetisation.

This question of 'image'-making, or what is often termed 'optics', has also been a defining feature of the last decade. I had argued that a general culture of vacuous consumerism over the decades had led to the cultivation of a middle-class sensibility geared towards instant and ready-to-consume ideas of cultural pride and nationalism. An example I had then cited was an image of the Burj Khalifa in Dubai lit up in the colours of the Indian flag on the occasion of India's Republic Day, forwarded repeatedly over WhatsApp by many whose interest in the history or meaning of Republic Day amounted to little more than such tangible symbols and affirmation.[40] I have mentioned that the advertisement model was appropriated to sell not just consumer goods and lifestyles, but brand leaders and parties as well. It also laid the ground for a vacuous cultural nationalism, dressed up in the technologically savvy format of media advertisements with the necessary 'feel good nationalism' factor (Chapter 11).

I would like to return to the matter of the poor. It is here that the BJP's targeted cash transfer to women, seen as key to the regime's success, ought to be studied carefully. The prime minister has successfully shifted the focus on women by talking about a host of women-centric schemes, such as 'Beti Bachao, Beti Padhao' or Ujjwala. But women essentially remain '*labharthis*' (beneficiaries) instead of equal citizens. The ugly instance of the State's treatment of India's Olympic medal-winning women wrestlers (which we shall return to later) exemplifies this.[41]

Third, foreign policy, which was seen as a marker of Indian national identity, has also been refashioned. It has moved away from the days of non-alignment (p. 9, fn 33), which would be read perhaps as both a sign of weakness and idealism today. Since India wished to be viewed as a global player, both economically and in international affairs, its shift from non-alignment to complete alignment was based on Realpolitik—a pragmatic decision based on a disregard for ethical considerations. The observations of a former National Security Advisor are pertinent here. The focus of India's foreign policy, he felt, should not be limited to issues such as seeking a permanent seat on the Security Council or extracting revenge for historical wrongs. It ought to be about welfare and peace. Peace is now seen as a sign of weakness, while bombing signals prowess and pride.[42] India's foreign policy's wishy washy stance and selective silence in the 2026 Iran Israel and US war is a tragic and definitive shift from what one had argued in the Introduction was a key element in the making of modern India's identity.[43] new authoritarian populist demagogues and a 'politics of emotions and resentment' that lead to 'hyper-nationalist tendencies' and a callous disregard for human sufferings.[44]

Recasting Gender, Public Discourse and Democracy

A key contention of this book is that gender is a pervasive presence in contemporary Indian media and popular culture. This visibility rested on (*i*) India's new economic policy, (*ii*) the Indian women's movement, and (*iii*) the publicity and media industry. Some of this has changed in the last decade. The uncertainty among global and national economies, mentioned at the beginning of this Epilogue, needs no further elaboration. While gender remains a constant presence in popular media, the women's movement, significantly, does not. This is not surprising, given that we have an authoritarian state that *sees* social movements as 'antinational'.[45] I emphasise the word '*see*' because social movements and protests have not stopped; however, the state has either decided not to '*see*' them or has chosen, with the aid of mainstream media, to '*see*' them as disruptors to 'normal', 'law-abiding', 'ordinary' people and the 'nation'. The farmers' movement and the role that women played in it was another such instance,[46] as was the extraordinary role played by women in protests against the Citizenship Amendment Act.[47]

What is more visible today is the instrumental use of women to specifically generate publicity for the State. A quote from a media analysis of the deployment of gender in the four-day war with Pakistan in 2025 conveys the point:

> The government of India named this military strike as 'Operation Sindoor'—a deliberate strategy to reduce women's identities to their marital status. The symbols sindoor (vermilion powder applied by a married woman's hair parting) and mangalsutra (a sacred neck jewellery worn by married women) are deeply ingrained in the traditional representation of a Hindu woman and her marital status. In the days following the terrorist attack, [an image of a woman] ... wearing a bridal attire sitting beside her husband's body was shared widely on the internet to garner widespread support in the country where the husband is seen as [a] woman's guardian and source of protection.[48]

Two women officers of the Indian army and air force gave a press conference after the Operation. 'The Indian news media outlets and liberal feminists celebrated this achievement of women's leadership in the operation as a message to the world on how progressive the country is.'[49] However, this strategic display of women in leadership roles in military action can also be read as a form of 'femonationalism'—an exploitation of 'feminist' ideals to advance nationalist and militaristic agendas. Indeed, governments worldwide are integrating women into violent security apparatuses purportedly as a sign of progress and equality, and 'weaponising gender' to transform their violent actions into moral and progressive acts.

Readers will recall that the third defining reason for the visibility of gender was the unprecedented growth of the media and communication industry, which owed as much to revolutionary technological innovations as it did to a political economy where communication, representation, and publicity increasingly define contemporary public culture. It is this mainstream media which, as we saw, has furthered 'the State's ideology and the violence that it espouses', apart from deploying 'covert tactics that encourage bias and discrimination against critics and dissenters'.[50]

I argue that it is within the two encompassing regimes of neoliberalism and authoritarianism that one must locate and map the ways that 'gender' is now a pervasive presence in public discourse, albeit often emptied of its core content of social justice, equal opportunities and democratic rights. It is also within these two crisscrossing processes that I find it productive to invoke Raewyn Connell's idea of hegemonic masculinity (Connell 2005 [1995]),[51] which offers us a lens through which to make sense of the intersections of patriarchy, the State, and the market in contemporary times. Bahubali, the strong man, is a current and widely used term in India, often deployed as a prefix to describe political leaders. It is still about the strong man and, strangely enough—or perhaps this is not so strange—is frequently used as a synonym for underworld Dons who not only wield enormous political clout but also occupy legitimate political positions. Bahubali, representing our current hegemonic masculinity, is the Strong Man. But his strength does not arise from self-endurance but instead rests on generating fear, exacting retribution and wreaking destruction on others.

I argue that the rise, visibility, and legitimacy of hegemonic 'masculinity' is a central component of the current populist and authoritarian project. The laudatory reference to the idea of a 'strong man' by the media and the larger public discourse is an endorsement of a 'strong State' that brooks no defiance, of a 'triumphant nationalism' and a concerted pushback to democratic processes that sought to change the social order defined by extant class, caste, and gender hierarchies understood as sanctioned by religion, tradition, and culture.

I seek here to unpack the making of this hegemonic masculinity in a context defined by, *one*, the rise of a State at once wedded to both neoliberalism and Hindu cultural nationalism; *two*, technological innovation, an exponential growth of media, a publicity industry, and a culture of image-building that dovetailed with the rise of populism; and *three*, a professionalisation of politics and public life within which gender, sexuality, and diversity became elements of marketing. Not surprisingly, the Ogilvy advertising firm oversaw the 2014 elections for the BJP, and the ad man in charge, Piyush Pandey, credited the BJP's success to the 'fantastic product' that it had in Modi and his ability to communicate with the people.[52] Unpacking this process is an ambitious task. I can only outline how key elements converged to construct an idea of a hegemonic masculinity, Bahubali.

While many countries have witnessed the growth of populism and personality-driven politics with an anti-gender rights agenda, it is important to address the historical specificities within which this populist storyline is played out. A few lines on the historical specificity of India and its tryst with British colonialism, a point emphasised in the Introduction, are therefore in order. It was in a colonially mediated modernity marked by economic devastation and deep cultural humiliation that the modern Indian intellectual critique, political struggles against colonial rule, and the engagement with democratic ideas of social justice, equality, liberty, and fraternity evolved. Movements that questioned the traditional social order were often accused of voicing Western colonial attitudes embedded in a deep racist ideology. This tension has defined modern India and created a fertile ground for cultural nationalism. Many viewpoints, including socialist ideas, became part of India's anti-colonial struggle and finally found legitimate space with the adoption of the Indian Constitution, where liberty, equality, and fraternity were enshrined as the goals of the Indian State.

The paradox lay in the fact that State laws were far ahead of social laws. This tension continues to haunt our present. B. R. Ambedkar, the central architect of the Indian Constitution, had alerted us to the grave danger that may emanate from the contradictions between political and legal equality in a context of deep social and economic inequalities. The point that I am making—and which is of relevance in contemporary times—is that even as social movements battled for democratic rights, there was fierce resistance to such changes. Debates within the Constituent Assembly (from 1946) and thereafter on the Hindu Code Bill highlight this opposition. As one of India's foremost feminists Amrit Kaur put it, the response to the mildest of reforms aroused an almost *fanatical opposition*. 'Religion in danger,' she observed, is 'a very potent caveat which scares even seemingly intelligent persons.' Today, this is not just the strident tone, but the most visible one. During the debate on the Hindu Code Bill that sought to extend certain rights to women, Shyama Prasad Mukherjee, founder of the Bharatiya Jana Sangh (the earlier avatar of the BJP), said that 'he had been reading books on psychoanalysis which suggest that the problems of Western society stemmed from sexual psychoses which he attributed to divorce'. Allowing women to inherit would lead to marriage going out of currency; he said: 'May God save us ... from having an army of unmarried women' (Chaudhuri 2005 [1993]). Nirmal Chandra Chatterjee, leader of the Hindu Mahasabha, commenting on the prohibition of bigamous marriages, argued that any Hindu who sought more than one wife could simply embrace Islam and come under a different personal law which still permitted polygamy. This is a discourse that is both overt and legitimate today. The point I seek to make is this: while such a line of thinking was a formidable presence, it was the constitutional vision that became the visible and official face of the Indian State and nation.

However, from the very beginning, the Indian Constitution of 1950 was itself seen by status quoist forces that sought to uphold the traditional gender order as a betrayal of tradition and culture. Cultural nationalism has always been a presence within India, but it was somewhat muted, reined in at times by the State; now, however, it has finally acquired legitimacy, strength, and hegemony that I argue would have been impossible without a confluence of the State, market, and media. Together, the rhetoric of a strong man (Bahubali) and a strong State has pervaded India's public discourse. It is therefore not happenstance that the Constitution itself is under attack, albeit not always overtly.

The complicit relationship between the media and populism has been widely commented upon. But here, too, one must note the historical specificity of India's public sphere. Scholars have commented that the European public sphere was social before it was political. In colonial contexts, political change came first while the social lagged behind. Anti-colonial politics led the Indian educated classes to engage in popular mobilisation against British rule, creating new modes of communication with peasants and workers. The bourgeois public sphere had to combine rational criticism with affect and image.

India's public sphere contained varieties of populism, where interest and identity served to mobilise people in combinations that are hard to anticipate. Rumour and superstition propelled campaigns that spread through print and digital channels, including Twitter (now 'X') and text messages. The technological basis of this public sphere is contemporary, yet it is dominated by crowds rather than individuals, often agitating over issues that appear to be traditional rather than modern. I want to draw attention to two aspects: *first*, the conflict between the State-led constitutional ideas of liberty, equality, and fraternity (the modern, democratic language) and society at large—a public for whom this was an alien language and worldview. *Second*, the conflict was not just about content, but form. India's public sphere was steeped not in the language of reason and deliberations, but in deeply emotive religious symbols.

As mentioned earlier, the rise of cultural nationalism coincided with the growth of India's economic liberalisation, technological changes, the exponential expansion of the media, and a certain mainstreaming of gender. *In hindsight, the shift from a public sphere of debate and discussion to a public sphere of image and spectacle could not have been easier. The Bahubali was waiting to happen.* The personalisation of political leadership has been a constant in India. The contemporary moment is but a dramatic instance of the same. It has suited well the global trend of mediatisation of politics, and dramatisation, entertainment, and sensationalism. The media has a far greater preference for stories about real people than it does for boring speeches or abstract issues presented in a bureaucratic style. There is a specific 'populist' communication style, of which appearance and attire are only one aspect. Childhood stories and favourite foods are another aspect. It fits into the '*story-telling' frames of media industries.*

The 2014 elections in India epitomised each of these dimensions. *Media management techniques were deployed to deal with the professionalisation of political action.* The last decade in India has seen a careful 'crafting' of political messaging. The entire BJP campaign, created by the agency Soho Square, a part of Ogilvy, was cinematic, evoking glamour, power, might, and the heralding of a new epoch.

An *entire ecosystem* of messaging was built up, pervading India's public discourse, down to the residential associations and ordinary everyday conversations. Together, they built up a message of a strong man, a strong State, and a triumphant nation. The shooting of alleged rapists in 2019 in Telangana by the police in what is known as an 'encounter' was heralded as the right step to teach criminals a lesson. All four accused in the rape and murder of a 25-year-old woman were killed, triggering a chorus of praise for what many saw as speedy justice, while also raising concerns over extra-judicial executions.[53]

The making of the strong man, the Bahubali, is a good example of this ideological ecosystem. The head of the Wrestling Federation of India, Brij Bhushan Singh,[54] was accused of sexual harassment by India's top women wrestlers in 2023. He too had been referred to as the Bahubali.

There are two elements in the larger-than-life construction of Bahubali (hegemonic masculinity), the 'individual persona' and, more importantly in our context, a figure who represents a dominant caste group, one traditionally associated with warfare and rulers in charge of the social order. Women are necessarily subalterns in this scheme of things. Those women who protest must be crushed. I argue, therefore, that the rise and legitimacy of Bahubali is antithetical to individual autonomy, freedom, and equality. The complicit relationship between populism and media is unambiguous, but how it plays out is context-specific. The relationship between authoritarian populism and gender is equally unambiguous, but, as mentioned earlier, historically specific. I wish to show how this is played out by drawing from two events: the 2012 Delhi gang-rape and murder of a young physiotherapy student dubbed 'Nirbhaya' (the fearless one) and the 2023 case of sexual assault against India's leading women wrestlers by Brij Bhushan Singh, a prominent BJP leader. Both saw widespread protests, demanding justice from the governments of the time. In 2012, the government led by Prime Minister Manmohan Singh, which was seen as having failed its citizens. The party in power lost in 2014, despite its belated engagement and setting up of some measures to address women's safety (see Chapter 10).

In 2023, however, matters unfolded very differently. A newspaper report stated that

> In 2023, several renowned wrestlers had protested for months in New Delhi, demanding the arrest of the then BJP lawmaker for allegedly sexually harassing women wrestlers, including a minor.... As the protest continued for weeks, the Sports Ministry had constituted an oversight committee to internally investigate the matter. The police filed an FIR against Mr. Singh after the intervention of the Supreme Court in May 2023. In June, a 1,000-page chargesheet was filed.... Within weeks of lodging the FIR, the Delhi police, in June 2023, filed its closure report in the court in the minor wrestler's case and sought cancellation of the case involving the girl after her father said that he had made a false complaint of sexual harassment against Mr. Singh to settle scores.[55]

Significantly, the minister in question was termed 'the Bahubali, who was a one-man federation':

> He ran the federation with his *strong-man instincts*; he was the *overall president, selection committee chief* and *chaired athletes' grievance panel*—was the *judge, jury and executioner.* And even as the protests by the wrestlers continue we hear of the Bahubali's huge rally on 10th April where he asserted that he shall fight ... fight ... the 2024 Elections. [56]

That on 27 May 2025, Singh was cleared on one count of sexual harassment by a court in Delhi tells us all we need to know about the rhetoric of gender empowerment and the ground reality.

Elsewhere, another chief minister, though dressed as a Hindu monk, is seen as the strong man who has purportedly quelled the underworld and terrorised the minority community. The government led by him has reshaped the meaning of the bulldozer—it is now a ruthless symbol of state administration.[57] This message has been amplified across media platforms. A song eulogising the might of Baba bulldozer is sung by a DJ at a wedding; a truck driver sings, '*Jab baba ke bulldozer chamak ke chale*... ('when Baba's bulldozer starts...'). This went 'viral' on YouTube, and social media was abuzz with songs about Bulldozer Baba that got lakhs of views.[58] A popular song states that when the bulldozer comes, the miscreants of society hide, while the powerful and the musclemen run away. This is the story not of the bandit, not of Robin Hood, not of any outlaw, but is the language of a weaponised state. These perhaps are the ways in which populism thrives, and neoliberalism and authoritarianism coalesce.

NOTES

1. See Sudha Pai, 'Shifting Identity Politics: The Dalit Move toward the BJP in Uttar Pradesh', Institute of South Asian Studies, 9 May 2024. Available at https://www.isas.nus.edu.sg/papers/shifting-identity-politics-the-dalit-move-toward-the-bjp-in-uttar-pradesh/ (accessed September 2025).

2. The Cabinet Committee on Political Affairs, chaired by Prime Minister Modi, has decided to conduct caste enumeration in the upcoming Census. See Sony Kunjappan and Amal Chandra, 'A different approach to the caste census: Explained', *The Hindu*, 12 June 2025. Available at https://www.thehindu.com/news/national/a-different-approach-to-the-caste-census-explained/article69684153.ece (accessed September 2025).

3. 'Beset by war, upended by broken supply chains, ravaged by a deadly pandemic and exacerbated by rapid inflation—the globalising forces that have long shaped our world threaten to come undone'. *Bloomberg*. Available at https://sponsored.bloomberg.com/article/sc/globalisation-isn-t-dead-it-needs-a-reset (accessed September 2025).

4. 'April 3, 2025 marks the formal, unceremonious death of the Globalisation era. With a pen stroke and a camera-ready grimace, Donald J. Trump did what he's always promised to do: pull the plug on what he considers the great con of the American century. This time, it's not rhetoric. The new tariffs ... are not just economic weapons ... they are funeral rites'. See Max Barahona, 'Globalisation is Dead', *Medium*, 14 April 2025. Available at https://max-barahona.medium.com/globalisation-is-dead-cd17e0824f44?source=rss------trump-5 (accessed

September 2025).

5. See '"Must remain alert": PM Modi's "Swadeshi" appeal for Indians; days after Trump's 25% tariff', *The Times of India*, 2 August 2025. Available at https://timesofindia.indiatimes.com/india/must-remain-alert-pm-modis-swadeshi-appeal-for-indians-days-after-trumps-25-tariff/articleshow/123063410.cms (accessed September 2025).

6. The May 2025 edition of the Chief Economists Outlook was published at a time of extraordinary volatility and uncertainty. The global economic outlook has worsened since the beginning of the year, as rising economic nationalism and tariff volatility fuel uncertainty and risk, stalling long-term decision-making. See World Economic Forum, 'Chief Economists Outlook: May 2025', 28 May 2025. Available at https://www.weforum.org/publications/chief-economists-outlook-may-2025/ (accessed September 2025).

7. Affluent households in urban India grew in 2024, while lower middle-class households saw a decline compared to five years ago, underscoring a widening gap between the socioeconomic class (SEC) in cities and presenting a dilemma for fast-moving consumer goods companies. See Sagar Malviya, 'Urban middle-class households shrink, rich club sees big jump', *The Economic Times*, 6 December 2024. Available at https://economictimes.indiatimes.com/news/economy/indicators/urban-middle-class-households-shrink-rich-club-sees-big-jump/articleshow/116019517.cms?from=mdr (accessed September 2025).

8. Neoliberalism's decline is not confined to shifts in trade policies or economic frameworks. It has also become visible in tangible and symbolic ways—most notably, the proliferation of physical border walls across the globe. See https://www.oiip.ac.at/en/publications/the-end-of-an-era-the-decline-of-neoliberalism-and-the-emerging-interregnum/ (accessed 26 March 2026).

9. As I write, the entire National Capital Region (NCR) stands witness to the razing of homes belonging to Bengali-speaking workers, on the ground that they are illegal migrants from Bangladesh. See Sreya Chatterjee, 'School over for me: Bengali speakers in limbo amid crackdown on illegal migrants', *India Today*, 29 July 2025. Available at https://www.indiatoday.in/cities/gurugram/story/school-over-for-me-bengali-speakers-in-limbo-amid-crackdown-on-illegal-immigrants-2762765-2025-07-29 (accessed September 2025). Significantly, the last BJP-led government had carried out a similar deportation drive (Chaudhuri 2005).

10. According to a report:

> India's private university boom bears an uncanny resemblance to the reckless expansion that triggered the 2018 NBFC collapse; only this time, the toxic assets aren't bad loans, but the futures of millions of students. What was once celebrated as educational liberalization now shows troubling signs of becoming a speculative bubble.... Since 2014, over

> 150 private universities have been approved in India under progressively liberalised norms. The University Grants Commission (UGC)'s 2016 amendment reduced the requirement for 'deemed-to-be-university' status from 10 years of operation to just five.... This policy shift led to a 153% increase in private universities, compared to a mere 12% rise in public institutions over the same period.

See Debdulal Thakur, 'Are private universities the next NBFC crisis?' *Deccan Herald*, 30 July 2025. Available at https://www.deccanherald.com/opinion/are-private-universities-the-next-nbfc-crisis-3655948 (accessed September 2025).

11. Both are run by BJP governments.

12. 'Partition as an ongoing project', *Political Line*, 9 September 2025. Available at https://www.thehindu.com/newsletter/newsletter-analysis/?utm_source=political_line_preview_link&utm_medium=website_nl-sub_page&utm_campaign=newsletter_signup (accessed September 2025).

13. Ibid.

14. Untouchability is illegal in law. Yet it persists, even as new forms of caste discrimination have emerged.

See 'Abolition of Untouchability', Constitution of India, Part III, Article 17. Available at https://www.constitutionofindia.net/articles/article-17-abolition-of-untouchability/ (accessed September 2025);

'The alarming rise of anti-Dalit violence and discrimination in India: A series of gruesome incidents since July 2024', *CJP*, 5 September 2024. Available at https://cjp.org.in/the-alarming-rise-of-anti-dalit-violence-and-discrimination-in-india-a-series-of-gruesome-incidents-since-july-2024/ (accessed September 2025).

15. Jehangir Ali, 'Day after Army Cancels Presser, Amit Shah Announces Killing of Three Pahalgam Attackers in Parliament', *The Wire*, 29 July 2025. Available at https://thewire.in/politics/pahalgam-attack-militants-killed-amit-shah-parliament-press-conference (accessed September 2025).

16. This is just indicative, pointing new directions, not an exhaustive study. See Vidya Subrahmaniam, 'In one corner of Delhi, an attack on religious freedom', *The Hindu*, 19 August 2010. Available at https://www.thehindu.com/news/cities/Delhi/In-one-corner-of-Delhi-an-attack-on-religious-freedom/article16137619.ece (accessed September 2025).

17. See p. 85, where I describe the early days of globalisation and consumerism in Vasant Kunj, where I continue to live. Communalism, casteism, and classism were below the radar back then, but are official now. But that is another story that I hope to write soon.

18. Leo Kelion, 'WhatsApp rises as a major force in news media', *BBC*, 22 June 2017. Available at https://www.bbc.com/news/technology-40340830 (accessed September 2025).

19. In the 2026 conflict between the United States, Israel, and Iran, it appears that all the countries agree on controlling the media.. Despite differences in their political system, all three governments follow an approach that prioritises 'national morale' and 'operational security' over press freedom and the flow of information. This approach redefines the concept of fake news and extends its authority to managing public sentiment, making coverage more 'positive' and 'optimistic'. The goal is unified: to turn media into a state mouthpiece that tells only the official narrative of the war (Al-Shammourie 2026).

20. A quick look at the list of schemes of the Government of India is illustrative. See https://en.wikipedia.org/wiki/List_of_schemes_of_the_government_of_India (accessed September 2025).

21. See Azadi Ka Amrit Mahotsav, Amrit Kaal and Vikshit Bharat as schemes for academic events.

22. Amit Sengupta, 'The Politics of Symbolism', *Lok Marg*, 7 May 2025. Available at https://lokmarg.com/the-sindoor-smokescreen/ (accessed September 2025).

23. Mukesh Singh Sengar, 'How Terrorists Killed in Op Mahadev were Identified as Pahalgam Attackers', *NDTV*, 29 July 2025. Available at https://www.ndtv.com/india-news/operation-mahadev-amit-shah-shares-crucial-evidence-linking-recovered-guns-to-pahalgam-attack-8972522 (accessed September 2025).

24. Amplifying biased hashtags that push a majoritarian narrative or headlines that repeat the government's version of the truth also contribute to this endeavour. Hashtags that champion the prime minister (#ModiCreatesHistory, #ModiStrikesBack, #ModiMeansBusiness, #ModiStrikesCorruption) and attack the Opposition (#SoniaCoverupExposed, #RahulInsultsMartyrs, #CongAdmitsCAALie, #TikaitExposed) are used frequently on these news channels, as are Islamophobic hashtags (#CoronaJihad, #LandJihand) or hashtags against the Farmers' Protest. See Pooja George and Vedika Inamdar, 'Mainstream news media and majoritarian state violence in India', *The Polis Project*, 9 December 2021. Available at https://www.thepolisproject.com/read/mainstream-news-media-and-majoritarian-state-violence-in-india/ (accessed September 2025).

25. The term 'new India' is, however, not new. It has had many avatars. In June 1914, Annie Besant purchased the 'Madras Standard' and renamed it 'New India', which thereafter became her chosen organ for her campaign for India's freedom. Today, we have the grandiose pomposity imprinted within the new India of Hindu majoritarianism and its relationship with big capital.

26. George and Inamdar, 'Mainstream news media'.

27. Ram Shengale, 'WhatsApp Statistics 2025: Usage Trends, Demographics and More', *WANotifier*, 29 May 2025. Available at https://wanotifier.com/whatsapp-statistics/ (accessed September 2025).

28. A study suggests that 'the "WhatsApp panopticon" was mobilized as a tool of everyday community care *and* surveillance to shape morality regimes and influence the compliance of residents with national and locally enforced rules'. It argues that

> digital socio-spatial practices of securitization, fear and compliance represent forms of 'grassroots authoritarianism' that echo and ensconce state-led ideological change in India. Building on 'everyday authoritarianism' we show how digital technologies and middle-class organizations are mediating India's authoritarian shift from below.

See Lipika Kamra, Philippa Williams, and Pushpendra Johar, 'Grassroots authoritarianism: WhatsApp, middle-class boundary-making and pandemic governance in New Delhi's neighbourhoods', *Territory, Politics, Governance* 11 (6), 2023, 1121–40. Available at https://www.tandfonline.com/doi/full/10.1080/21622671.2022.2160372#abstract (accessed September 2025).

29. Three principles—saffronisation, privatisation, and authoritarianism—have animated the BJP's education policy. Saffronisation tends to reinforce Brahminical stereotypes, glorify authoritarianism, demonise India's Muslim rulers, deny the historically-ascertained Aryan migration theory, and encourage communal polarisation. There is a refusal to acknowledge the deep caste, class, and gender inequalities that define our society. See Akash Bhattacharya, 'BJP lays siege to India's education system', *360*, 27 May 2024. Available at https://360info.org/bjp-lays-siege-to-indias-education-system/ (accessed September 2025).

30. A legal anthropologist writes:

> In Modi's Hindutva version of India, law now exists on two parallel planes. Constitutionally, it remains a secular democracy, committed to the idea of social and political equality. Yet on the level of policing, judicial interpretation, and—increasingly—legislatively, Indian state law has become a site where majoritarian Hindutva ideologies have reshaped ideas of justice and belonging.

See 'The authoritarian leader's playbook: how Narendra Modi captured India's legal system and is rewriting the country's history in his image', *The Conversation*, 11 April 2024. Available at https://theconversation.com/the-authoritarian-leaders-playbook-how-narendra-modi-captured-indias-legal-system-and-is-rewriting-the-countrys-history-in-his-image-226889 (accessed September 2025).

31. Marking the anniversary of the raid in 2023 on news website *Newsclick*, the Press Club of India, the Delhi Union of Journalists, the Indian Women's

Press Corps, Press Association, and the Kerala Union of Working Journalists passed a resolution that stated: 'The right to life, a fundamental constitutional right, cannot exist without the right to work. The two are inextricably connected'. 'Journalist bodies pledge to resist attacks on the freedom of media', *The Hindu*, 4 October 2024. Available at https://www.thehindu.com/news/national/journalist-bodies-vow-to-resist-attacks-on-freedom-of-media/article68714538.ece (accessed September 2025).

32. Groundwork by communal organisations is an ongoing effort. It is only in specific historical moments, particularly with the help of State power, that they gain ascendency in the national public discourse.

33. Sanya Mansoor, 'India's School Textbooks Are the Latest Battleground for Hindu Nationalism', *Time*, 7 April 2023. Available at https://time.com/6269349/india-textbook-changes-controversy-hindu-nationalism/ (accessed September 2025).

34. Maitrayee Chaudhuri, 'The Rhetoric, Routine and Ruse of a Regime: The Case of NCERT', *The Wire*, 25 August 2025. Available at https://thewire.in/education/the-rhetoric-routine-and-ruse-of-a-regime-the-case-of-ncert (accessed September 2025).

35. Mohammad Ali, 'Government is accountable, pro-poor, says Narendra Modi', *The Hindu*, 17 November 2021. Available at http://www.thehindu.com/news/national/government-is-accountable-propoor-says-narendra-modi/article8651361.ece (accessed September 2025).

36. Shivam Vij, 'With the anti-poor lockdown, BJP is back to its upper caste, middle class, urban roots', *The Print*, 1 April 2020. Available at https://theprint.in/opinion/anti-poor-lockdown-bjp-upper-caste-middle-class-urban-roots/392892/ (accessed September 2025).

37. 'Poor sleeping peacefully but corrupt troubled: Modi on demonetisation', *Hindustan Times*, 14 November 2016. Available at https://www.hindustantimes.com/india-news/poor-people-sleeping-peacefully-but-corrupt-troubled-modi-on-demonetisation/story-j4hQ5rkOww5CKkBGVloZhJ.html (accessed September 2025).

38. Vij, 'With the anti-poor lockdown'.

39. Ibid.

40. 'Colour of Indian flag on Burj Khalifa DUBAI!! Proud to be an Indian'. Available at https://www.youtube.com/watch?v=9EOrNBS2twc (accessed September 2025). The Crown Prince happened to be the Guest of Honour on Republic Day that year.

41. 'What has been missing in the wrestlers' story is the disappointing silence and lack of action by those who were expected to reach out to them. Despite so many women wrestlers complaining, the police did not file FIRs till the court instructed them to do so. But the court too kicked the can down the road.' Neerja

Chowdhury, 'Wrestlers' plight shows how women are seen as labharthis, not equals; our politicians fail to sense the shift', *The Indian Express*, 10 June 2023. Available at https://indianexpress.com/article/political-pulse/wrestlers-plight-shows-how-women-are-seen-as-labharthis-not-equals-8654911/ (accessed September 2025).

42. 'India's Foreign Policy should Look at Peace', *The Hindu*, 8 July 2022. Available at https://www.thehindu.com/news/national/telangana/indias-foreign-policy-should-look-at-peace/article65616909.ece (accessed September 2025).

43. Khanna, Swati. 2026. 'India's Foreign Policy Falters When It Abandons Its Own Goalposts'. LiveLaw.in, 25 March. Available at https://www.livelaw.in/articles/india-foreign-policy-us-israel-intervention-527804 (accessed March 2026).

44. Chowdhury, 'Wrestlers' plight shows how women are seen as labharthis, not equals'.

45. I have argued elsewhere that the pandemic and the lockdown allowed an authoritarian state to complete the ideological task of recasting India. Repression was a necessary tool for this project. A proposal for a war tank in campus was mooted to rein in JNU's belligerent teachers and students, and force them to learn the virtues of 'nationalism'. Maitrayee Chaudhuri et al 2022.

46. Jagmati Sangwan and Shamsher Singh, 'Women's Participation in Protests against the Three Farm Laws in India', *Economic and Political Weekly* 57 (43), October 2022. Available at https://www.epw.in/journal/2022/43/special-articles/womens-participation-protests-against-three-farm.html (accessed September 2025).

47. Ziya Us Salam, 'How the women of Shaheen Bagh stirred a nation to stand up for the "idea of India"', *Frontline*, 12 December 2023. Available at https://frontline.thehindu.com/books/how-shaheen-bagh-women-stirred-a-nation-to-stand-up-for-idea-of-india-anti-caa-protests-anniversary-book-excerpt-being-muslim-in-hindu-india-ziya-us-salam/article67630103.ece (accessed September 2025).

48. Jigyasa Agarwal, 'The Indian government's weaponisation of gender in Operation Sindoor', Institute of Development Studies, 9 May 2025. Available at https://www.ids.ac.uk/opinions/the-indian-governments-weaponisation-of-gender-in-operation-sindoor/ (accessed September 2025).

49. Ibid.

50. George and Inamdar, 'Mainstream news media'.

51. Raewyn Connell, 'Masculinities'. Available at http://www.raewynconnell.net/p/masculinities_20.html (accessed September 2025).

52. Gouri Shah, 'Narendra Modi was a fantastic "product": Piyush Pandey'. *Mint*, 16 May 2014. Available at https://www.livemint.com/Politics/RdNXMW4vv6eBIml741Q6QM/A-bad-product-with-great-communication-will-never-succeed-P.html (accessed October 2025).

53. BBC, 'Hyderabad case: Police kill suspects in rape and murder of Indian vet', 6 December 2019. Available at https://www.bbc.com/news/world-asia-india-50682262 (accessed September 2025).

54. Singh had as many as thirty-eight cases against him under various charges, including theft, criminal intimidation, murder, attempt to murder, rioting, and kidnapping. He was a six-time Member of Parliament. See https://en.wikipedia.org/wiki/Brij_Bhushan_Sharan_Singh (accessed September 2025).

55. Ishita Mishra, 'Court accepts closure report to cancel sexual harassment case against Brij Bhushan', *The Hindu*, 26 May 2025. Available at https://www.thehindu.com/news/cities/Delhi/court-acc epts-closure-report-to-cancel-sexual-harassment-case-against-brij-bhushan/article69622399.ece (accessed September 2025).

56. Mihir Vasavda, 'Brij Bhushan Sharan Singh: The Bahubali, who was a one-man federation', *The Indian Express*, 11 July 2023. Available at https://indianexpress.com/article/sports/sport-others/brij-bhushan-the-bahubali-who-was-a-one-man-federation-8656679/ (accessed September 2025).

57. Badri Narayan, 'Why "Bulldozer baba" Yogi Adityanath keeps using the machine for law and order', *The Print*, 17 June 2022. Available at https://theprint.in/opinion/why-bulldozer-baba-yogi-adityanath-keeps-using-the-machine-for-law-and-order/1000182/ (accessed September 2025).

58. Ibid.

SELECT REFERENCES

Al-Shammourie, Majdoline. 2026. 'How the US, Israel & Iran are controlling their media narratives'. *The New Arab*, 24 March. Available at https://www.newarab.com/opinion/how-us-israel-iran-are-controlling-their-media-narratives (accessed March 2026).

Chaudhuri, Maitrayee, 'The Concept of Culture in My Classroom and in Globalised Times', in Maitrayee Chaudhuri (ed.), *The Practice of Sociology* (New Delhi: Orient Longman, 2003), 370–402.

———, *The Indian Women's Movement: Reform and Revival* (Kochi: Palm Leaf, 2005 [1993]). Available at https://www.researchgate.net/publication/332442222_The_Indian_Women's_Movement_Reform_and_Revival (accessed September 2025).

———, 'Betwixt State and Everyday Life: Identity Formation among Bengali Migrants in a Delhi Slum', in Meenakshi Thapan (ed.), *Migration and Gender in Asia* (New Delhi: Sage, 2005), 284–311.

———, 'If Hate Has Been Normalised, Can WhatsApp-Triggered Lynchings Be Far Behind?' *The Wire*, 6 July 2018. Available at https://thewire.in/society/if-hate-has-been-normalised-can-whatsapp-triggered-lynchings-be-far-behind (accessed October 2025).

Chaudhuri, Maitrayee, 'Higher Education and the Social Sciences in a "Smart" India', in D. V. Kumar (ed.), *The Idea of a University: Possibilities and Contestations* (New Delhi: Routledge, 2021), 104–26.

———, 'Globalization in Indian Sociology: The Invisible and Hypervisible'. *Diogenes* 65 (2), 2024, 276–98.

———, 'Trivial, Dangerous or Just Routine: Unpacking the Many Responses to "Doing Gender"', in N. B. Lekha and Pradip Kumar (eds), *Beyond Boundaries: Intersections of Gender, Culture, and Development in India*, Routledge Handbook of Gender, Culture and Development in India (New Delhi: Routledge, 2025), 27–41.

Chaudhuri, Maitrayee, and Rituparna Patgiri, 'The Pandemic and Our Entangled Lives: Experiencing the Many Relations of Ruling', in Melanie Heath, Akosua Darkwah, Josephine Beoku-Betts, and Bandana Purkayastha (eds), *Global Feminist Autoethnographies During COVID-19: Displacements and Disruptions* (Abingdon: Routledge, 2022), 1–15.

Connell, Raewyn, *Masculinities*. (Cambridge: Polity Press; Sydney: Allen & Unwin; Berkeley: University of California Press, 2005 [1995]).

Pasquino, G., 'Populism and Democracy', in D. Albertazzi and D. McDonnell (eds), *Twenty-First Century Populism* (London: Palgrave Macmillan, 2008).

Bibliography

Adhikari, Gautam, 'Whose India is it? Today's intolerant hordes would do well to read the Constitution, plus Vivekananda', *The Times of India*, 2015. Available at http://blogs.timesofindia.indiatimes.com/just-graffiti/whose-india-is-it/ (accessed 20 June 2016).

———, 'The thrill is gone: Where India stands after almost two years of Modi's leadership', *The Times of India*, 2016. Available at http://blogs.timesofindia.indiatimes.com/just-graffiti/the-thrill-is-gone-where-india-stands-after-almost-two-years-of-modis-leadership/ (accessed 11 May 2016).

Agarwal, Bina, 'Gender and command over property: A critical gap in economic analysis and policy in South Asia', *World Development* 22 (10), 1994, 1455–78.

Al-Shammourie, Majdoline. 2026. 'How the US, Israel & Iran are controlling their media narratives'. *The New Arab*, 24 March. Available at https://www.newarab.com/opinion/how-us-israel-iran-are-controlling-their-media-narratives (accessed March 2026).

Anklesaria Aiyar, Swaminathan, 'Ten Commandments for Dr. Singh', *Sunday Times*, 10 June 2007, 24.

Agnes, Flavia, 'No Shortcuts to Rape', *Economic and Political Weekly* 48 (2), 2013, 1–4.

Altheide, David and Robert P. Snow, *Media Logic* (Beverly Hills: Sage Publications, 1979).

Althusser, Louis, 'Ideology and Ideological State Apparatus (Notes towards an investigation)', in Louis Althusser, *Lenin and Philosophy and other Essays*, (London: New Left Books, 1971), 121–73.

Anderson, Benedict, *Imagined communities* (London: Verso, 1983).

Ansari, Tariq, 'Is publishing a sunset industry', cited in Bhaskar Das, 'The Paper Chase', *Gentleman*, June 1999, 57–61.

Antony, Shiney, 'Defending marital rape means knowing a Miss can't let a man touch her, a Mrs can't tell him not to', 2016. Available at http://blogs.economictimes.indiatimes.com/et-commentary/defending-marital-rape-means-knowing-a-miss-cant-let-a-man-touch-her-a-mrs-cant-tell-him-not-to/ (accessed 21 June 2016).

Arora, Akash, 'Bhang, Booze and Bonhomie: Holi Mania Sweeps City', *The Hindustan Times*, 10 March 2001.

Asp, Kent, *Mäktiga massmedier: Studier i politisk opinionsbildning* (Stockholm: Akademilitteratur, 1986).

Badal, Kumar, 'Advertising Glory', *Rashtriya Sahara*, July 1997, 110–12.

Bakhtin, Mikhail, 'From the prehistory of novelistic discourse', in David Lodge (ed.), *Modern Criticism and Theory* (New York: Longman, 1988).

Bakhtin, Mikhail, *The Dialogic Imagination: Four Essays* (Austin: University of Texas Press, 1992).

Bal, Raka Singh, 'Sushma Swaraj: Wife, Mother Politician—a Woman of Our Times', *Life Review* March–April, 1999, 10–13.

Barthes, Roland, *Image, Music, Text* (London: Fontana, 1977).

Basu, Aparna, 'The Role of Women in the Indian Struggle for Freedom', in B. R. Nanda (ed.), *Indian Women: From Purdah to Modernity* (New Delhi: Vikas, 1976).

Basu, Srimati, *She Comes to Take Her Rights: Indian Women, Property, and Propriety* (New York: State University of New York Press, 1999).

Bathla, Sonia, *Women, Democracy and the Media* (New Delhi: Sage Publications, 1998).

Baviskar, Amita, Veena Naregal, and Nandini Sundar, 'Editorial: Celebrating 50 Years', *Contributions to Indian Sociology* (Special Issue) 42 (1), 2008, 1–5.

Baxi, Pratiksha, 'We must resist the cunning of judicial reform', *Kafila* 29 December 2012. Available at http://kafila.org/2012/12/29/we-must-resist-the-cunning-of-judicial-reform-pratiksha-baxi/#more-14996 (accessed 30 December 2012).

Bell, Norman W. and Esra F. Vogel, *A Modern Introduction to the Family* (New York: The Free Press of Glencoe, 1964).

Benhabib, Seyla, 'The generalized and the concrete other', in Seyla Benhabib and Drucilla Cornell (eds), *Feminism as critique* (Oxford: Blackwell; Minneapolis: University of Minnesota Press, 1987), 1–15.

Beteille, Andre, 'The Reproduction of Inequality: Occupation, Caste and Family', in Patricia Uberoi (ed.), *Family, Kinship and Marriage in India* (New Delhi: Oxford University Press, 1993), 435–51.

———, *Sociology: Essays on Approach and Method* (New Delhi: Oxford University Press, 2002).

Bhasin, Kamla and Ritu Menon, 'The problem', *Seminar* 342 (February), 1988, 12–13.

Bhattacharjea, Ajit, 'Fourth Estate no More', *Gentleman*, June 1999, 46–50.

Bhattacharya, Sabyasachi, 'Nationhood and frequently unasked questions', *The Hindu*, 4 August 2005.

Boltanski, Luc and Eve Chapello, *The New Spirit of Capitalism* (London: Verso, 2007).

Bourdieu, Pierre, *Language and Symbolic Power* (Massachusetts: Harvard University Press, 1994).

Breman, Jan, 'Return of Social Inequality: A Fashionable Doctrine', *Economic and Political Weekly* 39 (35), 2004, 3869–72.

BS Reporter, 'Ambani's RIL takes control of Network18', *Business Standard*, 30 May 2014. Available at http://www.business-standard.com/article/companies/

ril-to-acquire-control-of-network18-114052901661_1.html (accessed 30 May 2014).

Burke, Jason, 'Delhi rape: how India's other half lives', *The Guardian*, 10 September 2013.

Business Today, 'Nucleus Marketing', 22 February–6 March 1999.

Butalia, Urvashi, 'Community, State and Gender – On Women's Agency during Partition', *Economic and Political Weekly* 28 (17), 24 April 1993.

———, *The Other Side of Silence: Voices from the Partition of India* (Durham: Duke University Press, 2000).

Calfee, John E., 'How Advertising Informs to Our Benefit', *Span*, December 1998, 10–15, 58–60.

Cambell, John L., *Institutional Change and Globalisation* (Princeton: Princeton University Press, 2004).

Carey, J., *Communication as Culture: Essays on Media and Society* (Boston, MA: Unwin Hyman, 1989).

Castells, Manuel, *The Informational City: A Framework for Social Change* (Toronto: University of Toronto, 1990).

———, 'Materials for an exploratory theory of the network society', *British Journal of Sociology* 51 (1), 2000, 5–24.

Chakrabarty, Gargi, 'Rubbing people the right way', *Business Standard*, 7 January 1998.

Chakravarti, Uma, 'Whatever happened to the Vedic dasi?', in Kumkum Sangari and Suresh Vaid (eds), *Recasting women: Essays in colonial history* (New Delhi: Kali for Women, 1989), 27–87.

Chakravarty, Sukhamoy, *Development Planning: The Indian Experience* (Clarendon: Oxford University Press, 1987).

Chakravarti, Dipesh, 'Postcoloniality and the Artifice of History: Who Speaks for "Indian" Pasts?' *Representations* 37 (Winter), 1992, 1–26.

Chandhoke, Neera, '"Seeing" the State in India', *Economic and Political Weekly* XL (11), 2005, 1033–39.

———, 'Dumbing Down of Indian Politics', *The Hindu*, 2016. Available at http://www.thehindu.com/opinion/op-ed/dumbing-down-of-indian-politics/article8604008.ece (accessed 15 June 2016).

Chandra, Bipan, 'The making of the Indian nation', in Anand Kuman (ed.), *Nation Building in India: Culture, Power and Society* (New Delhi: Radiant, 1999), 9–22.

Chaney, David, *The Cultural Turn* (London: Routledge, 1994).

Chatterjee, Partha, 'The Nationalist Resolution of the Women's Question', in Kumkum Sangari and Suresh Vaid (eds), *Recasting Women: Essays in Colonial India* (New Brunswick: Rutgers University Press, 1989), 233–53.

Chatterjee, Shoma, 'Changing Sex Roles in Advertisement', 2006. Available at http://www.indiatogether.org/2006/jul/med-roles.htm (accessed 19 July 2012).

Chaudhuri, Maitrayee, 'Sociology and Studies on Women', *Social Scientist* October 1982, 21–29.

Chaudhuri, Maitrayee, *The Indian Women's Movement: Reform and Revival* (New Delhi: Radiant, 1993).

Chaudhuri, Maitrayee, 'Citizens, workers and cultural emblems: An analysis of the first plan document', in Patricia Uberoi (ed.), *State, Social Reform and Sexuality* (New Delhi: Sage Publications, 1996), 211–35.

———, 'Among my Own in Another Culture: Meeting the Asian Indian American', in Meenakshi Thapan (ed.), *Anthropological Journey: Reflections From the Field* (New Delhi: Orient Longman, 1998a).

———, 'Advertisements, Print Media and the New Indian Woman', *Social Action* 48 (3), 1998b, 239–52.

———, 'Models of development and images of women', in Anand Kumar (ed.), *Nation Building in India* (New Delhi: Radiant, 1999), 124–38.

———, 'Feminism in print media', *Indian Journal of Gender Studies* September 2000, 263–88.

———, 'Gender and Advertisements: The Rhetorics of Liberalisation', *Women's Studies International Forum* 24 (3/4), 2001, 373–85.

——— (ed.), *Feminism in India* (New Delhi: Women Unlimited; London: Zed Books, 2004).

———, 'A Question of Choice: Advertisement, Media and Democracy', in Bernard Bel, Jan Brouwer, Biswajit Das, et al. (eds), *Communication Process: Media and Mediation* (New Delhi: Sage Publications, 2005a), 199–226.

———, 'Moving Beyond "Cultural Dupes" and "Resistant Readers": Issues of Constraints and Freedom in Contemporary Indian Media', *Communicator*, 2005b, 1–26.

———, 'The Travels and Travails of the Concept of "Gender"', in Maitrayee Chaudhuri (ed.), *Sociology in India: Institutional and Intellectual Practices* (Jaipur: Rawat, 2010a).

———, 'Indian Media and its Transformed Public', *Contributions to Indian Sociology* 44 (1/2), 2010b, 57–78.

———, 'The Family and Its Representation: From Indology to Market Research', in Yogendra Singh (ed.), *Social Sciences: Communication, Anthropology and Sociology, History of Science, Philosophy and Culture in Indian Civilization*, Vol. XIV, Part 2 (New Delhi: Pearson, 2010c), 363–89.

——— (ed.), *Sociology in India: Intellectual and Institutional Practices* (Jaipur: Rawat, 2010d).

———, 'Feminism in India: The Tale and its Telling' (Féminismes décoloniaux, genre et développement'), *Revue Tiers Monde* 209 (March), 2012, 19–36.

———, 'Higher education in "global" India: The need for critical sociology', in Ishwar Modi (ed.), *Education, Religion and Creativity: Essays in Honour of Professor Yogendra Singh* (Jaipur: Rawat, 2013), 3–22.

Chaudhuri, Maitrayee, 'Gender, Media and Popular Culture in a Global India', in Leela Fernandes (ed.), *Routledge Handbook of Gender in South Asia* (New York: Routledge, 2014), 145–59.

Chaudhuri, Maitrayee and J. Jayachandran, 'Theory and Method in Indian Sociology', in Yogendra Singh (ed.), *Indian Sociology: Emerging Concepts, Structure, and Change* (New Delhi: Oxford University Press, 2014), 87–134.

Chaudhuri, Saumitra, 'Even as world changes under Trump, India's currency shortages will stay for months', 2016. Available at http://blogs.economictimes.indiatimes.com/et-commentary/even-as-world-changes-under-trump-indias-currency-shortages-will-stay-for-months/ (accessed 12 February 2017).

Chaudhuri, Utsav, 'Feminism and Chauvinism for Urban India: Perceptions of Urban Youth A Marketing Context', 15 March 2009. Available at http://www.slideshare.net/utsav_chaudhuri/feminism-chauvinism-for-urbanindia (accessed 26 May 2012).

Chauhan, Bhumika, et al. 'Anti-Rape Movement: A Horizon beyond legalism and sociology', *Radical Notes*, 10 June 2013. Available at http://radicalnotes.com/category/editorials/ (accessed 22 April 2014).

Chen, Martha Alter, *Widows in India: Social Neglect and Public Action* (New Delhi: Sage Publications, 1998).

Chilkoti, Avantika, 'Narendra Modi to be India's first social media prime minister'. Available at http://www.ft.com/cms/s/0/e347de5c-e088-11e3-9534-00144feabdc0.html (accessed 15 February 2015).

Chimni, Abhik, 'Demonetisation, National Anthem, and National Interest', 2016. Available at http://www.thecitizen.in/index.php/NewsDetail/index/2/9332/Demonetisation-The-National-Anthem-And-National-Interest-The-Political-And-The-Judicial (accessed 12 February 2017).

Chimni, B. S., 'Marxism and international law: A contemporary analysis', *Economic and Political Weekly*, 34 (6), 1999, 337–49.

———, 'International Institutions Today: An Imperial Global State in the Making', *European Journal of International Law* 15 (1), 2004, 1–37.

Choudhury, Kavita, 'Cong brainstorms media strategy for D-Day', *Business Standard*, 2014. Available at http://budget.businessstandard.com/news.php?id=40&bs_autono=114051000952 (accessed 21 June 2016).

Chowdhry, Prem, 'Widow Remarriage in Haryana: Law Strengthens Repressiveness of Popular Culture', *Manushi* 82, 1994, 12–18.

Curran, James, 'The impact of advertising on the British mass media', *Media, Culture and Society* 3 (1), 1981, 43–69.

Das, Bhaskar, 'The Paper Chase', *Gentleman*, June 1999, 57–61.

Das, G., *Indian Social Institutions* (New Delhi: Manu Enterprises, 1994).

Das, Veena, 'Masks and Faces: An Essay on Punjabi Kinship', *Contributions to Indian Sociology* (n.s.) 10 (1), 1976, 1–30.

———, 'Voice of Children', *Journal of the American Academy of Arts and Sciences* 1991, 91–108.

De, Barun, 'A preliminary note on the writing of the history of modern India', *Quarterly review of historical studies* 3, 1963–64.

De, Shobhaa, 'Be Smart and Shut up a la Hillary Clinton', *The Week*, 28 March 1999.

———, 'Politically Incorrect: Cheeni Kum', *Sunday Times*, 10 June 2007, 24.

De Souza, Alfred and Walter Fernandes (eds), *Ageing in South Asia* (New Delhi: Indian Social Institute, 1982).

Desai, A. R., 'Gender role in the constitution', in Lotika Sarkar and B. Sivaramayya (eds), *Women and the Law: Contemporary Problems* (New Delhi: Vikas, 1994), 41–49.

Desai, I. P., *Some Aspect of Family in Mahua* (New York: Asia Publishing House, 1963).

Desai, Santosh, 'Anybody in there? When silence killed the star economist', *Outlook*, 2014. Available at http://www.outlookindia.com/printarticle.aspx?290702 (accessed 12 April 2015).

———, 'Manufacturing Bias', *The Times of India*, 2015. Available at http://blogs.timesofindia.indiatimes.com/Citycitybangbang/manufacturing-bias/ (accessed 21 June 2016).

Deshpande, Satish, 'From Development to Adjustment', *Review of Development and Change* 2 (2), 1997, 294–318.

———, *Contemporary India: A Sociological View* (New Delhi: Penguin/Viking, 2003).

Dhir, Gangan. 1998. 'Man to Women', *Delhi Times*, *The Times of India*, 9 December.

Doshi, Anjali, 'Marriage by Mouse: Matrimonial Websites', *India Today*, 18 October 2004, 50.

Doshi, Anjali, Nirmala Ravindran, Uday Mahurkar, and Arun Ram, 'Rearranging Marriage', *India Today* 2004, 40–50.

Dube, Leela, *Anthropological Explorations in Gender: Intersecting Fields* (New Delhi: Sage Publications, 2001).

Dube, Muchkund and M. K. Jabbi, *A Social Charter for India: Citizen's Perspective for Basic Rights* (New Delhi: Pearson Longman, 2009).

Dutra Sachdeva, Sujata, 'India Emerges Key Driver of Global Television Market', *Times Business*, 28 May 2007.

Elshtain, Jean Bethke, 'Sovereignty, identity, sacrifice', *Social research* 58 (3), 1991, 545–64.

Engels, Frederick, *The Origin of the Family, Private Property and the State* (Moscow: Progress Publishers, 1948).

Ewen, S., *Captains of Consciousness: Advertising and the Social Roots of the Consumer Culture* (New York: McGraw Hill, 1976).

Faludi, Susan, *Backlash: The Undeclared War Against American Women* (New York: Crown, 1991).

———, *Backlash: The Undeclared War Against Women* (London: Chatto and Windus, 1992).

Fernandes, Leela, 'Theoretical Reflections on India's New Middle Class,' in Amita Baviskar and Raka Ray (eds), *Elite and Everyman:* The *Cultural Politics of the Indian Middle Classes* (New Delhi: Routledge, 2011), 58–82.

Forbes, Geraldine, *Women in Modern India* (Cambridge: Cambridge University Press, 1999).

Fraser, Nancy, 'From Redistribution to Recognition? Dilemmas of Justice in a "Postsocialist" Age', 1998. Available at http://ethicalpolitics.org/blackwood/fraser.htm (accessed 29 April 2015).

———, 'Transnationalizing the Public Sphere', 2005. Available at http://www.republicart.net/disc/publicum/fraser01_en.htm (accessed 29 April 2015).

———, 'Feminism, Capitalism and the Cunning of History', *New Left Review* 56, 2009, 97–117.

Freed, S. A. and R. S. Freed, 'The Domestic Cycle in India: Natural History of a will-o-the Wisp', in P. K. Roy (ed.), *The India Family: Change and Persistence* (New Delhi: Gyan Publishing House, 2000), 73–98.

Friedman, Thomas, *The World Is Flat: A Brief History of the Twenty-first Century* (New York: Farrar, Straus and Girous, 2005).

Friedan, Betty, *The Feminine Mystique* (New York: Laurel, 1983).

Fruzzetti, Lina and Rosa Maria Perez, 'The Gender of the Nation: Allegoric Femininity and Women's Status in Bengal and Goa', *Etnográfica* VI (1), 2002, 41–58.

George, Nirmala, 'India's Gay And Lesbian Community Demands End To Discrimination At New Delhi March', *Huffington Post*, 2014. Available at http://www.huffingtonpost.com/2014/12/01/new-delhi-gay-lesbian-march-_n_6245802.html?ir=India (accessed 14 April 2014).

Gera, Nish, '800 Million Voters in World's Biggest Election: Are Gay Rights on the Ballot? *Hiffington Post*, 2014. Available at http://www.huffingtonpost.com/nish-gera/800-million-voters-in-india-gay_b_5176179.html?ir=India (accessed 14 April 2014).

Ghosh, Deepshikha, 'Congress Concedes Weak Campaign, Failed Media Strategy'. Available at http://www.ndtv.com/elections-news/congress-concedes-weak-campaign-failed-media-strategy-562211.

Goffman, Ervin, *Gender Advertisements* (London: The Society for the Study of Visual Communication, 1976).

Gopal, S., *Jawaharlal Nehru: A Biography, 1889–1947*, Vol.1 (New Delhi: Oxford University Press, 1975).

Gore, M. S., *Urbanisation and Family Change* (Bombay: Popular Prakashan, 1968).

Government of India (GoI). 'Women in India', Country paper (New Delhi: Ministry of Social Welfare, 1985).

———, *Country report. Fourth world conference on women. Beijing* (New Delhi: Department of Women and Child Development, Ministry of Human Resource Development, 1995).

Gandhi, Gopal, 'Why 2014 was an extraordinary year for our republic'?, *Hindustan Times*. Available at http://www.hindustantimes.com/gopalkrishnagandhi/why-2014-was-an-extraordinary-year-for-our-republic/article1-1300688.aspx (accessed 12 April 2015).

Gandhi, M. K., 'Speech at second Gujarat educational conference, Broach, 20 October 1917', in *Collected works of Mohandas Karamchand Gandhi* (CWMG), 14, 31–36.

———, 'Appeal to the women of India', *Young India*, 1921, CWMG 20 (11 August), 195–97. Available at http://www.gandhi-manibhavan.org/eduresources/article9.htm (accessed 7 April 2017).

———, 'Gandhi's speech at Women's Christian College, Madras, 24 march', 1925, *CWMG*, 26, 395–98.

Garfinkel, H., *Studies in Ethnomethodology* (New Jersey: Prentice Hall, 1967).

Gatade, Subhash, 'For a New Rendezvous with Dr Ambedkar', countercurrents.org, 2 May 2016. Available at http://www.countercurrents.org/gatade020516.htm (accessed 22 March 2017).

Geetha, V., 'Periyar, Women and an Ethic of Citizenship', in Maitrayee Chaudhuri (ed.), *Feminism in India* (New Delhi: Women Unlimited, 2004), 156–74.

———, 'On Impunity', *Economic and Political Weekly* 48 (2), 2013, 1–3.

Ghosh, Avantika, 'Opposition to govt: When migrants can't vote, why the rush to let NRIs?', *The Indian Express*, 2015. Available at http://indianexpress.com/article/india/india-others/opposition-to-govt-when-migrants-cant-vote-why-the-rush-to-let-nris/ (accessed 5 May 2015).

Ghosh, Avijit, 'Bhojwood Dreams Big', *The Times of India*, 27 May 2007.

Ghosh, Palash, 'Delhi Gang-Rape Victim: Global Reaction', *International Business Times*, 31 December 2012. Available at http://www.ibtimes.com/delhi-gang-rape-victim-global-raction-983484 (accessed 20 April 2014).

Ghosh, Sagarika, 'Target: Media', *The Times of India*, 2015. Available at http://blogs.timesofindia.indiatimes.com/bloody-mary/target-media/ (accessed 13 April 2014).

Ghurye, G. S., *Family and Kin in Indo-European Culture* (Bombay: Oxford University Press, 1955).

Giddens, Anthony, 'Institutional Reflexivity and Modernity', in *The Polity Reader in Social Theory* (Cambridge: Polity Press, 1994), 89–94.

Gokulsing, K. Moti and Wimal Dissanayake, *Popular Culture in a Globalized India (*Abingdon: Routledge, 2008).

Gordon, Michael D., Hellen Tilly, and Gyan Prakash, *Utopia/Dystopia: Conditions of Historical Possibility* (Princeton: Princeton University Press, 2010).

'Gossip!', *Times Life, The Times of India,* 30 July 2006.

Gramsci, Antonio, *Selections from Prison Notebooks* (London: Lawrence & Wishart, 1971).

Goyal, Malini, 'Number Game', *India Today,* 20 September 2004, 14–18.

Guha, Ramachandra, 'How the Congress lost the Diaspora', *Hindustan Times,* 14 February 2015.

Guha Thakurta, Paranjoy, 'Mass media and the Modi "wave": What have been the consequences of the extreme mediatisation of the elections and how did we get here?', 30 June 2014. Available at http://himalmag.com/media-modi-elections/ (accessed 9 May 2017).

Gupta, Akhil, 'Blurred Boundaries: The Discourse of Corruption, the Culture of Politics, and the Imagined State', *American Ethnologist* 22 (2), 1995, 375–402.

Gupta, Sachdeva, *A Simple Study of Sociology* (New Delhi: Ajanta Prakashan, 1989).

Gupta, Smita, 'Anti-rape bill diluted, Cabinet approves new version', *The Hindu,* 19 March 2013. Available at http://www.thehindu.com/todays-paper/tp-national/antirape-bill-diluted-cabinet-approves-new-version/article4524019.ece (accessed 31 July 2014).

Guru, Gopal, 'Janus faced Colonialism', *Tarun Udwale,* 20 July 2005.

Gurumurthy, Anita, 'Introduction', *Feminist Media Studies* 11 (1), 2011, 139–49.

Habermas, Jurgen, *The Structural Transformation of the Public Sphere: An Inquiry into a Category of Bourgeois Society,* Thomas Burger (trans.), with the assistance of Frederick Lawrence (Cambridge: Polity Press, 1989).

Harris, Gardiner, 'India's New Focus on Rape Shows Only the Surface of Women's Perils', *The New York Times,* 12 January 2013. Available at http://www.nytimes.com/2013/01/13/world/asia/in-rapes-aftermath-india-debates-violence-against-women.html (accessed 20 April 2014).

Hasan, Abide, 'Experts divided over TRAI's move on cross media ownership', *Exchange4media.com,* 29 July 2013. Available at http://www.exchange4media.com/52126_experts-divided-over-trais-move-on-cross-media-ownership.html (accessed 2 October 2013).

Hasan, Zoya, 'Manufacturing Dissent: The Media and the 2014 General Elections', 2014. Available at http://www.thehinducentre.com/verdict/commentary/article5843621.ece. (accessed 20 June 2016).

Heckman, Susan (ed.), *Feminism, Identity and Difference* (London: Frank Cass, 1999).

Held, David (ed.), *States and Societies* (Oxford: Basil Blackwell and The Open University, 1984).

Hemer, Oscar, 'The challenge of the present continuous', 12 February 2013. Available at https://johnpostill.com/2013/02/12/the-challenge-of-the-present (accessed 30 April 2016).

Hensman, Rohini, 'Globalisation, Women and Work: What Are We Talking About?' *Economic and Political Weekly* 39 (10), 2004, 1030–34.

Hilgers, Mathieu, 'The Three Anthropological Approaches to Neoliberalism', *ISSJ* 202, 2011, UNESCO, 351–62.

Hood, John, 'In Praise of Advertising', *Span*, December 1998, 8–10.

Illaiah, Kancha, 'Cultural Globalisation', *Outlook.India.com*, 24 February 2002.

Inglis, Fred, *The Imagery of Power: A Critique of Advertising* (London: Heinemann, 1972).

Jayawardena, Kumari, *Feminism and Nationalism in the Third World* (Colombo: Sanjiva, 1986).

Kabeer, Naila, 'Is Microfinance a "Magic Bullet" for Women's Empowerment? Analysis of Findings from South Asia', *Economic and Political Weekly* 40 (44 & 45), 2005, 4709–18.

Kalpagam, U., *Labour and Gender: Survival in Urban India* (New Delhi: Sage Publications, 1994).

Kalra, Harsimran, 'Report Summary: Report of the Committee on Amendments to Criminal Law, 2013', *PRS Legislative Research*, 25 January 2013. Available at http://www.prsindia.org/parliamenttract/report-summaries/justice-verma-committee-report-summary-2628/ (accessed 9 October 2013).

Karkaria, Bachi J., 'Face it, the Change is More than Cosmetic', *The Sunday Times of India*, 18 January 1998.

———, 'When the Chairman is a Woman', *The Sunday Times of India*, 13 June 1999.

———, 'Marriages are made in heaven', *The Times of India*, 6 February 2005.

Kasturi, Leela (compiled and ed.), 'Woman's role in planned economy', Report of the Sub-Committee, National Planning Committee Series (1947), *Samya Shakti* 6, 1991–92, 110–25.

Kasturi, Leela and Vina Mazumdar, 'Women and Indian nationalism', Occasional paper No. 20 (New Delhi: Centre for Women's Development Studies, 1994).

Kaur, Ravinder, 'Across-region Marriages: Poverty, Female Migration and the Sex Ratio', *Economic and Political Weekly* 39 (25), 2004, 2595–2604.

Kaviraj, Sudipta, *Imaging History* (New Delhi: Nehru Memorial Museum and Library, 1988).

———, 'On State, Society and Discourse in India', in James Manor (ed.), *Rethinking Third World Politics* (London and New York: Longman, 1991), 72–99.

Khandekar, Nivedita, 'AAP launches web TV to reach out to NRIs', *Hindustan Times*, 2014. Available at http://www.hindustantimes.com/india/aap-launches-web-tv-to-reach-out-to-nris/story-oFmg7nLHOV5GT3B6bY98TJ.html (accessed 23 June 2016).

Khanna, Swati. 2026. 'India's Foreign Policy Falters When It Abandons Its Own Goalposts'. *LiveLaw.in*, 25 March. Available at https://www.livelaw.in/articles/india-foreign-policy-us-israel-intervention-527804 (accessed March 2026).

Khilnani, Sunil, 'A democratic asteroid that wiped out many old habits', 18 May 2014. Available at http://articles.economictimes.indiatimes.com/2014-05-18/news/49925938_1_india-s-narendra-modi-indian-history (accessed 5 February 2015).

Kishwar, Madhu, 'Why I Do Not Call Myself a Feminist', *Manushi* 61, 1990, 2–8.

Kotiswaran, Prabha, 'Unintended consequences of feminist action: Prabha Kotiswaran', *KAFILA* 18 February 2013. Available at http://kafila.org/2013/02/18/unintended-consequences-of-feminist-action-prabha-kotiswaran/ (accessed 31 July 2014).

Krishna, K. B., *Plan for Economic Development of India* (Bombay: Padua Publication, 1945).

Krishna, T. M., 'Conversation flows, ideas don't', *The Hindu*, 24 November 2012. Available at http://www.thehindu.com/opinion/op-ed/conversation-flows-ideas-dont/article4127471.ece (accessed 31 July 2014).

Krishnaraj, Maithreyi, 'Research in Women Studies: A Need for a Critical Appraisal', *Economic and Political Weekly* 40 (28), 2005, 3008–17.

Kumar, Radha, *The History of Doing: An Illustrated Account of Movements for Women's Rights and Feminism in India, 1800–1990* (New Delhi: Zubaan, 1997).

Kumar, Tilak, 'INS wants higher FDI ceiling in print media', *The Times of India*, 1 October 2013. Available at http://timesofindia.indiatimes.com/business/india-business/INS-wants-higher-FDI-ceiling-in-print-media/articleshow/23327919.cms (accessed 2 October 2013).

Herzfeld, Michael, 'History in the Making: National and International Politics in a Rural Cretan Community in Europe', in Jao de Pina-Cabral and John Cambell (eds) (Houndsmills, England: MacMillan Press, 1992), 93–112.

Jagannath, Thejas, 'From Littering to Spitting: Sanitary Problems in India's Public Spaces', *Urban Times*, 12 February 2013. Available at http://urbantimes.co/2013/02/from-littering-to-spitting-sanitary-problems-in-indias-public-spaces/ (accessed 30 May 2014).

Jeffrey, Robin, *India's Newspaper Revolution: Capitalism, Politics and the Indian Language Press* (New Delhi: Oxford University Press, 2000).

Jenkins, Henry, *Convergence Culture: Where Old and New Media Collide* (New York & London: New York University Press, 2006).

Jetley, Neerja Pawha, 'More Than Just Mothers', *Outlook*, 24 August 1998, 46–47.

Jhally, S., *The Codes of Advertising* (London: Francis Pinter, 1987).

John, Mary, 'Gender and development in India, 1970s–1990s: Some reflections on the constitutive role of contexts', *Economic and Political Weekly*, 31 (47), 1996, 3071–77.

———, 'Feminism, Internationalism and the West: Questions from the Indian Context', Occasional Paper No. 27, Centre for Women's Development Studies, New Delhi, 1998a.

———, 'Globalisation, Sexuality and The Visual Field: Issues and Non-issues for Cultural Critique', in Mary E. John and Janaki Nair (eds), *A Question of Silence? The Sexual Economies of Modern India* (New Delhi: Kali for Women, 1998b), 368–96.

John, Mary E. and Janaki Nair (eds), *A Question of Silence? The Sexual Economics of Modern India* (New Delhi: Kali for Women, 1998).

Joseph, Ammu, 'The Broadcast Bill and the Public Interest', *The Hindu*, 1 July 2006.

Kapadia, K. M., *Marriage and Family in India* (London: Oxford University Press, 1955).

Kapoor, Coomi, 'New Age Journalism', *The Indian Express*, 7 September 2014. Available at http://indianexpress.com/article/opinion/columns/inside-track-lead-drummer/ (accessed 20 June 2016).

Karve, Irawati, *Kinship Organization in India* (Bombay: Asia Publishing House, 2e, 1965).

Keane, John, *The Media and Democracy* (Cambridge: Polity, 1991).

———, 'Public Life in the Era of Communicative Abundance', *Canadian Journal of Communication* 24 (2), 1999.

Khare, Harish, 'The *Dhanatatra* age begins', *The Hindu*, 7 July 2004.

Kaushambi, 'Women Bosses in Indian Corporates: What is Driving Their Growth?' 30 March 2012. Available at *http://trak.in/Tags/Business/women-ceos-in-india/* (accessed 23 May 2012).

Lakshmi, Rama, 'India's Cheeky "Chick Lit" Finds an Audience', *Washington Post* Foreign Service, 23 November 2007. Available at http://www.washingtonpost.com/wp-dyn/content/article/2007/11/22/AR 2007112201415.html (accessed 28 May 2012).

Lal, Rasmee Roshan, 'No Respite for Disenfranchised Indian in UK', *The Times of India*, 30 May 2007, 15.

Landes, J., *Women and the Public Sphere in the Age of the French Revolution* (Ithaca: Cornell University, 1988).

Lasch, Christopher, *The Culture of Narcissm* (New York: Warner Books, 1978).

Lash, Scott and Jonathan Friedman, *Modernity & Identity* (Oxford: Blackwell, 1996).

Lee, Martyn J., *Consumer Culture Reborn: The Cultural Politics of Consumption* (London: Routledge, 1993).

Leighley, Jan E., *Mass Media and Politics: A Social Science Perspective* (New York: Houghton Mifflin Company, 2004).

Lerche, Jens, 'Transnational Advocacy Networks and Affirmative Action for Dalits in India', *Development and Change* 39 (2), 2008, 239–61.

Liebes, Tamar and Elihu Katz, *The Export of Meanings: Cross Cultural Readings of 'Dallas'* (Cambridge: Polity Press, 1993, 2e).

Lilleker, Darren, *Key Concepts in Political Communications* (London: Sage Publications, 2008).

Lodge, David (ed.), *Modern Criticism and Theory: A Reader* (London: Longman, 1978).

Lodziak, Conrad, *Manipulating Needs, Capitalism and Culture* (London: Pluto Press, 1995).

Martel, Frédéric, 'The different identities of the Internet'. Available at https://www.youtube.com/watch?v=x_wv6U_2UWo (accessed 2 February 2017).

MacIntyre, A. C., 'A Mistake about Causality in Social Sciences', in P. Laslet and W. O. Runciman (eds), *Politics, Philosophy and Society* (Oxford: Blackwell, 1962).

Madan, T. N., 'The Hindu Family and Development', *Journal of Social and Economic Studies* 4 (2), 1976, 211–31.

Mankekar, Purnima, *Screening Culture, Viewing Politics: Television, Womanhood and Nation in Modern India* (Durham/London: Duke University Press, 1999).

Marx, Karl, 'Results of the immediate process of production', in *Capital* (Vol. 1) (London: Pelican, 1976).

Marx, Karl and Frederick Engels, 'The German Ideology', in Karl Marx and Frederick Engels (eds), *The Individual and Society* (Moscow: Progress Publishers, 1984a), 138–63.

———, 'From economic and philosophic manuscripts, 1844', in *The Individual and Society* (Moscow: Progress Publishers, 1984b), 80–104.

Mazumdar, Vina, 'Whose Past? Whose History? Whose Tradition? Indigenising Women's Studies in India', *Asian Journal of Women's Studies* 7 (1), 2001, 133–53.

Mazzarella, William, *Shoveling Smoke: Advertising and Globalization in Contemporary India* (Durham, NC: Duke University Press, 2005).

McBride, Meredith, 'INDIA: A Heartless Nation for Women', *Asian Human Rights Commission*, 16 April 2013. Available at http://www.humanrights.asia/news/ahrc-news/AHRC-PAP-001-2013 (accessed 28 April 2013).

McCann Erickson, 'The Indian Woman Consumer Focus', *Insight Quarterly* Inaugural Issue, 2000, 6–7.

McDermott, Patrice, 'On Cultural Authority: Women's Studies, Feminist Politics, and the Popular Press', *Sign: Journal of Women in Culture and Society* 20 (31), 1995, 668–84.

Mehta, Pratap Bhanu, 'Contradictions in the Modi government are still muddying its identity', *The Indian Express*, 2016. Available at http://indianexpress.com/article/opinion/columns/narendra-modi-government-bjp-achievements-failures-progress-economic-contradictions-at-play-2819273/ (accessed 27 May 2016).

Mehta, Ruchika, 'Like Daughters, Like Mothers', *The Times of India*, 6 November 2004.

Menon, Nitya, 'Broadcast Battles', *The Hindu*, 11 January 2014. Available at http://www.thehindu.com/features/magazine/broadcast-battles/article5562685.ece (accessed 9 February 2015).

Menon, Ritu and Kamla Bhasin, *Borders and Boundaries* (New Jersey: Rutgers University Press, 1998).

Mies, Maria, *Indian Women and Patriarchy* (New Delhi: Vikas, 1980).

Misener, Jessica, 'Vagina Bleaching Ad Sparks Controversy Over Who Needs A Paler Va-Jay', 2012. Available at http:// www.dnaindia.com/blogs/ post_fair-and-lovely-kaale-ko-gora-bana-de_1581513 (accessed 25 May 2012).

Mishra, Pankaj, 'Narendra Modi and the new face of India', *The Guardian*, 2014. Available at http://www.theguardian.com/books/2014/may/16/what-next-india-pankaj-mishra (accessed 11 April 2015).

Mike, F., *Consumer Culture and Postmodernism* (London: Sage Publications, 1991).

Minault, Gail, 'Purdah politics: The role of Muslim women in Indian nationalism 1911–1942', in Hanna Papaneck and Gail Minault (eds), *Separate Worlds* (New Delhi: Chanakya, 1982), 245–61.

Misri, Urvashi, 'Child and Childhood: A Conceptual Constructions', *Contributions to Indian Sociology* 19 (1), 1985, 115–32.

Mohanty, Manoranajn, 'On the concept of empowerment', *Economic and Political Weekly*, 17 June 1995, 1434–36.

Murdoch, G., and P. Golding, 'Ideology and the mass media: The question of determination', in M. Barret, et al. (eds), *Ideology and Cultural Production* (London: Croom Helm, 1979).

Murthy, Mahesh, 'The Other Voices: From Politics to Bollywood, Here are the Virtual Movers and Shakers who Wield the Maximum Online Chat', *Brunch*, 11 March 2012. Available at http://issuu.com/brunch/docs/brunch-ll-march-2012 (accessed 11 June 2012).

Myers, Kathy, 'Understanding Advertisers', in H. Davis and P. Walton (eds), *Language, Image, Media* (Oxford: Blackwell, 1983), 205–23.

NDTV, 'Badaun Rape Case', 2 June 2014. Available at http://www.ndtv.com/topic/badaun-rape-case (accessed 8 August 2014).

Nally, Preethi, 'Gender Issues Could Be a Game Changer in India's Elections', 14 April 2014. Available at http://time.com/61122/india-womanifesto-election-women-voting/ (accessed 14 April 2014).

Nambath, Suresh, 'Economic reforms and the Hindutva project', *The Hindu*, 2015. Available at http://www.thehindu.com/opinion/op-ed/economic-reforms-and-the-hindutva-project/article6831123.ece (accessed 29 January 2015).

Narayan, Badri, *Fractured Tales: Invisibles in Indian Democracy* (New Delhi: Oxford University Press, 2016).

Natarajan, Jayanthi, 'A political hypocrisy', *The Hindu*, December 1996.

Nehru, Jawaharlal, *A Bunch of Old Letters* (Bombay: Asia Publishing House, 1958).

———, *Glimpses of World History* (London: Lindsay Drummond, 1962).

———, *The Discovery of India* (New Delhi: Asia Publishing House, 1966).

Neimark, Jill, 'Why we need Miss America', *Femina*, 1 February 1999, 50–52.

Nelson, Dean, 'Female tourists shun India after rape attack', *The Telegraph*, 31 March 2013. Available at http://www.telegraph.co.uk/news/worldnews/asia/india/9963608/Female-tourists/shun-India-after-rape-attack.html.

Ninan, Sevanti, *Headlines from the Heartland: Reinventing the Hindi Public Sphere* (New Delhi: Sage Publications, 2007).

O'Sullivan, Claire, 'India's Rape Shame', *The Irish Chronicle*, 23 March 2013. Available at http://www.irishexaminer.com/lifestyle/features/indias-rape-shame-226260.html (accessed 20 April 2014).

Omvedt, Gail, 'Capitalism and Globalisation, Dalits and Adivasis', *Economic and Political Weekly* 40 (47), 2005, 4881–84.

Oommen, T. K. (ed.), *Critizenship and National Identity. From Colonialism to Globalism* (New Delhi: Sage Publications, 1997).

Outlook, 'Britain Issues Advisory for Women Travelling to India', 18 March 2013. Available at http://www.outlookindia.com/news/article/Britain-Issues-Advisory-for-Women-Travelling-to-India/792870 (accessed 30 May 2014).

Padmanabhan, Chitra, 'NDTV's Ravish on the Dark World of News Television', *The Wire*. Available at http://thewire.in/22267/ndtvs-ravish-on-the-dark-world-of-news-television/ (accessed 21 June 2016).

Pandey, Devesh K., 'Need for proper verification of domestic help', *The Hindu*, 5 February 2005.

Parashar, Swati, 'The Gender Report Card of the Indian Elections', 2014. Available at http://past.electionwatch.edu.au/india-2014/gender-report-card-indian-elections (accessed 20 June 2016).

Parekh, Bhikhu, 'Putting Civil Society in Place', in Marlies Glasius, David Lewis and Hakan Seckinelgin (eds), *Exploring Civil Society: Political and Cultural Contexts* (London: Routledge, 2005 [2004]), 14–23.

———, 'The Constitution as a Statement of Indian Identity', in Rajeev Bhargava (ed.), *Politics and the Ethics of the Indian Constitution* (New Delhi: Oxford University Press, 2008).

———, 'Bapu and the Pravasi: What Gandhi would have said, had he spoken at the Pravasi Bharatiya Divas', *The Indian Express*, 10 January 2015. Available at http://indianexpress.com/article/opinion/columns/bapu-and-the-pravasi/ (accessed 10 May 2015).

Patel, Akaar, 'Narendra Modi is good with words, but it comes with a fondness for empty wordplay', *Hindustan Times*, 2015. Available at http://www.hindustantimes.com/analysis/narendra-modi-is-good-with-words-but-it-comes-with-a-fondness-for-empty-wordplay/story; http://www.hindustantimes.com/business-news/ (accessed 20 June 2016).

Patel, Vibhuti, 'Women's Liberation in India', *New Left Review* 1 (153), 1985, 75–86.

———, 'Campaign against Rape by Women's Movement in India', *GandhiTopia* 20 December 2012. Available at http://www.gandhitopia.org/profiles/blogs/campaign-against-rape-by-women-s-movement-in-india-vibhuti-patel (accessed 27 September 2013).

Pateman, T., 'How is Understanding an Advertisement possible?', in H. Davis and P. Walton (eds), *Language, Image, Media* (Oxford: Blackwell, 1983), 187–204.

Pathak, Rahul, 'The New Generation', *The Week*, 30 May 1994, 73–87.

Pathak, Zakia and Rajeshwari Sunder Rajan, 'Shahbano', *Signs* 14 (3), 1989, 558–52.

Patil, Vimla, 'Miss India: The Search for the Complete Woman', *Femina*, 23 April 1992, 6-8.

Patnaik, Prabhat, 'Manmohan Singh and Colonialism', *Peoples Democracy*, 17 July 2005.

———, 'Decision to Demonetise Currency Shows They Don't Understand Capitalism', *The Wire*, 2016. Available at https://thewire.in/79419/demonitesation-interview-prabhat-patnaik/ (accessed 12 February 2017).

Peck, Jamie, *Constructions of Neoliberal Reason* (Oxford: Oxford University Press, 2010).

Phadke, Shilpa, 'Thirty Years On: Women's Studies Reflects on the Women's Movement', *Economic and Political Weekly* 38 (43), 2003, 4567–76.

Pisharoty, Sangeeta Barooah, 'Crowning the Kind King', *Metro Plus, The Hindu*, 8 November 2004.

P. Prabhu, H., *Hindu Social Organization* (Bombay: Popular Prakashan, 1955 [1940]).

Prabhudesai, Arun, 'The Indian Women CEO Have Arrived and How?' 13 July 2000. Available at http://trak.in/tags/business/2009/07/13/top-powerful-indian-women-ceos-have-arrived/ (accessed 23 May 2012).

Prakash, Satya and Harish V. Nair, '16/12: A crime that changed rape laws in India', *Hindustan Times*, 11 September 2013 (accessed 11 October 2013). http://www.hindustantimes.com/India-news/DelhiGangrape/16-12-A-crime-that-changed-rape-laws-in-India/Article1-1120370.aspx.

Prasad, Chandra Bhan, 'Wealth in the Bhopal Meet', *The Pioneer*, 21 January 2002.

Probyn, Elspeth, 'Mc-Identities: Food and the Familial Citizen', *Theory, Culture & Society* 15 (2), 1998, 155–73.

Purie, Aroon, 'From the editor-in-chief', *India Today*, 20 September 2004.

Radhakrishnan, Mita, 'Feminism, Family and Social Change: Myths and Models', *Social Action* 44 (4), 1994, 34–53.

'Open letter to Muslims', Translated and reprinted from the original in *Inquilab* 13 November 1985.

Rajagopal, Arvind, 'Ram Janmabhoomi, Consumer Identity and Image-Based Politics', *Economic and Political Weekly* 29 (27), 1994, 1659–77.

———, 'Thinking About the New Middle Class: Gender, Advertising and Politics in an Age of Globalisation', in Rajeswari Sunder Rajan (ed.), *Signposts: Gender Issues in Post-Independence India* (New Delhi: Kali for Women, 1999), 57–100.

———, *Politics after Television: Hindu Nationalism and the Reshaping of the Public in India* (Cambridge: Cambridge University Press, 2001).

———, 'On Media and Politics in India: An Interview with Paranjoy Guha Thakurta', *South Asia: Journal of South Asian Studies* 2016.

Rajghatta, Chidanand, 'Indians now face a Green Card Gridlock: Professionals Lose out to Illegal Immigrants', *The Times of India*, 10 June 2007a.

———, 'Immigrant Swansong', *The Times of India*, 10 June 2007b, 24.

Rao, Leela, 'Facets of Media and Gender Studies in India', *Feminist Media Studies* 1 (1), 2001, 45–48.

Rao, Nirupama, 2016. Available at http://www.thehindu.com/opinion/lead/lead-article-by-nirupama-rao-on-indiaus-bilateral-relations-contours-of-a-natural-alliance/article8710549.ece (accessed 15 June 2016).

Rao, Ursula, 'News for consumer citizens: Corporate Pressure, Political Criticism and Middle Class Assertion in the Indian Media', *PORTAL* 9 (1), 2012, 1–19.

Ravindran, Visa, 'The Two Sides of Femininity', *The Hindu*, 13 June 1999.

Reeves, Geoffrey, *Communications in the Third World* (London: Routledge, 1993).

Rege, Sharmila, 'Dalit Women talk Differently: A Critique of "Difference"', and 'Towards a Dalit Feminist Standpoint Position', *Economic and Political Weekly* 33 (44), 1998, WS 39–46.

———, *Writing Caste, Writing Gender: Narrating Dalit Women's Testimonies* (New Delhi: Zubaan, 2006).

RINA, 'Women's groups and activists on latest anti-rape Bill', *RINA* (*Rabita Islamic News Agency*), 17 March 2013. Available at http://www.rina.in/news/women%E2%80%99s-groups-and-activists-on-latest-anti-rape-bill/ (accessed 17 November 2013).

Rhode, Deborah L., 'Media Images, Feminist Issues', *Signs: Journal of Women in Culture and Society* 20 (31), 1995, 685–709.

Robinson, William I., *A Theory of Global Capitalism: Production, Class and State in a Transnational World* (Baltimore: Johns Hopkins University Press, 1998).

Robinson, William I. and Jerry Harris, 'Towards a Global Ruling Class? Globalization and the Transnational Capitalist Class', *Science and Society* 64 (1), 2000, 11–54.

Rowlatt, Justin, 'Why beef ban in Indian state undermines secularism', 4 April 2015. Available at http://www.bbc.com/news/world-asia-india-32172768 (accessed 13 April 2015).

Roy, Anupama, *Gendered Citizenship: Historical and Conceptual Explorations* (New Delhi: Orient BlackSwan, 2005).

Roy, Kumkum, 'Where women are worshipped, there the gods rejoice: The Mirage of Ancestress of the Hindu Woman', in Tanika Sarkar and Urvashi Butalia (eds), *Women and the Hindu Right: A Collection of Essays* (New Delhi: Kali for Women, 1996), 181–215.

Roy, Mary, 'Women and law: Striking down a Succession Act', Paper presented at the 5th National conference of the Indian Association for Women's Studies at Jadavpur University, 9–12 February 1991.

Rukmini, S., 'Modi got most prime-time coverage: Study', *The Hindu*, 2014. Available at http://www.thehindu.com/elections/loksabha2014/modi-got-most-primetime-coverage-study/article5986740.ece (accessed 21 June 2016).

Sahay, Uday, *Making News Handbook of the Media in Contemporary India* (New Delhi: Oxford University Press, 2006).

Sangari, Kumkum, 'Perpetuating the myth', *Seminar* 342 (February), 1988, 24–30.

Sangari, Kumkum and Sudesh Vaid, *Recasting Women: Essays in Colonial History* (New Delhi: Kali for Women, 1989).

Sarkar, Sumit, *Modern India, 1885–1947* (New Delhi: Macmillan, 1983).

Sassen, Saskia, *Global Networks: Linked Cities* (New York: Routledge, 2002).

Sen, Illina (ed.), *A Space within the Struggle: Women's Participation in People's Movements* (New Delhi: Kali for Women, 1990).

Shah, A. M., 'Changes in the Indian Family-An Examination of Some Assumptions', *Economic and Political Weekly* 3 (1–2), 1968.

———, *The Household Dimension of the Joint Family in India* (Berkeley: University of California Press/Delhi: Orient Longman, 1973).

———, *The Family in India: Critical Essays* (New Delhi: Orient Longman, 1998).

Shah, Nandita and Nandita Gandhi, *The Issues at Stake: Theory and Practice in the Contemporary Women's Movement in India* (New Delhi: Kali for Women, 1992).

Sharma, Jyoti, 'Petri Dish Population', *Delhi Times*, *The Times of India*, 6 November 2004.

Sharma, Sanjeev K., *Depiction of Women in Indian Media—A Case of Introspection for Media Planners, Samaj Vigyan Shodh Patrika*, Amroha, 1 (1), 2005, 32–36. Available at http://www.ijps.net/images/Depiction%20of%20 Women%20 in%20India%20Medi.pdf (accessed 20 June 2012).

Singh, Yogendra, *Modernization of Indian Tradition: A Systematic Study of Social Change* (New Delhi: Thompson Press, 1973).

———, *Indian Sociology: Social Conditions and Emerging Concerns* (New Delhi: Sage Publications, 1986).

———, *Ideology and Theory in Indian Sociology* (Jaipur and New Delhi: Rawat, 2004).

Singharoy, Debal K., 'Peasant Movements in Contemporary India: Emerging Forms of Domination and Resistance', *Economic and Political Weekly* 40 (52), 2005, 5505–13.

Sinha, Mrinalini, *Colonial Masculinity: The 'Manly Englishman' and the 'Effeminate Bengali' in the Late Nineteenth Century* (New Delhi: Kali for Women, 1997).

Smart, Barry, *Economy, Culture and Society: A Sociological Critique of Neo-liberalism* (Buckingham: Open University, 2003).

Southard, Barabara, *The Women's Movement and Colonial Politics in Bengal 1921–1936* (New Delhi: Manohar, 1995).

Srichand, Monisha, 'Gender Stereotypes', 2012. Available at http://www.talkitover.in/self/gender-stereotypes/ (accessed 29 May 2012).

Srilata, K., 'The Story of the "Up-Market" Reader: *Femina's* "New Woman" and the Normative Feminist Subject', *Journal of Arts and Idea* April (32–33), 1999, 61–72.

Srinivas, M. N. (ed.), *India's Villages* (Bombay: Asia Publishing House, 1960).

Stancati, Margherita, 'Foreigners Ask: Is India Safe?' *India Real Time* (posted by *The Wall Street Journal*), 18 March 2013. Available at http://floost.com/wsj-post-foreigners-ask-is-india-safe-3752859 (accessed 1 June 2014).

Stuart, Hunter, 'India Refuses to Co-Sponsor UN Resolution to End Child Marriage', *The Huffington Post*, 16 October 2013. Available at http://www.huffingtonpost.com/2013/10/16/india-child-marriage-un-resolution-sponsor_n_4108408.html (accessed 2 June 2014).

Subramaniam, Banu, 'Imagining India: Religious Nationalism in the Age of Science and Development', in Kum-Kum Bhavani, John Foran and Priya Kurian (eds), *Feminist Futures: Re-imagining Women, Culture and Development* (London: Zed Books, 2003), 160–77.

Subramaniam, Indhu, 'Is It Post Feminism Yet?' 13 December 2007. Available at http://youngfeminists.wordpress. Com/2007/12/13/is-it-post-feminism-yet/ (accessed 24 May 2012).

Subramaniam, Vidya, 'PM Admits to Gender Insecurity', *The Hindu*, 12 April 2013. Available at http://www.thehindu.com/todays-paper/pm-admits-to-gender-insecurity/article4608628.ece (accessed 17 November 2013).

Sunder Rajan, Rajeswari, *Real and Imagined Women. Gender, Culture and Postcolonialism* (London: Routledge, 1993).

——— (ed.), *Signposts: Gender Issues in Post-Independence India* (New Delhi: Kali for Women, 1999).

———, *The Scandal of the State: Women, Law, and Citizenship in Postcolonial India* (New Delhi: Permanent Black, 2003).

Suroor, Hasan, 'Year Modi lost the Plot', 2016. Available at http://www.tribuneindia.com/news/comment/year-modi-lost-the-plot/336324.html (accessed 11 February 2017).

Swain, M. A. Kharabela, 'Farming the farmer: By tying peasants to land, political parties propagate an insidious new caste system' 23 April 2015. Available at http://blogs.timesofindia.indiatimes.com/toi-edit-page/farming-the-farmer/ (accessed 25 April 2015).

Taghizadeh, Negar, 'Media-Inspired Images of Women in Post Feminist Context: Angela Carter's Wise Children', 2011. Available at http://www.inter-disciplinary.net/critical-issues/gender-and-sexuality/femininity-and-masculinity/ project-archives/1s/session-8-postfeminism-is-now-new-perspective-on- feminism/ (accessed 24 July 2012).

Taylor, Steve, 'Emotional Labour and The New Workplace', Paper presented to the 14th Annual International Labour Process Conference, University of Aston, Birmingham, 1996.

Teltumbde, Anand, 'Ambedkar In and For the Post-Ambedkar Dalt Movement', 1997. Available at http://www.ambedkar.org/Babasaheb/postambedkar.htm (accessed 27 April 2016).

———, 'Delhi Gang Rape Case: Some Uncomfortable Questions', *Economic and Political Weekly* 48 (6), 2013, 10–11.

Tenth Five Year Plan, 2002–07, Governance and Implementation, Vol. 1, 2003. (New Delhi: Government of India, Planning Commission).

Thapar, Karan, 'Pertie and the Prime Minister', *Sunday Sentiments, Hindustan Times*, 3 June 2007.

The Sub-committee on Labour (Bombay: Vora, 1947).

The Sub-committee on Population (Bombay: Vora, 1947).

The Times of India, 'Kutting Kake with Karan', *Delhi Times*, 25 May 2007a, 1.

———, 'Pay Check: Capping CEO Salaries will Shackle Private Enterprise', 26 May 2007b, 1, 22.

———, 'Country of Consumers', 27 May 2007c, 22.

———, 'Fresh Sting Tapes Entangle Kulkarni', 2 June 2007d, 2.

———, 'Anti-rape Bill debate in Lok Sabha: Who among us have not followed girls? Sharad Yadav asks', 19 March 2013a. Available at http://timesofindia.indiatimes.com/india/Anti-rape-Bill-debate-in-Lok-Sabha-Who-among-us-have-not-followed-girls-Sharad-Yadav-asks/articleshow/19070842.cms (accessed 2 June 2014).

The Times of India, 'India has half the world's modern slaves: Study', 18 October 2013b. Available at http://timesofindia.indiatimes.com/india/India-has-half-the-worlds-modern-slaves-Study/articleshow/24313244.cms (accessed 20 April 2014).

Therbon, Goran, 'The Rule of Capital and the Rise of Democracy', *New Left Review* 103, 1977, 3–42.

Thompson, John, *Studies in the Theory of Ideology* (Oxford: Polity, 1984).

———, *Ideology and Modern Culture* (Cambridge: Polity Press, 1990).

———, *The Media and Modernity: A Social Theory of the Media* (Cambridge: Polity Press, 1995).

Trawick, Margaret, 'The Person Beyond the Family', in Veena Das (ed.), *The Oxford India Companion to Sociology and Social Anthropology* (New Delhi: Oxford University Press, 2003), 1158–78.

Tully, Mark, 'PM Modi is not a listener; so be prepared for it', *Hindustan Times*, 31 August 2014. Available at http://www.hindustantimes.com/analysis/not-listening-to-experienced-voices-can-isolate-modi-from-reality/article1-1258325.aspx (accessed 5 February 2015).

Uberoi, Patricia, *Family, Kinship and Marriage in India* (New Delhi: Oxford University Press, 1994).

———, 'The Family in Official Discourse', in *Second Nature: Women and the Family*', *India International Centre Quarterly* Winter, 1996a, 134–55.

———, *Social Reform, State and Society* (New Delhi: Sage Publications, 1996b).

———, 'The diaspora comes home: Disciplining desire in *DDLJ*', *Contributions to Indian Sociology* 32(2), 1998, 305–36.

———, 'The Family in India: Beyond the Joint and Nuclear Debate', in Veena Das (ed.), *The Oxford India Companion to Sociology and Social Anthropology* (New Delhi: Oxford University Press, 2003).

———, *Freedom and Destiny: Gender, Family and Popular Culture in India* (New Delhi: Oxford University Press, 2006).

Udupa, Sahana, 'Aam Adami: Decoding the Media Logic', *Economic and Political Weekly* 49 (7), 2014, 13–15.

Van Zoonen, Liesbet, 'A Tyranny of Intimacy: Women, Femininity and Television News', in P. Dahlgren and C. Sparks (eds), *Communications and Citizenship* (London: Pandora Press, 1991).

———, *Feminist Media Studies* (London: Sage Publications, 1994).

Varma, Anuradha, 'It's a corporate take over', *Times Life*, *The Times of India*, 19 April 2009.

Varma, Pavan K., 'Of Images and Perceptions', *The Hindu*, 6 May 2015. Available at http://www.thehindu.com/opinion/lead/jdu-mp-pavan-k-varma-writes-about-of-images-and-perceptions/article7173965.ece?textsize=small&test=2 (accessed 10 May 2015).

Vasudeva, Shefali, 'What Men Want: Exploring the Libido of the Indian Male', *India Today*, 20 September 2004a, 26–50.

Vasudeva, Shefali, 'Rearranging Marriage', 2004b. Available at http://indiatoday.intoday.in/story/indian-wedding-mart-matchmaking-in-india-becomes-flexible-practical-and-adaptable/1/195162.html (accessed 21 April 2017).

Vasudevan, Ravi S., *Making Meaning in Indian Cinema* (New Delhi: Oxford University Press, 2000).

Verma. Ravi and Vaishali Sharma Mahendra, 'Construction of Masculinity in India: A Gender and Sexual Health Perspective', *The Journal of Family Welfare* 50, 2004, 71–78.

Virani, Pinki, 'No Kids, No Compulsions', *The Sunday Times of India*, 11 October 1998.

Vishnu, Uma, 'The Census Truth: More Indians Have Access to Phones than to Toilets', *The Indian Express*, 2012. Available at www.indianexpress.com/news/thecensus (accessed 16 March 2012).

Vishvanathan, Shiv, 'An Indianness that needs no Aadhar', *The Hindu*, 13 April 2015. Available at http://www.thehindu.com/opinion/lead/indian-minorities-are-selfconfident-cultures/article7095727.ece (accessed 13 April 2015).

Wajihudin, Mohammed, 'Why Some People want to be Poor', *The Times of India*, 27 May 2007, 23.

Walby, Sylvia, *Gender Transformations* (London: Routledge, 1997).

Warner, Michael, 'Publics and Counter Publics', *Public Culture* 4 (1), 2002, 49–90.

Wayne, Mike, *Marxism and Media Studies: Key Concepts and Contemporary Trends* (London: Pluto Press, 2003).

Wearing, Betsy, *Leisure Feminist Theory* (London: Sage Publications, 1998).

Williams, Raymond, *Marxism and Literature* (Oxford: Oxford University Press, 1977).

———, 'Advertising; The Magic System', in *Problems in Materialism and Culture* (London: Verso, 1980), 184–91.

Winch, P., *The Idea of a Social Science and its Relation to Philosophy* (London: Routledge, 1958).

Woman's Role in Planned Economy, 1947 (The Sub-Committee on Woman's Role in Planned Economy) (Bombay: Vora).

Wolff, R. B. Moore and H. Marcuse, *A Critique of Pure Tolerance* (London: Jonathan Cape, 1969).

Wollstonecraft, Mary, *From Vindication of the Rights of Women* (Harmondsworth: Penguin, 1975 [1792]).

Yuval-Davis, Nira and Floya Anthias, *Woman-nation-state* (Basingstoke: Macmillan, 1989).

ONLINE REFERENCES

'E-governance brings empowerment, equity and efficiency', https://in.finance.yahoo.com/news/full-text-of-the-president-s-speech-to-parliament-074449489.html (accessed 10 June 2014).

http://www.firstpost.com/india/republic-day-blunder-modi-govt-ad-omits-socialist-secular-from-constitution-preamble-2066447.html (accessed 15 June 2016).

http://www.outlookindia.com/news/article/minorities-in-india-facing-violent-attacks-under-new-govt-us-panel/894471 (accessed 1 May 2015).

http://www.hindustantimes.com/analysis/indian-media-ignored-suffering-of-quake-hit-survivors-in-nepal/article1-1345319.aspx (accessed 11 May 2015).

'The rapidity of change has changed', https://www.jimcarroll.com/2005/04/the-rapidity-of-change-has-changed/#.VyhnOmOKe8U (accessed 3 May 2016).

http://indianexpress.com/article/india/india-news-india/dalit-student-suicide-full-text-of-suicide-letter-hyderabad/#sthash.rgCeUHY5.dpuf (accessed 3 May 2016).

http://atlantablackstar.com/2016/05/02/blackness-around-the-globe-dark-skinned-dalits-fight-an-oppressive-caste-system-whatever-is-black-is-not-welcomed/ (accessed 3 May 2016).

https://greatbong.net/2011/08/13/patriotism-and-the-nri/ (accessed 14 May 2016).

http://www.ndtv.com/india-news/2-videos-of-jnu-event-manipulated-finds-forensic-probe-sources-1283105 (accessed 14 May 2016).

http://www.hindustantimes.com/columns/a-knowledge-of-history-is-an-antidote-to-hubris/story-y6Cuh9xhC8Zk0EdGj9pRxK.html (accessed 15 June 2016).

http://www.thehindu.com/news/national/government-is-accountable-propoor-says-narendra-modi/article8651361.ece (accessed 15 June 2016).

http://www.firstpost.com/india/republic-day-blunder-modi-govt-ad-omits-socialist-secular-from-constitution-preamble-2066447.html (accessed 15 June 2016).

http://publishing.cdlib.org/ucpressebooks/view?docId=ft8r29p2ss&chunk.id=ch2&toc.depth=1&brand=ucpress (accessed 16 June 2016).

http://www.pressreader.com (accessed 12 June 2016).

http://www.thehindu.com/news/national/its-a-contest-of-two-of-two-competing-ideals-of-india/article5941163.ece?ref=relatedNews (accessed 27 April 2014).

http://www.thehindu.com/news/national/capt-amarinder-reaches-out-to-nris-via-skype/article8524733.ece (accessed 28 April 2016).

http://indianexpress.com/article/cities/chandigarh/bsp-reaches-out-to-dalit-nris/#sthash.I1iGBTZl.dpuf (accessed 4 May 2016).

https://in.finance.yahoo.com/news/full-text-of-the-president-s-speech-to-parliament-074449489.html.

http://www.business-standard.com/article/companies/lakshmi-mittal-household-name-in-france-for-all-the-wrong-reasons-112112900034_1.html (accessed 14 May 2016).

http://www.thatscricket.com/news/2010/12/16/ipl-scandals-and-controversies-of-2010.html (accessed 13 May 2016).

http://www.india.com/news/india/rajdeep-sardesai-quits-twitter-after-allegedly-hurling-abuses-in-direct-messages-to-haters-1149466/ (accessed 21 June 2016).

http://scroll.in/article/762857/the-ravish-kumar-interview-our-lazy-liberal-class-was-always-opportunistic (accessed 23 June 2016).

http://economictimes.indiatimes.com/news/economy/policy/india-unveils-budget-for-recovery-and-the-poor-after-cash-crackdown/articleshow/56927634.cms (accessed 2 February 2017).

https://www.theguardian.com/business/2016/nov/17/does-trumps-election-spell-end-for-globalisation (accessed 3 February 2017).

https://dalitnation.com/about-3/ (accessed 3 February 2017).

http://www.ndtv.com/india-news/mayawatis-elephant-gives-social-media-a-chance-online-blitz-coming-soon-1648362 (accessed 3 February 2017).

https://www.youtube.com/watch?v=9EOrNBS2twc (accessed 4 February 2017).

http://economictimes.indiatimes.com/news/politics-and-nation/how-the-great-upstart-aap-and-the-foreign-hands-of-diaspora-are-changing-politics-in-punjab/articleshow/56975837.cms (accessed 5 February 2017).

'Female Bosses in Sportsworld: Gayari Reddy. Owner of IPL Franchise, Deccan Chargers', http://sports.in.msn.com/gallery/female-bosses-in-sportsworld (accessed 23 May 2012).

'Moving Women to the Top: McKinsey Global Survey Results', http://www.mckinseyquarterly.com/Moving_women_to_the_top_McKinsey_Global_Survey_results_2686 (accessed 9 June 2012).

'The Axe Effect on Deodorant Ads in India', 1 June 2011.

http://www.tmrcrescarch.com/2011/06/the-axe-effect-on-deodornt-advertisements-in-india/ (accessed 25 May 2012).

http://www.dailymail.co.uk/news/article-1294649/Facebook-app-Indian-men-users-look-paler-face. html#ixzzlvxr0Vdmn

http://www.tmrcresearch.com/Home (accessed 22 June 2012).

'The Axe Body Spray Destroys Indian Culture', http://gawker.com/5047155/axe-body-spray-ads-destroy-indian-culture (accessed 11 June 2012).

http://article.wn.com/view/2012/04/12/Vagina_Bleaching_Ad_Sparks_Controversy_Over_Who_Need_A_Pale/ (accessed 25 May 2012).

http://indianfusion.aglasem.com/ban-skirts-in-schools-safety-of-women/ (accessed 21 January 2013).

http://www.thehindu.com/news/states/other-states/child-marriage-as-remedy-for-rape-sparks furore/article3984623.ecen (accessed 21 January 2013).

http://travel.state.gov/travel/cis_pa_tw/cis/cis_1139.html (accessed 21 January 2013).

http://www.sundayguardianlive.com/news/8941-bjp-woos-backwardsbihar; accessed 12 May 2017.

http://www.bbc.com/news/world-asiaindia-34943206; accessed 20 April 2017.

http://www.hindustantimes.com/india-news/womenrights-is-a-development-issue-don-t-politicise-triple-talaq-pm-modi/story-VDaGsDF4isPDsOuOdM94YM.html; accessed 18 April 2017.

http://www.ndtv.com/india-news/yogi-adityanathbelittled-women-in-article-should-apologise-congress-1682656; accessed 18 April 2017.

https://thewire.in/74667/triple-talaq-statement-muslims/;accessed 18 April 2017.

https://credoinunumdeum.wordpress.com/2007/07/21/c-l-stevenson-on-the-emotive-meaningof-ethical-terms-a-review-and-critique; accessed 17 April 2017.

http://www.thehindubusinessline.com/todayspaper/tp-opinion/when-liberty-becomes-licence-dictatorship-is-near/article2168908.ece; accessed 17 April 2017.

https://blogs.wsj.com/indiarealtime/2013/03/20/in-anti-rape-debate-indian-mps-revealsexism/; accessed 4 May 2017.

http://www.hindustantimes.com/comment/barkhadutt/pm-modi-must-take-a-clear-stand-against-motor-mouth-mps/article1-1298366.aspx#sthash.7IWcAGPf.dpuf (accessed 20 December 2014).

'About India Real Time', *Indiarealtime* (Blog), http://blogs.wsj.com/indiarealtime/ (accessed 2 June 2014).

'Age of Sexual Consent', *AVERT*, http://www.avert.org/age-sexual-consent.htm (accessed 2 October 2013).

'India Readership Survey 2008', *publicitas*, 24 April 2008, http://www.publicitas.com/zh/home/media-news-events/news-detail/?newsid=22413&title=india-indian-readership-survey-2008-irs-round-1#UC_o2Pc1kl (accessed 31 July 2014).

'Mother India (book)', *Wikipedia*, http://en.wikipedia.org/wiki/Mother_India_%28book%29 (accessed 25 April 2014).

'One Billion Rising', *Wikipedia*, http://en.wikipedia.org/wiki/One_Billion_Rising (accessed 11 September and 2 October 2013).

'Roop Kanwar', *Wikipedia*, http://en.wikipedia.org/wiki/Roop_Kanwar (accessed 11 October 2013).

NEWSPAPERS AND MAGAZINES

Business Standard, 7 January 1998
eLAN: the Magazine for Successful Women, August–September 1999.
The Economic Times (Brand Equity), 16–22 June 1999; 19 October 1999
Elle, October 1999.
Femina, 1 February 1999; 23 April 1992.
Hindustan Times, 1 February 2005
Gentleman, June 1990, 1999
Gladrags, 1999.
The Hindu, 19 October 1998; 16 November 1998; 13 June 1999; 15 September 1999; 12 November 1999; 1 March 2002; 11 February 2005; 17 February 2005
India Today Woman, January 2008
India Habitat Centre Notice, November 2007
Life Review, March–April 1999.
New Woman, February 1999; March 1999; May 1999; October 1999
Outlook, 4 May 1997; 9 July 1997; 31 January 2005
Parenting, February 1999.
Rashtriya Sahara, December 1996; July 1997
Savvy, October 1998.
Society, September 1994.
The Sunday Times of India, 18 January 1998; 8 March 1998; 7 February 1999; 13 June 1999.
The Times of India, 20 October 1994; 25 February 1995; 16 June 1995; 16 August 1995; 9 December 1998; 7 November 2004; 30 May, 1 & 2 June, 2007; 18 April 2009
Vasant Kunj Times, December 1996.
The Week, 30 March 1997; 30 May 1997; 28 March 1999
Women's Era, 1 August 1994; 2 January 1999; 2 February 1999.

INDEX